THOMAS AQUINAS
THEOLOGIAN

——— ✛ ———

Thomas Franklin O'Meara, O.P.

University of Notre Dame Press
Notre Dame and London

Copyright 1997 by
University of Notre Dame Press
Notre Dame, IN 46556
All Rights Reserved

Manufactured in the United States of America

Library of Congress Cataloging-in-Publication Data
O'Meara, Thomas F., 1935–
    Thomas Aquinas theologian / Thomas F. O'Meara.
       p.   cm.
    Includes bibliographical references and index.
    ISBN 0-268-01898-7 (alk. paper). — ISBN 0-268-04201-2 (alk.
    paper)
    1. Thomas, Aquinas, Saint, 1225?–1274. I. Title.
230' .2' 092—dc20   96-26438
                                                           CIP

For
My Dominican Brothers
in the Province of St. Albert the Great (U.S.A.)

✛

CONTENTS

———— ✢ ————

PREFACE

———— ✝ ————

I want to thank Lawrence Cunningham, Robert Krieg, and James Langford who read parts of this manuscript; and to remember Walter Principe who encouraged this project and read the opening chapters.

Fr. A. M. Carré, O.P., preacher at the Cathedral of Notre Dame and member of the French Academy, wrote some years ago a book to which he gave the title *Ces Maîtres que Dieu m'a donnés*, "These Teachers God Gave Me." This book led me to recall that in three ways providence drew me into the circle of Thomas Aquinas: through membership in the Dominican Order, through the variety of my education, and through the times in which I have lived. Thus various teachers have introduced me to Aquinas. Some were my teachers in the provincial Dominican studium in the American Midwest, while others in Europe, a few as teachers in Munich and others as advisers at the Ecumenical Council Vatican II, led me by their lectures and books to broader paths and showed how theologians and theology could renew the church and the world. To these teachers and to my brother Dominicans in my province (and in the Vice-Province of Nigeria) this book is dedicated.

While I have wanted only to present and explain the theological patterns, themes, and insights of a medieval theologian, my examples are sometimes contemporary; they are, however, intended to illustrate Aquinas' own ideas and not to imply that he knew about galaxies or viruses. These pages have attempted two difficult tasks, to present the thought of a genius and to do so in a somewhat vivid, contemporary exposition. And so I must ask in advance the reader's indulgence because in both directions I have had meager success.

INTRODUCTION

— ✟ —

A man for every hour.
Francisco de Sylvestris, O.P. (+ 1525)

There are about a half dozen outstanding Christian thinkers in Western civilization: Thomas Aquinas is one of them. Twice since the Renaissance and the Reformation the Catholic Church has revived his theology and has presented Thomism as an outstanding interpretation of Christian faith. His way of seeing the world and his vitality in explaining the gospel of Jesus Christ have influenced scholars, mystics, politicians, and artists for well over half a millennium. This book is a guide to his theology, to its world, and to its influence.

I. A Guide to Thomas Aquinas

These chapters introduce Thomas Aquinas in the vocation and profession he chose for himself: theologian. He was first and always a theologian: in the university and in the Dominican *studium*, in the pulpit and in his room writing. Whether commenting on Scripture or assembling opinions from past philosophers and theologians to flesh out his original, systematic conception of Christianity, he wrote to help the Christian message address sympathetically new problems and thought-forms. European scholarship in this century has reemphasized Aquinas as theologian, clarifying the relationship of philosophy to theology in his thought. The work of scholars as diverse as M.-D. Chenu and Etienne Gilson, Bernard Lonergan and Jean-Pierre Torrell have expanded greatly our understanding of the approach and depth of his theology.

Often the approach to Thomas Aquinas during the neo-Thomist revival from 1850 to 1960 was to describe a philosophy.[1] During that

xi

time far more books treated his philosophy than his theology. Central theological areas like the missions of the Trinity, the New Law, or the headship of Christ were neglected, while in the books on Thomist philosophy a concluding section of "theology" dealt not with the God of revelation but with the Cause of metaphysics. A search through a library catalogue or a perusal of a bibliography of articles on Aquinas written prior to Vatican II yields more material on the metaphysics of an unmoved mover or the abstract description of philosophical virtues than on salvation by Jesus or the role of a sacrament.

A number of introductions to Thomas Aquinas were written between 1920 and 1960, for instance, by A. D. Sertillanges, G. K. Chesterton, or Gerald Vann.[2] Some were biographies of a saint; some were introductions to a philosopher. Some have fine insights, and others, passing beyond the legendary and the edifying, describe the achievement of a controversial and courageous life. A few illumine the thought of the Christian theologian. Decades ago, I read these literate biographies and introductions (often several times) as an escape from neo-Thomist tomes holding only definitions and divisions, for they did bring color and insight into the career and thought of Aquinas. This book finds an initial inspiration in their pages.

At the same time, other scholars were at work on a deeper understanding of Aquinas, historical and theological. The historical study of the Middle Ages is a gift of this century, and it has enhanced the understanding of scholastic philosophy and theology enormously. Great spirits from Martin Grabmann to Etienne Gilson described the colorful worlds of the thirteenth century and also presented various theologies from that age. The prominent theologians of Vatican II like Yves Congar, Edward Schillebeeckx, and Karl Rahner were often particularly insightful in their views on Aquinas. If there is a rich literature in French, Italian, Spanish, and German, among Americans there appeared in 1974 James Athanasius Weisheipl's *Friar Thomas d'Aquino*, an internationally recognized presentation of the life and works of Aquinas.[3] That anniversary year of 1974 witnessed a flood of volumes and articles on Aquinas, while in the decades since important studies continue to appear, for instance, the articles of Walter Principe or Servais Pinckaers, and the books of Otto Pesch and Torrell. The following pages claim little originality but they do come from an apprenticeship with scholars from several generations.

Although it intends to introduce Aquinas in the light of scholarship from the past decades, this book, nonetheless, must be more than a chronology and a bibliography. Thomas Aquinas' theology mirrors the creative directions of his personality and his age: his originality gave life to several traditions in Western Christianity. His theology deftly employed the cultural and scientific (what we would call philosophical) forms and insights available to him. Themes like divine wisdom, graced humanity, and continuing incarnation have served as catalysts for the theologies and organizations of Catholicism far after the thirteenth century.

It must be said here at the beginning that this brief study has not been written by a medievalist nor by a researcher into texts or chronologies from the time of Charlemagne or Innocent III. The author's qualifications for offering an exploration of this theologian are only personal and practical: seven years of studying (almost exclusively) Thomas Aquinas in a Dominican *studium* prior to 1964 and twenty-five years of teaching his theology at various educational levels and in different cultures.

These pages have not been written by an apologete for yet another neo-scholastic revival but by a working teacher and theologian. A good way to understand Aquinas is to teach his theology, because teachers learn old ideas anew through the apprenticeship of bright students. In the last analysis, Aquinas wrote as a teacher. To draw a student to a great thinker is to lead both teacher and learner further into a world which is harmonious and gracious, human and mysterious.

The following chapters will inevitably reflect the approach and interpretation of the Dominican school. That collective understanding of Aquinas reaches back six centuries: it includes artists, popes, and preachers as well as theologians like Thomas de Vio (Cardinal Cajetan), Francisco de Vitoria, and Reginald Garrigou-Lagrange. In figures as diverse as Savonarola, Bartolomé de Las Casas, Walter Farrell, and Yves Congar the Dominican school is present with its emphases on supernatural grace, active realism, and a harmony between faith and philosophy. There are other schools of interpretation and they have their important contributions. But this writer has been immersed in one tradition and admits that its dominant perspective took hold of him through his education within the Dominican Order.

I have experienced in my life five different kinds of "Thomism":
(1) the texts of Aquinas in the interpretive tradition of Cajetan, John
of St. Thomas, and Garrigou-Lagrange; (2) a rigid, diluted neo-
Thomist reproduction of some segments or principles of Aquinas'
thought, usually philosophical; (3) the European rediscovery of
Aquinas in its medieval context; (4) the dialogue between Aquinas
and modern philosophy; and (5) the application of Thomist perspectives by great theologians to the themes of Vatican II. I have studied
Protestant theologians like Paul Tillich who understood Aquinas'
role in the history of Western Christianity, and have studied with
Catholic theologians like Karl Rahner who shaped theology for the
post-conciliar period by pursuing an energetic dialogue between
Aquinas and modern philosophical theology.

An introduction is a beginning. Far from looking for combative syllogisms or for an apologetic
imposition of Latin phrases, the goal of this guide is to understand the
faith and vision of Aquinas. He worked to attract hearers and to meet
positively one of the great cultural changes in Western history; he
refused to parrot the past's authorities or to silence his contemporaries. The dynamic structure of this theology helped to form the
Middle Ages even as that cultural epoch was reflected in it. Some
thinkers—and Aquinas is one—survive the onslaught of time. If few
theologies have a voice long after their first appearance, Aquinas has
influenced Western Christians for seven centuries, centuries which
have tested and continued his wisdom. He still fashions ways in
which Roman Catholics think. Research into the world and sources
of Aquinas should always be complemented by some contact with
his theology as it is active in the life of the Catholic Church today.
His influence, consciously or unconsciously, is inevitable in the
Catholic mind. Catholics absorb something of a Thomistic world-
view from their church's attitude towards politics and sacraments,
psychology and mysticism.

An introduction is a beginning. *Intra-ducere*—these pages would
lead within, that is, they would lead readers into an understanding of
Thomas Aquinas. One can notice in lines of Aquinas some naive exegesis, some limits of past science, and a sparse view of history. Some
moderns have been distracted by the un-modern pattern of centering
all on God or by the teleological dynamic. Limitations, however, do
not silence the voice of genius. If some ideas are antiquated, many of
the theological perspectives have proven fruitful century after cen-

tury. They contributed to the Renaissance in which Raphael painted his *Stanze* in the Vatican, and they have been at work in theologies of liberation for the Americas, those in the early sixteenth century and those in recent decades.

An introduction written at the end of the twentieth century, however, cannot begin without noticing the conflicts (even the injustices) which the exposition and interpretation of Aquinas in the past hundred years has occasioned. The most recent neo-Thomist revival reaching from 1850 to 1960 and occurring largely in Catholic seminaries was a campaign, fortified by papal statements and canon law, which sought to make Aquinas the sole teacher in the church. In some circles this became an impossible quest to build a prison of the past around Spirit and revelation. Some turned the dialectical research of his world-view into an ideology aimed at conflict, while others took a theologian whose method was inclusive research and made him into an inquisitor of anything new or different. An imperial neo-scholasticism, reaching from Vatican I to Vatican II, attained its climax in the years just before the Ecumenical Council began in 1962. But the decades before the Council had also been setting Aquinas free, balancing off rigid forms of neo-Thomism with philosophers and theologians who sought a dialogue between Aquinas and thinkers from both the early church and the modern world. Neo-scholasticism faded away after Vatican II (in chapter four we will see why) even as the Council's documents mentioned Aquinas with praise; the vast influence of Aquinas in schools throughout the world diminished in the 1960s (too many students had met Aquinas only in boring lectures and memorized assignments). This diminution of derivative Thomisms was necessary so that the Christian gospel could find in other theologies, new and old, ways of reaching contemporary lives and of finding access beyond Europe to other cultures. Precisely by being part of the recent renewal of the Catholic Church Aquinas' theology has retained its vitality,

This book's chapters offer something of the context and content of that theology. A first chapter looks at the life, career, and works of Thomas Aquinas. The central source for a discussion of his theology is the *Summa theologiae* (*ST*),[4] the climax of his life's work and his synthetic masterpiece, and so chapter two explores that work's theological structures, and chapter three presents its central motifs. From the fourteenth to the twentieth century Aquinas' writings passed through various revivals and declines, and so the fourth chapter sketches a history of the traditions of interpretation in schools and religious orders. A final chapter shows in some areas of religious and cultural life how Aquinas' influence is active today.

What is more interesting than to enter into the world of a great thinker? What is more exciting than meeting someone who saw the world in an original way? One imagines spending time with a great artist or interviewing a great politician from the past. But they are gone. Sometimes they have not left much of their personalities and lives behind. But other times, their writings or their paintings do give access to that personality which was so creative or resolute, so imaginative or holy.

II. How to Study a Great Thinker

How should one read a great theologian? The wrong introduction renders a theological genius dry and tedious and turns intellectual excitement into boredom. A rigid or misguided teacher can transform the world of Aquinas into something distant or irrelevant. Naturally, by encountering the theologian and the man, we want to enter into his vision, to feel something of his energy. Today we can do this only in his writings. But that does not command us to hand our intellectual pursuit over to a diffident reading of texts. We read the pages holding the perspectives of both a metaphysician and a mystic to find in them an inspiring access to the real. His texts are guides and witnesses to life.

There are several ways *not* to study great thinkers. It is preferable not to study them solely on one's own. The breadth and depth of the writings can discourage and the neophyte might conclude after a short time that they can be easily understood, and then shallow or incorrect interpretations replace insight. Ghirlandaio's frescos, Beethoven's late string quartets, James Joyce's novels need a guide—and so does Thomas Aquinas.

A beginner does not attain in a few months a balanced or insightful knowledge of Plato, Origen, or Schelling. Perhaps that is why Aristotle said that metaphysics was best pursued after the age of fifty. The theologian and historian Yves Congar once told young Dominicans that it would take them fifteen years to grasp Aquinas.[5] In my experience an initial understanding of a great thinker is possible only after five to ten years of study—and a mature interpretation comes later. A great artist or physicist is more than a source of information to be stored. Periods of reading and discussing and the leisure for pondering the patterns in great works are needed to fathom the work of Wagner or Cézanne. But our society moves rapidly. It is fashionable today to appropriate great ideas instantly, but then quickly to discard them and their creators like old soccer balls or used cars. The search for the sensational, the exaggerated rediscovery of the forgotten, the showcasing of the trivial are the enemies of meeting greatness. For when novelty fades, greatness too is discarded. This mentality is particularly unsuited to learning about and from Thomas Aquinas. His life was a contemplative one, and the theology he produced is best understood in a contemplative atmosphere.

There are different ways in which Aquinas can attract disciples, and not all of them are healthy. Some adopt the name and the authority of this medieval teacher without understanding him to any great extent; others claim to have the sole or best interpretation of his thought for all time while ignoring the variety of Thomistic traditions. Not a few are attracted to his tight logic without realizing that it is a scaffolding for sacramentality, while others search desperately for a closed philosophical logic, not realizing that Aquinas' theology is open, transcendental, and transcendent. History shows sadly that Thomism can hold a perennial attraction for compulsive, anxious, and fundamentalist minds. They seek there—beyond the ambiguities of Bible, life, and church—rational defenses or deductions which are little more than games.

Intelligent disciples, however, soon learn that a historical interpretation along with the history of interpretations is the place to begin, and that this encourages Aquinas to speak anew, showing how his theology is multi-layered and open to further insights. The revivals of Aquinas occurring in history achieve more than a recovery of a past terminology. They reshape the ideas and conclusions of the master: not to rearrange a text but to address the issues of an age.

Why is a thinker great?

I once asked a class why important modern theologians and philosophers were difficult to understand. The answer came back: "Because they wrote in German!" In comparison to many philosophers and theologians Aquinas' language and terminology are not difficult. His process of thinking is straightforward, the brief and logical sentences are direct. But his thought is more than definitions and conclusions. His ideas live from a way of seeing a world which includes multiple beings and divine presences.

Great minds are difficult because they write in a kind of code. The "code" is expressing ideas within the thought-forms of a culture; it bears (but does not create) the influential insights of a new thinker. The code exists not to hide but to disclose; it offers not esoteric or effete metaphors from the libraries of academia but insights into the real world, ways of seeing, thinking, and living. Theologians or philosophers are not difficult because they put down on paper curious information or prolix theories. The writings of an Aristotle or a Kant offer not so much facts as perspectives, ways of understanding self and society. These approaches and principles might be cosmic or personal, static or changing, God-centered or political. A lastingly influential theory is, of course, written in a particular language. Aquinas' Latin was the easy vehicle for medieval teachers and students working in a second language, while Hegel's dense German of idealism is aimed at a cultured class. The language (which every translation weakens) is itself a code and a thought-form; it leads into a constellation of thought-perspectives and models beyond the terms and data. The medieval thinker does not provide just terms like *"esse"* and *"actus"* but patterns and principles. The greater the creative spirit the more an introduction needs to go beyond facts. A theologian is a theoretician of life and history within the mystery of the presence of the divine. A guide to a theology points to what is unseen as well as to what is seen. A thinker is great not because his books offer abstract laws, but because they offer a new perspective about the human and the divine. How should I live on this planet and at this time in history? Where lies my destiny? Is there an unseen God, and how does a supreme being (lover or judge?) relate to me? Theologians employ philosophies, aesthetics, or sociologies not to prove the content of Jesus' revelation but to express the Word and its words to a particular culture.

If the writings of a great theologian offer approaches and insights, why do students need a teacher? A teacher leads others to pass beyond the code: to understand the models and the thought-forms, the themes and their perspectives. Someone who over time has come to understand a great religious or philosophical view of people and God—understanding is not the same as memorizing or repeating—can unlock the coherent fabric of ideas. A teacher who is successfully self-taught in a major thinker is rare. Furthermore, to appreciate a creative spirit from a different age is not easy, for one never escapes her particular culture or science. A beginner should seek out a teacher (or, at least, a knowledge-able and mature written guide), a teacher who leads into a world not only by study but by experience and sympathy. Who would recommend a doctoral student intent upon the ideas of John Locke or Thomas Cranmer studying that figure with a French Jesuit whose specialization lies with Robert Bellarmine or Pierre Teilhard de Chardin? It is not easy to learn about the structure and insights of a distinctive perspective from writers who are ignorant of the cultural world from which it emerges, or from those who find the thought basically in error. The worst thing is to read alone (or to discuss with amateurs) a few books on Plato only to decide that Plato is confused, limited, and passé. One learns not just from the text but from what experts, past and present, write about the text. Studying an original thinker like Aquinas requires modesty and patience. Part of being introduced to a great thinker is to realize that only an introduction has taken place.

We remain inevitably outsiders to the life and thought of thinkers and artists from other ages. There are, however, ways of entering their world. One can study in the institutions of a tradition or a school founded by or devoted to them. A student can seek out people who because of ties to a university, a religious order, a church, or a center of a spirituality have links to founder and teachers. One can also look at the art and architecture which an age produced and see the motifs and aspi-rations of an age which might be present in literature or philosophy.

Curiously the time spent in learning about one person's world some-how aids the appreciation of other ages. Understanding that theologian or this architect helps us understand others. To study one great artist or thinker is to see and understand a little about all human greatness and all human suffering. We are touching not only the genial humanity of a Rembrandt or a Mozart but humanity itself.

III. A Theologian and His Age

Mysteriously God created the human race in a historical mode. History unfolds amid diversity: Assyrian cities and Hong Kong sky-scrapers, Benin villages or Alpine Baroque churches incarnate human aspirations and gifts. If there is a community in the human race, nonetheless, there is no evidence that human beings—past and pres-ent, in Nebraska or in Senegal—think exactly the same way. Human language and customs imply the opposite. Neo-scholasticism from 1860 to 1960 was mistaken in its Eurocentric ideology: the human mind is not "naturally Aristotelian," just as society is not naturally feudal or Leninist. Aquinas was aware of the greatness and the limits of an Augustine or a John Damascene. With enthusiasm he examined Greek, Latin, and Arab philosophers, and found the variety of Christian theologians invigorating. God created a human race which delights in time. The drama of political conflicts, the opportunities for exploration, the invention of machines, the creation of music form a culture—and a Christian theology expresses revelation, faith, church, and morality for a particular time. Yves Congar wrote: "From any point of view, Thomas Aquinas remains one of the greatest masters of Christian thought, an exceptional moment in the chain of tradition. To study him historically, far from diminishing him, makes him appear even greater."[6]

Aquinas was not primarily a philosopher or a monk or a physicist. He was a teacher and preacher of theology: this was his vocation and ministry. He argued calmly and directly, stressed nothing unduly, and betrayed his interests simply. There are no trivial creatures, and everything is great and divine as it reflects its Author. "All things which have been or can be shine in God as in a kind of mirror, for God is all things in God-self" (I, 12, 8, 2). University professors, *"magistri,"* gathered and discussed opinions, and, even though they were not bishops, gave mature resolutions about particular problems within their own interpretation of Christianity. The Dominican saw theology as more: it was a reflection of a deeper human life and destiny revealed in Christ; theology was not a search for shocking theories or a condemnation of people but a sharing in God's view of earth. With a special gift for borrowing, arranging, and evaluating, out of multiple intellectual pieces and despite difficult problems, he fashioned a harmonious totality. For Aquinas the pursuit of and instruction in truth was a high human vocation and responsibility. In a rare burst of emotion he wrote in 1270: "If anyone wishes to express something against what we have written let him not speak in corners or before the young who cannot judge difficult problem, but let him write against our text—if he dares."[7]

❖ ❖ ❖

It is now time to enter the age of Thomas Aquinas and meet his theology. We will be assisted by valuable mentors, living and dead, people from different expertises and different times. Whether from Italy or Canada, whether from the sixteenth or the twentieth centuries, experts on medieval culture and on theology, they are our guides.[8]

1. The Life and Career
of Thomas Aquinas

✛

The dispute [in Job] between God and a mortal may seem inappropriate because of the great distance between them. But where truth is concerned differences between persons are relatively unimportant. To proclaim the truth is to render that person invincible no matter who the adversary might be.

Commentary on Job

An age with its culture, a life with its individuality—these, though broad and elusive, are the forces behind every great man and woman. Out of culture and time thinkers, scientists, and artists find and experience their world, and then a few fashion a work which survives time. The first step in understanding great human creations is to set them aside for a while and learn about the age and the person who produced them.

I. A Time of Change

Thomas of Aquino was born between 1224 and 1226 at the castle of Roccasecca near Aquino. His birth came only five years or so after the death of Dominic, the founder of the new religious community which he would join, and a year or so before the passing of Francis of Assisi. Thomas was the youngest son of Landulph of Aquino (d. 1243), master of Roccasecca and Montesangiovanni, and of his second wife, Theodora (d. 1255) of the Rossi branch of the family Caracciolo, a woman of the Naples region but with some Norman ancestors. Thomas had five sisters, four older brothers and at least three half brothers.[1]

Aquino was an ancient town (the Roman poet Juvenal was born there in A.D. 60, and the important Roman highway, the *Via Latina*, was not far away), and this place-name indicates the lineage and land-holding origins of Thomas' family. The area of Aquino and Roccasecca lies in Lazio (the ancient Latium occupied by Etruscan and Latin peoples prior to its conquest by Rome) and is situated about midway between Rome and Naples. It is a countryside of towns and castles perched on high hills above fertile valleys. The Kingdom of Sicily, ruled by the Emperor Frederick II in Palermo from 1220 to 1250, reached so far north as at times to include Landulph's holdings. Aquinas' family was in the service of Frederick and so was involved in the emperor's struggle with strong popes like Honorius III (1216–1227) who had approved the foundation of Dominic's order of preaching brothers. Thomas' brother Aimo fought together with the emperor on the fifth crusade and was captured and held for ransom on the island of Cyprus in 1223. Released from Muslim prisons through the efforts of Pope Gregory IX, he switched allegiance from empire to papacy. In 1240 another brother Rinaldo began service as the emperor's page, but in 1245, when Frederick II was deposed by Innocent IV at the Council of Lyons, he too changed allegiance. A year later he was involved in a failed attempt to assassinate the emperor and was executed by Frederick's orders. The family considered him a "martyr" to the dictatorial designs of the emperor.

Thomas was born at an important cultural moment. Pope Honorius III was continuing the renewal and prestige of Innocent III; Frederick II reigned as Holy Roman Emperor from Sicily to Germany; Louis IX was about to begin his long reign as king of France. The Muslims continued to expand in parts of Spain, while the Latin Kingdom of Jerusalem established by the Crusades became increasingly fragile. Western crusader lords occupied parts of the eastern Mediterranean, and far to the north and east the Mongol invasions disclosed something of Asian peoples. Thomas' life more or less corresponds to the time of the High Middle Ages with its study and integration of the new sciences recently received from ancient Greek works, and with its new arts of building and decorating churches.

The thirteenth century was a time of economic growth and social evolution throughout much of Europe. In that century the West was moving from one cultural milieu to another. Favorable climatic conditions furthered an increase in population and the clearing of new land. Business was facilitated by the circulation of money just as agriculture was improved by advanced tools and skills. Feudalism, centered on a rural life and agrarian economy, declined, whereas cities devoted to commerce extended their walls. Great resources were expended in construction programs, as stone church buildings with vast proportions and interior richness arose to proclaim a city's pride and to attract commerce and tourism. In France between 1180 and 1270 a population of less than eighteen million produced eighty churches of cathedral size and hundreds of abbeys. To focus on one example, Chartres, a community of ten thousand citizens, rebuilt in one generation its cathedral on a grandiose scale. A mercantile middle class was flourishing, and taxes drew off some of this prosperity to the nobility and royalty. The urban middle class sent its sons to the universities, and, since the earlier social fabric of clerical benefices that had supported students was not adequate to the explosion of people seeking the new learning, the university rented larger halls and introduced fees. The French Dominican medievalist M.-D. Chenu wrote of the special cultural age which would frame Aquinas' life:

> It is not unimportant that in the days of Saint Louis and of Frederick II, Saint Thomas should arrive at Paris at a time:
> —when, in a new society just entered upon a communal era, it was in the corporate university body that intellectual eagerness and curiosity were concentrated and were to introduce Aristotle and ancient reason to Christian thought;
> —when the cathedral of Notre Dame of Paris was being completed and the *Romance of the Rose* written;
> —when Europe was entering on a new era in which it would cease to be a theocratic entity;
> —when the Muslims were hemming in the Western world by their military successes and seducing it by their science and philosophy;
> —when, finally, merchants and missionaries were pushing their way into the region of Cathay and discovering the world's dimensions and the variety of its civilizations.[2]

In 1231, at the age of about six, Thomas was entrusted by his parents to the Benedictine monks of the Abbey of Monte Cassino for elementary education according to the custom for noble families. Some biographers observe that his family thought he might one day become abbot of that ancient monastery where a distant relative Landulph Sinnibaldo was then abbot. The impact of the monastic life in that great and ancient institution—communal order in graced tranquillity, education joined to liturgy—must have impressed the young Thomas. Its very location perhaps captured his personality and imagination; Angelus Walz speculated on the influence of the hills of the area upon the ideas and faith of Aquinas. "Cassino towers majestically above the Campania Romana and dominates the valleys of the Liri and the Garigliano which meet near Cassino. There is an immense prospect over the highlands of the Abruzzi and the hilly district that lies along the Tyrrhenian Sea."[3].

Frederick II, infuriated by yet another papal excommunication, sent troops in 1239 to occupy Monte Cassino and to use it as a fortress. Thomas was sent home in the spring of that year (he was about fifteen) by the abbot, perhaps with the recommendation that he should pursue studies at the recently founded "general center of studies," the university at Naples. This institution had been founded by Frederick II in 1224 as a rival to Bologna and to other institutions under papal influence. The Neapolitan university, with its faculties in arts, ecclesiastical and civil law, medicine, and theology, reflected the atmosphere of Frederick's court at Palermo where Latin, Muslim, and Jewish scholars exchanged ideas, where Arab astronomy and Greek medicine met, and where the texts of Aristotle and his Arab commentators were being discussed and translated into Latin. There from about 1240 to 1244 Aquinas studied the seven liberal arts. When his basic education was complete, he was taught natural philosophy and most probably the metaphysics of Aristotle. Michael Scotus' translation of some parts of Aristotle (1231) had been done under the patronage of the emperor. At a time when lecturing on the writings of "the Philosopher" was forbidden in Paris (they could, however, be read and cited), Naples was beginning to be a center of study for the ancient but controversial science recently arrived in Europe.[4] Thomas was introduced to Aristotelianism by Peter of Ireland.[5] Peter was a lecturer in natural philosophy and formed part of an Aristotelian movement generally associated with the court of Frederick II. He was an early pioneering figure in the introduction of the works of the Arab interpreter of Aristotle, Averroes. His sparse Aristotelianism would have an influence on Aquinas, and through him on the West.

II. Friar Thomas of Aquino

Thomas lived at a time when new perspectives, without banishing the wisdom of the past, gave a new role to the riches of Aristotle and Plato, of Eastern Christian theologies, and of Arabic and Greek viewpoints. Thomas was affected by the lectures he heard on new ideas, while in the streets of Naples he walked past the changing face of urban medieval life. He was encountering the two forces, original and creative, which would direct his life: the thought of Aristotle and the way of life in the Dominican Order.

One of the great innovations in Western monastic life was occurring: the success of the newly founded religious orders called "the friars," "the brothers." In their origins, as they began shortly after the beginning of the thirteenth century, they were a group of traveling preachers, a part of a spectrum of evangelical movements beginning in the previous century.[6] An idea, a spirit had been moving many women and men before Francis and Dominic to imitate what they pictured as Jesus' simple life of itinerant preaching. In contrast to the stability of noble families, rich merchants, and monasteries (large, land-owning centers of education and liturgy), bands of people, ordained and non-ordained, took to the roads to pursue "the apostolic life." A few ended up in communes of immorality or nests of sensational heresy, but many pursued the ideal of Christ-like evangelization. Francis of Assisi in Italy was the charismatic climax of this age of wandering evangelists; its organizer was Dominic in Southern France. Franciscans, Dominicans, and Carmelites drew numbers of men from the merchant class or the lesser nobility to their urban priories. Their vowed life was original because it blended study with community life, liturgy, and urban apostolates. The decision by the friars to settle in the cities and universities was a consequence of some of the new orientations in society and church. In place of isolating themselves in rural enclosures, silent cloisters, they built their priories just inside or outside the town walls. When their ministry became expansive and influential, space was established in front of the friars' churches where the *frati* could preach to crowds, piazzas of ministry. Their lives shared the agitations and the miseries of the growing city and they understood the aspirations of its merchants and artisans. Their practice of poverty in the narrow streets was a dramatic break with the economic organization supporting monastic life. These begging clerics ("mendicants") asked no more of the citizens than alms while they offered them in their churches sacraments and sermons. How did they move from the evangelization of towns to the universities of cities? Dominic, imagining from the beginning that his preaching brothers would be educated, had sent some of them to the universities. Then too, the ministry of preaching was soon joined to that of hearing confessions; both required education and books, and so the Dominicans became not only students but writers and teachers.[7] The Dominicans joined study to their imitation of Jesus the preacher and their commitment to poverty. They were gaining many recruits, largely from the urban middle class. Pierre Mandonnet wrote:

> The founding of the Order of Friars Preachers was very closely bound up with the general needs that were making themselves felt in the Christian world at the start of the thirteenth century. Having encouraged religious life in this new stage of development, the church of Rome decided to make use of it in order to solve some of the urgent problems confronting the church. . . . The ministry needed an ecclesial militia that was both well-educated and directly in contact with the social life of the times. The friars preachers with their new type of religious life and an original mode of organization were the answer to the needs of the new age.[8]

At least by 1243 Thomas had become attracted to that brotherhood with its new manner of religious life: striving to imitate Jesus' ministry rather than to work and pray in a monastery, it was a life intellectual as well as meditative. One friar, John of S. Giuliano, befriended him and encouraged his independent interest in the new Order of Preachers. With the energy and hope of youth and with a casual dismissal of family plans for his future, Thomas at the age of nineteen entered the Preaching Friars at their priory in Naples in 1242 or 1243. The priory had been founded in 1231 and dedicated in 1234 to Dominic, by then not only founder but canonized saint. There Dominic's successor, Jordan of Saxony, had preached to university students in 1236. The originality of Thomas is present in his vocation and his obedience to it. He understood his future life as a call by God: to follow the example of Jesus, to help others through a ministry of the Word, and to enter into a world of schools and books. The young man's choice was neither a reluctant selection of some romantic isolation nor the first step in an unclear and paradoxical mission. The combination of forces around him were fashioning his destiny and his ministry. Evidently his personality was such that he could receive various influences and mold them in his own life, and his age would offer him the atmosphere and tools for his work of theology. The enthusiasm of youth met the creativity of an age. A healthy and happy personality began to see that truth is not excluded from any realm where there is being.

Chenu thinks that the break of Thomas with his family is as significant as the similar decision, thirty years earlier, of Francis of Assisi.[9] But Thomas was leaving not a mercantile family but a world of the lesser nobility and monasticism. He wanted not only prayer and discipleship but a formal, ecclesial ministry which would have an impact upon the people around him. Jean-Pierre Torrell observes: "Certainly Thomas had perceived quite early that his penchant for study would be better pursued in the new order, and that, according to the theory he developed later, while it is good to contemplate divine things, it is better to contemplate them and communicate them to others."[10] The following theological observation written years later gives a hint of the firmness of the young friar's vocation: "When parents are not in a situation where they have serious need of the help of their offspring, they can leave the service of their parents and enter religious orders, even against their objection" (II–II, 189, 6).

Thomas' novitiate year was not to be pursued in Naples because the Dominicans had already had some bad experience with sons from noble families who forcibly tried to reclaim their scions from the friars. The feudal class did not have children so they would be free to pursue their own lives but so that sons and daughters could further the family's fortunes and the security and well-being of the family network. The Dominicans, aware of this, sent Thomas to Rome, and from there, accompanying the Master of the Order, in May 1244 he headed toward Paris. Learning of her son's entry into a mendicant order—a form of church life which appeared radical, irresponsible, and without prospects—his mother Theodora (his father Landulph had died not long before) sent word to Rinaldo to intercept his younger brother in Tuscany (her soldier son was then with the emperor's forces), and to bring him to her. Thomas was kept in a kind of house arrest for over a year, but the arguments and appeals of his mother made little impact on his resolve (he had the leisure to read the Bible and theological texts[11]). Theodora permitted him to return to the Dominicans in Naples in the summer of 1245.[12] What is surprising about this incident is not the forcible return of Thomas to his home but the insight of his mother permitting him after a relatively short time of disagreement to follow a risky and dubious path. As later years show, this early opposition did not alienate Thomas from his family, for he visited them and advised them in their legal and financial problems.[13]

Destiny can appear as journey. As a young man of about sixteen he was sent away from Monte Cassino and then went to the University of Naples—and that trip set in motion (and even summed up) his life. Thomas' journey down from the hill-town of Roccasecca to Naples is an image for his personality and career. He was moving from the feudal castle-towns of the lesser nobility to the expanding cities, from the venerable past to the change-filled present, from the monastic centers of trades and schools to the new universities, from theology as Platonic-Christian spiritual reading to theology as faith seeking new understanding through Aristotelian science, from the centuries of Augustinianism to the future theology about to be born, from the rural monastery to the house of the Friars Preachers, from a life of stages of asceticism and contemplation to the ministry of following Jesus Christ. Although he would later walk, ride, or journey by boat back and forth from France to Germany and from France to Italy, no journey would be as important or as determinative as those miles which led, fatefully and providentially, into his future. They drew him to the city, the university and the Dominicans; drew him into the several worlds which would fashion his life, alter Western civilization, and express the gospel in a new way.

III. Universities, *Studia*, and Albert the Great

In Naples, in Paris, in Oxford, the Dominicans were already associated with university theology and with the intellectual freedom to search out ideas. Thomas would have been taught in his novitiate year about the order's desire to espouse broad and new ministries. One Dominican meeting in those years expressed their spirit: "Let the brothers not mix in the wars of princes, in the decisions and opinions of bishops or in the business of municipalities; we must show that we share in the life of all, that we are ambitious seekers for the salvation of all living in the same time as our own."[14] The Dominicans at the time of Thomas understood their community life as extending outward through various ministries. They spoke of their fellow friars as co-workers; their houses held teams of scholars, preachers, or missionaries.

In 1246 Thomas was making a second dramatic journey, for he was then traveling north to Paris and its schools. Chenu wrote: "Thomas Aquinas at his birth was involved in a high feudal dynasty whose family traditions destined him for one of the most powerful abbeys. But he entered, by a liberty gained through his vocation, into a journey which was to lead to the most agitated and most representative of the urban schools, to the very heart of the new society, to the University of Paris."[15] To that university Dominic, in a move away from his apostolate of preaching among largely rural Albigensians, sent preaching friars in 1221. Shortly before the beginning of the thirteenth century which would hold Aquinas' life and career, Gui de Bazoches wrote:

> I am in Paris, in that royal city where abundance of natural wealth not only holds those who live there but also attracts those from afar. Just as the moon outshines the stars in brilliance, so does this city, the seat of the monarchy, lift her proud head above the rest. . . . Two suburbs extend to right and left. . . . The first—great, rich, trading— is the scene of seething activity; innumerable ships surround it, filled with merchandise and riches. The Petit Pont belongs to the dialecticians who walk there deep in argument. . . . [16]

Aquinas came as a student to the Paris of the new kind of teachers balancing opinions and pondering sources, the "dialecticians." To Paris the manuscripts of Aristotle and the neo-Platonists flowed along with the texts of medical theorists and Arabic commentaries. In that city of majestic towers and beautifully painted statues, new artistic styles conversed with theology and philosophy. The university with scholastic science was the gift of medieval and Gothic culture. The shifts in art after the twelfth century displayed views about the human person: the realism of muscular structure and the emotion of facial expression reveal the arrival of Aristotelianism emphasizing the individual being. Otto von Simson notes:

After the "shift in style" from the eleventh to the twelfth century
a new view of pictorial representation takes over. The composi-
tions become clearer and simpler, and with a quite new, firm and
often radiant clarity and dignity the theme of the picture expresses
its meaning. This movement . . . finds after 1150 a particularly
striking expression in the French "Early Gothic" which will determine European art for two centuries.[17]

A new art for a new culture brought a spirituality of light and a
theology of the real. Christian faith offered wide realms for Greek
thought to enter and to explore.

In Paris and Naples, the Dominican houses and schools where
Thomas lived stood in some relationship to a university. The origins
of the universal or general school lay in the twelfth century with edu-
cators like William of Champeaux lecturing at the cathedral school of

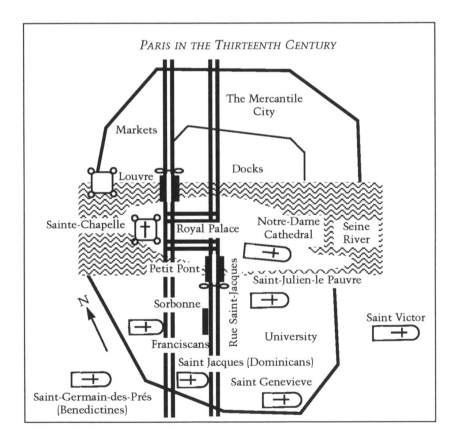

PARIS IN THE THIRTEENTH CENTURY

The Mercantile
City

Markets

Louvre

Docks

Sainte-Chapelle   Royal Palace   Notre-Dame
Cathedral   Seine
River

Petit Pont

Saint-Julien-le Pauvre

Sorbonne   Rue Saint-Jacques

N

Franciscans   University   Saint Victor

Saint Jacques (Dominicans)

Saint-Germain-des-Prés
(Benedictines)   Saint Genevieve

Paris and with Abelard founding a new kind of school on the outskirts of the same city. The latter school attracted crowds of students with its freedom of investigation and its technique of contrasting opinions about science prior to finding a synthetic resolution. A university had a structure: it was a collection of schools in a city, an institution owning a rigor and freedom (and a certain secularity) which the monastic schools could not achieve. The schools with their faculties in liberal arts, science, philosophy, theology, and law represented the intellectual side of the vitality of the Middle Ages. Their motivation was research, their method was dialectical, and their interests ranged widely. The university was a corporation in an age when new social collectivities were frequent. As teachers and students gained national and international attention and some stability, they had to fight for their right to exist over against the local church of the bishop or the powers of city and duchy. They had, however, as a defender the papacy.[18]

In the thirteenth century the many students at the collectivity of schools were divided into "nations": the French, the English, the Scandinavians, and others. They took as their common means of communication a direct if simple Latin. The students were avid for new knowledge but also for singing and drinking, for torch light processions and brawls. The tapestry of their urban, university life had religious strains woven through it: festivals on days of special saints led to theological study and discussion. Jacques Le Goff observes: "One finds in university imagery a persistent corporate tendency to blend intimately the sacred world with the profane world of professions. Images evoked Jesus among doctors and represented saints, dressing them in teacher's robes and equipping them with the accouterments of masters."[19] Both students and professors were at times involved in conflicts or even strikes. In 1229, when students died in bloody battles with royal police, the university went on strike and moved to Orleans. Louis IX's recall of the university to Paris was accompanied by a broader recognition of the schools' independence. Like apprentices in guilds, the students living and studying on the left bank in the "Latin Quarter" had a basic education in arts over six years. For more specialized courses they had particular masters whose lectures they were to attend for a certain period. At the end of a specified time a bachelor, an advanced student, was examined orally by three or four masters. If he passed this examination, after further studies on basic texts he was raised to the position of a master amid public banquets and celebrations, and he could teach on his own.

The university had its proper and original way of thinking: that of the schools, "scholasticism." That style of thinking and of discourse among scholars was at its birth not a dusty academic machine but an original way of dealing with intellectual and cultural life. Suited to a cultural world which was less monastic and isolated, the open discussion of a topic through different opinions and distinctions appeared to some dangerous but to others a liberation. The scholastic had a language (Latin), a terminology (Greek philosophy), and appropriate thought-forms (science). Scholasticism was a process of reasoning about realities as analyzed by science but it was also an intellectual construction which began with authorities and their interpretations. Through logic and dialectic it arranged a variety of opinions and authorities in the exposition of an area by means of the resolution of questions. Scholasticism had limitations and dangers. Did it appear to give the final judgment to reason? Was it too enthusiastic about each and every science? Was it too quick to follow non-Christian authors, too confident about its capabilities?

Because of the prominence of clergy, theology was at the center of the university, and theology led to the involvement of the church in this new institution. It soon became clear that university masters (professors) had more independence than teachers at episcopal or monastic schools. Chenu wrote: "Theirs was an intermediary status that was to remain non-existent in the Eastern Church. In the field of sacred doctrine, the doctor in theology or the *magistri* (masters), as they were collectively called, made up a sort of new department in which the teaching of the truths of faith expressly enlisted the services of natural reason or its philosophy in order to bring into being an organized science, a scholastic theology."[20] Paris, "the noblest of all university cities,"[21] was in many ways the leading *"universitas"* of schools, although Bologna, famous for law, was its rival. Paris was known for its faculties of liberal arts and theology. To this city Aquinas came as a young teacher, and years later he would take up a professorship there a second time. Chenu concluded: "Thomas outside of Paris is inconceivable."[22]

It is likely that it was in Paris that Thomas passed the year-long novitiate (resisting an offer by ecclesiastical authorities of a church office, something his family had arranged as a second attempt to persuade him to leave the Dominicans[23]). Many now think that Thomas' first time in Paris included contact with teachers in the arts and with some informal study with the man who would be his providential guide, the Dominican Albert of Lauingen (1200–1280).[24] Rudi Imbach concludes: "Thomas was too little advanced in the curriculum of his studies to become an official student of Albert, but it is nonetheless possible that he heard the lectures of Albert. What is certain is that Thomas at that time heard lectures on Aristotelian ethics in the faculty of arts . . . something which contravened the regulations forbidding lecturers to clerics to treat Aristotle, a regulation the Dominicans in 1228 had put in their constitutions."[25]

Albert from Lauingen on the Danube was called first "Albert the German" (he was the first German Dominican to be a professor at Paris) and then "Albert the Great." Born around 1200, he had studied in Padua, and after 1223 had entered the Dominican order, doing his novitiate in Cologne. After 1233 he taught in the Dominican houses of studies in Hildesheim, Regensburg, and Strassburg, while from 1245 to 1248 he was *magister*, professor, in Paris and in Cologne. Albert lectured in Paris and Cologne on the theological text of the time, the *Sentences* of Peter Lombard (+ 1164). Lombard had in Paris arranged on a large scale theological topics and patristic opinions, using a systematic and dialectical style. The Franciscan Alexander of Hales began to use the *Sentences* as a basis for his lectures about the time that Thomas was born, and it became a required university text in theology. That text was explained by a bachelor preparing to become a master in the faculty of theology. In the 1240s Albert was becoming famous in Paris for interpreting Aristotle in a creative and mature way (one that had satisfied or transcended the prohibition of Pope Gregory IX in 1231). Albert had to lecture outdoors at Saint-Jacques to accommodate the numbers of students and faculty.

In the year 1248 the Dominicans found in Cologne a further general center of studies, what the friars called a *"studium,"* a Dominican school of theology and philosophy mainly for Dominicans but open to others. It would be the first center of the new university world of studies in the German-speaking world. Thomas moved with Albert to Cologne in the summer of 1248 and studied with the older Dominican for four years. While he continued to lecture on the *Sentences* Albert undertook a revolutionary step: first he lectured on the writings of pseudo-Dionysius, and then he lectured on Aristotle's

Ethics. Thereby he drew Aristotle's corpus into a parallel consideration along with theological texts.[26] His Dominican brothers, Albert wrote, had been asking him to write on the natural sciences, including not only a general philosophy of nature but studies on meteors and stones or on the classification of animals and plants. He began in 1251 (continuing the work for over fifteen years) a large set of commentaries on the many texts: it would make Aristotle "intelligible to the Latins."[27]

One can grasp the breadth of Albert—he was introducing Aristotle and offering neglected neo-Platonic thought to theology—from his observation at the beginning of his commentary on Greek logic: "The sciences are not all constituted; there remains still a good number for us to discover."[28] Albert, J. A. Weisheipl concluded, was basically an Aristotelian in philosophy; in fact some scholars see him as the Latin interpreter of Aristotle par excellence.[29] Not only had he accepted and incorporated fundamental Aristotelian ideas into his own world-view, but he expounded Peripatetic thought in a way that would be intelligible to his Latin contemporaries. If Aristotle was central, there were also facets of Platonic teaching from pseudo-Dionysius, Augustine, and even Proclus; Avicenna too played a role. Albert was influential in his synthetic and explanatory writings but his style and innovations in the practice of philosophy as teaching led students to see how the unfolding content of the texts led to contemplation of world and God. If Albert's lectures resembled those of a natural scientist, it was because his career of teaching was both an overview of science which was living and a life of thinking. Thus Albert offered a model of a teacher of metaphysical theology who applied its principles to the Christian life.[30] Albert knew that his exposition of Aristotle placed him at the center of a battle spreading through Europe. He complained (and he was including some of his own Dominican brothers): "Our opponents are too lazy to study these works; they merely leaf through them in order to charge us with whatever heresies and errors they may run across, and so they feel that they are doing Christendom a service. They are the ones who murdered Socrates, who drove Plato away; their machinations have banned Aristotle from the universities."[31]

Through the Dominicans educated there, Cologne during the thirteenth and fourteenth centuries extended its intellectual influence along the Rhine. That school gave birth to theologians other than Thomas Aquinas. Albert himself could absorb and hand on both Aristotelian and neo-Platonic thought. Thus he furthered not only the genius of Aquinas but also inspired another line in medieval theology, a direction different from the Aristotelianism which attracted Aquinas; there philosophical and theological minds were drawn to the neo-Platonic Augustine and pseudo-Dionysius as well as to Avicenna, Averroes, and Maimonides. That second school used a methodology which moved from the philosophy of nature through the knowing and praying human being to the divine ideas. It elaborated the motifs of a divine fullness of being and of God giving birth to words which were creatures, finite beings set free in the realms of existence and knowing. Thus Albert the Great founded two influential currents of the thirteenth and fourteenth centuries.

Thomas' studies were to be done within the milieu of Dominican schools and of the universities. During the Cologne years Thomas passed from age twenty-four to twenty-seven, and we can imagine the impact which having a great teacher, contacts with a generous and creative spirit, must have made. Weisheipl concluded: "It would seem that throughout his active life Thomas kept very much in touch with the writings of St. Albert, but we cannot be sure that Albert bothered much about the writings of his favorite disciple."[32] A theological student spent some years being introduced into the methodical study of the Bible and then to the entire course of theology. We can surmise that Thomas also pored over texts recently accessible, the entire corpus of Aristotle and not just the philosophy of nature and logic. In Cologne, Thomas wrote down his teacher's lectures on Aristotle's *Ethics* and also Albert's pioneering lectures on the Syrian neo-Platonist pseudo-Dionysius—a mystical theologian of fifth-century Syria who was incorrectly identified as that Dionysius reported in the Acts of Apostles (17:34) as Paul's convert, and also revered as the missionary bishop of the Parisians. Perhaps as a novice-teacher, a "bachelor" under Albert, Friar Thomas gave his first lectures, explanations of the prophets Jeremiah and Isaiah. Back at Paris for four years he studied and explained the *Sentences* of Lombard. A young bachelor was to explain the basic meaning of the biblical text with its grammatical and logical problems, while the master presented theological exegesis. There was also a kind of resource book, the *Glossa ordinaria* from the twelfth century, which gave for the Scriptures notes (beneath the lines and along the margins) on difficult words and on opinions from important theologians. Meanwhile, Albert became for a while provincial of the main German province in 1254 and then bishop of Regensburg in 1260 (he resigned after two years realizing that his intellectual career was a more valuable service to the gospel). After teaching during the 1260s in Würzburg and Strassburg he refused a second term as professor in Paris and suggested Thomas Aquinas.

IV. Teacher and Writer

Despite Thomas' youth and the turbulent situation for the mendicants at the university in Paris, the head of the Dominicans was persuaded by Albert to assign Thomas there. In 1251, he arrived to pursue the stages of a professorial career as a master in theology, living at the priory of Saint-Jacques thirty-five years after the first Dominicans had arrived there. By the mid-thirteenth century the Dominicans had control of two chairs at the University of Paris. Under his director, Elias Brunet of Bergerac (he had succeeded Albert in the Dominican chair reserved for professors who were not French), Thomas for several years studied and lectured on Lombard's *Sentences*. His biographers stated that in his lectures on Lombard and on the Bible he introduced new issues and resolved past questions in a strikingly clear and original way.

At this time Thomas wrote two youthful works: one on Aristotle's philosophy of nature, and one on the metaphysical structure of the world ranging from rocks to God. Tugwell sees in this second early work a major difference between Thomas and Albert.

> All the same, it [*De Ente et Essentia*] announces some of Thomas' distinctive views, and especially it already reveals his desire to upgrade "existence": the real mystery of things is not *what* they are, but *that* they are, and it is their sheer existence which leads us to talk about God. Here we can recognize both one of the major differences between Thomas and Albert and one of Thomas' most basic and pervasive convictions. Albert was fascinated by all the details of *what* things are and rejoiced to find traces of God in all the intricacies of his handiwork. . . . For Thomas, it is not really the marvelous complexity and ingenuity of things that alerts the mind to the reality of God; it is rather the metaphysical implications of very simple observations about things, beginning with the primary fact of their being there at all.[33]

1252–1256   Bachelor of the Sentences at Paris
1256–1259   Master in Theology at Paris (I)
1259–1268   Period in Italy
                Naples (1259–1261)
                Orvieto (1261–1265)
                Rome (1265–1267)
                Viterbo (1267–1268)
1268–1272   Master of Theology at Paris (II)
1272–1273   Teaching and Writing in Naples

Admiring the diversity of nature and grace, Thomas will more and more develop his philosophy and theology not only as an admiration of the ingenious variety of things but also as an expression of a wondering but scientific analysis of the forms of things, beginning with the original fact that they exist at all and in this way.

Tension grew between the priests attached to dioceses who had traditionally filled professorships and the new Franciscans and Dominicans. This controversy, as much as disputes over profound metaphysical and theological issues, disturbed Thomas' periods of teaching in Paris. The secular clerics (called "secular" because they were not monks or friars) resented the friars' independence and interest in new ideas and were jealous of the growing popularity of the mendicant masters at the university. Were not academic positions contrary to the friars' poverty and to their rejection of power? Because the friars-masters had refused to join with the faculties in calling for disciplinary measures against the townspeople for killing a cleric in a brawl, they were expelled in September 1253 from the "gathering of professors." The second Dominican chair, the one for which Thomas was preparing (that which Albert and then Elias had held), was particularly resented. From 1252 to 1256, as Thomas was lecturing on the *Sentences*, the conflict intensified. Sometimes the friars were afraid to set out on their daily rounds of begging in the streets, and on a few occasions the unrest around Saint-Jacques was so intense that Louis IX sent royal archers to protect the priory. Simon Tugwell writes:

While Thomas was studying and lecturing in Paris, the Dominican Order was passing through the worst crisis in its history. . . . Their increasingly effective public ministry cut across the traditional lines of pastoral responsibility, which antagonized some (though by no means all) of the clergy. And their powerful presence in the universities threatened the prestige and corporate identity of the secular masters. Also the friars represented a new internationalism in the church with their direct dependence on the pope and their considerable independence of the bishops. . . . They accordingly had to defend their right to be what they were, in particular, the legitimacy of their living in towns among people rather than in secluded monastic strongholds, and their right to live off alms and to preach and teach rather than engaging in manual labor with financial self-sufficiency.[34]

Both Thomas and Bonaventure replied in lectures and writings to the attacks of prominent opponents like William of Saint-Amour who called the brothers of the new religious orders false prophets leading to the anti-Christ.[35] Aquinas' lines could take on an unusual force when he was defending the existence of the Dominicans and Franciscans. "Those who embrace voluntary poverty, especially those who renounced all income, wish to imitate the nakedness of the cross. . . . So it is clear that the enemies of poverty are also the enemies of the cross of Christ."[36]

Paris was involved in several acrimonious conflicts: not only that between friars and secular masters, but one between the faculty of arts, recently receiving permission to teach Aristotle, and the more conservative faculty of theology.[37] In March 1256, Alexander IV ordered the chancellor of the university to grant Thomas Aquinas the license to teach even though he was under the approved age of thirty-five, and to arrange promptly for his inaugural lecture as a professor. But Thomas and his gifted contemporary, the Franciscan Bonaventure, still were denied full professorial rights, because the administration of the university refused to recognize their status. Only in 1257 were the two friars grudgingly admitted to the privileges of their university positions. Amid students and faculty, some enthusiastic and some hostile, Aquinas, the first member of his Roman province to become a master, gave his inaugural address.

In his inaugural lecture when he became a bachelor teaching the *Sentences*, Thomas had said that a good teacher should "teach the ignorant, interest the bored, and attract the disinterested."[38] Now the young professor's opening remarks described a "law" which God had eternally instituted: the gifts of providence reach creatures through the apt mediations of being and grace. Divine wisdom also flows into the minds of the professors of theology: their ministry is to direct the light of divine wisdom to their hearers. Aquinas then discussed four aspects of his new office and of his vocation: the loftiness of Christian teaching, the dignity of being its teacher, the students, and the mode of communication between teacher and students.[39] The young professor was an engaging teacher, something soon recognized. An early biographer wrote: "When Thomas entered upon his duties as teacher and began disputations and lectures, students flocked to his classroom in such numbers that the hall could hardly accommodate all of them. . . . The reason for this success was the terse, clear, and engagingly intelligible style of his lectures."[40]

In the Middle Ages the Bible was the basic text of the masters' lectures but its presentations unfolded in questions and elucidations drawn from philosophy, theological opinions, speculative theology, law, and church tradition. Weisheipl wrote: "Outstanding as Thomas was as a bachelor, lecturing between the hours of Tierce and Sext (9 A.M. to 12 A.M.), he matured enormously as a master. Although young, he took his responsibilities seriously. As master his task was to lecture doctrinally on the Bible between the hours of Prime and Tierce, resolve disputed questions in the afternoon, and preach to university clerics on special occasions."[41] Opportunity for displaying quickness and originality of intellect in theological solutions came in the disputations. Held several times a year they took place in both planned and impromptu formats. The impromptu disputations held before Christmas and Easter were open to the public, and members of the audience could pose a problem to be discussed and take a position on the question. Thomas' major series of formal disputations began with the topic of truth presented in Paris during the years from 1256 to 1259; he treated in Rome after 1265 God's power and evil, and upon his return to Paris in 1268 the soul, the virtues, and the incarnation. The *magister* supervised the later published text of his disputations which gave his opening presentation and an ordered selection of current, public objections. Aquinas showed a grasp of Greek philosophical directions and sources as he joined Platonic and Augustinian views to his Aristotelian approach in presenting and querying the Christian faith.[42] The teacher produced many writings in different genres. He wrote a commentary on the

Sentences of Peter Lombard, interpreted several books of the Hebrew Bible, and from the New Testament expounded the gospels according to Matthew and according to John, and the letters of Paul. Finally there are commentaries on writings by other theologians, for instance, Boethius. He composed three large theological projects beyond the commentary on the *Sentences*: the *Summa contra gentiles*, the *Summa theologiae*, and the *Compendium theologiae*. Added to commentaries and disputations are smaller writings and commentaries on Aristotle. For instance, in the year 1269 he was commenting on the Gospel according to John even as he was writing sections of the *ST*, moving through the ethical areas of personal decision and virtue up to the New Law and grace, and he was also explaining Aristotle's writings on natural philosophy. Summing up the style of the young professor, an early biographer wrote: "In his lectures he introduced new articles, resolved questions in a new manner and more clearly and with new arguments. The result was that those who heard him teach new theses and treat them with a new method were not able to doubt that God had let shine forth a new light."[43]

The unassuming young teacher, as he was explaining new models of metaphysics and theology, was, as we saw, repeatedly drawn into the two controversies which engaged him throughout his life: the legitimacy of using Aristotle in theology, and the legitimacy of the mendicant orders in church and society. While the young Aquinas in Naples had learned about Aristotle's physics when the philosopher's writings were proscribed in Paris, the novel realism of the new science was, years later, still disparaged and attacked. The logical works of Aristotle had never disappeared from European awareness, but contact with Muslim intellectual centers had introduced the rest of his corpus at the end of the twelfth century. "Aristotle" in the lifetime of Aquinas stood not only for a wider body of his writings but for the ensemble of Greek and Arabic science and philosophy then arriving in Europe. It brought a new world-view: realistic, based upon empirical methods of research, original in insight and organization. R. W. Southern wrote: "By 1250 virtually the whole corpus of Greek science was accessible to the western world, and scholars groaned under its weight as they strove to master it all. The days had gone when two large volumes could hold all that was essential for the study of the liberal arts. There was no time for artistic presentation and literary eloquence. This was a grave loss, but the achievement was there all the same. The main ideas of the earlier masters—the dignity of man, the intelligibility of the universe, the nobility of nature—not only remained intact, but were fundamental concepts in the intellectual structures of the thirteenth century."[44] This flow of Greek texts through Spain and Sicily, however, brought with them into Europe Islamic commentaries and interpolations which raised inflammatory issues: Had the universe existed eternally? Was there a super intellect guiding all humans? Were people free? Would not the scientific method of exploring a reality's causes undermine devotion? The papacy moved from condemning Aristotle (in 1231 and 1245) to requesting accurate texts. Roman authority saw in the new religious orders of the friars an instrument to draw two powerful cultural forces of the times into the ambiance of the church: the movements of apostolic discipleship, poverty and preaching and the new intellectual world of the universities with its science, including Aristotle. By 1244 Albert was commenting on the works in natural science and Robert Grosseteste was translating the *Ethics*. Chenu observed:

> In 1252, the year when Thomas began teaching his own doctrine, already conditioned by a deliberate and decisive choice for Aristotelian thought, the Stagirite's *De Anima* was listed among the texts to be used in the English nation section of the faculty of arts. In 1255 the whole of the Aristotelian corpus was placed on the curriculum. The masters had won over for themselves a complete cycle of philosophical teaching that went far beyond the propaedeutics of the seven liberal arts and of the ancient dialectic. This was more than enough to raise, within the institutional organization, the problem of a philosophy that was now set free from the superintendence of the theologians.[45]

If others were beginning to study and to propound Aristotle, Albert and Thomas viewed the understanding and propagation of the new philosophy as inspiring intellectual creativity, as calling for evangelization. They gave Aristotelian principles wider application and richer meanings, and—the most daring enterprise of all—they applied sharp and synthetic analyses to biblical revelation. For instance, one might view grace and virtues as something like the Aristotelian soul and faculties, or one might discuss the mystery of divine love for the human race by beginning with the Greek's understanding of friendship and love among equals. The *Summa theologiae* would offer 3,500 quotations from Aristotle.[46] At the same time, we must recall that, while the thought of Aristotle played a significant part in these synthetic works, the Aristotelian corpus had by this time been read and interpreted in some universities for thirty years. Hans Urs van Balthasar observed: "Thomas is himself a '*kairos*,' a historically transitory moment between an old world style of thinking in a monastic way and seeing (Greek or Christian) philosophy and theology as one, and an emerging dualistic world which (Christian and non-Christian) will attempt to tear philosophy and revelation's theology apart and then will try to make out of each a totality."[47]

V. The Idea for a Masterpiece

Around the new year of 1260 Thomas returned to his own Roman Dominican province, to the priory in Naples where he had received the friars' white habit and black cloak a dozen years before. His chair of theology at Paris was turned over to an English Dominican. On his route back to his homeland he preached in Milan and Bologna.[48] Perhaps he taught in the priory near the university. In Naples he worked on his first "*summa*," the *Summa contra gentiles* which he had begun in Paris, had expanded and revised over some years, and which would be completed in 1265.[49] The twelfth century had seen the origins of medieval speculative theology: collections of opinions on a topic were gathered together. After 1200 the *summa* strove for greater order and integration, and for an order which would assemble in logic and beauty more and more material. Building upon William of Auxerre, Alexander Hales, and Albert, Thomas' *Summa contra gentiles* was a presentation of the Christian faith in its teachings and in its philosophical underpinnings and implications. Scholars no longer think that it was written as a practical handbook for Dominicans in direct contact with Islam: rather, the "*gentiles*" indicate great past thinkers—Greek, Jewish, and Muslim—some of whose philosophical and religious views diverged from the Christian faith but which Aquinas met in an irenic way.[50] The later *ST*, however, will be the outstanding medieval *summa*. The struggle over the right form for a theological *summa* in the thirteenth century illustrates the great problem of forming a sacred history into an organized science.[51]

In 1261 he moved to Orvieto, a city with ancient Etruscan origins, then serving as the residence of Pope Urban IV. That urbane and educated church leader formed his central ecclesiastical administration, his "*curia*," in such a way that it attracted scholars and diplomats, bishops and preachers. The pope was unsuccessful in warfare against the Emperor Frederick, but he had his successes as a patron of philosophy and as an advocate of reconciliation between Rome and the Eastern churches (Urban had been in the East earlier in his life). The amicable pope appreciated the talents of Aquinas who was serving as the Dominican priory's theology teacher.[52] He asked him to address issues in the theologies and traditions of the Greek church in terms of reconciling them with Latin theologians: the result was the small work, *Against the Errors of the Greeks*. Orvieto gave to Aquinas a time of intellectual growth—for a while in 1262 Albert the Great was there with him—because he was able to make use of monastic libraries in the area and to assemble new material from theologians of the third to the seventh centuries. Written around 1264 and at papal request, a special kind of commentary on the Gospels, "a golden chain," set forth opinions by earlier theologians on each verse. This shows an advance in sources, for he cited twenty-two Latin but fifty-seven Greek theologians. Aquinas did not merely quote these works, some little known in the West at that time, but labored to enter into their thought. Scholars also think research done during the Orvieto period gave Aquinas more acquaintance with the acts of the first five ecumenical councils.[53] Certainly, the theology of Christ in the Third Part of the *ST* (1272) shows study of the texts of the early councils and of theologians like John Damascene. He also was gaining access to some late writings of Augustine and to ecclesiastical documents on the later stages of the Pelagian controversy, and these led him to give grace a more dominant place in human life.[54] Experts note a change in tone shortly after as the First Part of the *ST* was completed and Thomas moved further into his theology of the Christian life. There was a shift from metaphysics toward the complexity of the human person; there was an emphasis upon the affective and the intuitive, on graced virtue and the instinctual gifts of the Holy Spirit.[55] If Aquinas searched for new perspectives, still he revered the authorities of the past. He did not think any text held an inerrant, intimidating, or total authority; nor did he identify language with revelation, a linguistic phrase with the reality to be expressed. He approached Greek,

Christian, and Arab philosophers with an interested but critical mind. Coming to the end of a trip out to the Abbey of Saint-Denis with its apartments and tombs for the royal family and its library of Greek and Carolingian manuscripts, Thomas and his companion looked down on the recently built towers and buildings of the rich capital of Paris. The other Dominican asked if Aquinas would not like to own the striking city. Thomas asked, "What would I do with it?" and his confrere answered, "You could sell it and use the money to build houses for the Dominicans." The teacher replied "I would rather have the homilies of Chrysostom on the Gospel of St. Matthew."[56] This is not the rebuff of a pious academic but the cry of a scarcher for new ideas. The choice of the text is significant: the author of the sought-for book is a Greek theologian and the book is that writing of the New Testament which medieval scholars saw as focused on Jesus' humanity.

That busy time of research, writing, and teaching had to be interrupted for Dominican provincial meetings almost every year, for instance, in Perugia, Rome, and Viterbo. Aquinas moved to Rome from Orvieto in 1265 and taught at the Dominican priory of Santa Sabina until 1267 or 1268 when he began a short time of service (lasting to the autumn of 1268) at Viterbo where the papal administration of Clement IV was then in residence. Perhaps at Viterbo and Rome Thomas met his Dominican brother William of Moerbeke, who, though of Flemish parentage, was born in Greece and entered the Dominicans in the East. He began translating Greek philosophical works in 1253, and Aquinas prized his careful and mature realizations of Aristotle into Latin.[57]

In 1265 Aquinas was commissioned to organize a Dominican theological school at Rome (around that time he declined Pope Clement IV's request that he become archbishop of Naples). Historians think that it was in the cloister of Santa Sabina on the Aventine that the idea of a richer but more tightly organized synthesis came to him, the plan for his greatest *summa* of theology. As we shift our attention from Paris to Rome, we can recall that in 1221 Pope Honorius III gave to Dominic as a first central church and monastery the basilica of Santa Sabina. The church was over seven hundred years old when Aquinas worshipped in it. Inside, over the central portal, is still today the dedicatory inscription from 432. Its Latin letters in gold on a blue mosaic background mention the pope

at that time, Celestine. That pope had received in the fifth century the
first reports of difficulties with the bishop Nestorius over the being of
Jesus Christ. The Dominicans, whose order was only sixty years old
when Aquinas lived at Santa Sabina, had built a second floor on to the
cloister constructed some centuries earlier. Thomas, resting from the
physical and mental journeys he set for himself, and looking out on
imperial and medieval Rome from the quiet of the Aventine situated
above the Tiber, found his imagination picturing forms suitable to a
new kind of theology: motifs and patterns for the *Summa theologiae*.

At the age of forty and at the height of his powers, working on
philosophical and biblical commentaries, Aquinas began to "set forth
those things which pertain to the Christian religion . . . briefly and
clearly" (*ST*, Prologue). The First Part was probably finished before
Thomas left Italy to teach again in Paris. Did Thomas teach the material of the *ST* as he was writing it down in Rome? The *ST* was written
for use in a less formal setting for educating Dominican preachers.
Among the friars Thomas could present an innovative theological pedagogy which might have been unacceptable at a university. Certainly,
the originality in order, the ambition of the enterprise, and the departure from lecturing only on the Bible would have suggested to his community that here was a person of unusual gifts.

Thomas began a second period of teaching at the University of
Paris in 1268.[58] Why was he asked to return to Paris? Scholars believe
that Albert the Great had been invited to assume a vacant professorship in Paris to support the cause of Aristotelianism, but he declined
(he was seventy-five), and Thomas was the next choice. Paris was still
the battleground of the conflicts which disturbed Aquinas' personal
and theological career: the opposition to the mendicant professors, the
hostility of the theological faculty to Aristotle, the identification of
Aristotle with Averroism. Thomas engaged his powers on all these
fronts: he wrote two major works supporting the mendicant orders
(and we have sermons from the Christmas season of 1270/71 arguing
for evangelical poverty), and a number of works on the value, meaning,
and limitations of Aristotelian thought.

Why was the study of Aristotle viewed as dangerous? Augustinianism with its Platonic origins and its monastic setting was the
traditional, entrenched way of pursuing Christian theology. That
approach often centered on edifying arguments and allegorical interpretations of the biblical message. It rather implied that creatures and

ideas received their value in mirroring the divine and the eternal. The long history of Western monasticism had drawn faith and theology deeper into the realms of prayer and symbolism. To the meditations of the cloister, the argumentation and realism of the new Aristotelian approach seemed secular and independent. To analyze bishops and sacraments, physical emotions and divine grace in light of their actions rather than as inspiring symbols and pious hopes could be unnerving.

Weisheipl saw Franciscan opposition to the philosophy and theology developed by Albert and Thomas emerging; it wanted to preserve the older type of Augustinian doctrine with its origins in neo-Platonism and its goal in spiritual edification. At Paris the Franciscan John Peckham criticized Aquinas: "I do not in any way disapprove of philosophical studies, insofar as they serve theological mysteries, but I do disapprove of irreverent innovations in language, introduced within the last twenty years into the depth of theology against philosophical truth and to the detriment of the Fathers. . . . [This is] a doctrine which fills the entire world with wordy quarrels, weakening and destroying with all its strength what Augustine teaches."[59] Étienne Gilson thought that Bonaventure, the superior of the Franciscan Order with his headquarters at Paris, was the source of the difficulty, but Bonaventure never came out directly against Thomas—although scholars are uncertain about the personal friendship between them which tradition affirms. Bonaventure had observed: "Among philosophers the word of wisdom was given to Plato, while to Aristotle was given the word of knowledge. The first looked principally to what is higher, the second to what is lower. . . . But the word of both knowledge and wisdom was given by the Holy Spirit to Augustine."[60] Chenu thought that after 1267 Bonaventure became more anxious over the open discussion of Aristotle, particularly in theological questions, "making discrete allusion to those who, without falling into error, nonetheless pursue under any pretext a rationalist method."[61] This is the type of controversy that could well have caused the Dominican superior in Rome to take such an unprecedented step as this second assignment of a particular master to the University of Paris.

The advocacy of Aristotelianism by Albert and Thomas in the thirteenth century was not simply a debate over logic or metaphysics but marked a turning point in the history of Christianity and Western civilization. For the third time, after Origen in the third century and

Augustine in the fifth, the Christian faith perceived that it could employ (but not be absorbed by) the ideas of a new age, culture, and science. The struggle of the thirteenth century swirled around Aristotle, because he brought a spirit of criticism over against piety, a realism in the structure of the human personality over against the reduction of faith or grace to signs or stories. The instincts and faculties of human life enhanced (but did not rival or replace) the world of grace and faith. Faith was not just religious information about curious mysteries, but a knowing supported by the will, a cognition which gave access to a real world. To describe God's special presence, "grace," as a form resembling the human soul, as a life-principle for men and women journeying to a special destiny, seemed then quite scientific. Within a freedom of inquiry Aquinas' career unfolded around his constant and courageous assertion that Christian faith need not fear realistic world-views or sciences.

A second threat to the use of Aristotle came not from Augustinian theologies but from the very supporters of the new Greek science. Professors in the arts faculty cultivated the new science drawn from Arab commentators on Aristotle like Averroes and Avicenna to the extent that they accepted conclusions from Aristotle and his Arabic commentators which contradicted Christian doctrine. They resolved conflicts between Christianity and physics—an eternal world, a too determinative world-soul—by preferring science. This option for secular learning, while appearing to be a liberation, undermined when it became an ideology the world-view of the believer.[62]

Scholars disagree over Aquinas' goals in writings books on Aristotle and the accuracy of the Dominican's interpretations. Do the Christian's commentaries aim at reconciling a Greek philosopher with the faith? Do they present him accurately? Torrell observes: "With regards to the Aristotelian accuracy of his exegesis, historians have little by little become more critical. One recognizes an intelligent and profound, often literal, fidelity but it is one which, nonetheless, bends the teaching of Aristotle on certain points . . . e. g., a metaphysics of creation or an absence of polytheism." Thomas wished to understand the intention of the author and the meaning of the text, but this did not hinder him from setting them in a theological context. "Without turning it into a too bold apologetic which would ultimately be of no service to his goals, one can say that a balanced appreciation of his work occurs when one remembers that he undertook these commentaries out of an apostolic perspective to aid his profession as a theologian and to accomplish better a ministry to wisdom which he understood in terms of the dual school of St. Paul and of Aristotle: to proclaim the truth and to refute error."[63]

Medieval masters sought out and explained texts. But why did Thomas comment so extensively on Aristotle? Not because he wished to extract a philosophy independent of theology. Careful expositions of Aristotle were composed for young teachers in the liberal arts and philosophy or for students approaching the end of their theological education. Regardless, at the height of his career, he spent a great deal of effort offering clear and orderly expositions of what Aristotle said. His commentaries spotlighted the truth and value of this philosophy and defended it from past Arabic misinterpretations.[64] While he wanted to give the accurate meaning of Aristotle and thereby to show that Aristotle need not be feared by Christians, he also was very interested in introducing the valuable method and conclusions of Aristotle which would serve his own theological perspective. His attention to Aristotle (he wrote on Platonist works too) was pedagogical: after all, these writings were education and science par excellence. But an extracted philosophy, set apart for neutral or secular goals, was not Aquinas' purpose. Chenu concluded: "It would be to falsify . . . the intention of Saint Thomas to seek in the commentaries his personal thought and to build a Thomism whose theology would be in his *Summa* and philosophy in his commentaries on Aristotle. . . . It is very difficult to elaborate a Thomistic 'philosophy' from the works of Saint Thomas and from their concrete implications. But it is to pervert right from the beginning the components of the problem to state it in those terms. It would also be a misunderstanding of the historical and doctrinal relations between Aristotle and his commentator Saint Thomas."[65] Scholars agree that the commentaries on Aristotle's psychology and ethics were written as Aquinas composed the first part of the Second Part, and that the Dominican commented on them in his role as theologian. Walter Principe writes:

> Like his teacher, Albertus Magnus, he saw no opposition between nature and grace or between truths discovered by reason and those revealed by God. It cannot be stressed too much, however, that Thomas intended to be and always was primarily a theologian: even

his commentaries on Aristotle were done for theological purposes. To treat him as a philosopher and to extract a "Thomistic" philosophy from the theological context in which Aquinas uses philosophy is a disservice too frequently done by many professing to follow him. Divorced from its living theological context, such a desiccated body of doctrines loses the force and vitality of Aquinas' thought and is at least partly responsible for the current neglect of his teaching in many quarters.[66]

The theological vocation of Thomas Aquinas and the religious context of the friar's presence in university life offer the setting for all the philosophical writings. Ludwig Hödl notes: "Thomas is concerned exclusively with the philosophical pre-work for his *Summa theologiae.* In what does this preliminary work consist? Thomas was working within the basic philosophical concepts which are also necessary for understanding moral theological statements. The concepts are studied in their general determination and thought-forms which also are valid in theology because theology basically has no other mode of thinking even if it employs these insightful ideas differently."[67] In short, philosophical analyses of being, even when separated from their employment in explaining, for instance, the missions of the Trinity or the Incarnation, do not assume from a historical or doctrinal point of view an independent life of their own.

Aquinas returned to Paris probably in the autumn of 1268. The capital of Louis IX held within its gates along the banks and islands of the Seine new churches and castles, particularly the completed cathedral of Notre Dame and the spectacularly adorned Sainte-Chapelle, a seven-story architectural reliquary of stained glass constructed to house Jesus' crown of thorns. The king, biographical anecdotes tell us, was a patron of Aquinas; he invited him to court and provided him with secretaries to copy texts and take dictation. Thomas was particularly busy, lecturing, preaching, and disputing, while trying to find time to write systematic and exegetical works.[68] In terms of the *ST*, the second half of the Second Part and segments of the Third Part were written during this second period in Paris. At the same time Aquinas found time to compose a commentary of particular serenity and depth, one on the Gospel according to John which scholars rank with those on Romans and Job as his finest.[69] The series of Aristotelian commentaries begun in Rome was continued: work after work found a detailed exposition, e.g., the *Physics*, the *Nichomachaean Ethics*, *On Interpretation*, and the *Metaphysics*. To works of commentary and of original composition are to be added an extraordinary number of disputations, and ad hoc philosophical works on topics ranging from the elements of matter to astrology, angels, and political theory. Torrell has estimated that from October 1268 to May 1272 he produced the equivalent of 4,000 pages in today's books. To accomplish this he would have to have written 2,500 words, that is about three and a half pages, every day. This productivity would be possible only with secretaries, indeed, with an "atelier" of copyists, researchers, and clerks for dictation.[70]

Because he drew the method of Aristotle into theology, Aquinas was seen in the turbulent world of Paris as an innovator, as an avid, even risky, explorer of new ideas, and as an original creator of syntheses for being and faith. At the end of 1270, the Bishop of Paris Stephen Tempier condemned propositions drawn from Latin Averroism. Their kind of Aristotelianism could be read as involving the Dominicans, although Albert and Thomas had always rejected those directions. (This prepared for a further condemnation in 1277, three years after Aquinas' death, in which he could again be construed as included.)

After four years, however, Aquinas was again to leave Paris. The university was caught up in administrative conflict, and his Dominican province had plans for him. Despite protests from young teachers and students in the faculty of arts (some saw themselves to be disciples of his exposition of Aristotle), he left Paris in the spring of 1272. The provincial chapter held at Florence (the friars representing their priories at this assembly received letters from professors in Paris asking for him to return[71]) requested him to establish a general *studium*, a school for Dominicans. He traveled to Naples where he would remain until his last journey north in 1274. In Naples, Thomas lectured and directed disputations in the halls of the priory of St. Dominic. The priory then was next door to the University of Naples, and in fact served as the faculty of theology in the university. Thomas was lecturing on the Pauline letters and working on the *ST*. Weisheipl commented:

> Thomas had been working at a high pitch for the preceding five years, ever since his return to Paris in 1269, when he seemed to realize in a new way the great need for his apostolate. A kind of fever seemed to possess him, so that "he was continuously occupied in teaching, or

in writing, or in preaching, or in praying, so that he devoted the least possible time to eating or sleeping." The quality of his work never suffered. On the contrary, he continued to mull over problems and their solution, trying to improve his grasp of the truth. In the odyssey of his thought he progressed from imperfect solutions to more perfect expressions of the truth. He modified earlier opinions and sometimes changed them significantly.[72]

In Naples transition became crisis. As his biographer Bartholomew of Capua put it, "It was the common view that he had wasted scarcely a moment of his time."[73] But even a genius with a sound constitution could not keep up such a pace of teaching and writing, or face the relentless challenges of expressing the old in the new. Thomas' productivity slowed—perhaps out of fatigue. It would not be surprising to think that he was saddened by the attacks on him he had learned were taking place in Paris. Still, he had the strength to continue work on his great *summa* in its sections on Christ and the sacraments. He preached a Lenten cycle of sermons in Naples during 1273. After Mass on the feast of St. Nicholas in December 1273, in the words of an early biographer, "He neither wrote nor dictated anything; in fact, he hung up his writing instruments." To his assistant inquiring why he had completely stopped work on his many projects, Thomas replied, "I cannot go on. . . . All that I have written seems to me like so much straw compared to what I have seen and what has been revealed to me."[74] A visit to his sister Theodora at the castle of San Severino near Naples did not rouse him from his increasing lethargy. Returning to Naples in early January 1274, it was evident that Thomas was ill, exhausted, uncertain, and introspective. He was physically and mentally unable to continue his past life of teaching and writing: the following months saw what must have been for him a painful asceticism, the acceptance of inactivity. Weisheipl did not discount the mystical side of the experience in which Aquinas saw the limitations of his work in comparison with God's being, but he also noted the likelihood that this had a physical cause in some kind of stroke or brain tumor (brought on by overwork) whose symptoms included the depressing inability to focus attention or to work.[75] The suddenness of Aquinas' lapse into inactivity and the subsequent occasion of his death a few weeks later, hitting his head against the limb of a tree, argue for a neurological factor.

Gregory X was elected pope in 1272, and to initiate reforms in the Western church and to further reunion with the Eastern churches he convoked the Second Council of Lyons to which he summoned the Dominican theologian. At the beginning of February 1274, a group of Dominicans were traveling north from Naples to Rome from where they would continue on to Lyons and to the assembly. There, it was rumored, Thomas Aquinas would be made a cardinal. On the journey north he planned a visit to his family. After injuring his head Thomas continued for a few hours but then asked to stop at Maenza where his niece lived (Maenza was not far from Roccasecca where he had been born). As he became increasingly weak, he asked to be moved to the Cistercian Abbey of Fossanova where after a month's decline he died on March 7th in his fiftieth year (Bonaventure died four months later in July). The life of a person of extraordinary energy in traveling, lecturing, and writing, in gathering texts and creating new syntheses, had ended abruptly, and yet, his spirit had found before death a brief time of reflection and contemplation. How shocked his elderly teacher Albert must have been to receive the news that his extraordinary student was dead.[76]

VI. Personality and Genius

In the following chapters we want to understand Aquinas both as a theologian of the Middle Ages and as a religious thinker whose influence reaches up into our own times.

A culture is first a birth, a moment, a time; subsequently it is a struggle, a conversation with the unexpected. His ideas were called forth by a historical self-awareness, that is, by his creative perception of what was beginning. We should attempt to understand him as man of his age. The more we know about the world of a thinker the better we understand that particular way of thinking. We can learn something about his personality from his career and writings. Chenu established a basic principle:

> The course of Christian history is the source of theological knowledge, especially when for the sake of our understanding theology presents faith to new generations in new ways. . . . All the metaphysics of Aristotle, all the psychology of Augustine, all the mysticism of Dionysius, all the science of the Arabs, all the asceticism of

Gregory and the contemplation of the Victorines—these did not make up the spirit of Friar Thomas. His consciousness assimilated all of this, but that assimilation, that "reduction" of five civilizations into the unity of one spiritual life, is itself an object for us to study. The beautiful form which is the intellectual approach of Aquinas is not an angelic form: it was born, it lived, it attained a concrete realization; [his theology] existed in a time, in a climate, in a context, in a body.[77]

Recent historical scholarship has helped to dispel the clichés of English-speaking prejudice in the nineteenth and twentieth centuries accusing Aquinas of compulsive rationalism, of pursuing irrelevant topics, of being ignorant of the Bible, or of lacking a mystical spirit or a human tone. It is hard to imagine that only fifty years ago some universities and churches presented Thomas as a superstitious monk lost in something named the dark ages. We at the end of the twentieth century are, fortunately, heirs to the scholarship which has uncovered the rich historical world out of which the *ST* was written.

His early biographers too often changed traits of his personality into arguments for canonization and depicted him as either a "saint" or a "character." There are a number of stories told about Aquinas which have no historical fact. He seems to have been tall, large, blond, and balding, but we do not know that he was very fat (the regimen of the Dominicans, the long days of work, and frequent walks or travels would make that unlikely), or that he was excessively quiet (speculative gifts, composing several large works simultaneously would lead to some inner preoccupation). The story that Albert defended him against his fellow Dominican students who were calling him a "dumb ox" is legend and presents a childish view of teacher, student, and confreres. Chenu points in a different direction:

We must first free ourselves from the sketchy, devotional image where St. Thomas is presented as an abstracted, solitary person, which contemplation and his profession have removed physically from the conflicts and squabbles of his century. That century, however, was the century of summas and of cathedrals, and of the royal holiness of Louis IX. Only a facile romanticism can remove that time from its own reality where violent spirits, even among believers, struggled with the coarsest social customs. This sentimentality cannot be harmonized with either historical truth nor with the personal generosity of Aquinas.[78]

A realistic approach to his personality ponders how his choices and accomplishments reflect the person (after all, according to Aquinas' theoretical psychology, actions reveal the agent). We know about his professional life as a teacher and theologian. Let his life, then, disclose the personality.

At seventeen Thomas determined the direction of his future: the young student left the feudal and monastic world which was declining and entered enthusiastically his changing age, so rich in ideas and opportunities. Chenu observed how early decisions gave him an unusual freedom: "He broke totally with the established regime (of feudalism and monasticism) and conquered for himself a spiritual and intellectual freedom, the institutional freedom of the Order as well as its liberty for religion. . . . Thomas was the audacious and balanced master of the cultural and intellectual strategy which created a civilization."[79] Those decisions tell a great deal about the man, about clarity and energy, characteristics which, if we look closely, are also present in his writings.

Thomas of Aquino must have been a man of unusual energy, generosity (he composed twenty-six works at the request of others), and courage. Some have estimated that on his trips across Europe he walked over 9,000 miles.[80] Fatiguing travels did not discourage him, for they enabled his educational enterprises and research. M.-H. Vicaire saw a paradox: "An apparent conflict between the dramatic career and the serene work is present in the Dominican's life— in his childhood and religious vocation, in his education at high levels and in his teaching—and his mature years are its climax. Under the impersonal construction of the *ST* are hidden strong positions, dramatic decisions, controversial conclusions some of which his opponents will try to have condemned."[81] People who knew him described him as approachable, patient, and kind. His writings present the same image of their author.

We do not know that he was withdrawn or prayed all the time, that he never left the priory or school, or had no interest in people. Thomas' personality was bright and not intimidated; it was not only receptive to the new but its seeker and its lover. He prized the enthusiasm, poverty, and ministries of the Dominicans and gave up a comfortable and secure life to enter their brotherhood. He would not have identified the friars-preachers of Dominic exclusively with the university, and throughout his life Thomas remained a preacher. Decisively avoiding ecclesiastical offices and honors, he was a tireless evangelist. Theology should not be apologetic but essentially ministerial. The Word and words of God were about life and had many consequences. His life was one of searching and researching, always sharing generously and tirelessly knowledge with others. He joined the attainment of a high position in the intellectual life with a mystical intention to follow Jesus literally. Far from being an ascetic introvert, he was interested in everything, in details and in small issues. He puzzled over the different activities of the godhead or over the precise geographical location of the garden of Eden. That powerful genius (who described humility as an active orientation neither to undertake what is beyond our powers nor to stay with what lacks all challenge [II–II, 161, 1]) devoted himself not to overturning the past or demeaning the present but to service and creation. Originality met with reality; objectivity emerged within arrangement.

Aquinas' theological project reflects his personality, suggesting that he was optimistic and generous, capable of living in the middle between the universe and the reign of God. Neither new movements and ideas nor the range of people in medieval society frightened him. The serenity of his mind did not lead him to judge people haughtily or to withdraw from conflict. The writings of Aquinas, however, tell us little of the private views of this theologian. Those pages are serene, lofty, human but rather anonymous—like a fresco painted by Giotto. The writings come from someone who is hardworking, respectful, and modest toward others, but who is also aroused by what creation and grace present. Logic and order always serve the human and the divine. Torrell concludes: "We should recall how that portrait has nothing to do with the timeless thinker which has been the result of phrases like 'Common Doctor' and 'Angel of the Schools'. . . . The man we venerate as a saint should not lead us to neglect the person who has been a model of the Christian life he incarnated. Certainly there is a continuity between the man who wrote hurriedly and the one who was not slow to challenge his adversaries and who was irritated at their inconsistency."[82]

Aquinas' theology offers better intimations of his personality than do later, fabricated, pious stories. We might sketch his theological mentality in this way: he was consistent but not predictable, interested in resolving theological issues but not dogmatic, curious and broad in his projects but respectful of tradition and church. Enthusiastic for the gifts which both the universities and the friars could bring to society, he was fond of study and research and unsympathetic to uninformed interventions of authorities. He was permeated by the quest for order, and yet his writings reveal originality, spontaneity, and imagination. He was not a rationalist, for his rational exposition was moving toward intuition and mystery. He preferred the ordinary to the miraculous. He was enthusiastic about the capabilities of human powers, and yet he believed that in metaphysics and revelation one could touch something of the knowledge that God has of himself and of his works. His writings reveal a sense of tranquillity: an appreciative contemplation of the structure of the cosmos is joined to a calm openness to all that exists.

A close examination of the few surviving manuscripts gives us a picture of the writer whose traces have survived in paper and ink. Aquinas' handwriting, the expertise of P.-M. Gils concludes, has an Italian style and was set down on quite poor paper and with pens and ink of low quality; it is not elegant or beautiful. Signs of rapidity suggest someone pressed for time and caught up in his own studious reflections. He has to find time for writing among his obligations of teaching and preaching, and often the hour seized upon is only enough for a few dozen lines, rarely more. "St. Thomas is a busy man. He is always faced with the demands of his writing. He is constantly being distracted and these distractions oblige him to interrupt what he is doing and then to return to it later. He struggles with how to order his thought and with the means of expressing it. He is careful in details but also unconcerned about the results, for there is always an irresistible drive within him to go forward."[83]

We do not have the amount of first-hand information about Aquinas we would like. For instance, what were his precise role and his impact at the papal court? How did students and colleagues in Rome react to the new theological program of the *ST*? How did a young friar of talent and energy, supported by both Pope Urban IV and King Louis IX, fit into his Dominican priory in Paris and into his Province in Italy? We suspect Thomas had a sense of humor, succinct and dry: in the sublime articles on charity he asked: "Who would be so foolish to assert that one could be friends with wine or with a horse" (II–II, 23, 1), and in the rough and tumble of public disputations he takes on topics like the possibility that God can sin and the way in which Jesus' blood shed in crucifixion returns to the risen Christ, about the legal relationships of traveling crusaders to their families, or about the physical nature of the fire of hell.[84]

No great thinker or artist should be presented as the replacement or opponent of all predecessors or contemporaries. Richard Wagner does not remove J. S. Bach; Monet does not overshadow Raphael. Aquinas expressed his gratitude to all who had worked to find truth, for all had disclosed something of the real—the real which was also the good, the beautiful, and the true. Aristotle said that scholars and scientists should thank even those who have spoken superficially in investigating the truth and whose opinions no one would follow. Thomas sought many viewpoints and truths in every thinker. His delight (like that the of the master architect supervising the decoration of Notre Dame in Paris in the 1250s) was to arrange a vast number of ideas around a central insight. In Thomas Aquinas there was joined in an uncommon way two intellectual characteristics which are often found only separately: independent reflection, and research into the past. A speculative bent was focused by locating questions in a wide view of the world.

Aquinas thought that the truth of an idea and not its author or past source should hold our allegiance. Ultimately every truth, no matter who says it, is from the Holy Spirit (I–II, 109, 1, 1). While grace and morality further an intellectual life, they do not substitute for native ability; neither research and education nor grace and faith provide automatically intellectual truth. A pious Carthusian might express false ideas and a Muslim true ones. "Study . . . does not aim merely at finding out what others have thought but how the truth of things presents itself."[85] The mosaic of thousands of opinions in the *ST* is sustained by clarity and balance. "In selecting and re jecting opinions a person should not be led by love or hate concerning who said them but by the certitude of truth. So he [Aristotle] says we should love both: those whose opinions we follow, and those whose opinions we reject. For both study to find the truth and in this way they are our collaborators."[86] Thomas was interested in distinguishing between what is passing and what is eternal, and in discussing both he prized originality as well as judgment.

Increasingly he sought to express the true and the real in ways by which it could be glimpsed that they were also anticipations of the divine.

VII. The Theologian

Aquinas saw his life's work clearly. In a broad sense, it was to be a teacher of theology. Some preaching, much teaching of the Bible, formal and public disputations, and writings books responding to queries—these made up his profession and his ministry. The composition of the *ST* occupied him for the last ten years of his life. That work, as we will see in the next chapter, interpreted Christianity as a panoramic unfolding of the wisdom and love of God reaching from a myriad of natures (in what we now know are billions of galaxies) to God's love for each person. It was a kind of physics of the realms of life and grace in motion. His theology of the Christian gospel is realistic, intellectual, and optimistic; it is also sacramental and analogical, multi-faceted and incarnational. Those characteristics have given to his pages a circulation beyond European culture.

Thomas, in his personality and profession, was certainly an intellectual. A. D. Sertillanges wrote of the harmony between personality and his work: "He was distinguished first and foremost for his power of intellect which in him was not so much a particular trait as the very essence of his life. It gave a unity to his whole life. His profession was that of teacher. In his preaching he mainly simplified and elaborated his doctrine and adapted it to the exigencies of the pulpit. In his poetry, he sings in concerts. His mysticism is intellectual rather than emotional, and even his prayers are didactic in form like the articles in the *Summa*."[87] An Aristotelian wanted to see things scientifically, that is, to see them in their properties, causes, and relationships. That meant throwing a spotlight on being and action, letting each form stand out. Aquinas expected theology, like the human psyche and the universe, to make sense. Through many ways one could touch a God whose wise plans overflow in power and love. Thomas was not a logician or a rationalist: his subject was not the mind but the human personality vivified by the grace of Trinity. At the end of his psychology of grace he discerned a special offer to men and women of the highest wisdom: born of the impetus of grace-in-love, it was a quiet, intuitive contact with God, a gift of the Spirit of Jesus.

The biblical scholar and philosophical teacher was also a preacher in the church. Torrell has looked at Aquinas' sermons and finds some traces of the preacher who delivered them.[88] There is a clarity and a directness, an attention to the theological. The preacher avoided bizarre if pious stories which had assumed earlier in that century an undeserved prominence. Biblical allusions and quotations (not so much to prove as to remind) permeate the sermons, a preaching which often was to their hearers and copyists a chain of scriptural images and lines. Concrete problems like justice in the marketplace or the harm of unjust governments are considered, and there can be a striking illustration of the sublime by the vivid: "People who are drunk are outside of themselves; so it will be with the saints in heaven."[89] The sermons hold recurring themes: the centrality of love within Christian life, the imitation of Christ, a theology of the creation and restoration of each human being as the image of God.

The intellect, Aquinas often stated, seeks and loves truth. Truth is also a theme of Aristotle and of the Gospel according to John. Ideas and words alone do not satisfy it is truth which is the tranquil telos of the mind. Truth is found in propositions but more deeply in realities which concepts and judgments mirror. Reflection begins where data and history stop. Truth is primal (God) and truth is total (the universe); truth is judgment (a sentence) and truth is real (this orchid). Jesus Christ, the Incarnate Word as a man, was truth as a living pattern in a historical life. Christ, the "*magister*," the teacher of the science of God, appeared often on the central column at the main entrance of the great cathedrals. Better to know a little truth than to have a great deal of information, Aquinas thought, and the best knowledge is profound truths about ourselves and about God.

As we saw, this teacher was surrounded by innovation and conflict. Vicaire drew attention to Aquinas' courage. There was courage in public disputations (some threatening his ideas as well as his career and religious family), courage amid new ways of thinking, and courage in different schools and countries.

The most courageous and profound activity of Thomas, perhaps not exceeding the public expression of his thought, lies at the heart of his intellectual activity, the act of being a theologian. Theological truth is his highest ambition, indeed the ambition of his life for

Christ. . . . All who study frequently the text of Thomas know how he joins his own identity to the idea and method of his sources, and how, accepting their proper role, he never sacrifices one or the other in a false concordism. This obliges him to be constantly renewing positions he has already taken. Before a fixed and lazy traditionalism, he appears as an innovator. He is an innovator with and through his vigorous respect for authenticity, an innovator in philosophy as well as in church tradition. His courage and absolute sincerity give a permanent value to his work. But in his career they also raised up around him hostile and inept opponents. Possibly the sufferings and sacrifices of Thomas brought a purification and a conformity to his own Master, Jesus. They helped him as a Friar Preacher to retain the desire to follow Christ completely and also to become himself.[90]

His subject matter was the reality and harmony of truth flowing from God and existing in creatures; his asceticism lay in his professional obligations; his cloister was the world of new and old sciences and theology.

❖ ❖ ❖

So now we can begin our intellectual journey. Aided by centuries of interpretation but motivated by the need to see his theology anew for our times, we move into his theological creation. It will be a journey into his world, a world with many beings vibrant with properties and activities. Their vitality, goodness, and generosity bid us welcome.

2. Patterns in the
Summa theologiae

✣

All beautiful attributes showered throughout the world in separate drops flow together whole and complete, and move toward the font of goodness. When we are drawn to the graciousness, beauty, and goodness of creatures, we ought to be borne away to the One in whom all these little streams commingle and flow.
Summa contra gentiles (2, 2)

Every project, every plan or enterprise, no matter how modest or how great, presupposes some seminal idea, some unfolding pattern. Nature reveals patterns, structures which join together the bones of the body or which link ecologically creatures along a seashore. In human creations, models arrange into order numerous, disparate entities. Data, facts, bytes are interesting and valuable but thin and partial: they await some further relationship and vitalization. In the arts it is not only color and sound but the variety and repetition within forms which give pleasure. This chapter on Aquinas' theology looks for the patterns he used in thinking about and expressing God and creation, Jesus and the human being. Even a few insights into the complexity of nature or into the project of a human life within God's presence are worth human pursuit. Aquinas thought he was fortunate to be able to spend his life thinking and teaching about realities which were gifts of divine truth. Science, psychology, theology, physics, music are finite expressions of divine intelligence.

Aquinas wrote well over twenty commentaries on the Bible and the works of Aristotle, and a dozen more theological works of broad synthesis or specialized investigation. The chapters of this book, however, are focusing on one of his works, the *Summa theologiae*. That distinguished product of his mature genius is his most successful work of comprehension and synthesis.

41

The opening of a masterpiece is important. The first lines of an epic poem state its theme, or a symphony's first notes may hold the tonality of the entire work. The opening lines of the *ST* are not simply an affirmation of God or a reverence toward Christ; they are a statement of the subject of the entire theological work, the reality which its many pages will study. In the first article of the *ST* Aquinas repeats four times the subject of Christian theology. Theology's theme is not the existence of God, nor God as an unfathomable deity. The *ST* is exploring a further, special, divine realm and power. A "sacred teaching" from God presents men and women with a special knowledge about the plan and empowerment from God for intelligent creatures—this will lead them to a destiny beyond biological life, to a supernatural and healing life and destiny given by God. "It was necessary for human salvation that there be a certain teaching revealed by God" (I, 1, 1).

Movement and activity, reaching from origin to goal, link God and creatures. Trinity, creation, predestination, the Christian life, incarnation, and the future—these flow out from and mark the divine presence inspiring men and women in their life and destiny. The *ST* is a plan of human life, a physics of God's presence, a psychology of grace.[1]

What makes a creative work attractive and profound is its form, its exposition of order. When we speak of patterns in Aquinas' thought we do not mean only the Aristotelian syllogism or the grammar of medieval Latin but structures which order, highlight, and explain Christianity. *Ordo* was a significant interest of medieval culture. There is order in the universe and a further order of grace. It belongs to the university professor or the wise person to see and to unfold the realms which make up the world and life. M. D. Chenu wrote:

> Thomas extols the virtue of wisdom. *Sapientis est ordinare* ('The task of wisdom is to give order.'): the philosopher seeks to penetrate to the ultimate sources of reality, to understand the why and wherefore, and to rest only when necessity has been found. The word *intelligere*, Aquinas likes to think, is derived from *intus legere* (to read within). The world is for him intelligible; let it then render an account of itself.[2]

Aquinas prized the ability of the human mind to reach reality, to find through outward and inward exploration the forms of each being in lucid patterns. Order only enhanced diversity. Each being would stand forth as itself, as the loved gift of divine wisdom. It would give "an account of itself."

Standing forth, existing, being in contact with other beings—this ultimately is truth. Reality gives access to truth and invites knowing. The realm which wise teachers enter and meditate upon is truth.[3] Corresponding to being as the dynamic gift of God, truth is the satisfaction of the intellect, the joy of the mind. If truth means God, this is no pious invocation, because God is "first truth," not as an intellectual principle but as the prior reality planning and causing all realities. Christ, the Word in a human being, is truth as a living pattern in historical life. Order is important for itself but also because it enhances reality and thereby draws forth truth.

Data, contingent truths about ichthyology or cuisine are valuable, but the best knowledge, even though sparse, expresses truths about God and about ourselves, "a kind of impression of what God knows" (I, 1, 3, 2). Theology is a search for truth, and truth's realms, creation and grace, result when God puts divine truth into action. Truth is mentioned in the opening words of Aquinas' two systematic masterpieces: in the "Prologue" of the *ST*, and in the first pages of the *Summa contra gentiles*. Faith too gives access to truth because faith is a kind of knowing, a dark seeing, a reception of information supported not by the senses but by the commitment of the will to the revealed word of God. The truth of faith is not a substitute world but an insight into the real world of grace and sin in which each person exists. Theology is a kind of knowing, a knowing dependent upon and expressive of faith. The Dominican's theological personality was marked by an appetite for knowing, for contemplating realities seen and unseen. Order and truth were served by the harmony between knowing and being, between truth and reality, between personality and grace. The follower of Aquinas is the person courageous enough to see the truth, that is, to see what something is and what it is not— and to accept the insights of science and faith concerning the deeper realms of truth, even of Truth itself.

I. A Composer of *Summae*

Thomas wrote four comprehensive works in theology: a commentary on the *Sentences* of Peter Lombard (1252–1256), the *Summa contra gentiles* (1259–1265), a *Compendium theologiae* (1269–1273), and the *Summa theologiae* (1266–1273). The last three works one might call *summae*. Overviews of creation and revelation, they explain the major truths of Christian revelation through philosophy. The affluent Middle Ages and the new universities provided the background for Aquinas' writings while the communities of friars provided teams of scholars seeking out and translating the ideas of Aristotelian, Platonic, and Arabic thinkers. A pioneer of medieval studies Martin Grabmann wrote: "The works of Aristotle, only now accessible, powerfully widened and re-enforced the philosophical substructure of theological speculation, while at the same time enriching the doctrinal structure of theology with new architectonic motives."[4] Aquinas expounded the messages of the Scripture and of secular knowledge, and with an inborn gift for synthesis, he gathered the insights of science, philosophy, and law to unfold Christian faith. He fashioned a theology which neither piously distorted belief nor confused mathematics or psychology with revelation; he affirmed both grace and being by highlighting the power and the distinctiveness of each. The reader of Aquinas does not find in his writings an eclecticism, despite the citation of so many sources, but rather an extraordinary gift of assimilation. Using the forms and language of the Bible and Greek philosophy, his writings treat traditional problems but also issues in his age which were quite new. Grabmann concluded:

> The great scientific life-work of Thomas is the independent penetration and appropriation of Aristotelian philosophy, and it is the organic linking in a scientific mode of that philosophy with the world-view of Christianity offered by Augustine and earlier scholasticism. In short, [this is] the creation of a Christian Aristotelianism in philosophy and the construction of a speculative theology with the means and forms of this adapted Aristotelian philosophy without abandoning the great lines of the traditions of church and theology.[5]

Through the centuries various schools and disciples have advocated the thought of Thomas Aquinas, but few have understood the structure of his theology. Too often, Aquinas has been presented in a digest of texts, in boring summaries, or in authoritarian lists of conclusions—and often they offered a static Aristotelianism rather than a vital Christianity. One consequence of the past exposition of Thomism as a philosophy is that the thought of Aquinas became abstract and remote. But his theology illustrates the gospel of Christ, precisely because the gospel is the truth about a real realm, the kingdom of God, a supernatural order to which life points and which revelation expresses.

Order, existence, reality, truth—these are architectonic motifs in Thomas Aquinas' theology.

II. Medieval Culture and the *Summa theologiae*

Ordo attracted artists and lawyers, theologians and architects. What was more exciting or profound than order—subtle or bold—drawing a diversity of motifs and media into a harmonious whole? From the twelfth century on there had been a search for patterns wherein a myriad of elements could achieve an effect greater than their parts. The churches of St. Denis or Chartres displayed large pictorial windows or ensembles of sculpture which presented in theological and artistic patterns biblical stories and lives of saints. In elaborate but coherent iconographic plans the images offered their narrative.

The society was delighted by its awakened capacity for creativity, and a desire for masterful arrangement was enkindled. In art the medieval mind selected a central theme of magnitude: for instance, salvation-history prior to Mary and Jesus, or kingship from Melchisedech to Christ crowned with thorns and further on to Louis IX. Hundreds of scenes with countless figures were arranged in logical and religious patterns. The same quest for multiplicity and unity appeared in the sciences subsumed under philosophy. Music in the thirteenth century expressed a novel multiplicity in the motion of independent parts. Polyphony did not begin at Notre Dame after 1160, but it did find there an acceptance of innovation. Above a sustaining line of Gregorian chant, sung at a slowed tempo, improvisations were added, the tropes of other melismatic vocal lines. Tonal diversity was organized; musical intricacy emerged from a desire for simultaneous variety, and soon the motet was at hand.[6]

That world, intrigued with unity and diversity, manifested forms and figures in the facade, the rose window, the tympanum, the disputation, the *summa,* and the hymn. History and law also sought a *summa*-like format. Experiencing multiplicity in arrangement, the direction of the master theologian or of the master architect was to ensure that the whole would enhance and be greater than its pieces. Through patterns, elements should stand out even as they support and integrate the total fabric. In formal organization the *summa* of the thirteenth century went beyond the less comprehensive and less successfully organized collections (Lombard's *Sentences*) and so expressed the energetic breadth of the age.

Imaginative orders arrange forms to achieve a transcendent effect. The sight of a Gothic cathedral would impress the minds of the thirteenth century not only by the stonework of a large building, but by its soaring structural lines intimating transcendental longings from reason and faith. Otto von Simson wrote: "The Middle Ages was the age of the cathedrals. This extraordinary structure owes its emergence to the conviction that metaphysical truth could become transparent in the beautiful."[7] The particular world of the cathedral cannot be taken in from one position or glance but must be explored, walked through, contemplated from different perspectives. Art historians note how in Gothic buildings the individual enters into a larger world where a religious aesthetic draws the human spirit upwards and beyond. It is difficult to imagine the effect these sacral castles of colored light made upon those walking into them in the thirteenth century. Most men, women, and children lived in constricted areas (every inch of space was valuable), having few openings to the outside and filled with the smoke and smells of the living quarters. The cathedrals, sponsored by civic initiative and by religious and business interests, were themselves a kind of *summa:* an order giving to many media an arrangement according to theological and iconographical plans. Arnold Hauser's view of Gothic art recalls the role played by integral arrangement as well as by the motif of journey in the *ST:*

> The basic form of Gothic art is juxtaposition . . . [drawing on] the
> principle of expansion and not of concentration, or co-ordination and

not of subordination, of the open sequence and not of the close geo-
metric form. . . . The beholder is, as it were, led through the states
and stations of a journey. . . . Gothic art leads the onlooker from one
detail to another and causes him, as has been well said, to "unravel"
the successive parts of the work one after another.[8]

The Middle Ages fashioned *summae* in stone and stained glass as
well as in theology. In the twelfth century a new architecture (what
would later be called pejoratively "Gothic" in contrast to the earlier
"Roman" style) produced a building out of freedom and synthesis.
Sharp arches pointed toward heaven and, since the arches could sustain more weight, the wallspace was free. Some creative personality
suggested filling it with windows of red and blue, yellow and green
glass. Colored light poured in. The artists with their theological con-
sultants faced in the rose windows of the cathedrals the same questions of multiplicity and order as did the university professors in planning their summary works of theology. Just as light comes from the
sun and pours into the church through colored windows, so God passing through the events of salvation-history pours grace into the individual spirit. It was, Chenu observed, an age of energetic creativity.

> The men who built the cathedrals could hardly become bogged down
> in the writing of commentaries. They built *summas*, but . . . imita-
> tion of the Ancients did not snuff out inspiration, especially religious
> inspiration. The medieval rebirth and the Gospel movement were
> creative movements, within the *renovatio temporis* of which Francis
> of Assisi and Thomas of Aquino became the masters. . . . Whether
> the Medievals did little thinking about their own dynamic qualities,
> and if they might have been wanting in historical sense, neverthe-
> less, at times they had astonishing strong foresight about the pro-
> gressive elements that tend to stir up the successive generations of
> humanity.[9]

Gothic architecture through a system of skeletal supports—ribs,
buttresses, arches, and vaults—freed wall space for light. Two aspects
of Gothic are without precedent and parallel: the unique relationship
between structure and appearance and the use of light. Gothic lines
direct light into the church and then draw the light, and the human
spirit, upwards and outwards. In the interplay of light and glass and

stone we see a parallel with Aquinas' theology of grace enhancing the human. "Grace is caused in people by the presence of the divinity as light in the atmosphere by the presence of the sun" (III, 7, 12). The technique of stained glass rose to the occasion, providing shimmering pictures where pieces of glass outlined dozens of figures, stories, and symbols in one window. By the year 1200 the colors had been deepened, and naturalness and realism had touched the figures. If the impetus to expand the use of stained glass came from Arab technology and Aristotelian realism, the theology behind it was a neo-Platonism coming from the royal abbey of St. Denis or from the Parisian center of St. Victor.[10] The stained glass windows of the Gothic, replacing the frescoed walls of Romanesque architecture, not only opened the walls to admit light but held patterns and pictures. Suger, the abbot of St. Denis who furthered the building of the first church in Gothic style, described the effect of the windows:

> When out of my delight in the beauty of the house of God, the loveliness of the many-colored gems has called me away from external cares, and worthy meditation has induced me to reflect on the diversity of the sacred virtues by transferring that which is material to that which is immaterial, then it seems to me . . . that by the grace of God I am transported from this inferior world to that higher one. . . .[11]

A century later, the walls of brilliant windows at the Sainte-Chapelle brought a climax to this style of image in light. Thus in form and image theology found an aesthetic counterpart, and art an incarnational content.

Aquinas, as he composed the *ST,* drew the content of the gospel into the forms of Greek philosophy just as the structures and colors of a Gothic rose window, set alight by the sun, presented a history of God's salvation on earth. History and culture provide the unavoidable context of a thinker's creation. Chenu observed:

> To analyze the historical and social conditions of Aquinas' work is the best way of observing the truth of his teaching in relationship to its place in civilization and in the course of theological development. We find this realism again today as we understand better how the Word of God is incarnate in the history of humanity, in the worlds of space and time. Theology should not be a closed chapel

set apart from people but a faithful experience and elaboration of the Word of God in a mature faith. To accomplish this was the genius of Thomas Aquinas.[12]

As order progressed in architecture and the arts, theology developed from arranged collections of opinions to the synthetic *summa*. Before Aquinas, William of Auxerre and Alexander of Hales had written *summae*, as had the Dominicans John of Treviso and Roland of Cremona. Seeking to find the breadth and order which would fashion a successful *summa*, Albert the Great and his Dominican pupil, Ulrich of Strassburg, as well as Henry of Ghent wrote comprehensive theologies. Von Simson noticed similarities between architecture, science, and theology in the age of cathedrals.

> In gothic architecture, the wonderful precision with which every single block was shaped in the vault (leaving no ragged joints that it was necessary to conceal) suggests a new esthetic appreciation of the dignity of structural perfection. This tectonic system is never concealed but rather underscored by Gothic wall painting. Even the stained glass windows submit, in composition and design, increasingly to the pattern of stone and metal armature in which they are set. The esthetic function of these windows is not only the creation of a new luminosity; the light they admit dramatically underscores the web of tracery, ribs, and shafts.[13]

Erwin Panofsky also described how the development of the *summa*-form paralleled the structure of the cathedral. The organizational spirit of medieval culture aimed at *"manifestatio."* This manifestation required: (1) totality of treatment, (2) arrangement of equal parts, as well as (3) distinction and interrelation.[14] To walk into a Gothic church is then to see that each of the members of the ensemble of the arts has a role, and to grasp that together they compose a summa as an event of art and theology.

Medievalists have referred to the thirteenth century as a century of "spirituality full of light."[15] Light playing on stone might have set Aquinas' intellect and imagination in motion, for act and light became motifs for his explanation of God and world. Divine light in grace and revelation enlivens the figures and events which are the sacraments or the jeweled images of salvation-history. The biblical narratives are real, just as the window's designs are real, and without them we would not see light. Both Gothic architecture and Aquinas' theology pass through the three dimensions of time. The past is prominent in the prophets, apostles, and philosophers whose thought is symbolized in their statues. The present moment is one of contemplation, of the application of the art's symbols and narratives to oneself. The future exists ahead and above: not as the continuation of the line of history but as a world beyond time and as a fulfillment of the present. Anyone entering a Gothic cathedral also encounters incarnation: spirit in stone, color in glass and air. Gothic space is both sacral realism and sublime activity, while medieval theology presented the Holy Trinity active on earth. Outpourings of color and light lead the believer in the church to return spiritually to the One, the Source, the Godhead. Yet, the goal of religious history and of the window is not the figurative events, but human contact with the Mystery of God.

The *Summa* is not an encyclopedia. There were anticipations of encyclopedias at this time, and they too illustrate the medieval interest in the accumulation of information. During the twelfth century Gratian produced a systematic compendium of patristic sources, and of conciliar and papal pronouncements upon which he commented and which became a theoretical introduction and pattern for canon law. Abelard's *Sic et Non* began the theological style of the schools which debated real problems with arguments on both sides. Those collections initiated a struggle for the professors to find a suitable theological arrangement. "*Summa*" in the language of the twelfth century stood for a collection of topics and opinions by revered experts, and, as Chenu noted, it was "no longer a simple compilation of the testimonies of the Fathers and of the ancient writers . . . but an organized and elaborate assemblage of materials, although it still remained very close to the texts which it collected and arranged."[16] Abelard called the *Apostles Creed* a "*summa*," but his own arrangement for theological issues was the awkward triad of faith, charity, and sacrament. "In the thirteenth century . . . the word *summa* designates a literary work undertaken with a threefold purpose: first, to expound, in a concise and abridged manner, the whole of a given field of knowledge (this is the original meaning of *summa*); second, to organize, beyond piecemeal analysis, the objects of this field of knowledge in a synthetic way; finally, to realize this aim so that the product be for teaching students."[17] So in the decades just before Aquinas intellectual pursuits in the new world of the universities sought multiplicity and comprehension. Richard Heinzmann concluded: "The systematic works of scholasticism give access not just to one work or to one writer but, when we are considering a thinker of some importance, they open to our understanding an entire epoch."[18]

Aquinas saw how the architect supervised on the Isle de Paris amid the lumber, stones, and pulleys of a construction site the totality of the medieval building being built. Supervisor of all the arts ranging from planning towers to selecting themes for sculpture, he was like a *"master,"* he was a professor among the stone masons and sculptors. He was like the teacher of theology whose activity involved being the director of several fields and whose wisdom sought the causal forces which were most sublime and most extensive (I, 1, 6).[19] God, of course, was the architect of the universe, but human beings too, as they engaged in wisdom and art, could fashion materials into new forms.

III. A Textbook for Dominicans

It was long thought that the *Summa theologiae* was written for university students, for those who had finished their studies in liberal arts, had some philosophy, and were beginning theology ("Prologue" to the *ST*). Leonard Boyle, however, has argued that the *ST* was written not in Paris but at the *studium* of the Dominican Order at Santa Sabina in Rome. Moreover, this *summa* was originally conceived as a work on moral theology (hence its lengthy Second Part) for the Dominican theological students in Rome preparing for the proper Dominican ministry of preaching and hearing confessions.[20]

In 1259 Aquinas worked with Albert on a commission (*de studiis*) which was composing a plan of education for Dominicans. In late 1261 Aquinas came to Orvieto where he lectured on Scripture in the Dominican priory and where he might have offered his views on moral issues of the time during public discussions. Then, as we saw, Aquinas was asked in 1265 to set up a school, a *studium* at the priory of Santa Sabina on Rome's Aventine hill where he remained for three years until he returned to Paris in 1268.

At all events, the *studium* at Santa Sabina probably was no more
than an attempt by the Roman Province to allow select students to
prepare themselves under a single Master, Thomas, for the priesthood and the Dominican apostolate. Basically the course there
would have had the same pastoral orientation as that in which we
presume Thomas to have been engaged for the previous four years at
Orvieto.[21]

In his first year in Rome he lectured on the *Sentences*. His experience
teaching Dominicans through courses employing practical guides for
preaching and hearing confessions written by early Dominicans like
Raymond of Penafort convinced him that pastoral ministry needed a
deeper foundation, a work which was more than a handbook on
moral problems. Boyle suggests that Aquinas' creativity as a theologian was stimulated by the influx of new texts, by his experience as
an educator in various settings, and by his contact with preachers and
confessors who were being challenged by new ethical issues. All this
led him to give to "practical," i.e., moral, theology an original and
broader setting. "By prefacing the Secunda or moral part with a Prima
pars on God, Trinity and Creation, and then rounding it off with a
Tertia pars on the Son of God, Incarnation and the Sacraments,
Thomas put practical theology, the study of Christian man, his
virtues and vices, in a full theological context."[22]

A philosophy might conclude that God is the source of rational
creatures in a metaphorical or a metaphysical sense, but Aquinas was
describing the human situation in light of God's revelation and as
known by faith. The human life of moral decision was enabled by
grace and destined for a future in the kingdom of God. A higher mode
of divine contact furthered a life surviving death in resurrection.
"First we shall treat of God, secondly of the movement of the rational creature towards God, and thirdly of Christ who—as a human
being—is the way for us of tending towards God" (I, 2). Virtue was not
an exercise in self-control, and moral theology was not confessional
casuistry: both were grounded in the dynamics of *vita* and *gratia*
reaching from God to the individual Christian.

Christian morality, once for all, was shown to be something more
than a question of straight ethical teaching of vices and virtues in isolation. Inasmuch as man was an intelligent being who was master of

himself and possessed of freedom of choice, he was in the image of
God. To study human action is therefore to study the image of God
and to operate on a theological plane. To study human action on a
theological plane is to study it in relation to its beginning and end,
God, and to the bridge between, Christ and his sacraments.[23]

Aquinas worked for seven years, in Rome, Paris, and Naples, on his
masterpiece while at the same time writing commentaries on nine
works of Aristotle. In the three groups of writings from the period of
his maturity one sees how his theological system drew from the speculative stimuli of the biblical texts while both of them found interpretive resources in the philosophical commentaries.[24]

Table 1. Writings during the Composition of the *Summa theologiae*

Commentaries on the Bible	*Summa Theologiae*	*Commentaries on Aristotle*
Job (1269–70)	*I* (1266–68)	On the Soul (1269–70)
John (1269–72)	*I–II* (1269–70)	On the Physics (1269–70)
	II–II (1271–72)	On the Ethics (1271)
Psalms (1272–73)		On logical works (1269–72)
Romans, First Corinthians (1270–1272)	*III* (1272–73)	

Although the Bible and Aristotle nourished the sections of the
speculative ST, how difficult it must have been for Aquinas to find
time from varied occupations to conceive and write out his own original theological system. Boyle concludes: "This persistence at least
suggests that for Thomas the *Summa theologiae* was something out
of the ordinary, and, indeed, meant much to him. It was, one may
suggest, his legacy as a Dominican to his Order and to its system of
educating the brethren in priories all over Europe."[25]

IV. Structures in the *Summa theologiae*

There are various patterns in the *ST*, and they exist at different levels. Of course there is a general interest in the meaning and usage of
words, in the combination of words with their ideas in the dialectic
of discussion, and in the roles assigned to opinions and authorities.

There are organizational patterns (the parts, the questions, the articles), and there are intrinsic patterns like theocentricity, nature and existence, or being and fulfillment. There are Aristotelian patterns of nature and action and neo-Platonic ones of participation. There are influences from sources, e.g., Origen or Gratian, and biblical patterns either from an individual book (the Gospel according to John) or from one scriptural theme (Word, faith). Finally there are theological motifs like law, grace, or light. Albert Patfoort begins his book on the keys to Aquinas' theology with these words: "It is not a question of composing a list of themes or of major points in the large theological works of Thomas. Rather we will try to discover the organization, the subject of deep reflection, which, full of wisdom, has been given to the ideas . . . to offer a key needed to enter into this monument of Christian thought, the theology of him who has been called the 'Common Doctor' of the church."[26] The structures of the *ST* are like the arches and vaulted ceilings of Gothic buildings: they sustain basic ideas and principles. They present the lines by which the work arranges and vivifies the topics of faith and life, of theology and philosophy. Patfoort writes: "If there is a practical conclusion to be drawn from the dynamic development we have observed, it is clearly that one must avoid at any price presenting the *Summa* in a linear and abstract way, remaining content with a static and isolated reading of its different parts. Rather we must always be sensitive to the ceaseless and multiple connections between the different areas."[27]

Aquinas' great *summa* begins with several general preludes: a prologue for the readers, a discussion of the nature of theology, proofs for the existence of God, and a consideration of the divine being leading on to a higher world of Trinity and grace. The opening "Prologue" announces that the text would present "those things that pertain to the Christian religion in a manner befitting the education of beginners." There were obstacles facing students beginning theology in a medieval school, whether university or priory. The works of theology they might consult were verbose, detailed, and repetitious. The order of treating Christianity was unsystematic: first because the *Sentences* of Peter Lombard was based upon the concatenation of articles in the creed, and second because the Bible lacks a logical order and repeats its great themes.

Which pattern was to give order to a *summa*? There was a tension between an approach from the biblical history of salvation (Hugh of St. Victor) and an approach based upon pedagogy (Abelard). Aquinas chose a format which combined the two. He brought into his *ST* all the information he could gather—the Scriptures and particularly Paul, the canonists, the Greek Fathers and especially John Damascene, the Latin Fathers and Augustine, Platonists and Aristotle, biological and astronomical works—but he also searched for the right arrangement.[28] To see the form which guides all this material, one should first look at Aquinas' own words introducing the major sections. Following the etymology of theology, the opening of each of the four parts is about God, but they are clearly about the God who is sharing a life deeper than biological existence with men and women. These prologues are about the nature and telos of humanity. "After we have treated the exemplary cause, God and those things which proceed from divine power and decision, now we should consider God's image, the human being, as endowed with free will and power for activities, the source of its own enterprises" (I-II, "Prologue"). They are all, in a sense, about incarnation, that is, about a special presence of God in us, and, par excellence, in the Word incarnate in Jesus. First and foremost, the *ST* is an ordered presentation of God-in-act. Beings emerge in the glory of their capacities for act and in the aura of their destinies. In plan and creation, through the missions of revelation and grace, the Trinity reaches men and women in their concrete world, the world studied by scientists, philosophers, religious prophets, and theologians. Consequently, a basic theological pattern is that of being-in-action: natures, whether this species of hawk or that sculptor, sustain their being and manifest themselves through their proper activities. One can see in the three parts on God, humanity, and Christ traces of patterns of being, activity, and process.

Confident that human reason and faith can soar to heights of exploration, and that the God who is the source of all being and truth is intelligible and good, Aquinas set out to compose a new way of looking at Christianity in which a multitude of sources were summoned to explain revelation in Christ. What is evidently important for Aquinas is that his work pursue a pedagogical order, a unified and systematic organization of what pertains to Christian faith. The chosen order is not that of canon law or that of the author of the Gospel according to Mark but the order of a teacher. Aquinas employed in the *ST* various patterns, logical, philosophical, and theological. Later

we will look at inner patterns of themes and sources, but first we
need to become acquainted with the two basic structures which organize an immensity of theological data: the overarching pattern and
the structure of the basic unit.

A. THE MACRO-STRUCTURE

Dozens of works, large and small, have been written as guides, expositions, or summaries of the *ST*. Some are bland; many are dull. Not
a few are a thin summary or an overly logical paraphrase of pieces of
a theology. Many studies of value have been written, ranging from the
commentary of Cardinal Cajetan in the sixteenth century to those of
Reginald Garrigou-Lagrange in the twentieth, but remarkably most
have left undiscovered the patterns in the *ST*. Most Thomists from
the seventeenth to the twentieth centuries paid little attention to the
missions of the Trinity, the New Law of grace, or the life of Jesus,
since, too interested in logic and metaphysics, they neglected the theological vein. Chenu uncovered a basic structure within the *ST*, and,
although scholars have suggested elaborations and modifications, his
study remains important.

> In order, therefore, to understand the *Summa theologiae* as well as
> the purpose of its author, it is important to perceive the *ordo disci-
> plinae* that is worked out in it—not only the logical plan of the work,
> with its divisions and subdivisions, but also that inner flow of move-
> ment giving life to the structure after having created it. . . the scien-
> tific reasons that govern the whole arrangement, the intellectual
> options by means of which it was decided, here and there, to lay
> stress on this or that part, or to locate it just there.[29]

Is Aquinas' theology, in its form, a tower, a mosaic, a chain? What
could join all the authorities and topics in the thousands of segments? Which pattern of patterns would bring harmony out of the
old theologies and the new sciences and give unity-in-diversity with
clarity and organization? Curiously, Aquinas turned not to Aristotle
but to a neo-Platonic way of viewing the world.[30]

For Chenu one grand organizing pattern joined the three parts of
the *ST*: this structure gave an *ordo* which was methodological, pedagogical, and aesthetic. Beyond the building blocks of Aristotelian sci-

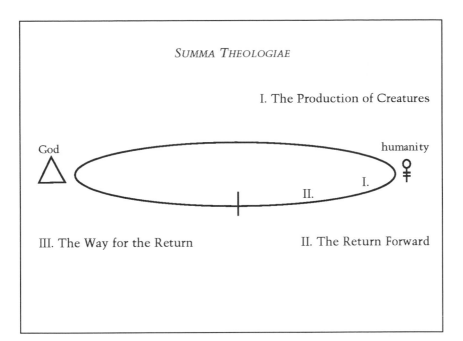

ence, Aquinas drew upon the theme of emergence and return. The young theologian teaching the *Sentences* had already employed the pattern of the procession outwards of creatures from the first principle and their movement toward fulfillment in their ultimate cause.[31] In theology all things are studied in their relationships to God. Production and destiny, every being, and every action could be located and known in the lines of process God has set in motion. The pattern is Christian as well as neo-Platonic: a divine creation and process on to fulfillment might also have been planted in Aquinas' mind by Augustine or Pseudo-Dionysius. The monastic writers used this pattern to describe prayer, and Bonaventure employed it for his journey of consciousness to God.

Exit and return, procession and fulfillment. This pattern implies movement and life. The telos, the ever-attracting goal in the future, need not, however, be conceived as a "return," a backward move. The emergent being does not exist only to collapse backwards or be absorbed in the original birth which is now a death. The process can be a drawing forward; creation can become history. We might best imagine the course of the *ST* not as circular return but as upward spiral. Aquinas said that this was the approach of Pseudo-Dionysius to

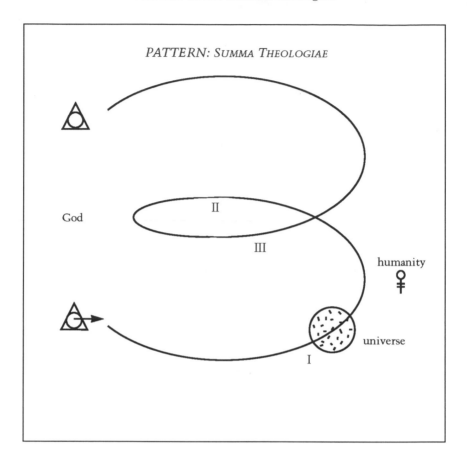

PATTERN: SUMMA THEOLOGIAE

God

II

III

humanity

universe

I

divine realities: to circle them in contemplation.[32] The human being moves toward its destiny through a kind of spiral (a perfect figure) manifesting the movement of eternal love, from good and toward good. This dynamic movement can be seen in the creation of the universe but also in human life, and even in the Incarnation. "The totality of the divine work finds its fulfillment in the fact that the human being, the last creature created, returns to its source by a kind of circle in such a way that with the work of the Incarnation it finds union with the very source of all things."[33] The goals of being and grace draw creatures not backward but upward and forward. Aquinas spoke not of a return but of a journey, a way. "Before God one journeys not with steps but with the . . . activities of the mind."[34]

Aristotle's science certainly supported the pattern of movement.

Beings by their nature and existence are in motion toward future realization. The movement outward of beings through their forms and
toward their goals includes even God in a Trinity of active persons,
giving and receiving eternally. For all things God is the term of their
procession and return—but in different ways. Creation continues but
individual beings pass away as the procession mirrors and moves forward toward God.[35] From revelation we learn that parallel to the
degrees of being is a history of grace, missions of Word and Spirit to
men and women. Thus the pattern of procession-toward-destiny is a
cord of several threads, matter and spirit, cosmic forces and human
history, nature and grace. "There is a double 'procession from God':
one according to the gifts of nature, and one according to the gifts of
grace and salvation. In both cases, the creative action of God continues in divine government."[36]

If the *ST* intends to give order to realities in creation and grace
(and so pedagogically to help the theology student), nonetheless, this
approach does not completely eliminate history. It is not simply a
neo-Platonic emanation but includes the history of salvation. Men
and women are offered a share in God's life described in the preaching of the Incarnate Word Jesus, and so the human being, set forth in
nature and grace at the end of the First Part, does not in the Second
Part turn back but moves forward to its destiny. According to Max
Seckler,

> If according to the Bible all things proceed from the hand of God
> according to his plan and work of salvation, and then return to the
> one who is Alpha and Omega, so the theologian according to the
> demands of that science treats reality in relationship to God, as ori-
> gin and goal. But in a surprising way the source and goal of history,
> the source and completion of being, the first and last cause of under-
> standing all have a close correspondence with each other, so that the-
> ology is not only a "science" of salvation history but bears the his-
> tory of salvation in its basic plan.[37]

The *ST* is an interpretation of salvation-history as well as being a
physics of being and a psychology of grace.

The *ST* is not studying God as only the creator of the universe but
mainly as the author of a higher order for men and women, grace perceived by faith, a supernatural order: the reign of God preached by

Jesus Christ and the life in the Spirit described by Paul. Congar observes: "Medieval theologians, Thomas in particular, loved to locate human realities within a general order which revealed in various ways analogous structures. If the world is the work of the Word-Wisdom of God, still a further order will enter, that of supernatural life."[38] After treating God and creation, the history of salvation with its biblical events does not at first continue in the Second Part, but the *ST* continues a theology of the created images of God, every man and woman, on the journey to their destiny. This journey assumes again something of a historical course in the Third Part with Jesus Christ.

Consequently, one cannot describe this theology with the chain of terms, "One God–Trinity–Creation–Anthropology–Christology;" not with "nature–grace–Christ" nor "God and Trinity, Creation and Covenant and Incarnation." Nor can one compare it with the order of logic or the structure of mathematics, for the new presences of the Trinity, the individuality of men and women, and the dynamics of creation and grace are always moving through the work. The structure of the *ST* is multi-layered. God is always present as the bestower of both natural and supernatural being; the human is always present touched by one form or another of creation and incarnation. Ultimately the theology of the entire *ST* is a history of graced beings and not a metaphysics, although just as creation is the place of grace, metaphysics offers a framework for theology. The salvation described is not Christology alone, although all grace flows from the Word through Jesus Christ; theology is not retelling the narratives of the Bible but presents the life of the Spirit to which all of the Bible points.

In the "First Part" of the *ST* all things move outward from the Triune God in a diversity of beings—suns, bacteria, persons, cacti, snakes—and in creation's climax, the human person. Men and women exist as finite beings but also as knowing and loving images of God who out of their animality and spirit are called to a deeper life which is an intense gift of God. (See figures 4a and 4b.)

The "Second Part" concerns the human personality on that journey which is life and which leads to a destiny enabled by a special life-force, grace. Its topics are not mainly figures like Moses or Jesus, or the church. The "First Part of the Second Part" describes the psychological principles (human and divine) of a life-journey with choices, emotions, faculties, intuitions, accomplishments, and misdirections: and

Figure 4a

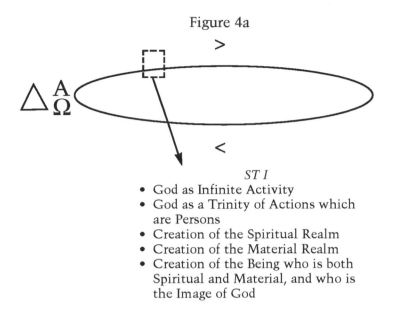

ST I
- God as Infinite Activity
- God as a Trinity of Actions which are Persons
- Creation of the Spiritual Realm
- Creation of the Material Realm
- Creation of the Being who is both Spiritual and Material, and who is the Image of God

Figure 4b

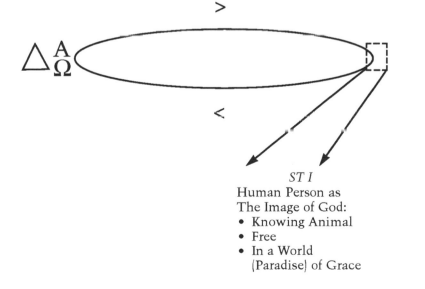

ST I
Human Person as
The Image of God:
- Knowing Animal
- Free
- In a World (Paradise) of Grace

Figure 4c

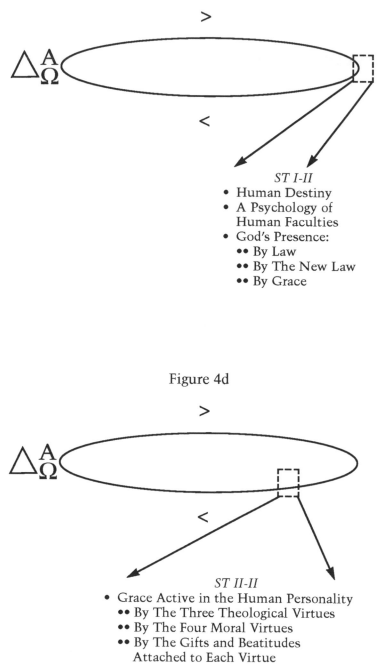

ST I-II
- Human Destiny
- A Psychology of
  Human Faculties
- God's Presence:
  -- By Law
  -- By The New Law
  -- By Grace

Figure 4d

>

<

ST II-II
- Grace Active in the Human Personality
  -- By The Three Theological Virtues
  -- By The Four Moral Virtues
  -- By The Gifts and Beatitudes
     Attached to Each Virtue
- Grace Active in Social Roles

next, God's help of grace. How will we reach a destiny beyond us? Aquinas responded by considering at length two principles: psychological life and the grace of God. (See figure 4c.)

The "Second Part of the Second Part" brings together two forces: human personality and God's grace. The human is the place of grace. The framework for this detailed psychology of grace is the three theological virtues (faith, hope, and charity) and the four moral virtues (prudence, justice, temperance, and fortitude). Under each is arranged sub-virtues (and countering vices), a Beatitude from Jesus' Sermon on the Mount, and complementary gifts of the Holy Spirit. (See figures 4d and 4e.)

The "Third Part" of the *ST* presents Jesus Christ as the model for the journey; he is the living portrait of God's wisdom. We learn in the First Part that missions of the Trinity found a concrete expression in the historical man Jesus of Nazareth who is the incarnation of the Word of God, and in his Spirit active in human lives. The Third Part gives a presentation of the being, life, and work of Jesus; second, of the Incarnation continuing after Jesus' departure in the sacraments; and finally, of life beyond death. Just as Jesus' work on earth will be completed by his second coming, so the graced life of the Christian finds beyond death the triumph of grace as resurrection and vision. (The final sections of the Third Part, however, Aquinas never wrote, since death interrupted him in the midst of treating the sacraments.) (See figure 4f.)

All three parts of the *ST* have a similar structure. What is at first general and basic becomes concrete: the theology of God is followed by the world of creatures; the human person in psychology, law, and grace leads into the virtues of graced life; the Incarnation of the Word is a life, a teaching, and a redemption.[39] Similarly one can find themes which appear in all three parts: for instance, divine procession and mission, image of God, love, or teleological desire.[40]

The macro-structure of emergence and destiny is, then, a line of activity reaching from the missions of the Trinity through creation, human history, and incarnation to the eschaton. Moving forward, or circling upward, empowered by God, this teleological process orders hundreds of "questions" and thousands of "articles;" they are the building blocks of the areas of theology illumined and joined by the patterns and principles.

Figure 4e

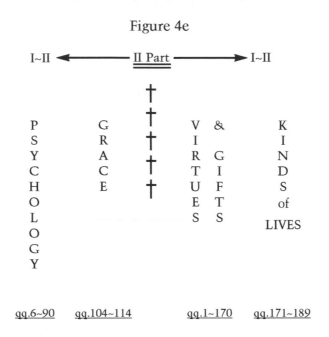

I~II ◄─────── II Part ───────► I~II

P   G   V &   K
S   R   I   I
Y   A   R G   N
C   C   T I   D
H   E   U F   S
O   E T   S
L   S S   of
O   LIVES
G
Y

qq.6~90   qq.104~114   qq.1~170   qq.171~189

Figure 4f

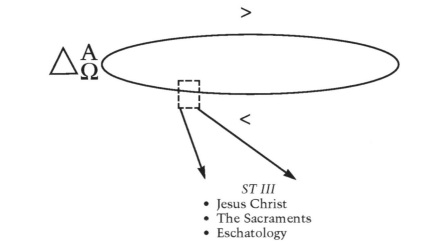

ST III
- Jesus Christ
- The Sacraments
- Eschatology

B. THE MICRO-STRUCTURE

The *ST*'s parts are made up of "questions" containing "articles." The questions are arranged into clusters of questions (about thirty-eight) like divine knowledge, sacraments, or a particular virtue like hope. The microstructure of the *ST* is the question with its articles; a question treats a larger or smaller topic through articles which are the basic investigative units of the work. The four parts are made up of 611 questions with well over four thousand articles.

Aquinas followed Aristotle's methodology by arranging his inquiries into Christian faith around four basic questions: Does something exist? (Or in theology, Why is it suitable or helpful for it to exist?) How does it exist? Are there different kinds of this reality? What is its nature? What are some of its special characteristics or properties? The articles of this *summa* combine the dialectical method of the universities going back to Abelard—the discussion of both sides of a theological issue—with Aristotle's questions pursuing science. Chenu wrote:

> The medieval *lectio*, in like manner, was to give rise to *quaestiones* that went beyond the mere explaining of the texts, the latter, however, still furnishing the substance with which they dealt. In these *quaestiones*, together with the resources of the ancient dialectic and latter of demonstrative logic, came into play with the great complex of problems instigated during the thirteenth century by the entrance of Aristotle and the new surge of inquisitiveness in theological matters. With the "questions" scholasticism reached the peak of its development. In them, it found the literary medium best answering its creative inspiration in philosophy as in theology.[41]

The scholastic approach of the new universities was precisely not an approach of authority or piety but one of scientific investigation. Abelard, not content with devotional symbolism, had inquired into the real reasons and causes of things. The contemporaries of Albert and Bonaventure referred to university professors as "dialecticians," because they were discussing both sides of an issue. Aristotelian science sought the causes of each thing, and to find causes is the goal of the questioning inquiry in the *ST*. How do the characteristics of a human emotion correspond to its purpose? How does Jesus' death save? Can a sacrament cause grace? To explain a reality and to further basic scientific study, Aristotle spotlighted four causes:

- the material out of which something exists;
- the form ("essence" or "nature" or "species") which is the principle of a particular nature realized as an individual in matter;
- the efficient cause bringing this being into existence;
- its final cause, a goal or destiny.

Distinctions, reasons, divisions, definitions, questions, causes—this was the scholastic method.

The structure of each of the thousands of articles is the same.

First, there is a statement of the question to be discussed followed by a number of objections (about two to eight) which ordinarily support positions opposite to the one Aquinas will take. Between the objections offering fundamental problems and the treatment of the topic a line from an authority (a passage from Scripture, a sentence from Ambrose, a quote from Canon Law, or an axiom from a philosopher) challenges the direction of the objections. This countering opinion, it was long thought, is simply an authority rather indifferently selected to balance the negative tone of the objections, but now experts think that one can find indications not only of argument but of structure in those citations from Aristotle (frequent in the questions on God) or Augustine (frequent in those on the Trinity); they suggest subtle directions appearing in Aquinas' own theology. Then there follows the body of the article, the "response," where Aquinas gave his own views. There he first attended to the insight and weight of other opinions and then offered his own reasoned and creative presentation of the topic under consideration. Finally, he answered the objections, finding some truth in seemingly opposed positions.

The articles unfold the question. Each article depends upon its place in the question and in a cluster of questions. Previous topics provide the context and perspectives which will illumine what follows. Grabmann advised: "If we were to sketch a method of interpreting St. Thomas, and especially the *ST*, it would be necessary for us first to consider the *systematic study* of that work, a method by which one researches under all its aspects the meaning, the idea of each article in order to understand in a basic way all of the teaching contained in the entire span of the work."[42] The disputation, the public scholastic exercise in dialectic, was an important, if sometimes occasional, exercise for the professor, and its format and spirit were prominent in Aquinas' mind. The articles of the *ST* are micro-disputations: they are composed in a pointed but tranquil style of argumentation, of question and resolution. Aquinas' style, reflecting intellectual changes in the Middle Ages, calls into question opinions on creation and revelation not to remove their intellectual foundations or with the hope of finding a comfortable agnosticism or nihilism, but to spotlight important issues. The objections allow further issues to be treated. Amazingly these almost 10,000 or more difficulties with their responses are not random problems, but they focus on significant issues in a specific topic. In a spirit far from any inquisitorial mentality, Aquinas brought in other opinions, mustered not as errors but as stimuli for research into truth (truth, for him, is difficult to enclose and also difficult to escape). The meeting with a different opinion occurs within the atmosphere of dialogue and research. Other views are never fully rejected, because they too can have intimations of truth and can make contributions not only to discussion but to conclusion.

This theology proceeds:

- from the general to the specific;
- from unity to diversity;
- from how something behaves to what it is (from its activities to its nature);
- from the reality of something to our words, concepts, and symbols representing that reality;
- from the world of natures to the being and activity of God; and from nature to grace, a grace which essentially is God, incarnationally in Jesus of Nazareth, and is participatively in human beings.

In its relentless logic, unalterable format, and abstract language, the *ST* can bring fatigue or feed compulsion. It is helpful when pursuing a topic like "salvation" or "hierarchy" to read more widely than one article or question, and to use a concordance to the *ST*. Staying with terminology is to dally with a mechanical and positivist approach, one alien to this theology. To look closely at a set of articles is to see that Aquinas was not constrained by his structure but used arrangement to include much material in brief units. He was interested in logic, linguistics, or methodology only as helps to gain insight into faith. Combining observation and speculation, he pursued an intellectual approach of disclosure, revealing, setting forth, and unfolding, while avoiding both exaggerations and overly subtle questions. His spirit was never dogmatic or ideological; appeals to absolute authority are rare. "Two things should be avoided: asserting something which is false and opposed to the truth of faith. And, it is also not permissible to take whatever one might think is true and to assert at once that it belongs to the truth of faith: for then the truth of our faith becomes a matter of ridicule among non-believers . . . asserting something to be a truth of faith which most certain research and documentation shows to be false."[43]

V. A Biblical Theology

If the medieval teacher was interested in books and ideas, he treasured them because they gave access to reality, to worlds visible and invisible. In the thirteenth century books were being written in quicker scripts and were being produced more cheaply, copied not for a wealthy elite but for the growing class of scholars. Texts opened up networks of nature or that subtle realm of grace which faith affirmed to be "a new way of the divine existing in intelligent beings" (I, 43, 3). A university teacher of theology commented on Scripture. Hugh of Saint Victor wrote: "The cathedral of the professor is Sacred Scripture."[44] The composer of the *summa's* panorama was also the teacher of the Bible. Exegesis was work required by an academic position but it was subsequently a source of theological reflection. No matter how attractive and important the writings of philosophers and theologians, the scriptural text and the reality to which the text witnessed gave theology's first foundation and inspiration. Aquinas lectured on a number of biblical books. One of the signs that we love God, he said, is that we enjoy hearing God's word.[45]

In his two magisterial inaugurations—as a young professor and as a *magister*—Aquinas treated the theme of Scripture. Religious teaching should teach, delight, and inspire. The gospels are fulfillment, the Hebrew writings are revelation and anticipation (the frequently cited Psalms are a kind of bridge), and the epistles are theology and pastoral application. "The New Testament, ordered to eternal life, has not only precepts but the gifts of grace. The gospels give us the origin of grace; the letters of Paul give us the power of grace, while the other books give us the realization of grace."[46] How could those texts of revelation and wisdom be imparted to people? Aquinas stressed that the Bible used metaphors and analogies, mysterious links between the highest of teachings and the world of creation and humanity. "God communicates [this biblical wisdom] through a proper divine power . . . but teachers communicate it as ministers of this teaching."[47] His theology of the biblical text pays attention to how different writings explored the same word and the same theme, and experts see here signs of his employment of a concordance.[48]

The university teacher led students through particular books of the Bible. Theology presents a sacred teaching, a revelation, which is concretely proposed in the Bible, in those "pages which are sacred." As Aquinas was lecturing on the Bible and engaging in public disputations, he was also composing synthetic works offering his personal theology of God's revelation. The presence of Greek philosophy in them is evident, but how is the Bible present? Its role is formally discussed at the opening of *ST*—it is a privileged written witness—but its words are on every page. If theology should illumine biblical meanings and metaphors (I, 1, 8), the subject matter of Aquinas' theology, however, is not so much biblical phrases as the realities (this reflects the realism of Aristotle) to which they point: God active in history, covenant and incarnation, grace and life.

The "Prologue" to the *ST* indicates that Aquinas sought a less repetitive format than that found in commentaries on the Bible. In his systematic arrangement, order would illumine inspired writings. Research during the twentieth century has shown that medieval theology was hardly waiting for the Reformation's liberation of the Bible, and that Aquinas is not just decorating metaphysics with biblical citations. Similarly certain books of the Bible exercise an influence on particular areas of theology. We can see the role the Psalms play in moral theology, or the influence of the Gospel according to John in the theology of the Incarnation. His commentary on Romans illumines the centrality given to grace in the structure of the *ST*. All the Pauline letters, Aquinas says, have as their subject God's grace, but Romans is about grace "in itself," and the eighth chapter, its climax, describes how offspring and heirs of God act in the Spirit.[49] Research

has still not sketched sufficiently how biblical themes appear in clusters of questions or how they inform broad structures of the *ST*.
Aquinas' commentaries divide the text into its major and minor areas
of teaching, elucidate the major theological points, and, with the help
of earlier commentators, respond to difficulties about either the literal text or its implied theology. But Otto Pesch notes:

> The biblical commentaries of Thomas are quite often rather tire-
> some to read. The text is divided in minute detail, and this some-
> times results in a stark analysis which pursues the grammatical and
> logical connections. Often this is expanded by the exposition of var-
> ious possible interpretations among which Aquinas does not always
> decide. Sometimes the commentary becomes a mini-question or an
> article (as in the *ST*). Nevertheless, the faculty and the students saw
> this method as a decisive scientific progress beyond the meditative
> exegesis of Scripture in the cloisters of the ancient monastic
> orders.[50]

With some perseverance the reader needs to draw out the underlying
arrangement in sections of commentary, to see how exegetical exposition aims at a theological clarification or expansion.[51]

Aquinas followed his analysis of the different senses in Scripture.
There was, first and foremost, the literal sense, the meaning intended
by the author writing the book. There was also one or more spiritual
senses in which allegory and metaphor might offer to an individual
reader a personal application, a meaning stimulated by the text but
not placed there, except seminally, by the original author.[52] Particularly in theology, the tensions between words and meanings, and
even more, between words and the divine realms, are significant.
"Spiritual things are always hidden. Therefore, through the realities
of time they cannot be fully manifest, and so they need a diversity of
presentations."[53] Any reality is always richer than any verbal presentation; truth is always greater than the words of its expression.
Fundamental to this theology is that words do not collapse in upon
themselves, caught in their limitations and uncertainties. Rather,
words, although they are arbitrary signs of things, tend dynamically
toward the realities they would express. Is there a key for finding the
sense of a biblical author, for finding the first meaning beneath later
interpretations? One key lay in the actions of Jesus Christ. In him the

plan of the Trinity has its culminating point; to him the writings of the Hebrew Scriptures lead; in him men and women find the teacher of the reign of God, the icon and norm of the life of grace, the source of church and sacraments. "Whatever pertains to Christ or is about Christ—that is called gospel."[54] The *ST* in its theory and practice of scriptural interpretation holds exegesis, theological reflection, and ecclesial life together. M. A. Reyero notes:

> What results from a study of Aquinas' exegesis is that behind his teaching on the meanings of Scripture stand various but complementary ways of thinking which are used by Thomas to explain the basic truths of Christianity. This exegesis . . . is a many-sided totality whose individual parts can be distinguished by their philosophical, theological, moral, and mystical elements. And yet they do not introduce a strict separation between exegesis and theology, interpretation and pastoral life, exegesis and moral theology.[55]

For instance, the commentary on the Psalms from 1272 had the goal of making intelligible God's theology of covenant and Messiah, and of explaining the poems to Aquinas' Dominican brothers who recited them several times a day in choral prayer. In a prologue to this commentary he explored how the many songs first celebrate the universality and diversity of God's work in creation and redemption. Second, God's work historically expressed in other writings of the Hebrews is here developed poetically. Finally, the Psalms exist to inspire, to lift up the human spirit. "Whatever is said in other books [of the Bible] in various genres is here expressed in the mode of praise and prayer."[56]

Exegesis and theology go together. The words of the Bible are not verbal celestial magic but exemplifications of the interplay of the created and the graced. Not confusing literary forms, Aquinas within the limitations of his time sought to understand in the text an inspired meaning and then its relationship to science and life. Four gospels are needed because of an "overflowing richness in the works of Christ." And yet, "infinite human words do not explain one word of God."[57] Significantly, while God is an artist for Aquinas, he is not a poet. God's creation is a product, not a simile; salvation-history is not a novel. Pesch observes:

He could have admired the "poetic art" of God in his quite personal word, Holy Scripture, revealed as it is in such imaginative ways. But Thomas does not do that. Despite a rather agnostic element in his teaching on the analogous discourse of God . . . here he accentuates the few aspects of similarity within analogy . . . and emphasizes that analogy is highest when one can, even with only weak understanding, peer into the highest things. And so God is not a poet.[58]

Although he analyzed the metaphorical and the symbolic, Aquinas always sought to draw the diverse scriptural texts toward reality, divine or human but he did not always demand or produce a simple resolution to every exegetical problem. He pursued exegesis in light of how other great theologians had explained this or that text.[59]

To return to the *ST*, the Bible was important not only in providing a multitude of citations but in its structure. Biblical motifs and theologies are latent in this work like threads joining expositions and sections: Genesis' creation, the Johannine Word and missions, the law of the Jews, the life of grace, the love of God, the salvation of Jesus.

VI. Some Principles in Thomas Aquinas' Theology

We have been sketching theological patterns in the *ST*. Other kinds of organizing forces play an influential role throughout the work. We call them principles. They are themes or axioms, fundamental orientations or ways of grasping reality. Some principles of Aquinas' thought are philosophical and some are theological. Principles are philosophical when they give general perspectives on being; they are theological when they come from revelation. The *ST* is, of course, not a theological system in the modern sense of an elaboration of a basic principle begetting every facet of Christianity. But it is systematic in its organization and organic interdependence. Some of the following principles come first from the Aristotelian science which Aquinas drew into his theology to explain "divine realities," but they influence perspectives on both creation and grace.

Let us look at a few important theological and philosophical principles which are at work throughout this theology. They typify Aquinas' thinking, and as underlying motifs they serve to link areas and to vitalize their theology.

A. THE FORCE OF THINGS

God is a powerful and mysterious cause, the sovereign cause of all. A truly divine being is not jealous of creatures and their capabilities. Everything has a basic form, a specific principle of what it is. Its nature makes a chemical element or a bird to be itself. First and foremost, nature is the source and enabler of activities proper to the species. Creatures exist to act and to live, and the permanent intrinsic source of all that they do is the basic form of each. A nature gives the proper range of activities or the mode of life to each being, and then individuals realize that form through their unique existence. Actual existence is the highest gift of being, and each existent has an inner fecundity and energy, even its own generosity in sharing itself with others. The poet Gerald Manley Hopkins captured this in his poem, "As Kingfishers Catch Fire":

> Each mortal thing does one thing and the same;
> Deals out that being indoors each one dwells;
> Selves—goes itself; *myself* it speaks and spells,
> Crying "What I do is me: for that I came."

For Aquinas not only the intricacy and order of creation but the individual being and prowess of each creature, no matter how tiny or transitory, glorify God. To this Aristotelian reality is added a neo-Platonic idealism. These frogs or those palm trees in their temporality and limitations, in their specific form and individuality, realize God's ideas and wisdom.

God delights in giving beings life and existence and also in enabling them to be causes. A creature by action and by causality imitates the endlessly active reality which is God.[60] Consequently it is not preternatural tricks or natural disasters which suggest the divine power but the glory of the lioness and her cubs, or the whale in the ocean. To look in nature for the un-natural is to misunderstand God entirely. God is more glorified by nature's powers (and by the graced life of millions of men and women) than by visions and magic. The wasps' community, the spider's web trapping gnats, or even the bacteria whose own life-sustaining actions can make men and women ill are in their quest for existence and in pursuit of the goals of their natures manifesting God's intelligence and love.

B. THE GOALS OF BEINGS

Aristotle was originally a biologist and his realistic thought was thoroughly teleological. Some goal fulfills this particular form and a goal motivates this being into activity. We learn about beings from their activities: a run from potentiality to form, a flight to completion. Seeds are equipped, even disguised, to survive being eaten, and to float for miles in order to reach the right kind of earth so they can sprout as a plant. Bees have intricate guidance capabilities enabling them to find flowers' nectar in order to nourish the queen and to store honey for workers who will live in the hive through the threatening winter. For Aquinas the power and beauty of creation and of creation's God are to be found in the ordinariness of activity-to-a-goal. *"Causa finalis, causa causarum"*—"The final cause is the cause of all the other causes." Each being's nature (a bee is not a coal miner; a human body is not a tank or a church) finds its glory in activity, in activity specified by a goal. So the efficient, formal, and final causes will be similar; for instance, the bee's efficient cause is the queen, while its bee's nature gathers pollen and nectar for the over-riding survival of the hive.

The pattern of color in the dogwood flower is not formed by God for the purpose of depicting the nails of Jesus' cross but to attract insects. What piety might see as a trace of the divine, as when God is imagined to be directing birds to form a "cross" in flight, is for Aquinas an accident, chance. God plans nature's success, individually and overall, but an ecosystem is not the stage for a show of religious eccentrics.

Aquinas saw teleology as fundamental to beings. "In everything known by the human intellect order reigns" (I-II, 94, 2). The human being too lives and acts for a goal. But which goals satisfy human beings? What can exercise the strongest claim on us—wealth, fame, sensuality? Aquinas thought that only a destiny of some depth can satisfy the unquenchable search of humans for pleasure and joy. Jesus' revelation proclaims a special "reign of God," a deeper life for humanity. That is why Aquinas began the *ST* not with the crucifixion of Jesus or the authority of the church but with a statement that God has revealed a special world and destiny, one that is above nature but which also elevates and fulfills nature. Because the Kingdom of God exists as a supernatural future, men and women need to have a "form," a somewhat lasting source of activities, a life-principle to live now and in the future beyond death. The large Second Part of the *ST* does not retell Jesus' life but describes the two powers which will enable us to live within and for our destiny: the human personality and the life-principle called "grace."

Aquinas' principles are not opposed to the views of astrophysicists, paleontologists, or theologians who accept evolution in nature. Becoming does seem to dominate galaxies of gas and heat as well as biological life on earth. Aquinas stressed being, but, although he had little inkling of a world shot through with development and evolution, his theology nevertheless entertains stages in human life and history. Precisely his understanding of causality would have led him to appreciate a mature but delicate Power permitting worlds to unfold out of their inner capabilities. God is more glorified by an independent world of finite beings intricately emerging in time than by a planet where beings enter fully dressed like characters ready to act out a play.

C. THE DIGNITY OF BEING A CAUSE

That creatures are endowed with powers is a fundamental principle of Aquinas. God loves into existence the capabilities of every nature, whether it be the panda or the shark. He gives to creatures a wonderful endowment: the gift of being a cause. "On account of the abundance of his goodness (but not as a defect in his power), God has communicated to creatures the dignity of causality" (I, 22, 3). Causal creatures, whether young muskrats or radio waves, contribute to a world both stable and in movement. God's own causality possesses degrees which are so powerful as to permit the creature to be and to act. "It is not out of God's incompleteness or weakness that he gives to creatures causal power but out of the perfect fullness which is sufficient to share itself with all."[61] Not surprisingly, one of Aquinas' illustrations for independent causality was teaching: "For a professor does not just want his students to be knowledgeable but to be the teachers of others" (I, 103, 6).

There is only one "primary" or ultimate cause: that is God. But creatures—inevitably "secondary causes"—are not puppets. They are real agents, fashioning out of their nature's active forms this existence. A star burns, a tanager builds a nest. The power of God is revealed in the variety of creatures who are all proper causes of their actions. God appears supreme not by miraculously replacing them with unnatural displays of power but by endowing them with their own modes of activity. God gives independence to creatures "not by a lack of power but by an immensity of goodness; he has wished to communicate to things a resemblance to him in that they would not only exist but be the cause of others."[62] The Primary Cause is not glorified by interfering often in the course of its creation. In our world deadly viruses or multicolored sunsets are not produced on the spot solely by a distant but powerful deity. The divine source gives not only existence but causality and both summon up the image of God. Creation proceeds from and by proper, proximate causes. Who causes eagles? Other eagles, eagles feeding and training young eagles. Investigations can find the ordinary factors which influenced a car being hit by a truck or the production of a calf by a cow; the activity of God is not the proximate cause of most things. Aquinas' theology of causal interplays in nature and grace pervades his theology. "The one and the same effect is produced by the subordinate cause and by God, directly by both, though in a different way" (III, 70). To ignore the distinction between "primary" and "secondary" causality is to confuse the causalities of Creator and creatures, and to risk replacing God by a creature or the creature by God. When religion sets aside secondary causality, the modest activity of the creature, a fundamentalism enters to control miraculous divine activities. To some this appears to honor God but it in fact detracts from the divine plan and turns creation into a puppet show. On the other hand, atheism and an ideology of science reject any presence of the primary cause and any supra-natural empowerment of people, and affirm only what instruments can measure.

Aquinas dared to analyze the presence of grace in human life in terms of causes. The causal source of supernatural life could only be God. Formally, however, grace is a special principle of life by which men and women share in the life of God. Its matter is an individual personality, and its finality is heaven. For a theology of the reign of God the axiom of the three similar causes (efficient, formal, and final) holds: the cause of grace is the Logos in Jesus and his Spirit present in the world of people, and this deeper sharing in the life of God called grace, has, as its future, resurrection and eschaton. Aquinas' thought, refusing to choose secularism or fundamentalism, sets up a psychology of faith and grace which is an interplay of causalities where each is free to act and to relate with other causes.

D. BEING AND KNOWING

Among the many intricate natures of earth and the universe a particularly high form of existence is one that can know. Hawks, despite their volatile ingenuity, are quite determined and have capabilities for only a few enterprises. But members of a string quartet have a great deal of psychic space for choices. The higher the being, the more open is its field of action—a cocker-spaniel is more adaptable (and more interesting) than a worm. Knowing is the highest form of activity, for it can itself become all that exists. For that reason, freedom accompanies knowing.

Aristotle was a researcher for whom activities disclosed the essence of something living or inanimate. To watch a snake on a summer day is to see the species act and succeed. In a sermon Aquinas observed: "When Aristotle was asked where and how he had learned something, he replied: in things—they do not know how to lie."[63] Knowledge moves from the empirical to the intellectual, from the visible to the invisible. Whatever is in our mind somehow has entered through our senses. But knowing, calculating, or believing do not end with the data of the senses, or with ideas or sentences. The mind by employing concepts and language reaches the realities themselves. Knowing receives beings into our awareness as a mind represents intimately what lies outside. A. D. Sertillanges observed:

> Thomas explains that we understand by the impression which things make upon us. This impression gauges their intelligibility and our intelligence. It is the subject or the object which sets the limits as the case may be. The conditions of knowledge make us realize that the objects of experience are not entirely intelligible, and that we ourselves are not pure intelligence.[64]

Two consequences are unacceptable from the point of view of human experience: the denial of what is objective, and the evaporating of differences between the true and the false. Although error and misapprehension are not infrequent, what we know does reflect something of what exists outside our minds. There is an attention to subjectivity in

Aquinas but it never replaces or competes with objectivity. To say I see or I think this or that is to say at the same time, beings exist.

Human consciousness, however, is active as well as receptive. The human intellect receives the impressions of the senses, but it also forms them through arrangements, insights, abstractions, and fantasies. Aristotle and Aquinas thought the mind was fashioning what the senses brought to it. Knowing, reasoning, and insight are dynamic as they touch the world of objects and forces. With various and complex ways of knowing, human beings can devise imaginary animals on exotic planets, or ponder the near and distant future. A poet can be struck by something about this particular orchid, and a scientist can aspire to know the primal moment when the universe exploded.

How do we know God? Certainly we do not know what our senses do not, cannot contact. The human way to know the transcendent and the supernatural is called "analogical" knowing. This knowledge, more a form of not-knowing than knowing, lies between the extremes of agnosticism, affirming nothing about the immaterial, and anthropomorphism, affirming God as human or material. Analogical knowing is grounded in divine activity in the universe. Beings are the faint but accurate traces in the world of God's creative power. They presume in a real but very slight way that God originally caused the world. That act producing all things, despite an immense (indeed, an infinite) transcendence, leaves in creatures slight resemblances to the divine cause. Yet whatever similarity there is between earth's beings and God's being is faint, more filled with dissimilarity than similarity.

Knowing and loving can even touch the realm of the divine presence called grace. The human spirit can not only affirm metaphysical ideas about God but accept in faith the revelation of the Incarnate Word and the indwelling of the Spirit, a revelation expressed in human languages. Revelation is distinct from human life, but faith and revelation do not introduce the special effects of a Hollywood film portraying the Bible or science fiction. Christianity is not an assembly of hard truths and curious miracles turning creation topsy-turvy. The events of Jesus' preaching and ministry occurring long ago can be understood by people today: his triumph of life over death tell us of a further reality and future for men and women. The choices made by Peter and Mary Magdalen are not unlike our own quests for

meaning. When the gospel parables speak of God's love we understand that love through the moments of human love we have
enjoyed. Modern philosophers imitating empirical science and some
modern Protestant theologians guarding divine transcendence affirm
an unpassable abyss between human knowledge and divine being.
Aquinas' view is very different: he retained the faint traces between
Creator and creation, traces that glorify God. Then, revelation uses
ordinary human experience to speak of what is even more sublime. If
God transcends enormously the things we know, still they bear witness to creation's being, goodness, and activity which flow from that
of the divine cause, despite or because of the infinite difference
between God and creature.

Faith and theology, like all knowledge, can move beyond propositions in a particular language to attain the reality expressed (II-II, 1,
2, 2). Belief and love have a vital movement tending toward God.
While God, the source and ground of all truths, is the first truth, this
subsisting and originating truth is also personal and loving and wise.
Dynamic knowing, analogy, insight as well as reason, an apprehension and formation of what is objective and real—these are characteristics of Aquinas' philosophy. The modes of being in the created
world mirror faintly the being and activity of God in a reserved and
analogous way, and the revelation of Jesus has communicated to
minds elevated and empowered by grace God's plan for the human
race (I, 12, 13).

E. GOD AS MIND AND LOVE

Aquinas viewed God not first as a will but as an intellect. Not
from uncharted freedom, adolescent caprice, or the desire to dazzle
does God create but out of wisdom. In the divine intellect are countless ideas, species, individuals, and scenarios. Some are to be realized;
some will never exist except in the divine archive of unselected
choices. The decision to create, the selection of billions of suns with
perhaps endlessly varied planets and moons, the differences among
plants and animals—these exist from out of millions of options (some,
like gold and pink muskrats or very small giraffes, will not exist). All
that is comes from free choices born of sublime intelligence. Through
its relentless teleology, the universe points to a plan. God is well-
depicted as an artist whose genial ideas impelled outwards by love

the entire work. It remains to suggest briefly some other organizing forms which await further exploration.

VII. Patterns

Today there are different kinds of maps. Some not only reproduce the geography of a place but indicate through colors the place's degree of heat. We lack and need maps of the theological themes and thought-forms of the *ST.* Chenu complained of a void in his neo-Thomist education: "How often, in the interpretation of the *II Pars* in particular, I was shocked by the rigid and systematic way in which the Aristotelian structures present in the text were commented upon in detail, while the sap of biblical and patristic spirituality supplying life to these otherwise dead branches was ignored or glossed over."[66] What would these theological maps be like? One might trace how a particular theologian or philosopher influences Christology or sacramentology, or how great Christian themes appear in their proper questions and in other areas. Chenu encouraged students of Aquinas to write up their own plans of the *ST.* "The student, however, will find great profit in establishing on his own a plan of the *Summa,* whether of the whole or of a section of it, bringing all the while his effort to bear on the discovery beneath divisions and subdivisions of the internal unfolding of problems, the sources from which they spring and the manner in which they are brought up."[67] This is valuable advice. But unfortunately Chenu's project has rarely been pursued.

In the sweep of the *ST* there are lines linking different sections (Trinitarian missions lead to Jesus). There are anticipations and realizations (the material world prior to the sacraments), theme and variations (angelic psychology, human psychology and the psychology of the believer), and sources (this Greek or Latin theologian on the being of Jesus). The future understanding of Aquinas' theology should seek out the architecture in the large theological works.

The following are only an initial suggestion of patterns.

1) One pattern begins and pervades the *ST*: it is the activity of God. Beyond the Godhead as subsistent activity and source of Trinitarian processions, God creates through wise planning, execution, and providential ordering. Plans for free creatures and for a life of grace are put into effect. Then the missions of Word and Spirit,

extending into the psyche and history of creatures, become concrete through the incarnate Word, Jesus of Nazareth. Through the Spirit of the Risen Christ, God is actively present to beings in spirit, sacrament, grace, and church. Thereby the divine power extends in various ways into existence, nature, and love. Lafont concluded: "This seems to us to be the goal of the movement of the entire *ST*: the vision of God in God's self and of creation in God as it comes from the hands of the Creator and as it achieves the free participation of human beings in Christ. This dynamic seems to be animated by one grand Christian inspiration and at the same time to have a marked simplicity of line."[68] In a variety of modes, exerting divine influence but respecting each nature and each freedom, God is all in all.

2) Aquinas' works are explorations by a Christian theology of that horizon of reality called the "supernatural order." The *ST*'s opening lines announce a higher ordination, i.e., a plan and destiny for people. The entire work and each article are engaged by a teleology of the supernatural *ordo*. A divine plan (predestination) and a presence (Trinitarian mission) unfold that *ordo* in a new mode of existence, grace. The Word and Spirit of God come to people, live with them to summon forth and enable a special life and destiny under the leadership of Christ, the head of the new human race. Salvation is not ideas meriting a paradise or a transitory divine power warding off a devil but a deeper dimension silently offered to human life. Patfoort writes of three intensifications of the Spirit in the *ST*, of three "pneumatophanies" or "three zones of great pneumatological concentration: gifts, New Law, and grace."[69] The *ST* at its depth and in every moment is a theology of being and grace.

3) One can always ponder anew in this theology the interplay between Aristotelianism and neo-Platonism. It is also challenging to see how the patterns of Greek philosophy are joined to history. How does a psychology of grace fit into a history of salvation? Edward Schillebeeckx thinks that Aquinas struggled to integrate the process of creation and a history of salvation with the liberation and self-realization of a graced psychology and ethics. "Here the tradition of the Greek Fathers of *'paideiatou Christou'* ('education in Christ'), where the accent is placed upon the history of salvation in the world (where God liberates the image of God, the human being, from the darkness due to sin), is joined by Thomas to the vertical theology and interior subjectivity of Augustine. In other words, for Aquinas grace is always

composed essentially from two realities: a 'grace which is external' in correlation with 'a grace which is internal.' "[70] Pesch pursues this same theme.

> Thomas sketched in the first two books of the *ST* that underlying structure of salvation history which influences every human existence. This pattern always has a reference to Christ, but Aquinas sketches it to some extent in the purity of its emergence at creation, with the fact of sin and the special details of salvation-history bracketed. In this plan grace has the lofty assignment of being an ultimate, encompassing principle of activity whereby the human being through a radical interplay of inner activity and divine grace is brought to the level of divine life and therein is first made capable of that definitive determination which God has given to the human being from the beginning. . . .[71]

4) One form for the entire theology is incarnation. Incarnation, the most intense and concrete expression of God active within human nature, does not enter only with the Third Part. The Word's incarnation has various modes of presence. Introduced by the missions of the Word in history and with its climax in the being and person of Jesus Christ, incarnation animates the life and ministry of the savior. It becomes dominant in his headship, participative and unique, exemplary and causal, a headship of the human race redeemed. This union of the divine and the created does not cease with the end of the historical life of Jesus but reaches on through history in the new race, Christ's Body, and in its liturgy of sacraments. Finally the lengthy analysis of personality and grace in the Second Part contributes to an understanding of its cause and model, Jesus.

5) In the treatments of grace or incarnation one can see an approach which might be called that of a crescendo. Issues more general, more proper to nature or the human personality or to philosophical analysis begin a section, and the specific, grace-filled activity concludes a cluster of questions. Then a new development begins, slowly leading to another climax: for instance, the one God leads to the activities of the Trinity in human history; creation leads to the image of God constituted in grace; a psychology of the personality moves toward the conclusion of the First Part of the Second Part in the justification and merit of grace.

6) An individual theologian or philosopher can be traced through varying degrees of influence in different clusters of questions, e.g., Augustine in grace, John Damascene in Christology. The opening questions of the Third Part exemplify this. The "Prologue" cites only the infancy narrative in the Gospel according to Matthew, but the subsequent question on the suitability of the Incarnation cites this Gospel and that of John as well as the letters to the Romans and to Timothy. In terms of theological sources, Augustine is almost the sole theological source for the question on the suitability of the Incarnation. However, with the following questions on this union of natures and person a different selection of sources appears: there is Aristotle to explain "nature" and the Council of Chalcedon and contemporary theologians like Cyril and Gregory to offer the great conciliar sources for this mystery. Thus the selection of theologians and philosophers indicates the direction of the questions and articles. Sometimes one and the same authority links different sections of the work.

7) One could also explore with indexes and concordances how key terms, biblical or theological, are employed in different theological areas. For instance, the linguistic and epistemological presentations of "word" are countless, but they illumine each other. The divine ideas are words from which creation emerges, and Jesus is the Word of God. Other themes are "finality," "wisdom," "sacrament," or "connaturality." "Light" with its overtones from physics or medieval aesthetics would uncover relationships of sources and power. Creation begins in light; the power of knowing is a kind of light; faith is a dark light for knowing; grace is a light. Both biblical inspiration and the dawn of the eschaton appear as kinds of light. Seeing is the ultimate power, particularly in its intellectual form, so light has a priority, a universality in theology.

8) Broad theological motifs too are important. A theological area can be well understood only through its sources and relationships: for instance, the image of God in the human person, the shift in Christology due to more contact with Greek sources. There is the rich theme of "law" which begins as the divine intellect, finds realizations in natural law and the Jewish covenant, and then reaches a high point with a law which is no less than the Spirit of God.

9) These patterns lie within a system which itself undergoes some development in the career of Aquinas. Do his views change?

How? In the area of grace, when we contrast it with early writings, the *ST* emphasizes more the divine causality of grace and less the initiative of the human person.[72] The traditional virtues in the human being move from the rather general religious and Roman presentation of the time of Ambrose and Augustine toward greater realism and activity under the influence of Aristotelian psychology. It seems that Aquinas would mention a theological orientation, and then in later questions draw out its implications or complexity. His terse observation that God is not really related to creatures (I, 13, 7), understandable in a certain metaphysics of creation, is certainly modified or complemented by the missions of Word and Spirit (III, 7, 13).

❖   ❖   ❖

Ghislain Lafont, author of a valuable structural study of the *ST*, writes: "The Christian reality is too complex, in some ways even too unexpected for one simple outline. In this sense the *ST* is a difficult work and resembles the great churches of the Middle Ages. Its architectural perfection appears at once, but then with close observation it also reveals a richness of invention and adaptation, both in totality and in detail."[73] In general, Aquinas' genius gave to Augustinian teaching an expansion through Aristotelian psychology and metaphysics, but this theology was not the work of a short time, nor of a young and inexperienced mind but was the result of research and contemplation and insight. Sertillanges described the *ST* as a coherent reality, even as something living where every element under the influence of a guiding idea receives an orientation from and contributes to the entire work.[74] Chenu thought that with Thomas Aquinas dialectic reveals special creativity. "It is necessary then to pursue within a slow and tenacious maturing the grand intellectual perspectives in that work's constructions, and not to remain with anatomical analyses, no matter how precise."[75]

Patterns await exploration, and it is time to move from forms to ideas. The following chapter, surveying the theology of the *ST*, presents the important areas of Thomas Aquinas' theology and shows the above principles at work. Along the broad, neo-Platonic dynamic line serving a Christian theology but within a Aristotelian and scholastic methodology, his basic principles arrange a thousand or more topics in theology, with sources in hundreds of Roman, Greek, Jewish, Muslim, and Christian thinkers, into a coherent world-view.

3. A Theological World

———— ✛ ————

Just like light, divine grace makes things beautiful.
Commentary on the Psalms 25

To study, to ponder, to teach the theology of Thomas Aquinas is to see its great themes unfold, to see them illumine each other, as their patterns display his genius. These ideas offer a Christian interpretation of reality. Not a few theologians and philosophers have observed that when a system treats one area, other areas are implicitly considered. This is true in Aquinas' works: for instance, it is hard to learn about the Holy Spirit without considering human freedom, or to discuss baptism is to consider at the same time Jesus' life. Principles and key ideas appear within various topics, disclosing the networks of being and grace. The whole is in each part. While each page is about God, nevertheless, this is a God who creates beings, who lets creation act through its own powers, and who then shares an inner divine life with intellectual creatures.

This chapter surveys the main topics of Christianity as Aquinas saw them. The reader can join the movement of his thought as it proceeds through the *ST*: the vast roiling activity of God pouring forth within the life of the Trinity which then acts outward, setting forth a universe of natures, human life, incarnation in Jesus Christ, and sacraments of grace. To believe is to stand in a light which reveals God's plan; to do theology means to understand reality from the perspective which considers the activity of God as the source and destiny of men and women. Christian theology is about faith but about faith as both profound and patterned.

Thomas Aquinas was a theologian—but what is theology? Theology is investigation, orderly presentation, insightful teaching about what is believed. In its opening words the *ST* announces its field to be a "sacred teaching" and states that its theme is God.

87

Aquinas prized the contemplation of lofty forces and divine realities. When that professor in the new university world described theology as sacred teaching, he meant an activity, a process which included God's plan for and teaching about the economy of salvation, revelation as presented in the Bible, and faith's reflection in theological knowledge and the gift of wisdom (I, 1): theology explaining Christianity in a clear and orderly fashion. The divine source, the activity of salvation, and human reflection remain distinct, and theology is not revelation nor is it inspired as the Bible is. This subject matter, this kind of teaching, is multi-layered as it expresses the ways in which God instructs men and women through revelation climaxing in the Word, Jesus. Sacred instruction presents the procession of the cosmos and the history of God's saving presence on earth. That teaching becomes concrete in the Bible and in the writings through the centuries of great thinkers.

Yves Congar observed that sacred doctrine refers to the teachings of Christianity reaching from its inspired texts to tradition and creeds and then to theologies. Considering "teaching" in an active sense, this enterprise which is both divine wisdom and human education moves from the interior presence of the Trinity to ministries of teaching and preaching.[1] Aquinas distinguished clearly between various theologies, episcopal teaching, traditions and authorities, creeds, and conciliar dogmas. The theologian is not simply to repeat past authorities but is to present sacred teaching in an intellectual, interesting, and clear approach, one which draws on the thought-forms of the past and the present and which faces important questions and new issues. "The principal intention of sacred teaching is to give knowledge of God, not only as he is in himself, and, above all, as he is the principle of things and their end . . . particularly of the rational creature" (I, 2). Here God is not a principle in the sense of a static point but in the mode of a ground or primal cause whose sovereign power produces other beings. It is a "sacred teaching" about God's activity in the economy of salvation manifest in Scripture but capable of becoming, through faith, theological reflection and wisdom in individuals. The subject of theology is God, but God not as explored by human sciences but by faith's accepting perception of a supernatural order. God touches human destiny in two ways: people exist in the universe, and they exist within the gift of a further life called grace. Christian theology is thinking about faith, but faith, a dark knowing, is the acceptance of the revelation of humanity's "immediate orientation to God" and its "special ultimate happiness" (II–II, 2, 3). In Christian theologies God is not a missing factor behind particle physics nor the object of metaphysical logic. God appears in Christian theology as the source and goal of a special destiny which Jesus calls "the kingdom of God." Theology is a reflection (in the subway or in the library) about self and about the presence of God's Word in Jesus of Nazareth and in each human being. To give expression to the revelation of God theology draws on a dialogue with nature and culture. Thinking is not memorizing terms or piling up arguments but a calm and happy reflection. When we think about something, we circle around the subject, we explore it, we stand back and contemplate new perspectives. Thinking about the unseen but real, theology serves the individual and the church as it states the Christian message for new generations and new cultures. Aquinas had a particular audience in mind and his works show that he is addressing the issues of his age. "That particular kind of disputation proper to the theological professors in the schools aims not only at removing error but at instructing the audience, leading them to an understanding of the truth."[2] The opening of the *ST* spoke of how students were receiving a repetitious and boring theology. Theology is theory and praxis—"Theology is both speculative and practical" (I, 1, 4)—because it is theory destined for concrete life. As the highest knowing aided by the Spirit of God, theology is wisdom. Wisdom is a philosophical term for knowing in a particularly universal and insightful way, and it is a biblical term for God active among people. Human knowing directing men and women to God is wisdom, and God present to humanity is Wisdom. Faith and theology should further wisdom. In the opening pages Aquinas begins an original synthesis which will also pursue his task of interpreting texts and discussing current problems; the new theology will be expressed in the style of the university.

To view the medieval Dominican as a logician or an ontologist is to begin in error and to end in sterility, for the theme of his thought is life in the order of grace. An over-emphasis upon his philosophy is one reason why Thomas Aquinas was ignored during the Renaissance, the Reformation, the Enlightenment, and after Vatican II. Religion attracts people, and the *ST* has much to say about issues of church and family ethics, liturgy and spirituality. If philosophical sciences in the thirteenth century offered new perspectives, nonetheless, Thomas

Aquinas remained a Christian, a medieval, and a Western Catholic theologian. The realm of being and the kingdom of God are distinct spheres. Theology has an independence from the sciences, humanities, and philosophy, although theology uses their thought-forms, terminologies, and insights. While its subject matter is revelation and grace in life, the first principles of theology are drawn from the Bible and from the creeds and teachings of the church. Revelation, faith, and theology cannot find expression apart from human culture, but the role of culture's expressions is not to prove what is revealed but to explain it. A. D. Sertillanges wrote: "It was treason to give up an article of faith in favor of reason, but in Thomas' eyes it was just as bad to give up reason for faith. Indeed, the treason was fundamentally the same in each case: treason against God, the living truth."[3] There can be true and false philosophical propositions, there can be thought-forms and world-views which serve the continuing Incarnation of Christianity or deform it, but there can no more be a Christian philosophy than there can be a Christian biology. Christianity is essentially a revealed way of salvation and not a theodicy. One philosophy may be more compatible than another with Christianity, one may offer more helpful insights, but in the long run a philosophical system stands or falls on its own intrinsic merits or demerits. To have biblical texts or church authority supporting philosophy (or psychology or physics) is as risky as trying to deduce God's enactment of a history of salvation from metaphors or propositions. "Those who try to prove the Trinity of persons by natural powers of reason detract from faith . . . for the object of faith is invisible realities which are beyond the reach of human reason" (I, 32, 1).

The following sections lead the reader on a tour of the *Summa theologiae* (occasionally elaborated by other writings). They attempt the difficult task of summarizing and explaining the major Christian themes elaborated so profoundly in Aquinas' theology.

I. The Unknown but Present God

Theology is knowledge of God not as the object of philosophical proofs and examinations but God as the origin of realms of being. Above all, God is the source of the real life and destiny for men and women now and in the future which is a special one including and exceeding biological existence. Before exploring the two great realms of being and grace, however, Aquinas presented some proofs for the existence of an ultimate cause and some analysis of that being called "God." These opening areas, however, should not distract us from the *ST*'s theme of a deeper divine life in us through Word and Spirit.

The five proofs begin from five perspectives drawn from medieval physics; they move from facets dynamically present in all of creation to their ultimate cause. Even the divine being, unimaginable and transcendent as it might be, is, as cause, not utterly different from the universes of beings around us, and these lines of argument, these "proofs" inquire whether active beings in the world do not imply some cause, ground, or model. The arguments ponder the limits, the activity, or the contingency of every being, whether it is an otter or a quark. Is there not one necessary, all-influencing being? Aquinas noticed the omnipresent order in all of creation and asked: Who planned this? "Everything in nature is directed to its goal by someone with understanding" (I, 2, 3). Things are moving, contingent, directed—and this raises questions about what lies beyond various kinds of causes. The universe in its finite diversity mirrors the power and the beauty of One who is Act, Goodness, and Reality. (Perhaps, we could draw this search for lines of causality into the realm of grace—something Aquinas does not do in this introduction—by asking in modest and analogous ways about how human aspirations, arts, communities, and services suggest the presence of grace, how holiness and struggle point to life surviving death.)

If arguments can imply a single Absolute, still they do not tell us much about that being. Of course, they do not infer a necessary creation or presume to prove the Trinity sharing its life. These perhaps too famous five proofs and the subsequent description of God in a dozen or more questions do not substitute for the revelation of God by Jesus, although the God present in creation and the God of revelation and resurrection are one. "It is impossible to come to the knowledge of the Trinity of divine persons through natural reason" (I, 32, 1). Theology discerns different presences of God in life and history. Aquinas did not reject or confuse them, nor did he let revelation and metaphysics compete with each other. So those preliminary proofs are at best pointers towards a being utterly unlike ourselves and yet whose faint traces we see in that mysterious being's work, in minute enzymes or red giant stars. The cosmos mirrors the being of God but in tenuous ways. "A creature's likeness to God is not asserted by reason of agreement in form . . . but only by analogy, because God is essential being, whereas other things are being by participation" (I, 4, 3, 3). Thus God's reality is not an activity but activity, and God is not just living but is life (I–II, 55, 2, 3; I, 18, 3). While Aristotelian philosophy can consider the existence and essence of God, we should not think that those belong only to it, for revelation of the Trinity's presence also brings facets of the divine being to human awareness.

To speak of God is to speak of something which is ultimately scarcely known, indeed, which is not known. God lives "in a kind of darkness of ignorance, an ignorance pertaining to our state of life."[4] God is not a super-being, not a super-force, and not a gigantic version of a human mind or of a computer.[5] God is not one special being with a divine nature, nor is the divine the collection of all natures. When we consider the extent of the universe and then multiply it by all the possibilities in creation left unrealized, we begin to ask, How can God be grasped at all? Could a real God be known and loved by the human spirit? "The first cause surpasses human understanding and speech. The person knows God best who acknowledges that whatever is thought and spoken falls short of what God really is."[6]

Still, some words like "act" and "being," even while negating any definition of divinity, can be applied to God "in a more eminent way" (I, 13, 3). God is not encapsulated in our (univocal) terms and judgments, nor is he banished from any ability (equivocal) to know or worship. The basis for this is those facets of minute similarity from Creator to creature, and the dialectic of likeness and difference in human thought and language is called "analogy." Analogy is a juxtaposition of linguistic terms and mental ideas with the claim that the divine and human realms have a slight similarity: in the way the artist is in the art work, the creator is present in creation. "Whatever is said of God and creatures is said in virtue of the latter's relation to God as principle and cause in which all the perfections of things preexist in a more excellent manner" (I, 13, 5). Analogy is more than poetic metaphor and it asserts something real in God (for instance, love), but analogy also respects divine transcendence. The difference is infinitely greater than the similarity. Human knowledge has its source in what the senses perceive, and all that the intellect and imagination fashion from sensation extends only so far beyond sensible things and images. But words, and in a different way, ideas can be extended by the projection of understanding to imply and affirm that a created reality might exist in a more intense way in God. We know of divine love because we can project that love behind the goodness of our creation and life. When we say that God is loving, we affirm a love in God setting forth a world of beauty and light, but we do not have much information about what God's love is like. Ultimately we must find human ideas, images, and languages for the divine. Aquinas' theory of speaking about God permits and encourages discussing God while at the same time affirming mystery and transcendence.

Jesus' teaching used stories and images to proclaim a deeper love from God. Unavoidably the Bible employs human language to speak to human beings ("If you then who are evil know how to give your children what is good, how much more will the Heavenly Father give the Holy Spirit to those who ask him" [Luke 11:13]). The revelation of a higher love for humanity begins with human experiences of love on earth, for Christian revelation proclaims that life and love have been offered to us at a higher intensity. When we speak about God, we give words derived from human experience a certain boost and raise them to a higher power. In the last analysis, however, we have only touched, and not defined or described, the true God. "The ultimate in human knowledge of God is to know that it knows nothing of God" (I, 1, 9, 3). The reason we know little of God, however, is not because God is bizarre or monstrous, distant or angry, but because God so transcends the traces of his being and love. "God's way of being visible and lovable surpasses any human ways of seeing and loving because divine light and goodness are infinite. Consequently, God is not fully seen and loved by others, for only God sees the divine self clearly as it is."[7] Affirmations gingerly linking our perceptions to God conclude that the divine is not a commander-in-chief nor a giant among galactic clusters but a fullness of being; God is a sublime transcendence existing in countless, unknown modes of reality, a ground of creation infinitely different and distant from us. Vast in an actuality and potentiality of which we have a hint in the enormous universe around us, God is a surging fire of activity—but, most important, this boundless sea of being is first an intellect whose consciousness is love. God is as much subsistent wisdom and expansive goodness as limitless activity.

Philosophers and theologians have observed that God is immersed in the infinite. This unfathomable universe of plans, projects, decisions, and loves is embraced in an individual unlike any we can imagine.

Aquinas cited John Damascene's designation of God as "an infinite
ocean of substance," (I, 13, 11), that is, of reality. God is unimaginably
different, sublimely transcendent over all that can be conceived.

Out of a sovereign freedom, wisdom, and intense love God creates
that which is other to God's self. God is an actualization without
boundaries of all modes of reality, those actualized and those that
remain only possible. God's being includes all that can be imagined
(imagined by God and not just by us) in an infinite array of divine ideas
(I, 15, 2). The forms of the universe are like those of art in that they have
a twofold existence: one in the imagination of the artist and one in reality. God knows things in themselves and not through likenesses of
them; that knowledge is both contemplative (pondering the real and the
potential) and practical (productive of things). "There are many ideal
plans and natures, for God understands the divine essence to be capable
of imitation through this or that way."[8] Aquinas wanted to explain how
God can know all natures and yet can select from the range of potential
natures those which are to exist in reality; and further, he wanted to
defend the divine knowledge of individuals.[9] Amid the baffling array of
possible and real beings, ideas of worlds and species and individuals,
wisdom active in love leads the divine will to make its choices, to create fragile but independent beings (I, 14, 8; I, 15, 3).

The *ST* after treating the being of God considers the divine activities: knowing (which in a special way is divine life), willing, and
power. The limitations of God's activity are limits freely chosen by
God. When God set limits it is so that other beings, creatures, might
exist and act. Indecision and illness do not best characterize human
beings, and so too God is not passive or searching for an identity, not
paralyzed by sorrow over the casualties of history deformed by human
coldness, nor a heavenly watcher or repair-person, always judging and
always disappointed. A purely becoming god is a freak in a world out
of control; a suffering god is a momentarily consoling myth for the
sick but not a credible cause of the universe. God is not to be limited
by human psychology and earthly history. There can be many universes and countless worlds, all glorifying goodness, all mirroring
beauty. In Aquinas' theology God acts out of an abundance of goodness and not out of self-interest (I, 44, 4). In a being of infinite wisdom
and bestowal, causation and love have dramatic effects.

One God is lord of being and giver of grace. The goodness of creation and the generous activity of the Creator are remote preparations

for the possibility of humans sharing in some further way the divine life. The opening questions of the *ST* are an initial contemplation of God's life, an intellectual journey passing beyond metaphysics to deeper levels of the divine nature (I, 6, 4; I, 12, 13). God is not prior to or distinct from Father, Word, and Spirit, but there are levels of activities in God, something our knowledge and faith can faintly and partially glimpse. In the *ST* these activities of knowing and loving and creating increase the breadth of their activity, as we approach the mystery where person and activity are unique in God: the Trinity. From the depths of the Godhead through Word and Spirit people on earth receive a special love (I–II, 110, 1, 1). A religious philosophy leads to theology: being and activity move on to a history of salvation drawn forward by the Trinity; participation is illumined through analogous discourse.

II. God's Life in the Trinity

Out of a fullness of being and activity there proceeds—God's Word in the man Jesus tells us—a plurality, a community in God. Life in the divine reality, *"in divinis"* (I, 42, 3), unfolds in a Trinity of persons. There are not two divine beings; not a god who is a creator-logician, and then the Christian curiosity of the Trinity. One God exists beyond creation's forms and creatures' knowing for whom the Trinity is both the divine ground and the result. The divine nature's infinite realizations of activities are grounded in three eternal ones which are the realization and the source of God.

For Aquinas, the Trinity emerges first not as individuals, that is, as "persons" in the modern sense of distinct subjects, but as activities which eternally flow from the Godhead. These activities eternally bestow the three divine points of differentiated life which dogma phrased in Greek thought has called three persons. A ceaseless emanation of active and personal forces constitutes a God who is one and three. Aquinas sought to balance a theology of divine essence with a theology of persons, a theology of paternal origin with both the wisdom of the Word and the driving force of internal Love. This theology begins, however, not with divine persons but with activities. The two highest activities we know—knowing and loving—ground eternal relationships, and these activities mutually sustaining each other, are three persons, and the three persons are God as they share fully and equally the divine nature. Consequently, God appears as community out of activity. The *ST*'s concluding questions on God and the Trinity affirm that, while the activities within the Godhead bestow Father, Logos, and Spirit, they also extend outwards into the lives of men and women.

A creative aspect of Aquinas' theology was to note how the Trinity's inner threefold actions enter into human history and into each man and woman. The Father generates the Word and together they pour forth the Spirit (I, 28, 4), but this same circle of divine life by divine decision extends in time outward to some creatures. God's Trinitarian life grounds and touches a history of salvation on earth. Word and Spirit have special presences in human lives. These divine missions ("missions" comes from *missus*, "being sent," in the Latin translation of the Gospel according to John where Jesus speaks of being sent by the Father) offer to intelligent creatures a "new manner of existence" (I, 43, 1). The Word becomes Jesus of Nazareth whose followers form a collective self united to that Word, "the Body of Christ." The Spirit, love itself, the third person, vivifies their lives. "It is the missions of the divine persons that bring us to eternal happiness" (II–II, 2, 8, 3). Christ, Christian life, church as the body of Christ, baptism, Eucharist, and the other sacraments—these are meetings with the triune God. "In a generous way God communicates the divine self to creatures for their enjoyment" (I, 43, 4, 1). The triune God is the subject of Christian theology not because it dazzles with a mysterious logic or numerology but because the divine persons contact us, giving us a participation in divine life, love, and power. The life of any man or woman within the reign of God mirrors, shares a little in what love generates among the three divine persons. Aquinas dared to say that being a member of God's family was like being a person of the Trinity: "Adoptive affiliation is a kind of participated likeness in natural filiation" (III, 23, 3). What Christianity calls "grace" and what Aquinas calls "participation" is a presence of the Trinity. But of course, graced lives on earth do not encompass all that the Spirit enacts. The early theological debates and conciliar decisions understand that the "economy" of the Trinity in human history reflects the divine life, but they are not coterminous or identical. The supernatural order on earth is a real facet of divine life but only one of countless ways in which God is and lives. Torrell sees the specific role of the Spirit to aid in the journey of human beings toward God: the Spirit makes us through love God's friends, enables liberty, contemplation, freedom from sensuality, and finally an instinctual mode of living in the kingdom of God.[10]

Creation brings us the universe, and the revelation of the Trinity brings us a higher level of life. Creation and redemption flow from a goodness in God so intense that it impels (but not compels) itself freely to reach out to others (I, 44, 4; III, 1, 1). It is love which moves the Trinity to seek personal contact with intelligent and free creatures, to become Jesus of Nazareth, and to be present in each man and woman. The effect of the new modes of being in us is not first of all religion but presence (whose expressions religion serves). Love moves God to act, and the Creator-Redeemer is more deeply committed to our good, our life, now and in the future, than we are. Next Aquinas turned to the great effects of God: (1) the production out of nothing of elements and stars and animals; and (2) the gift of the presences of Word and Spirit as a life of grace. But faith's knowledge of God as the Trinity has expanded and reinforced the view that God's being is activity, intellect, and love. "The love of God is never idle, for wherever it is, it does great things" (III, 79, 1, 2).

III. The Choice for Beings

Gazing upon numerous alternatives and sublimely free, God chooses that there will be other beings. That primal choice emerged not from need but from love. God did not look out into an empty black universe and notice his aloneness or incompleteness and then hastily assemble other beings. Creation is not the amusement of a lonely deity. Nor is it the act of a being laden with untested powers, a demi-god who does not quite know how all these planets and species will turn out. Rather, with a delicate power God permits fragile, finite beings to exist. Creation is a first act presupposing no other action but which is presupposed by all else. Creation is an act about being: in the production of any plant or animal a radical power is intent upon existence, upon extra-mental and extra-divine reality. Creation, "producing something in terms of its very existence" (I, 45, 5), is an act unique to God and implies universal and sovereign powers. The young Aquinas spoke of rivers of goodness which God pours into natures and beings.[11] And yet, creation adds nothing to the infinite being which is eternally complete.

Today astrophysicists describe creation as an explosion. Six billion years ago a hot soup containing all the potentialities of the universe appeared where earlier nothing was. In the first minutes of our universe on a vast scale enormous forces of electro-magnetism, heat, and gravity were set in motion. Creation is an act before which there is no time or matter, an action concerning the "total substance of things" (I, 45, 2, 2). Sertillanges wrote of a paradox : "Creation, even when attached to the notion of beginning, cannot be regarded as an historical event. It is not an event at all because there is no stage at which this 'event' could be enacted; because nothing takes place; because no change is produced. There was no reality before the first instant of the world's existence, though there are subsequent realities and events."[12] And in an idea which anticipates future theories Aquinas noted that with creation all matter is present and the genera and species but not each and every thing or each individual person.[13]

A creature, a being, has two facets: one is its nature, and the other is its actual existence. Because no creature is unconditionally necessary, a species or one of its members are really distinct from their actual being, although in an existing being they appear intimately inseparable. Neither this species of cat nor this particular cat need exist. This distinction of essence and existence is, in Aquinas' view, most basic to creatures and explains their contingent fragility; at the same time, it points to a divine ground whose essence is its existence (I, 3, 4; III, 2, 2). With forms and beings finding their manifestation in activity the universe harmonizes countless activities through intricate laws. For the world of insects along a river or for the elements in the planet Pluto, the Creator is present as a source, a plan, and a goal. God does not just begin and construct a cosmos from outside but continues to sustain the being of creatures through the processes and goals which natures seek. What God makes is beings moving and acting out of themselves ("Every creature exists for its activity and fulfillment" [I, 65, 2]). Creatures give creation an independence, a development and growth. "To diminish the perfection of the creatures would be to diminish the perfection of God as cause" (III, 69). Simon Tugwell finds here an emphasis not just upon the natures of things and their mutual interplay but upon the striking fact of their existence: this he traces back to Aquinas' intellectual personality. "The fact that things exist and act in their own right is the most telling indication that God is existing and acting in them. Without this fundamental conviction, Thomas would never have developed his doctrines of creation and providence and grace."[14] God is not just a life but an eternal source of countless realms and individuals, the spring of all created life.

The entire *ST* strives for a dialectical affirmation of God's transcendent sovereignty in creation and of the stability and independence of the creatures. God is the efficient cause, the designing model, and the destiny "of every being in whatever way it exists" (I, 44, 1). Everything that exists is an idea and a love of God. Although there is an infinite distance between existing and not existing, God's delicate care and genius lie behind the flight of the eagle against a blue sky, or in the skating of the child on a frozen pond. Whatever a galaxy achieves in forming suns, whatever melodies come from the pen of a composer, every moment and every facet of all that we see and imagine retains relationships to that primal Source whose providence, through independent creatures, is drawing a wise plan forward. "For God in one act understands himself and all things. That sole Word expressing all is expressing not only the Father but also creatures" (I, 34, 3).

God can be compared to an artist: to an artist of furniture, or to an architect, or to a portrait painter. Their art causes what is made. Forms pass from the spirit of the artist into matter through talented activity. "The knowledge of an artist is the cause of what will be produced" (I, 14, 8). Every being on earth is a union of mind and matter, a work of art fashioned from plan and craft. The forms of thousands of species exist in the creative mind of God as a beautiful universe. Some species and some individuals of those species are selected for existence. God is the planning artist and the generous giver of various kinds of life, and animals and plants in form and act have their particular beauty. "In the organization of the world, the inequality of the parts . . . has as its goal the perfection of the totality—as we see in works of art" (I, 47, 2, 3). God not only selects natures and lets them be themselves, but he arranges the interplay within them—within species and within individuals—for yet more goodness and beauty. "The beauty of creatures is nothing else than the likeness of the beauty of God. . . . [and] the highest beauty is in the Godhead."[15] Creatures do not detract from God but lead to him.

There are unseen force-fields of spirit. There is a vast range in "being." "Just as the human being, when seeing that the concept of the mind cannot be sufficiently expressed through a single word, uses many and varied words to express diversely the conception of the mind, so the eminence of divine perfection can be seen only when the divine goodness (which in God is absolutely simple) radiates forth in the realm of the creatures in different and multiple ways."[16] We see its spectrum in the myriad of species just on earth, in the number of clusters of galaxies. But for Aquinas there are millions of further forms of being which are exclusively spirit. Human imagination must try also to picture beings and forces which are not material but spiritual. Religions call them angels, and Aquinas spoke of their "luminosity."[17] Science fiction, no matter how imaginative, does not succeed at passing much beyond the given of our universe, and it merely elaborates on the sensible, the quasi-human. Our minds are limited by sensate experience. But there can be minds and powers more diverse than the matter of chemicals and tissues.

The lengthy section on the angels in the *ST* explores such a universe of spirits. If the size of the universe of stars suggests that many planets might hold races where spirit and matter join in varied patterns, beyond that might lie universes of angelic spirits. Since there could be no material differences, each angel is its own species. They live eternally, move through our space instantly, think intuitively, love intensely. In a simple way Aquinas mentions that their range of being, neither human nor divine, completes the hierarchical order of the universe. But his exploration of their natures suggest that they are vastly different from men and women, intelligent animals on earth.

Creation flows from love. Love is always intent upon giving; love diffuses itself outwards. "God is by nature good" (I, 6, 1) means that God is totally and necessarily good, and that goodness is not an aspect of being-God but lies at the center of Godhead. While God inevitably and necessarily wills the goodness of all that is, in a further stage grounded in freedom and not blind volition, God—with characteristic love and goodness—chooses to let other good beings exist. The love of God is active and fertile, and its high form of charity creates a creature's dignity in the universe and a human's friendship with God. Hence the real God cannot hate or be destructive or vengeful (despite stories and metaphors in ancient religious texts). Aquinas employed the axiom, "Good tends to diffuse itself," to explain both creation and the incarnation. God pours forth goodness into things (I, 20, 2); that is, love carries the divine plans into external realizations. "God is a living fountain that is not diminished in spite of its continuous flow out-wards."[18] Love moves the divine mind to make goodness concrete in creation. Creatures glorify him not by challenging God or by keeping shy of achievement but by their activities, all originally his gift but now relatively independent. "God seeks from our good activities not something he needs but his glory, a glory which is the manifestation of his goodness, something he seeks from everything he does" (I–II, 114, 1, 2).

A painter is interested not in generalities but in individual figures drawn in color on canvases, and workers are responsible for assembling this particular truck. God loves individuals into existence. Individual moons and viruses flow from the ultimate cause even though their existence may come after a long evolution. God cannot be ignorant of how creation unfolds, for then he would be a watcher, a passive viewer of some vast cable-television collection of networks with millions of channels; moreover, the programs would determine God. Some theologians in the Middle Ages wanted to keep God's grandeur far removed from contact with individual creatures, while others have made God into a part of the universe. Aquinas insisted that God be sovereignly free from creation, infinitely different, and yet also be intimately directive of and present to each being. "It is necessary that the divine essence be a sufficient principle of knowing things which will come to exist through God—and not only in their universal nature but in their individuality" (I, 14, 11).

To some, the activities of God in creatures have suggested movement, even process and history in the deity. Aquinas asserts that basically God is unchanging. "God is totally immutable . . . for to change is to be in potency to something, but pure act is without any mixture of potentiality" (I, 9, 1). Obviously, since time and matter are God's products, God is infinitely different from them. God is neither life-less nor act-less, but God is timeless, that is, removed from a world in which the succession of events penetrates everything, bringing growth and decay. The beats of a heart or of an atom do not mark God's life, a life having neither past nor future but a wondrous present. How God is both one and triune, how God is outside of time but present in history, how God is the great initiator of change and changeless—these are topics which can be pondered, sketched, and admired, but hardly resolved.

Time, which we forget is also a creature, so permeates our minds that we cannot imagine timeless spirit in action. When we picture or measure God by time we meet great problems about the divine knowledge and power as it contacts our freedom. Aquinas was reserved about the divine life. If he set aside our ideas of process and growth in God, he did not diminish that creating and saving Life: "Human actions cannot increase or diminish God in the divine self, but, nevertheless, the human being has within itself the power to subtract from God or to enhance God to the extent that one keeps or does not keep the arrangement which God has instituted" (I–II, 21, 4, 1). The analogy of the artist helps us see how God relates to temporal creation. A playwright is not surprised by the final act of the play she wrote, but still something new comes into existence when actors come on a stage and speak the words which drive the plot forward. In a minor but real way the author of the galaxies rejoices in their courses. "God orders through his providence everything towards the divine goodness as to its goal. This happens not as if the divine goodness could experience an addition but rather so that things, as far as possible, gain a similarity to the divine goodness."[19] Creatures are something new, new in the Pleistocene period and new in the twenty-first century. For these mysterious topics, mysterious because they are divine, Aquinas offered not resolutions or definitions but clarifications. Theology ends in a dark human unknowing about God which can for some be the result of encountering intense light.

As we saw, the First Part of the *ST* has some resemblance to a neo-Platonic scheme. Nonetheless, in its exposition of the procession of creatures it is also following Genesis' account. A philosophical theology sustains the inception of creation, but then the narrative of biblical history makes this description concrete. Creation's problems are explained by ideas from medieval natural sciences and metaphysics which, while distinct from faith in their science, lead to a God whose deeper life is Trinitarian and is destined to be shared by angels and humans.[20] Sertillanges concluded: "Thomas held that being emanated from God and strove to be united to him; that this desire actuates reality and accounts for the ceaseless travail of all creation. Each being tends towards God according to its own nature. All travel by the same route, but not all go equally far towards God."[21] Nonetheless, creatures sometimes lack something nature intends, or there is a certain violence in nature's processes, and finally there is an activity which distorts action, an act whose means to a goal are ultimately defective: sin. Why are there different forms of evil, whether the failure and violence of nature or the choice of violence in free creatures? Aquinas' answer is more metaphysical than theological; it seeks an illustration rather than an original cause. "The perfection of the universe requires a certain inequality in beings so that all levels of good can be present. . . . God makes what is better in the totality but not in each part . . . and if there are in the universe some beings which can defect from good, at some time some of them will defect. Still it belongs to providence not to destroy nature but to preserve it. . . . God is so powerful that he can even do well from evil realities" (I, 48, 2, 3). Sin in the fallen angels (some spirits could not yield the mastery of their brilliant natures for that moment when they would gratefully receive grace) and in human beings is analyzed early in the ST after creation is complete. Nonetheless, it is kept apart, kept at a lower level, from the panorama of God's realization of beings (I, 44; I, 63). Later the theologian faced how individual men and women are marked by sinful acts.

At this point, however, the world of billions of harmonious beings is not a stage for tragedies, and the human person is not formed corrupt or defective. The universe is not a hospital or a junk-shop where a god is a sympathetic nurse or a defective machine. A god who can only watch and weep is not divine. God loves, creates, sustains people on earth, but God's vision and life are much broader than the limits of humanity in this solar system. God is not a failure observing human history which in its misdirected freedom inevitably disappoints him, an unpredictable trickster whose divine performance might upset the laws of physics. Nor would he repress and then assist the aspirations of humans just to dazzle and amaze. A God who is wisdom and love cannot be a universal hater of his own creation, a director planning a fiery apocalyptic end to the world engulfing innocent beings in suffering.[22]

After creation God does not depart to watch, to ignore, to judge. Finite beings need the invisible sustaining direction of the planner. "Providence" means to Aquinas the patterns of all of creation. Words like "plan," "will," "providence," and "predestination" express a divine intelligence. Creation points to God as generous, and nature indicates an abundance of forms and intricate patterns. The generous give generously. M. D. Chenu observed: "'Providence' is not a nice supplement given to us for our insufficiencies, something to console us, but the act by which we are able to realize our destiny. There appears in this an eminent mode of a high existence [men and women] with a creative liberty, the image and likeness of God. But every creature has its own being and activity, which clearly proceeds from God, but proceeds in a complexity of reality. The presence of God is the consecration of that complexity."[23]

There is a further, deeper providence. The sustaining presence of God in the kingdom of God is called predestination to grace. Predestination should not be a fearful term: it is providence for men and women in the order of grace. If richness exists in the world of matter (Aquinas drew this conclusion often), how much more generous must God be in the realms of spirit and grace where the divine can be even more shared. God has predestined every human being to live in a higher order of life called "graced" or "supernatural." Yet this original predestination, antecedent to the course of each life in freedom, does permit human wills to turn against nature and grace, to choose to fall away from the journey to God (I, 23, 3). Predestination is neither an arbitrary choice of some for heaven nor a force fixing freedom. For Aquinas predestination is a plan effecting an order of grace offered to all who in their lives affirm its gift. History is filled with suffering, but God is working to empower holiness and community in men and women living on earth. What predestination announces, a world of grace, is the great theme of the *ST*.

A theology of God as artist and lover, as transcendent and intimate, is the first response to the questions of how God touches billions of men and women. God is not the only answer to every theological question, nor is God the cause investigated by the many sciences. God is the remote cause of everything—beavers and vines, symphonies and bridges—but theology is interested in the close, proper, effective causes of things. "The eternal law . . . is made known to us in some way: either through our natural reason which is derived from it as its true image, or through revelation given beyond reason" (I–II, 19, 4, 3). Aquinas kept the orders of being and grace distinct as he showed how grace and humanity are not disparate or mutually hostile. Canadian geese flying south are driven by their own biology, not by an angel or by an instinct leading them to form crosses in the sky en route. Their life and not an imposed religious symbolism glorifies their maker. For questions about human death, about the role of the Bible in politics, or about the choices of a life, "the will of God" is not the best answer. God's creation is intelligible, his plans are good, his grace is revealed. Coincidence, violent natural forces, sins, or the effects of a history of oppression are the proper causes of evil. Consequently, Aquinas' theology discourages making God into the proximate and direct cause of human events, good or bad.

Despite its clear distinctions, Aquinas' thought opposes dualism. The human being is constituted as a single being where matter and spirit (body and animating principle) are principles of one living nature. Chenu described this anthropology in this way: "A human being is constituted by one sole being whose matter and spirit are consubstantial principles of a precise totality. . . . The soul is the 'form' of the body in a most intimate way . . . *It is the same thing for the body to have a soul as for the matter of this body to be in act.*"[24] The human being, where matter and spirit interact, sums up all the modes of being from mineral to spiritual. Aquinas concluded: "The human being is a kind of boundary line of spiritual and corporeal creatures, existing in a horizon of eternity and time, reaching from the lowest realm and approaching the highest."[25] As he was not a dualist, Aquinas was not a materialist nor a spiritualist. Natural life, whose principle is called "soul," is not an interior treasure house, nor a place of grandeur apart from the vitality of a face, the sensuality of the body, or the morality of actions. "Just as the body gets its being from the soul as from its form, so too it makes a unity with this soul."[26] The human being is not a stranger or prisoner in the world but lives at home in nature's network. Every inner principle of life, whether the soul of a gorilla or of a dolphin, whether the instinct of an athlete or that of a clarinetist, gives spontaneous activity.[27] The human being, then, is not locked in a metaphysical Aristotelian cage of causes and categories but is an individual who lives amid creation and grace, and who has a central position in the world (as the structure of the *ST* shows). Nevertheless, the soul and body and their relationship are subject to limits and to sinful disorientation, and they await a further enhancement through a grace in which their powers will be freed from violence and decay.

Central to Aquinas' world-view is the wonder of the human being, its powers of knowing, its creativity, its freedom. His thought cannot, however, be invoked to permit an exaltation of humanity at the expense of nature. Although he would not understand the terms "capitalism" or "ecology," his theology gives all natures, all agents, all individuals their due. Each being is loved by God so much that it exists—but it exists within a variety of beings. A theology of divinely planned communities—whether that be the cosmos or the human state—locates tranquilly each creature within networks of other beings. Each has its goals, its rights, its duties—and these glorify God. While human beings can employ creatures they do not have a dominion over all; that belongs to the total good of the universe and to the glory of the Creator (I, 65, 1, 3).

However great his genius might have been, Aquinas' thought could not escape that time and culture which gave to him forms and ideas. He wrote little about the differences or relationships between male and female in the human race; this is not a theme for him, as it will not be for centuries after him. His theology treats human persons in general in the orders of nature and grace. The differences of the sexes comes from nature and not from the fallen human condition or from sinful drives. Since nature is good and in need of procreation, human sexuality is good. His view of women is conditioned by a biology of the thirteenth century recently enhanced by Aristotle's *De generatione animalium* where the man is active and the woman is passive in conception. The female is indirectly produced by the species and because of this her roles in conception, manual labor, and political leadership are minimal.[28] If Aquinas' view of women was impaired by Aristotelianism, it was also injured by the book of Genesis. He several times mentioned women being in a "state of subjection" (I, 92, 1). While this could be a description of woman's social and political condition in the thirteenth century, he linked subjection to the religion of Genesis (3:16) where it was part of humanity's punishment for the primal sin. Beyond the textual influences of the philosophers and the Scriptures there was the social situation of feudalism where the public roles of women were few and most work appeared to be done by men. In Aquinas' defense one can note that in the few passages (more than a dozen in the entire *ST*?) where women appear in negative stereotypes, he is either presuming Aristotelian biology or explaining passages from the Jewish law.[29]

> If you collect random observations, then Thomas certainly appears as a dark misogynist. In fact, his observations, few and scattered in this enormous work, apart from the treatment of the biblical record of creation and the issue of ordination, appear most of the time in oblique observations and marginal statements. And equally impor-

tant: in these issues Thomas is not in the least original but repeats the knowledge and views of his time.[30]

Aquinas, however, held that the natural diversity of men and women before the fall contributed to the varied glory of the world (I, 92, 1, 2), and that men and women are equal in the future intensification of life. Moreover, at the level of the grace of Trinitarian presence there is no inferiority based on biology or society. The human being who is closest to the source of grace and so most graced because of her role in salvation-history is Mary (III, 27, 5). Aquinas' theology then gives two openings beyond what we might expect of a medieval theologian: an ultimate equality in the order of grace, and an argument about public roles based not on natural law or on gospel mandates but upon social subjection.[31]

A theology of the human being as the image of God concludes the First Part and serves as a bridge to the graced anthropology of the Second Part. The image and likeness of God linked the questions of creation with those of life in grace. Men and women are a place where grace can enter, where a silent revelation can speak. Trinitarian images build upon creation's images. Pesch observes how creation, mission of the Spirit, and indwelling are the same activity but in different modes. "This means nothing less than that the human being as the image of God is the goal of all of the divine activity for happiness and salvation, beginning with the creation of the human being in grace and concluding with the fulfillment of the mission of the Spirit which looks toward the end of time."[32] The image of God in us is several things: it is the receptive place of grace and sanctity; it is a reminder that religion and faith aim at beauty; it is an anticipation of Incarnation. The book of Genesis described men and women as the "image and likeness of God" (1:29), but in the *ST* the image is not first something supranatural but the human faculties to know and to be free. J. Tonneau wrote: "To be a human being, that is, to be intelligent, endowed with free will, master of self and of one's works, this is to be the image of God. To be a human being, to act like a human being . . . this is literally to follow one's vocation, to do one's job as the image of God."[33] This image, the openness of consciousness and freedom, enables contact with God beyond our biological nature, and so likeness to God is understood secondarily as the life of grace.

> The image of God in the human being can be considered in three
> ways: in one way through the human natural aptitude to know and
> love God . . . in another way in the actions and habitual orientations
> toward knowing and loving God (albeit imperfectly), and this image
> is through the conformity of grace. . . . In this way there is in human
> beings an image of God, both in the line of divine nature and in that
> of the Trinity of persons, for in God himself one nature exists in three
> persons. (I, 93, 4 & 5)

We never lose being the first mode of the image of God—even by the
sinful rejection of the reign of God on earth. The human aptitude to
know and to be free remains although it can be clouded by sin or
weakened by mental illness. A person can never be despised by the
Creator; image in nature and predestination to grace exclude being
cast off, being foreordained to some alien hell. To turn from God is
possible, but the image remains, attracting to us the redeeming love
of God who always seeks out all human beings. The biblical parable
of the good shepherd seeking the lost and rejoicing over each individual who abandons the path of death—Aquinas paraphrased that story
in his own way: "The good of grace in one person is greater than the
good of nature in the whole universe" (I–II, 113, 9, 2).

Thus the *ST* concludes its first part, a tour of the universe, with the
climactic introduction of the human being, body and consciousness, as
the image of God. Does this give a certain human focal point, a modest
anthropocentrism to the theology of Aquinas? C.-J. Pinto de Oliveira
observes that Aquinas surrounded human activity with "a luminous
crown of relationships. . . . Each of the three parts of the *ST* treats the
bearer of these acts, the human person, and the activity of God in people."[34] The human being is a high point where spirit and matter, intelligence and corporeality emerge in one creature. Like the first act of a
play the appearance of the image of God leads to what follows.

IV. A Special Life on Earth

From the triune depths of the Godhead comes the outpourings of love,
billions of creatures the edges of whose being are shaped by the knife
of finitude. As we saw, considering millions of optional plans, the
divine mind, moved by the deepest freedom and the wisest love,
decides to bestow real existence upon some species and some indi-

viduals. The divine mind chooses various plans—ecosystems, galactic clusters, laws of matter and of spirit—to exist. Further choices, however, await. The Trinity also selects a plan for our planet which includes not only the creation of matter and life culminating in conscious and free creatures but the offer of a higher degree of life to human beings. God could have chosen other plans: perhaps there are planets where people in blissful ignorance are content to cease to exist at forty, or where sin is unknown as are forgiveness and mercy; perhaps there are angels whose activity remains within their powerful minds but for whom God is only a cold, distant, neutral point. But for earth there is longing, faith, new life, promise.

The Second Part of the *ST* charts a human journey: this is not a geographical trip but life itself. "We arrive at happiness through actions" (I–II, 6). This journey builds upon and makes explicit and detailed the previously described theological psychology. This Part's two sections (I–II, II–II) with their almost three hundred questions focus on the presentation and interplay of the two important factors at work in life's journey: (1) the powers of the human personality, and (2) divine grace.

The force impelling every nature is its end or destiny. Having concluded the First Part with the human image of God existing and alive in the order of grace, Aquinas thinks that the first important issue concerning human history and salvation-history is destiny. What does it mean to be a human being? Where are men and women headed? As the very first article of the *ST* spoke of the special destiny given to human beings, so the opening of the second and third parts talks about that destiny as happiness for us. Thus there is a certain centrality of the human person at the key moments of the large sections of this work.

Surprisingly the life of knowing, faith, and love has for its specifying goal not religious obedience but happiness. If happiness is the first attraction for the human journey through life to God, this should not surprise us for God's life is joyful and people exist not for servitude or frustration but for happiness. "The reality which is desired as a goal is that in which this particular being's happiness consists and which makes it happy" (I–II, 3, 4). The motivation of human activity is not religion but happiness. But what is real happiness? What motivates human activity? Aquinas concluded that it cannot be anything material; no matter how great the wealth, fame, or political power, it will not satisfy or last. Human destiny must be something delighting our spirit, something without end, something almost infinite. That can only be God, and not the God of science or theodicy but the God who is a friend, and after death an intimate. God is not the goal of the human being because God has dictated this as a religious law. Rather, all that we seek, all our many finite quests search for an infinite fulfillment—and that is God.

Divine plan (predestination to grace), mission (incarnation), being, and grace—in the First Part of the *ST* these unfold an *ordo:* a real, concrete milieu in which the human race will live. That world, that destiny is ours, but we need a revelation to know that plan and a divine empowerment to enter it. The incarnate Word of God, Jesus of Nazareth, taught a plan for humanity. He directed attention to a further realm of divine presence which he called "the kingdom of God" and what theologians after St. Paul have named "grace." This reality, this life is in a special way the subject of theology. What is grace? A gift of a particular love for us? Some kind of participation in the life of God? Yes, but like every dynamic principle it is glimpsed in its effects. Grace is an extrinsic force to the extent it comes from God, but it is intrinsic to us as a principle vivifying the personal. Grace is not a transient, heavenly jolt, not God's will. In Aquinas' Aristotelian terms, grace is "a kind of quality" or "a created form."[35] Grace is a new life-principle given by God (normally but not exclusively at baptism or at conversion), and as such it is an underlying form with an array of powers. Thus the Second Part of the *ST* presents the means, internal and external, for human beings, by living in the Spirit, to journey to their destiny, means rooted in our personality and God's grace.

Thus in the *ST,* between a theology of the Trinity and a theology of Jesus Christ, a lengthy Christian anthropology unfolds. First, there is an Aristotelian psychology of faculties, activities, virtues, and other habits. "The nature of a being is constituted principally by its specific form, i.e., by the intrinsic element which defines this being . . . [We find] particularly manifest in nature an interior principle of activity, especially among living creatures . . . , its proper nature."[36] Second, because our destiny and life move along a supernatural plane, a further divine power enters. If the reign of God on earth is a special life, then like every life it has a principle, grace. Grace is not just a divine acceptance or favor but divine life shared. Grace brings a further image of God, one of some intensity by giving a share in some aspects of God's life: in love, in life beyond death, in mercy. "Since the Son is like the Father in essence, the human being will necessarily be made like the Father when it is like the Son" (I, 93, 5, 4). Image directs behavior. People struggle to recover an honest and attractive image for themselves. "The image of God is seen in the soul in so far as the soul is carried (or is born to be carried) towards God" (I, 93, 8). The presence of God in us is the presence of his likeness in our own spirit through the Word, Jesus. God begins this presence in persons, but they act under grace, directing graced actions (I–II, 111, 2). Aquinas strove to give an intensity to both God and the human personality, to let each retain its different identity, and yet to bring both together in intimacy. This transcends a crass interventionist theology of God working spasmodically in a biblical pageant or in an arena of miracles. We are most truly human when we are raised to the level of the divine, and this elevation is congruent with being human. Nevertheless, since grace is the Spirit of God, Aquinas gave a certain priority to the divine presence even as that presence on earth touches human lives.

Grace assists human beings to reach a life and a destiny which is both human and divine. Religions call this salvation and resurrection. The life grounded in grace is given solely by God and is not merited by human goodness. "For just as it is impossible for anything to make something fiery but fire alone, so it is necessary that God alone should make godlike by communicating a share in his divine nature" (I–II, 112, 1). Grace draws each man and woman to an individualized destiny as it also allays the wounds of sin. Grace is not a general electric current turned on by rituals and statues, or a purity solely accessible to cloistered monks and children, but a particular love of God for each person. "Inasmuch as through the Holy Spirit we are made into lovers of God, it is through the same Spirit that we are led to respond to God's requests."[37] Grace is not a possession and yet it is a new personal dynamic; the gift of grace is not purchased from God and yet without human cooperation it will fade.

This special presence of the Trinity is a dynamic thread running through the entire *ST*. Expecting to find realities behind biblical phrases, Aquinas set forth an incarnational theology, incarnational by its extension of the life of Jesus Christ into circles and realms of human history. The Christian idea of grace, however, was interpreted in the terms and insights of Aristotelian psychology. The *ST* within its emanation pattern (a metaphysics in the mode of Exodus) becomes an Aristotelianism of grace within human activities: it expresses the teaching of the Gospel according to John on "life" and that of the Pauline writings on the "Spirit" in perspectives both psychological and metaphysical.[38] The psychological approach of Paul's Letter to the Romans and of Augustine has been joined to the cosmic theology of the Letter to the Ephesians, and of the perspectives of the Greek theologians and the Eastern churches. The concrete source of grace is Christ and his presence continues after Pentecost in the sacraments. Nevertheless, while the Christocentric tonality of grace is important, Aquinas emphasized the human milieu of grace. Pesch observes:

> No student of Aquinas can overlook what a strong accent Thomas placed in treating creation from the perspective that God's own creative activity does not remove the proper activity of creatures but grounds them—and that is due to God's greatness. . . . This illumines the quite differently fashioned structure of thinking which Thomas developed for the description and interpretation of the created character of grace. Grace is not "created" as an independent reality. Rather the "special love" of God must have necessarily a created and creative effect in the human being.[39]

The human personality on its journey to the eschaton is instructed by God and then aided by God's grace. The instruction Aquinas called "law," and his developmental theology of law is particularly original. Is not law the opposite of grace? Not for Aquinas. Law is not a set of rules but a realm of reality, a realm of the world as it is understood by the human intellect. Medieval society lived from two legal traditions: there was the data of Roman law, and the interpretations of custom and law by the legal theoretician of the twelfth century, Gratian. To this was added the Platonic and Augustinian theology which related all laws to an eternal prototype, and more recently the thought of Aristotle had brought its perspectives. Aquinas drew these currents into a synthesis, an interplay of theologies of law, happiness, grace, and eschaton. He avoided the politics of autocratic rulers or the ethics of demanding authorities (including God); he was not content to rest with religious or legal positivism.[40] The laws of earth are areas of creation and life, and these laws, ways by which God instructs the human race, are presented in a developmental pattern. Divine wisdom in creation, the law which is nature, and that which is human nature lead to the Mosaic law of religion and revelation, and then on to the new law of Jesus' proclamation of the Spirit's presence. The divine law is first the divine being, the result of sublime mind and ceaseless love expressed in forms and plans for creation. The natural law is the human mind recognizing the plans impressed by God in nature. This law mediates between the actions of creation and human understanding; it has degrees of certitude about moral issues and cases (I–II, 94, 2). There is an early religious law in the history of grace that was active on earth before Christ: this occurs in the human recognition of natural law and perhaps in the laws and forms of religion symbolized by Noah. God, however, presents a more articulate law. It is found in the Jewish covenant which holds a high level combining revelation, religious ceremony, and natural law prescriptions (I–II, 98, 105), and also in the law of grace, revelation in Christ. Aquinas understands that some of the Mosaic law is a statement of the law of nature but he also spends many pages on how it is revelatory and sacramental and not solely judicial or inspirational. For Aquinas, the doctrinal and milieu of the Jews before Christ is a passage from natural law to revelation in Christ, and he can both highlight its sacramentality and insist upon its limitations and weakness (I–II, 100 & 101).

Before we enter upon the laws of nature and religion finding explicitness and power in the "law of the gospel," we should notice the motif of development, the movement of crescendo here as elsewhere in the *ST.* The different faculties of the human personality brought us to different realms of structures ("laws"), and through them, nature, religion, the chosen people, the dignity and destiny of men and women was illumined. Now the entire I–II is reaching its climax, a law which is explicit but of the Holy Spirit, a teaching which is also a power within us. As creation and revelation complement each other, social structures and laws lead to grace. The new law of Jesus is not really a law; it is new and original in that it is not an external list of commands but the presence of grace. "That, however, which is most powerful in the law of the New Testament and in which its entire power consists is the grace of the Holy Spirit given by Christ to believers" (I–II, 106, 1). Ultimately God instructs not through epiphany but through presence. The New Law is the Spirit of the Risen Jesus in women and men. This life is described by Jesus' teaching and life, particularly by the Sermon on the Mount. The essential gift and message of the Christian revelation, then, is an inner presence of the Holy Spirit which is a charismatic source of a new life for human beings. To it all religious laws and rituals point.

Sometimes readers mistakenly think that Aquinas is discussing grace when he offers preliminary and oblique observations concerning a constant divine force continuing on after creation to hold creatures back from non-being. "Every creature to the extent that it is (and acts) according to its nature is of God" (I, 60, 5). This philosophical tenet of Aquinas is not convincing to all, but it is important to understand that it describes something utterly distinct from grace. Such passages are clearly metaphysical and should not lead to a confusion of the orders of being and nature with those of revelation and grace. Aquinas thought that God is active in a mysterious intensity in every created being and act. At the level of being, affirming both the fragile existence and the independence of each creature, Aquinas posited a sustaining divine presence. If this is true, every time we touch the networks of being and activity we touch the ground of being, God. Prior to a discussion of grace he wrote: "Whatever potentiality any nature, corporeal or spiritual, possesses, it cannot proceed to its own activity unless moved by God" (I, 109, 1). Creatures exist on their own, and yet there is in the depth of each creature a radical dependence which affects the finite being. Chenu notes:

> Even as creation, at the heart of being, is received from God, this ontological link, this pure relation which expresses the indigence of that which has been created, the creature so referred to God is posited in its being. To be created is first of all to be, to be a dependent being, one totally suspended from the source of being, but whose very dependence possesses reality only because, first of all, some thing *is*.[41]

Christian revelation, however, is about a special presence in human consciousness and will, one far beyond that of the powers of nature. God is present to human beings in a richer way than existence, and the New Testament's theologies of God's "kingdom," "family," and "friends" express this. Reginald Garrigou-Lagrange wrote: "This [graced] life is more precious than sight, than bodily aptitudes or the talents of reason; more precious than the gift of miracles or of tongues or of prophecy, for these charismata are, so to speak, only exterior, supernatural signs, which can point out the way that leads to God but they cannot unite us to him as can grace and charity."[42]

"Knowing" for the medieval university professor meant knowing "*per causas,*" "through causes." One omnipresent structure of the *ST* is the articulation and ordering of different modes of causality, in God as well as in us. Can the delight of Thomas Aquinas in independent creaturely activity (in "secondary causality") extend even to the realm of grace? Since grace is of God—indeed grace is God—no being other than God, no creature, can cause grace (I–II, 110, 1 & 2). But do we act with the Holy Spirit? If grace is a life-principle enabling faith, hope, love, mercy, we must be active in grace. People in the realm of God are described in the gospel not as puppets or slaves but as heirs and friends.

> It is not suitable that God provide more for creatures being led by divine love to a natural good than for those creatures to whom that love offers a supernatural good. For natural creatures God provides generously . . . kinds of forms and powers which are principles of acts so that they are inclined to activity through their own beings. . . . Even more for those moved to reach an eternal supernatural good he infuses certain forms or qualities of the supernatural order according to which easily and enthusiastically they are moved by God to attain that good which is eternal. And so the gift of grace is a kind of quality. (I–II, 110, 2)

There is, nevertheless, a paradox in the interplay of the human and the divine: the more rich and lofty a creature's life, the more it needs, or rather, calls for God.

How do we act in the milieu of grace? Grace is not a source of miraculous powers for curing cancer or handling poisonous snakes. Aquinas was little interested in the miraculous (which he defines as a rare, visible interruption of universal laws of nature by solitary and extraordinary divine power), but he returned again and again to the invisible Spirit of Jesus working in people powerfully but respectfully. Speaking of the calling of Jesus' disciples, he wrote: "Public preaching which is merely external will only be frustrated unless the grace of the Redeemer is present. For people are drawn [to Christ] not by human power but by the work of Christ. That activity brings the highest dignity, for, as Dionysius says, 'Nothing is a more worthy enterprise for human beings than to become the co-workers of God.' "[43] Aquinas never tired of pondering the causal relationship of the predestining God to human activity, the relationship of grace to personality. God's presence somehow enables and sets free my activity, and in a harmony so extraordinary that I do not feel any duality: my personality and the divine presence seemingly act as one agent during the sweep of life. God, like a mature parent, creates beings and sets them free, free for a successful and happy but independent existence, and yet one which at a deeper level owes each facet of being to the enabling Creator. To detract from the perfection of a creature is to detract from God's power.[44] Cathedral preacher and member of the French Academy, A. M. Carré has described the panorama of the *ST*: "So I take my place in a universe on the move. And God himself proposes my destiny to me. But this destiny I must make my own."[45]

Aquinas' theology is the opposite of every religious viewpoint which is world-hating, of every religious ideology which believes that human beings and cultures are largely sinful, and of every pessimistic psychology which holds that religions are inevitably dangerous or demonic. Because grace is both divine and ordinary and because human nature is good, this theology is the polar opposite of any fundamentalism.[46]

Every agent has limits placed on its action and causality. God as infinite, however, is a different kind of being and has an unlimited ability to act in countless modalities. The Trinity is not a watcher, not a larger version of ourselves but infinite and eternal act. God's power is so delicate that it can influence the free creature in its freedom. After all, the being who creates freedom can act towards that free being in a way which respects the divinely bestowed modality of human freedom. Does this theology support a divine prominence? It is theocentric—not only in the order of the *ST* but in its emphasis upon God's sovereignty (joined to love) within a vast world. Interestingly, this theology also exalts creatures and people. Human beings know, love, create, act, and are free. The self is not demonic nor an animal to be beaten into submission. Human reason is not suspect; freedom will not, when left ungoverned by laws and fear, always choose evil. Happiness is not a grudgingly given gift from a cosmic judge who prefers human beings to feel guilty. Delight should be the companion of religious and moral life. God's salvation does not replace our humanity, nor is human nature—baptized or unbaptized—something shameful and hated by its Creator.[47]

Individuality too is taken into account. The charismatic structure of grace and the circumstances of ethical decision enhance individual life. As we saw, Aquinas emphasized that it was the individual who really existed. This principle would apply for the realm of grace. The missions of the Trinity come to us not as batteries needing a charge but as unique individuals whose lives are the particular object of God's love. Each day adults begin anew: they re-choose life by small or important ways which touch other people and God. Days of difficulty and joy unfold within a universe manifesting the plan and love of God.

Aquinas did not overlook the shadow side of humanity. Earth's misery and violence were all too apparent in his society. The sinful condition of humanity magnified by its own sins wounds people (grace is a remedy for these attractions of evil) but does not imprison or corrupt them. People are sick but they are not intrinsically perverse or demonic. "From the turning of the human will away from God proceeds disorder into all the powers of the soul. So the form, the determining moment in original sin is the lack of primal order through which the will was in harmony with God; all the other disorder in psychological powers is related to this original sin like the material for sin, or like its particular moments" (I–II, 82, 3). This lack of order includes lack of life and grace as well as a psychological proclivity to evil. Aquinas did not simply take over Augustine's too precise location of original sin within rampant sensual desires. He placed this debilitating condition in a psychological troika: a tendency of the practical judgment toward egoism, emotions which are too strong, and a will which is too forceful or too weak (I–II, 82). The will ought to be harmoniously leading the mind and emotions to what is good, but these three forces are too often misconnected. Aquinas did not see human nature as so corrupted that it was inevitably driven toward evil and stamped in every deed with rebellion. A person who has driven away grace can perform actions which we evaluate as good: design buildings, love children. While original sin, the sin of the proto-parents, weakens every human will and frequently misdirects it toward sensuality or power, Aquinas did not make individuals responsible for the fallen condition of humanity: men and women do not establish the misorientation running through all people as through one corporate body. Nevertheless, if humans are not guilty of their fallen condition, nevertheless, they can be responsible for the sins flowing from it (I–II, 81, 1).

Does God cause evil? Nothing is clearer than that before the principles of Aquinas' theology God could not be directly involved in evil, for whatever is bad is the opposite of the supreme Good, the wisest Plan, the most loving Source. Sin, an individual's deliberate and precise bad action, follows from a misguided action. Sin is not only an evil act but one flowing from an intelligent and free creature. God permits men and women to commit their own personal sins, that is, to pursue individual acts of selfishness and violence. The overarching power of the First Cause does not exclude the proper power of lesser causes which are so free that they can sin. "So the effect of the divine will can be impeded through the misdirected activity of the created cause, and in this sense the will of God is not always fulfilled" (I, 19, 6). As much as we can be shaken by the devastations of a war or the injustices of a prison camp, their malicious instigators and directors can be identified, and the explanation for immense suffering lies in their choices. God in bestowing freedom lets that freedom run its course. If the inner presence of grace tries to dissuade an individual from evil, the human will has within its scope of power a sometimes awful freedom for violence. To ask why God does not halt each train of suffering set in motion by this man or woman is to request God to interrupt or replace lesser levels of free action. On earth God has evidently chosen not to do this: human responsibility perdures. In a profound sense what evil humans do is an attack on God, not on his essence or his emotions but on his greatest gifts: freedom, life, grace (I, 19, 9).[48] Thus sin is not the courageous rebellion against a tyrannical super-being but the breaking off of friendship, the ending of intimate love.

God's compassion reaches toward an individual even as he or she pursues evil. The grace of Christ's cross redeems the human race for a happier future, but mysteriously it does not eradicate its propensity for evil. "The beings of nature are produced by the divine art; so in a sense they are the works of art of God himself. Every artisan intends for his work the best over-all disposition; not in an absolute sense but in terms of its own goal. . . . Thus God gives to each natural thing its best disposition not absolutely but according to its own purpose" (I, 91, 3). The plan for the good of the universe is that it includes process, life and death, history. The choice of that plan, while also ultimately good, introduces limits and conflicts for individual beings. As we saw, God has chosen not to interfere in the lines of causality in creatures, but to direct them toward the furtherance of the whole. From the point of faith, the divine being's goodness is such that it not only creates patterns of limited goodness but through a higher order sustains intelligent creatures in life and meaning, that is, through and toward incarnation and resurrection. Because of freely chosen violence, social and personal, grace has a harder, a dual task. The Trinitarian presence acts to overcome the violent forces of sin which block its silent yet efficacious invitations. That is what Aquinas meant when he wrote: "Because there is evil, God exists."[49] If there are disruptive forms, there must be first the goodness they disfigure.

How does grace touch human life? No topic occupied Aquinas more than the close interplay of grace and person following upon the consideration of those two principles.

V. Human Life amid God's Spirit

As we have seen, the world of Aquinas is one of active and colorful diversity: blue dragon-flies are equipped like amphibious airplanes to skim across the water searching for food or partners; out of its life-principle the deer finds food and shelter in the forests of summer and winter, while above, far away, suns are being formed from fiery elements. God works in creation—but he works even more powerfully and subtly in the special reign of God. Grace lives in the depth of our personalities, empowering prayer, decision, compassion.

In the Second Part a graced psychology becomes a moral theology. Its many questions, however, do not give a set of rules or a collection of answers to ethical dilemmas but present a picture of Christian life. Chenu notes:

> In Aquinas we have . . . a moral science which is different by being *theological*. This lofty knowledge both theoretical and practical has as its goal to see and to situate all beings in their relationship to God from which they emanate in a participation which itself determines their return to him. Goodness, virtues, laws, asceticism, customs are certainly the matter of a discipline charged with directing human action,

but this discipline already has gained a prior theological understanding of its object—the human person in the universe.[50]

The ethics of Aquinas develops not what a person vis-à-vis God and society ought to conclude but what the graced human personality can and should do. The *ST* is not a philosophy about ethics for a secular society disdaining mysticism and faith, but a psychology of grace looking back to the missions of the Trinity and ahead to the redemptive leadership of Christ.[51] Christianity announces a life which is much more than a cultivation of natural virtues or propositions about religious duties. The Spirit of Jesus subtly acts within our personality. The special divine presence—Aquinas called it "a friendly and intimate conversation" of God with us (I–II, 65, 5)—leads men and women to act. Thus daily life summons forth and realizes grace.

Part Two of the Second Part looks at the various modes, activities, and principles which flow from the personality enlivened by grace. The human personality is analyzed through its activities and the principles of those activities. To the human life-principle, the soul, which vitalizes the person, there corresponds the "soul" of grace; for the faculties, knowing and willing and feeling, there is an array of virtues infused from the Spirit. Grace-in-action unfolds in three modes: life-principle, virtues, the instinctive modes of the spirit (III, 62, 2; I–II, 66, 2). Virtues are not trophies for good behavior but modes of action, and in human history every action occurs amid the atmospheres of sin and grace. In the natural order, our intellect, senses, and drives spring from the principle called "soul": in the supernatural order, from sanctifying grace received in the soul there emerges infused virtues and the gifts of the Holy Spirit. "Just as in natural things nature itself is distinguished from its motions and operations, so in the realities of grace there is a difference between grace, love, and the other virtues."[52] Chenu notes: "Grace is in us like a [super] nature, i.e. like a most interior principle, most ours and at the same time most divine, possessing a dynamism which makes us capable of vital communion with God."[53] In the *ST* Aristotelian psychology (an analysis of faculties, activities, virtues and other habits) leads through the second life-principle, grace, to a presentation of different virtues.

Thus the lengthy Second Part of the Second Part is an applied theology of grace through the description of many virtues. Aquinas arranged the Christian virtues of faith, hope, and love, prudence, justice, temperance, and fortitude to correspond to the Aristotelian psychology of intellect, will, and emotions. Then he drew in the gifts of the Holy Spirit (mentioned in the Hebrew Scriptures and in Paul) and the Beatitudes of the Sermon on the Mount—Jesus' blessings which contain "all full happiness."[54] Just as each virtue finds its psychological, instinctive, and charismatic climax in a gift, so its relationship to the beatitudes links it to the life of Jesus. His moral teaching finds its epitome at the Sermon on the Mount and gives the virtue some content. Virtues give the pattern to Aquinas' ethics. The virtues, habits of grace, are sub-sets of the grace-principle, grace-vitalized "sources of action" (I–II, 62, 1). The potentialities for Christian life flowing from grace ("infused virtues") retain a certain continuity with the habits we acquire psychologically. To describe grace, Aquinas used the metaphor of light passing through air, and we can elaborate this by seeing grace like light touching a crystal and diffusing itself into a spectrum of colors, colors representing the seven central virtues, their sub-virtues, and their corresponding gifts of the Spirit.

The Aristotelian model of forms and activities is used to explain how life becomes concrete in virtues. Prudence, filial respect, generosity, love—virtues flowing from their life-principle of grace—enable human beings to move forward to the eschaton. The virtues, living in mutual harmony, are rooted not in a program for self-improvement nor in a slavish imitation of Jesus but in a knowing which is supernatural, a hope in life now and in the future, and a love which itself is a gift of Supreme Love.

Let us pause and look briefly at a few of the many virtues Aquinas considered.

Faith has a primacy, because it is a kind of knowledge. Faith gives access not to a metaphysics of the Creator but to the Trinity's supernatural order of life. If what we know comes through our senses ("While the soul is joined to the body it understands by turning to sense images; it cannot even understand itself except . . . through an idea taken from sensed realities" [I, 87, 1]). Nevertheless, faith is not a suspension of judgment before the paradoxically miraculous or celestial but a kind of knowing. In this special kind of knowing the will and grace help the mind affirm what it has not contacted empirically. Faith means the risked acceptance that there is something more than the laws of physics and the daily reports from the stock markets. This "more" is a special presence of God in society and creation. By faith we become Jesus' disciples and live in Jesus' Spirit. We affirm what we cannot see, affirm it as real on the word of Jesus and his followers, and so faith's act of acceptance and knowing must be especially willed. Since the act of religious faith flows from the mind, the object of revelation is the true (II–II, 4, 2). Thus faith and theology pursue not sheer obedience or self-debasement but the intelligibility even of revealed truth: the plan beyond nature, Trinitarian salvation-history, grace, moral authenticity, liturgical rite—these will be related to truth and judged by it. Nor do divine mystery and supernatural sublimity remove our halting efforts to be hearers of the Word and disciples of Light.

In Aquinas' realism the plan of grace for us now and beyond death is a realm of reality. Faith touches a real, albeit invisible, world (II–II, 2, 3, 3). The existence of salvation and salvation-history cannot be proven (its presence and power escapes every mode of electronic detection) but, nevertheless, Christian faith asserts them to be realities. "The objective realm of faith is divine reality not seen" (III, 7, 3). Faith is valuable because it knows something of the world of grace, that atmosphere of God's love which, in fact, is more real than the models of atomic particles or the reports of corporate headquarters. For Aquinas faith is not fantastic beliefs, not a set of religious words, and not mythical past events. Ideas express our faith, and faith is a realization of grace assisting us to accept and express God's invisible presence. Recent theology has often cited Aquinas' words: "Like knowledge our faith does not end with ideas but with the realities themselves" (II–II, 1, 2, 2).

How curious that a few, in different ages, have been drawn to Thomas Aquinas through the mistaken conviction that they will find there a fixed logic of revealed propositions. Aquinas observed that all intellectual truths, even religious ones, are finite and fashioned by human minds. Church authority can give some texts a special importance, but ultimately their power and truth rests upon their expressing truth and being grounded in God as First Truth. Faith dwelling in the depths of the personality is an acceptance of God's revelation and morality found in the teaching of Jesus. As science measures things, and as music comes to life in performance, faith appears in teaching, morality, service, and worship. Just as love is waiting to become joyful possession, faith is waiting to unveil the future, to disclose life beyond death. Faith's reality is waiting for the revelation of vision. "Eternal life has already set its beginning in us" (II–II, 4, 1).

Love is faith's affection and virtue's empowerment. Aquinas called love the form of all the virtues, because love pervades all that grace suggests we do. Love gives a special dynamic and orientation to justice, enflames mercy, makes prudence not calculating but wise. Love is the Spirit of Jesus and the gospel's law because love does not halt at ideas and words but touches directly what it loves. Love moves through the hundreds of articles of the *ST*, from Love creating to Love redeeming. Born of goodness, the Creator's love drew a universe out of nothingness, and love led the Word of God to become a human being. Jesus' parables describe in story and image the love of God, a particular and ceaseless love for each and all (II–II, 23). In a universal community of those loved and loving the Eucharist and the Bible express and intensify life.

For Aquinas God's love for us brought a kind of friendship; that is, friendship explains how God views and relates to people. This theology used Aristotle's ethics of friendship to explain Jesus' observation that he calls us friends (John 15:15). "Nothing is so characteristic of friends than that they live together."[55] This love of friendship means communication and sharing. But what could we share with God? "The divine essence itself is charity just as it is wisdom and goodness. Now we are said to be good with the goodness which is God, and wise with the wisdom which is God, because the very qualities which make us formally good and wise are participations in the divine goodness and wisdom" (II–II 23, 2, 1). The whole of the Second Part of the *ST* is to be read in the light of love. Since it has one ground, the Spirit of the Risen Christ, love of God, self, and neighbor, as the Hebrew Scriptures saw, are closely related. Nor is one to be sacrificed for the other. "Well-ordered self-love is right and natural; a self-love by which one wishes for oneself what is suitable" (I–II, 77, 4, 1). Human efforts, desires, and accomplishments are vitalized by the love of God, that is, by a love which influences us to live in a certain vital interaction with God. Through the missions of the Trinity we are in the words of Paul's letter to the Ephesians (2:19) "citizens with the saints and members of God's household" (I–II, 63, 4). Ultimately love and friendship are not impossible strivings but the result of divine life shared.

To turn to a third virtue, prudence is the right way of acting. It is not a carefulness or shyness which avoids commitment or which chooses the easy path of not acting. Just as there is in men and women an inclination to intuit basic principles of knowing, for Aquinas the personality has an inclination toward moral principles at the practical level. An individual has certain inner promptings, some cognitive and some emotional, to choose this or that option in a morally challenging situation. Then the general principles of doing good and avoiding evil, of seeking life not death, do not remain ethical axioms but are put into practice by reflection, experience, and decision. The individual applies moral insights through conscience. Prudence is a psychological modality of grace which considers for action concrete cases. "Prudence not only considers an action but applies that consideration to action" (II–II, 47, 3). Mistakes in human decisions can occur for two reasons: first, because the principle or insight applied is false, or second, because a correct principle is not applied to a concrete moral case properly.[56]

For Aquinas, generally people should follow their conscience. "Conscience is nothing other than the application of knowledge to a particular action" (I–II, 19, 5). This follows from a theology where natures are basically good and intelligence is capable of information about the world. To a personality not trapped in arrogance or addiction God's grace lights up the mind and guides desires. Naturally we should take measures to inform our knowing and acting, and conscience does not usually advocate destructive evil. Nonetheless, people in some occasions may be following (and may be bound to follow) a conscience even when it is wrong. "Quite simply, we should state that every act of will against reason, whether in the right or in the wrong, is always bad" (I–II, 19, 5). We act upon what we think or believe to be right as the result of our pursuit of truth. It is not only the right object which orients a life but the rightness of the individual's choices, and in the last analysis it is the individual's free choice which empowers the moral life. That action which is loving or just from our perspective furthers grace in us—and this could happen even if an objectively immoral action seems good to the individual. "To believe in Christ is good in itself, and necessary for salvation. But the will is not born toward this unless it is proposed by the intellect as such. So if it is proposed by the intellect as something evil, the will is moved to this as something evil: not because it is evil in itself but evil under a particular aspect according to that particular apprehension by the mind" (I–II, 19, 5).

For an ethical life, church and Bible exist not to replace freedom and charism but to enhance them. The law of the Spirit, the Pauline letters repeat, is a law of liberty. "When there are rules, they are not removing the liberty of the believing people but are rather impeding the slavery of sin which is repugnant to spiritual freedom" (I–II, 108, 1). A reclusive piety and a self-denying obedience do not guide moral action well (indeed, they often lead to moral violence against others or oneself). Rather, it is an individual's practical judgment which, when endowed by nature and vivified by grace, acts prudently and morally. History bears witness to how many men and women, lacking good judgment, made wrong decisions for their lives or for those of others. Graced prudence assists in a range of activities from embracing marriage and raising a family to choosing the right job or supervising a business. A familiarity with moral issues allowed Aquinas to discuss dozens of concrete issues within his framework of the virtues flowing through prudence.

For each woman and man, deciding how to live and how to act is aided by God's plan and presence. Because human beings do not live only rationally and methodically but exuberantly and spontaneously, Aquinas described beyond virtue a particularly heightened dimension of grace: the gifts and the fruits of the Holy Spirit mentioned by Paul (Galatians 5:22f). "By the theological and moral virtues people are not complete in respect to their destiny; they stand in continuous need of being moved by yet higher promptings of the Holy Spirit" (I–II, 68, 2, 3). These contacts by the Spirit are not transitory "actual graces" but special, divinely infused dispositions silently influencing a person. Virtues and gifts are two different modes of grace prompting someone to follow God's plan: the first is frequent, deliberate, thoughtful; the second is more intuitive, prompt, supra-deliberative. What is most characteristic of the gifts is that they are inspirational and instinctual. The Spirit's gift is spontaneous, liberating, and energetic. It draws grace to ignite an emotional and insightful experience, a mystical glimpse, or a prophetic service in society. There can be other intense, occasional, transitory inspirations of the Spirit in life: these bear St. Paul's term, "charisms." Charisms for Aquinas are powerful but very rarely miraculous. Aquinas predictably observed that perduring grace "is much more excellent" than transitory charisms, no matter how unusual (I–II, 111, 5). This theology of the climax of grace in the Spirit's gifts implies that the highest and most intense form of human knowledge is intuition and that the divine Word and Spirit bring not only teachings and virtues but insight and communion.

Thus far Aquinas' moral theology has not described a deity or an archive of laws but human life: created, called, enhanced. The entire central section of the *ST*, the Second Part, is itself a *summa*, a synthesis of the presence of God in the powers of the human being, a work stimulated by all the sources which Aquinas could bring to bear upon these themes.[57] "We ought to consider human beings more worthy than other creatures and not in any way diminish human dignity either through sin or through an inordinate desire for material things. . . . Rather we ought to prize ourselves in the way that God made us."[58] People live amid two atmospheres, sin and grace. The entire *ST* unfolds Aquinas' axiom, *"gratia perficit naturam,"* "grace brings nature to its full destiny." Cosmos and church, being and life, art and ecstasy do not point to death but to life; the Catholic mind (as the final chapter of this book explores) delights in the ways in which the Incarnation continues. Even life beyond death will not be totally new or extrinsic to us. That life-force which overcame death in the resurrection of Jesus is already present in us through baptism's waters. In this way the *ST* expresses in terms of Jesus' kingdom of God the terse Aristotelian insight that efficient, formal, and final causes are similar in form. If grace is God's presence now, heaven is its future.

Before this theology which is both centered in the Trinity and in the human person false spiritualities wilt. The asceticism which punishes the personality for being itself or which disciplines every personal preference or individual ability is rejected. Thomist theology is alien to the ideology which considers every religious idea to be divine and every event miraculous; and foreign also to a modern theology which delights in a crippled human nature and a weak God. The divine enhances the human, so the glory of a woman's life is to find individuality within the help of grace given to her particular personality (and not the past precise saintliness of Francis of Assisi or of Mary Magdalene). Grace from God is individualized and coherent; it is not a blanket affirmation thrown over Christians or a random force prodding reluctant faithful to do good actions. To be a saint is to be someone in whom individual nature and God's grace have joined successfully.

Next we consider the central Christian mystery: Jesus of Nazareth who, Word Incarnate, is the source, the pattern, and the goal of eschatological life.

VI. God's Word Incarnate in Jesus

This summary has reached the Third Part of the great *summa*. There the Savior, the sacraments, and life beyond death are treated. A theology of Christ, of his continuing incarnation in sacrament, and of the incarnation's fulfillment at the end of our and earth's history enter "to complete this entire theological enterprise" (III, Prologue). Each of these three subsections discloses a facet of God active in human lives: the Savior is the cause of graced human life, the sacraments continue his work, and the future fulfills it.[59] "Our Savior Jesus Christ . . . has shown forth the way to truth for us in himself, the way through which we by rising [from the dead] can reach the happiness of immortal life" (III, Prologue). The "Prologue" to the Third Part also states that Jesus is Savior (his Hebrew name means "one who saves" [III, 37 2, 1]), that is, he acts as the source (empowered by his suffering and resurrection) of eternal life.

When this final part opens, it sets the mission of the Savior within God's effusion of being and grace. Recalling the First Part, the text suggests some similarities between creation and incarnation. In each God takes the initiative; both are in time, both are born of wisdom and love, and both conclude with a gift of a particular mode of being. The Third Part of the *ST* resembles too the Second Part. In the latter, analyses of grace and personality led to the activities of life in the spirit, while in the Third Part the Word's incarnation in Jesus became tangible in the life of the Savior, and both find continuance and fulfillment amid people through sacramental signs and benevolent actions.

The Third Part is about the presence of God's Word on earth. We have already seen that the Son as Word is generated out of the Godhead through the divine intellect, and that the Word is the pattern of all creatures, the exemplar containing all realized and potential ideas (I, 34, 3; I, 93, 8, 4) "The being of things flows out from the Word as from an absolute starting point" (I, 58, 6). The creative Word which is present in the minute, faint mirrorings of creatures is the same Word which becomes flesh in Jesus of Nazareth. The divine Word comes through Jesus as a human being and that special presence of God in a member of the human race extends to all people.[60] We are adopted by the Son to be daughters and sons not just through a message but by a sharing in the divine life (III, 23). The Word as man is the truth of human life in history; he is the model for our journey along the way he has taken; he is the head of the new human race. Way, truth, life, future—these are the gifts Jesus Christ brings to human beings. Jesus the Christ teaches the truth about God's presence, saves people from their sins and gives familiar access to the Trinity (III, 40, 1). Aquinas described Jesus as the way of truth and as the primal cause of grace. Human beings live through what they sense and touch, and the opening of the Third Part gave Paul's theology—we come to the invisible things of God through the visible (Romans 1:2)—a wider application. The great example of the unseen in the seen, of the divine in the human is the incarnate Word of God, Jesus, son of Mary. Aquinas' Christology, following the Aristotelian pattern of nature grounding actions, treats first the subject of the union, the Word in Jesus of Nazareth; then the event of the incarnation leads into the psychology and activities of the prophet who was to be a savior; and third, the events in Jesus' life are presented.

Aquinas' seemingly tardy location of Christ in the *ST*'s Third Part never ceases to raise questions.[61] Should not Jesus appear first in any theology? Is not Christology on a higher level than a Christian psychology of grace? Is he not more important than our lives and stories? Some have implied that Jesus is marginal in this theology which may be only a philosophy adorned by occasional dogmas. Others have countered by stating an exaggerated Christocentrism. Aquinas has retained for his entire work the pattern of process, a process which flows from God and which includes the human being. While Jesus of Nazareth, the incarnate Word of God, is the pattern and the cause (both rooted in his historical existence) of redemption and salvation, nevertheless Aquinas evidently did not want to interrupt the broad movement, true of the past and of the present, reaching from Trinity to each man and woman. He did not want to stop and insert the biblical events of Jesus' past life. Aquinas has retained the protology and eschatology of the Bible in the pattern he selected for theological education: procession and movement to destiny of all things. In the central sections of the *ST* he has pursued, however, not narrative but psychology; now he shows how Jesus Christ, in his life and risen state, is the power and climax of the process.

In fact, the Savior has already entered this theology. Articles on the Word as the plan of creation, the missions of the Trinity, the Hebrew covenant and the gospel law, the predestination of humanity in Christ, and Jesus' preaching as a guide to virtue anticipate what will be a fully developed Christology. The first two parts of the *ST* are incarnational or theandric (the divine acting in the human) not because they are marked by biblical phrases about Jesus in Galilee but because they draw humanity from and to Jesus the Word. These laid the foundation for Jesus' birth at Bethlehem, his ministry, and his death on Calvary. Clearly in the mission of the Logos as Jesus (III, 1) some of Aquinas' grand motifs come together: the generosity of God toward the spheres of being and grace; the love of Wisdom for humanity; the value of the concrete individual; the enactment in the Logos of the higher destiny for men and women (even in the face of sin). Since Word and Spirit on mission offer modes of life, a physical and metaphysical incarnation, a union of human nature and divine being retaining duality and oneness, a union of nature and grace is not surprising. Chenu concluded: "Redemptive Incarnation is the very substance of the Christian economy, and yet the basic source of its meaning is the fact that it is presented as a means. The incarnation is inserted within the ontological framework of grace. But this does not minimize its marvelous unfolding in time."[62] Jesus Christ is not an unusual humano-divine hybrid but the new Adam for a renewed race. He too is a means, a servant of graced history. He restores what was injured in human existence, re-creates the image and likeness of God, and initiates a new human race into future life.[63] His entry here in the Third Part gives an intensification and fulfillment to the previous theology of God and humanity—Jesus leads the virtuous life of grace in exemplary intensity even as his life is mysteriously the cause of the Trinitarian life as it touches others. It is true that the dynamic of grace is not only centered in Jesus but caused by him, but how there is a historical unfolding of grace is a problem which Christianity itself presents, because for it definitive revelation occurs in history. "Thus by understanding this in a general way according to the entire time of the world, Christ is the head of the human race but in different degrees" (III, 8, 3).

Jesus is a complex being: fully human and yet grounded in the organizing point of the divine Son. A member of the human race, he is an independent learner and yet his mind and will are in profound contact with the mind and will of God. Clearly Aquinas begins not with Jesus' actions but with the fact of the incarnation accepted by faith; he looks at its suitability (III, 1), the union of the incarnation (III,

2), the divine person and the human nature (III, 3–6); then he turns to Jesus' grace, knowledge, powers, and humanness (III, 7–15), to aspects of Jesus as a religious individual mediating the human and the divine, and to his relationship to God the Father (III, 16–26). Following upon the theology of Jesus as Word and man are the many questions on the earthly life and destiny of the Savior (III, 27–59). Throughout that Christology, drawing on works of John Damascene and Augustine, upon the gospels according to John or Luke, and on Isaiah, Psalms, and the wisdom literature, Aquinas sketched deftly the forces influential in this mysterious oneness of the Word and Jesus.

It is with transition rather than with revolution that Aquinas introduced the figure of an Incarnate Word to redeem and to deepen human life. "The nature of God is goodness. . . . The nature of goodness is to be communicated. . . . It belongs to the highest being to communicate itself in the highest mode" (III, 1, 1).[64] Becoming-a-human-being is an ultimate expression of love. To be incarnate is to become the other. To exist physically and metaphysically in another is to be the one who is loved. If, as Aquinas concluded from the Scripture, the Logos became a human being so as to enter into our fallen history and save us from its atmosphere of evil and sins, there are other motives at work here too. When Aquinas explained the passage from Ephesians on the depth and breadth of the wisdom and mystery of God in the incarnation of Jesus, he dwelt not on atonement but love: "Whatever there is in the mystery of the redemption and the incarnation of Christ—all of it is the work of love."[65] To recall that God's love for men and women is a friendship (friends like to be with their friends [23, 1, 1]) is to understand incarnation not as a freakish miracle but as the fulfillment of a loving plan for the human race: a familiarity, a shared life. Because it is difficult to believe in the love of God, God proves it by the event of incarnation: "God wished to draw near to us and he did so by taking our flesh" (III, 1, 2, 3).

Aquinas was intrigued by metaphysical and psychological analyses of the God-man. This Christology develops two biblical directions in an original way. On the one hand, the incarnation is an event of the Word, not of the three persons or of the Godhead; on the other hand, this powerful sustenance of Jesus of Nazareth does not remove his human individuality. We see in the gospels how Jesus is free, makes choices, weeps in pain, takes pleasure in the experiences of nature or of wedding feasts. Jesus' teaching, example, and redemption come not from God inside a human body or from a pitiful deity enclosed in the suffering son of the carpenter but from the man whose ultimate ground, his metaphysical person, in being as well as in grace, is the Word of the Trinity: "For nothing can be thought of which is more marvelous than this divine accomplishment: true God, the Son of God becomes true man."[66]

The Greek theologians and early councils (some of whose texts Aquinas had found as he was composing the *ST*[67]) gave to Christian tradition a metaphysical understanding of person for Christology, not a modern psychological one. A person in Greek metaphysics means the point of unity of an individual intelligent being and not, as in modern psychology, a personality type with a set of inclinations. The "hypostasis" or "person" of the Word is the metaphysical organizing point of the man Jesus, and divinity and humanity in Jesus are united in one subject, the one person of the Word (III, 2, 2, 3). Since he has a human nature, and since the ecumenical councils proclaimed him totally human, Jesus has (in the medieval sense) his own array of emotions and his personal and cultural orientations. The one divine person (in the Greek sense) of the Word affirms one subject, one identity, one individual in Jesus, Son of God, but it does not deny the full humanity. There is no absorption of the human into the divine, no tragic dialectic of two beings, each of which is incomplete. There is only one subject for the man and the divine nature. If there are not two persons, there is also not a humanity which is only a bodily shell, and the human nature is not humanity in the abstract but one destined to be an individual human being (III, 4, 4, 3). Nor does Aquinas imply that a human being of male sexuality is the object of the incarnation in the way that soul, body, and intellect are: the Word becomes an individual human being but it is the Trinitarian person who brings individual personhood to the humanity (III, 4, 5).[68] What belongs to the Word of God and what belongs to human nature belong to Jesus Christ; separate natures and powers are united in one subject (III, 2, 3). Thus the incarnation is a dialogue, one of particularly great intensity, between God and a creature. A new earth, a new people, and a new heaven are the gift and goal of the mystery of the man Jesus who is the Word of God (III, 1, 3, 1; 5, 1 & 2).

Two minor topics in the opening questions of this Christology are worth noting briefly. God is not contained, that is, not localized or physically enclosed in the man Jesus (III, 5, 2). Jesus is a mission, an extension of the Word into terrestrial history, but not its tempo-rary enclosure. Second, an incarnation in Jesus of Nazareth does not exhaust the activity of the Logos. The Word or the Spirit draws at any moment upon infinite power within the Godhead and can have countless effects in the universe. The Word could be incarnate in sev-eral intelligent creatures, even at the same time (III, 3, 7).

After considering three topics—the incarnation in the union of God and man, the agency of the Word, and the divine and human natures—this Christology looks at facets of Jesus within salvation his-tory: at his grace, his knowledge, and his power. Within this area Aquinas examined the precise linguistic problems involved in speaking of a human being who is God. Then he turned to the issues of the sev-eral relationships of Jesus' being to the One who sent him, God: prayer, predestination, adoption, and mediation between humanity and divin-ity. Aquinas emphasized the human activity of the incarnate Word by discussing Jesus' feelings, his will-power, his freedom, and his prayer. Jesus' humanity is not absorbed by the Word (III, 7, 11), nor is the man Jesus a totally independent subject operating in tandem with God.

The metaphysical analysis of the Word in the incarnation (twenty-five questions) can deflect the reader from the remaining Christology of Jesus' life and ministry. Aquinas devoted an equal amount of space to Jesus' birth in human history, the progress of his life and ministry, his departure from life through his execution, res-urrection, and exaltation. We learn about someone by what they do. Jesus instructs us by his life and destiny. Medieval people were very interested in questions about Jesus' being (a divine person within a human being). Among medieval theologians, scholars tell us, Thomas stood out for his interest in Jesus' human life.[69] Aquinas asked: Why did the Messiah choose a lowly state of life: being a craftsman and a traveling preacher? He responded that, if Christ had lived in wealth, power, or great dignity, it could be construed that his doctrine and miracles had been accepted by people out of deference or ambition (III, 40, 3). Jesus was not a miraculous display of divinity but the visible witness, the teacher, and the exemplar of the mission of the Word. The daily life of Jesus is the framework for a history to narrate the prophetic life and work of this man who, grounded in the person of the Word of God, is the new head of the redeemed race. The son of Mary is not a demi-God nor a magician. The Logos of the

Trinity is incarnate not in a bodily shell or in a brain but in a real human being whose human nature is permeated but not disturbed by the Word (III, 4, 3). That Jesus learned and learned from experience is affirmed, but what Aquinas does not elaborate—this comes from the constraints of Aristotelian philosophy—is how Jesus developed as a man. How did experience shape him? How did he come to know his identity and his public role? How were his conscious and unconscious knowing touched by Jewish life or by Roman politics?

Aquinas' mind was always searching for proper causes, and, as a result, a causal analysis is prominent in his Christology. According to the Gospels Jesus is the source of grace for us. How do divine and human forces combine to effect salvation for "all people" (III, "Prologue")? In the headship of Jesus Christ, grace, causality, and history meet. Passages from the Gospel according to John, "And from his fullness we have all received, grace upon grace" (1:16), are joined to the Pauline understanding of the head of the church (Colossians 1:18). Jesus' grace flowing from the union of the being of the Word with the individual Jesus of Nazareth culminates in his leadership of the new humanity not only at the level of teacher but at that of inner life. Jesus is the unique but causal intensification of the order called supernatural, and so Aquinas noted what resulted from the Word of grace in Jesus Christ (III, 7, 13, 2). Pesch writes:

> Union is for Thomas the essence of grace, but in the incarnation God's salvation [grace] takes visible form and clear features. Salvation is precisely the form of this "union". . . . Consequently, for Thomas grace is not something abstract but, because it is necessarily incarnational and Trinitarian in its structure, has an essentially personal dimension. It is a grace which experiences concreteness in and through the events of human life, events belonging to being the Son, and thereby because they are accepted as lived in a human way . . . reveal at the same time grace and human being-graced.[70]

Grace meaning God's self-giving to a human being can include incarnation as well as sanctification, but "the reality [of the union of the Word in Jesus] is, of course, far above any participated likeness to it" (III, 2, 10, 1). Jesus has a life of grace (grounded in but independent of the hypostatic union) like all men and women: that grace unfolds in a new head of the predestined and redeemed human race. Christ is "a kind of universal principle in the genus of those graced" (III, 7, 9). In the world of grace a kind of Platonism exists: The Word in the man Jesus contains the fullness of the reality of grace which is offered to others. The books of the Bible, however, modify this by describing God's covenant and presence as moving through history. The incarnation did not happen at the beginning or at the end of human history because God's goodness follows the stages of human history (III, 1, 5).

But can a human being be a cause of the divine? With care Aquinas applied to his incarnational theology the theology of the instrument (the instrumental cause) drawn from John Damascene. This gave to Jesus a proper activity but it did not unrealistically fix properly and permanently in the Nazarene carpenter's brain and hands a divine capability of producing grace or miracles. Jesus was a human instrument of the Word, an instrument of a special kind, existing in a modality suited to an individual with freedom. This theology keeps the Word divine but lets Jesus be an agent. The result is that the events of Jesus' life are sacramental; in this or that biblical event, striking or ordinary, the divine is extended through the man Jesus. There is no miracle which is purely divine, no touching gesture which is only human. The narrative of the ministry of Jesus and its results in people is important, because they are teaching and sacrament. "Every action of Christ is there for our instruction" (III, 40, 1, 3). Jesus' life resembles the overall structure of the *ST*: it has its emergence through the Word from God, its beginning in Jesus' birth, its progress in his growing up and teaching, its exit and fulfillment in the Cross and Resurrection. "We have access to the Father through Christ, because Christ works through the Spirit. . . . And so whatever is done by the Holy Spirit is also done by Christ."[71]

Jesus is not first an expression of my needs, sorrows, or incompleteness, but of God's love, power, and glory in a human life. He is someone whose actions express divine wisdom and generosity, a missionary with a message about past religion and future life, a redeemer to heal failings, wounds, and sorrows. Jesus' preaching is treated only in a few articles examining his audience and style; the content is not mentioned. Why? Because the teaching of Jesus is the "sacred teaching" which is the subject of the entire *ST*, it is found in almost every question. Jesus is often portrayed on the central portals of medieval cathedrals as a teacher holding a book, accompanied by the Apostles who are also teachers of the world. For Aquinas, Jesus is a "master," a "doctor," a universal and convincing university professor of God's plan. "Christ is the most excellent and sublime *magister*, and therefore his students are the most privileged students."[72]

This revered teacher, however, ends up executed as a criminal. God's Word is stifled by trial and crucifixion, and the head of the new race is buried. This torture and death are not a bizarre ritual but should be interpreted within the entire *ST*, within the context of love and incarnation, freedom and violence. Jesus' death is redemptive. The bloody destiny of Jesus was not a matter of direct divine decree (III, 47, 1 & 3), not the inexplicable decision of a twisted or imponderable deity. The divine freedom, so broad in its wisdom, could have enacted other ways of salvation (III, 46, 2). Calvary is not the only possible redemption but the result of the Messiah living courageously amid the violence of earth. The sufferings of Jesus do, however, have a certain suitability, i.e., they correspond to our condition because they emphasize the physical and the spiritual, obedience and love. Nonetheless, God was not directly the cause of Jesus' death: his persecutors were the direct and proper agents (III, 47, 1). When we inquire whether God pre-ordained this violent mode of salvation, we are led to see how some divine actions take into account human freedom. God may permit conditional and optional plans suited to the human situation (III, 47, 3; 46, 2 & 3). A good God would not indifferently hand an innocent human being over to a cruel death. As the months of his public ministry unfold, the Word inspires Jesus to follow his mission and to accept in redemptive love the consequences of that fidelity (III, 47, 4, 1). According to Aquinas, religious and political enemies of Jesus freely pursued their course of violent evil which led to the arrest and execution of the innocent prophet. The Jewish leaders (but not the Jewish people who are ignorant of Jesus' person and innocent of his suffering [III, 47, 5]) bring Jesus to the occupying Roman authorities who are the proximate agents of his death (III, 47, 4). God did not miraculously halt those forces but turned their violence to good. Thereby Jesus' death becomes the causal source of all redemptive grace. Nevertheless, God is not an angry and vindictive tyrant satisfied by bloody disgrace and execution: "The least suffering of Christ would have sufficed to redeem the human race from all of its sins" (III, 46, 5, 3). In the last analysis it is God's countering moves of love which save humanity, for Calvary is an example and climax of divine activity struggling with evil in history. Jesus, alive, dying, and

risen, is the instrumental cause of redemption (III, 48, 6). Jesus' journey is, as Aquinas stated in his plan for the *ST*, the center of the wider
journey, the process of all from and to God. With Calvary God's Word
can be consoling to each human journey and death. "By his blood, he
has opened heaven for us; that is, he has opened it to us by going ahead
as the first, [journeying on] a new way . . . a way which permits us to
enter heaven. It is new because before Christ no one could open it."[73]

Aquinas, drawing on Augustine and pointing to Dante by making
Jesus our way forward, redirected the theology of Christ and
Christians from a static symbolism of order to one of journey.
Christology receives its beginnings at Christmas, its contradictory
efficacy from Good Friday, and its telos from Easter. Clearly this theology of Jesus is not permeated by a tonality of pain but by a theology
of life. "The sufferings of Christ worked to our salvation properly
speaking by removing evils; but the resurrection does so by beginning
and exemplifying good things" (III, 53, 1, 3). God raised Jesus from the
dead, a resurrection coming from the Word united to Jesus. But that
resurrection continues on in human beings. "The resurrection of
Christ acts in virtue of divine power . . . for it is from God that the
soul lives by grace and that the body lives by the soul. As a result the
resurrection of Christ has instrumentally the effective power of res-
urrecting bodies and souls, and it is the exemplar of the resurrection
of our souls" (III, 56, 2). Out of a human life with its coherence and
difficulties, with its joys and sufferings, Jesus preaches, exemplifies,
and incarnates the kingdom of God. Jesus' life, on earth and in the
future, is for all men and women. "Christ and the church can be
taken as one person."[74]

A summary of this Christology might be: in Jesus the wisdom
and love of God are one with the image of God restored and intensified, now and in the future.

VII. The Continuing Incarnation

In a universe of beauty but on a fallen planet, Jesus of Nazareth
became the cause, the sacrament, and the exemplary path of a life
called supernatural. The effects of Jesus' life continue after his departure from earth; he offers the Spirit's life through the biblical writings
and the sacraments, and through the lives of his followers. Chenu
noted:

The Gothic age was involved more and more audaciously in a spirituality of *incarnation* rather than in one of *the sacred* (so characteristic of Carolingian and Romanesque times). There is a progressive affirmation of the human being, and that affirmation of the human affirms the world. From an idealist universe one passes on to a world where the vitality of realistic novels, nature, science, history, and activity find realization in the birth of secular art. The encyclopedia, *Mirror of the World,* composed by Thomas' confrere Vincent of Beauvais, adviser and librarian to Louis IX, gives to this vision in its great panels of nature, thought, tradition, and history a significant expression."[75]

Grace continues on, expanding not as judgment but as sacrament. The *ST* devotes many questions to the sacraments, for they are precise and important modes of that continuing incarnation. "Veneration in religion is given to images not for themselves as things but because they are images leading to God incarnate" (II–II, 81, 3, 3).

The New Testament describes grace not only in people but in movements, not only in the individual but in the church. Before we look at the sacraments, we should inquire into Aquinas' theology of the church. Aquinas did not compose an ecclesiology, that is, a section for the *ST* on church forms. Why? Perhaps because he did not view ecclesiastical structures to be on the same level with Godhead, grace, or incarnation. He understood that faith and theology, life and liturgy are lived within a context which was the church. But the church was secondary, offering the places and instrumental forms for the realization of grace. The church is not on the same level as God or Christ or grace but is the place, the instrumental means, the voices of their special presence.

For Martin Grabmann, the treatise on the law of the gospel gives sources for an ecclesiology, while for Yves Congar the union of grace and humanity suggests the church be viewed as a kind of sacrament, as "the plane of grace and divine-theological life."[76] When Aquinas explicitly treated topics about the church, this occurred in the areas of Christ's leadership, the virtue of faith, or the states within society. Congar wrote: "Because, relative to Christ as its standard, leader and principle, this 'work of grace' merits the name of 'body of Christ,' Thomas conceived the mystical body first simply as a 'society of

saints' without including at this level the note of visibility or of hierarchical structure. Finally, in terms of human beings, one can say
that the church, at the most basic level, encompasses totally the
return to God, *reditus ad Deum*, i.e., the entire Second Part of the
Summa theologiae."[77] Congar saw an ecclesiology in the articles of
the *ST* devoted to Jesus Christ as the head of graced humanity. At the
same time there were sacramental and social dimensions. A people
and a liturgy celebrate the incarnation—and it is also a kind of city or
community with its customs and forms of life: "For St. Thomas the
church is the whole economy of the return towards God . . . in short,
the *II Pars*. . . . Christ bears the economy of the new life, the entirety
of humanity reborn and moving back to God; the church, the same
reality, is a kind of overflow of a fountain or an unfolding and development of what was from the beginning realized in Christ."[78] The
influence of Jesus upon the fallen human race, from birth to resurrection, is the church's service and presence.

Aquinas applied many metaphors to the church—ship, ark, spouse
of Christ—but he offered his own perspective in terms like "people,"
"the congregation of believers," or "the mystical body of Christ."[79]
Both institution and community, the church strives to be the body of
Christ amid human society in history. Christ, church, and liturgy follow a similar pattern—divine grace active in human lives—and thus
the church is the background to sacrament, word, and life.[80] The
church has an inner vitality and a public concreteness: "The beauty of
the church consists chiefly in an inner life, in inner acts [of grace]. But
external activities also belong to this beauty in so far as they proceed
from the interior [reality] and carefully preserve its inner beauty."[81]
Liturgy, particularly the Eucharist, nourishes service and spirituality.
Even while being a visible society with its failings and sins, the church
furthers the power of God's grace for the world.

Not a sacral state nor a community of elite charismatics protect-
ing people from history and society, the church exists to preach the
gospel's view of salvation-history and to further love among human
beings. Love is the source and the soul of the church, and love is the
community's goal. "When someone joins the army of a king, he
wears his insignia; the insignia of Christ are the insignia of love."[82]
As a kind of city or people, it has customs and should display the benefits of living together. In the Aristotelian mode it is a collective person with body and soul. The Holy Spirit giving life to the church is

"the soul" of the Body of Christ,[83] while the virtues, gifts, charisms, and ministries give to grace concrete forms and voices. Because of the presence of God and the dignity of men and women the church cannot be simply a tribe or theocracy but is a community of persons and charisms. Congar summed up: "This church encompasses all those who believe in Christ, whether to come (in the Old Testament) or now come; this is the theme of 'the church from Abel' or the 'universal church.' So the church is seen as the ensemble or supernatural unity of spirits vivified by the grace of Christ, a 'work' or 'effect' of 'grace.' "[84] Touched by the depths of the life of the Trinity, men and women, images of Christ, form a collective Christ, the church.

Although only God is the proper cause of grace and creatures cannot be the controllers (but only the instruments) of grace, the ministers and people of the church are sacramental causes, "The spiritual physician Christ works in two ways: interiorly through himself as he prepares the human will to will good and hate evil; in another way through ministers externally offering sacraments" (III, 68, 4, 2). More perhaps than Aquinas grasped, his theology offers a supernatural dynamism and realism which enhances the church but which also can be critical of institutional forms.

The thirteenth century was molded by the neo-Platonic theology of ecclesial authority, namely, hierarchy. In that society the pattern of descending levels of beings or offices molded mysticism, aesthetics, and politics. Because the sources and antiquity of this theology (Plato, and a Dionysius understood to be both the convert of the Areopagus and the bishop of Paris) were unassailable, hierarchy was a structural model for much of medieval public and ecclesiastical life. Church offices (mirroring those of the angels) were rungs on a ladder of descending illuminations; the lower was perfected and directed by actions moving downwards but not upwards. The levels of the facade of a French cathedral present the thought-form of hierarchy. In layers of statues a vertical line ascends, representing in images an elevation from the material to the spiritual. To the one approaching the entrance of Notre Dame in Paris the lowest level contains sculptured signs of the zodiac, the seasons and their occupations, the moral virtues. Then the eyes are drawn to the figures framing the doors: Christ the teacher and the Apostles who have taught the cities of the world (their characteristic urban outlines hover above them in stone canopies). And then up to the angels, and, as if to leave not only earth but creation itself, the towers and spire soar into the sky. Historicity was not prominent, as knowledge of and belief in the transcendent held sway. So ministerial and magisterial aspects of the church were constrained by a vertical hierarchy.

Aquinas defines hierarchy rather broadly as the leadership of one directing an ordered multitude (I, 108, 2), but he could criticize immorality and rigidity in the political orders.[85] Moreover, there is a place for diverse roles in Aquinas' ecclesiology. The church is not simply a chancery of honors for the powerful. The universal vivifying principle of the one body is not the bishops but the Holy Spirit. Membership in the congregation of the faithful is not differentiated according to ecclesiastical status, but grace comes according to the receptivity and capability of the personality and according to God's plan for that individual. Christ is the head, but according to external roles and inner gifts all can share in the communion of goods of the society given by the Spirit. Congar continues:

> The church is both anthropological or moral, and pneumatological or theocentric. The substance of the church is composed of the new life which people receive by the three virtues of faith, hope, and love. This life is driven Godwards, for it has God for its end and the divine life as its determining principles. The church is the whole economy of the return towards God. . . . Its movement and return find in the Holy Spirit its power and agent, the principle of the divine life which is influencing the dynamic movement towards the objects of the life of God; the soul of the church.[86]

The church is universal in that all people and all peoples may belong to it, universal in the gifts of grace to each man and woman. It is universal in time, because it has in some way existed from the beginning of the human race but not in the same form.[87] Existing within a single, initial predestination to grace, Jesus Christ is one head redeeming the human race for the original plan of life above nature. "There was no period," Aquinas wrote in the *Sentences,* "in which human nature was excluded from the way of salvation, and so there is no time of life in which an individual human being is excluded from the way of salvation."[88] Consequently the mystery of Christ's Incarnation was believed "in all ages and by all peoples in some fashion but in ways differing with the differences of times and peoples" (II–II, 2, 7). Just as the individual response to grace is not a passive state but occurs in actions at points in time, apparently the efficacy of Christ's mysterious headship upon church members would not be inevitably monoform but diverse. John Mahoney thinks that Aquinas was able to view the succession of changing ecclesial customs and forms in a positive light; it was something encouraged and directed by the Spirit. Aquinas did not absolutize practices of the past which were not central to the life of the Spirit and could be burdensome. On the other hand, he could view liturgical innovation as dangerous because it too casually sets aside what the Spirit in the central traditions of the church has prompted.[89]

These pages have just inserted a constellation of theological themes which experts have selected as offering insights for a theology of the Christian community, an ecclesiology which Aquinas did not compose.[90] Our summary now returns to the *ST*: there the theme of incarnation is extending beyond the Risen Christ to the sacraments of the church. Aquinas had prepared for a theology of incarnation and sacramentality by exploring human nature (I, 75), men and women as the images of God (I, 93), and grace in freedom (I–II, 110). The sacraments (and this includes all forms of ritual and liturgy) continue the Christ-event precisely by being material and visible. David Bourke writes: "If there is one key idea which lies at the very roots of St. Thomas' treatise [on the sacraments] as a whole it is the idea that the new life of the redemption wrought by God in the incarnate Word is communicated to man through created media, physical things, or acts combined with words."[91] If the man Jesus renders concrete the missions of the Son and Spirit in history, they continue through all kinds of realities which are not only symbols but channels of divine presence. Countless forms from statues to banners, from water to incense point to an unseen divine presence. What is a sacrament? It is a sign of a sacred reality acting in the mode of a cause (III, 62, 1, 1). The cause, the deepest reality, and the effect of a sacrament is grace.

Christ enters human life in two ways: mentally through faith, bodily through the sacraments (III, 69, 5, 1). In a theology which sees the world sacramentally, liturgy is more than rituals. In liturgy Aquinas insisted upon the incarnational presence of grace within the movement, matter, and symbol of worship. This rejects any reduction of public liturgy to marginal devotions or private prayer, and it expects the liturgy to avoid automatic mechanics. Like grace and nature, inner life and outer forms belong together. Striving to present the divine to the consciousness of believers, liturgical forms are instruments for people's lives even as they are communal celebrations which delight and bind a community together.[92] Aquinas emphasized the visible in church and sacraments, because the spiritual touches us first through our senses. Just as the words of the gospel are witnesses to the historical life of the Word in Jesus, the words of the liturgy explain and point with images and symbols to spirit-in-matter. In human life reason and grace are realms of the real, and so too in sacraments and statues, celebrations and decorations, the real—the reality of grace, the visibility of sacrament, the activity of community—remains paramount (I–II, 108, 4).

We noted earlier that one could characterize Aquinas' theology as a theology of light; it is also a theology of seeing. Creation mirrors the divine, and men and women are the images of God. Jesus is the icon, the exemplary cause, of the new creation—and sacraments are further signs of grace. Words are important but they are invisible. With words God speaks in stories and poetry, but through things the divine touches concreteness. Various kinds of symbolic actions signify grace and make people holy: colors, water, wine, and light (III, 60, 2 & 3). The colors and movements of sacramentality are arts referring to God invisible. Liturgy exists in an aesthetic mode. The historical life of Jesus continues on through his Spirit active in the symbolic rituals of the community.

The Dominicans developed in the thirteenth century their own version of the Western Christian liturgy, their rite. They had a fixed tradition of proper feast days, and of music, processions, and devotions. Although the Friars Preachers had shortened the time spent singing the liturgy, their chanted public prayer—particularly Matins, Eucharist, and Compline—were important sources of intellectual and spiritual reflection. For an international community of priories, the Dominicans after 1254 copied for every priory the texts of their rite which drew on liturgical texts, music and actions from the English Sarum rite, the church in Paris, and the monastic Cistercians. Thomas Aquinas worshipped during his life as a friar in this Dominican rite, and anecdotes relate how moved he was by some of the pieces of music and their texts.[93] His was not a pre-Incarnational God rejoicing in a chilly transcendence and holding out only a spiritual or future religion. Oil, bread, and fire are not simply inspiring occasions of faith but events of grace. "As Christ by his visible appearance in the world has given to the world the life of grace (according to John 1:17, 'Grace and truth has come through Jesus Christ') so, coming sacramentally into a person he brings about the life of grace (as John 6:58 says: 'Who eats me, lives by me')" (III, 79, 1).

Why are there sacraments? Aquinas did not cite biblical prescriptions or legal canons. There are sacraments because men and women are animals and not angels: they need the visible, the tangible. "Through the sacraments, things which strike the senses instruct people, spiritual and corporeal beings, in a way appropriate to their nature" (III, 61, 1). Since knowledge and emotional experience begin in the senses, sacraments are crucial. People do not live by their minds alone; ideas come and go; words are multiplied to infinity. Religion needs action and color; people are drawn to the invisible through the visible, and consequently liturgy is an education. The visible and tangible aspects of the sacrament—the bridal pair at marriage, the water of baptism, the anointing oil for the sick ("the real use of sacramental things" [III, 62, 6, 1])—are of the greatest importance: they both instruct us and bring the power of Christ's life and death to us. Ultimately the reasons for the incarnation are the reasons for sacraments. Through sensed signs and matter interpreted by words, grace born of the Word of God touches the lives of the individual (III, 60, 6).

Why are there several sacraments and countless sacramental rituals? Aquinas said that Jesus was the road by which we reach our destiny, a path into the healing atmospheres of incarnational presence. The sacraments also present a journey. The spiritual life has parallels with our human life: we are born, we act in society and church, we die (III, 73, 1). In his early works Aquinas arranged the sacraments around the forgiveness or avoidance of sins, but in the *ST* the Christian becomes more independent, more a participator in Christ's work. In a framework which recalls contemporary developmental psychology Aquinas gave as the reason for having a number of sacraments the exigencies and stages of a human life: birth, maturity, sustenance, healing, procreation. "The sacraments are set up for certain important effects which are necessary in the Christian life" (III, 62, 2). Aquinas combines life and redemption. "The sacraments of the church are constituted for two purposes: to lead the person to a maturity in those things which pertain to the worship of God according to the religion of the Christian life, and also as a remedy against the defect of sin" (III, 65, 1). The sacraments as a whole are designed to sustain Christ's Incarnation and Resurrection, and sacramental liturgy exists not to fulfill a religious duty but to nourish our lives, to confirm us as images of God and rebuff vice, and to strengthen us as heirs in the reign of God. Liam Walsh writes, "The form of grace in sacraments is, indeed, a humanly-made sign, and their finality is human salvation."[94] Sacraments are encounters between particular human beings and the unseen God.

The *ST* treats all seven traditional sacraments (although not all received the theologian's consideration before his death). We will look only at the Eucharist.

Aquinas began:

> What is most characteristic of friendship is for friends to be together, and because of this [Christ] has promised us his bodily presence as a [future] reward (Matthew 24:28). But meanwhile he has not wanted to leave us fully deprived of his corporeal presence during our journey of pilgrimage. So he joins us to himself in this sacrament through the truth of his body and blood. . . . This sacrament is the sign of the greatest love, a support of our hope because of the friendly presence of Christ with us. (III, 75, 1)

This Eucharistic theology joins the lofty role of the Hebrew covenant and the sacrifice and meal of Christianity with Augustinian, Platonic, and Aristotelian perspectives. Three motifs describe the Eucharist: presence, symbol, and cause of grace. It is not enough for God to act in the sacrament, but, as the New Testament indicates, Jesus must be really present in it as the source of grace. Nevertheless, the presence of Christ is not overly physical. There is one presence which is not divided between bread and wine, body and blood, eschatological spirit and historical body. In a theology of transubstantiation, he employed (but did not originate) that term to explain how the reality of bread is changed into the reality of the body of Jesus Christ. The verb "is" in Jesus' words of institution implies existence, reality, subject. In Aristotelianism those characteristics belong to substance, the independent subject underlying other aspects like color, texture, or location. In that philosophico-theological framework the reality of Jesus Christ (of the Risen Christ) cannot be marginal, that is, accidental.

Consequently the real presence is substantial, is one of a subject of a basic reality. Substance here does not mean the stuff of bread or some crass underlying matter but a specific reality. The Eucharistic subject's external accidents do not belong to the historical Jesus but to bread and wine. Certainly the seeing of the Eucharistic bread and wine is emphasized along with the meal, for in both ways the faithful can meet in a limited way Jesus of Nazareth. The bread and cup surrounded by candles draw the believer ahead toward the future realistic vision of God. Liturgy aims at enhancing the symbolic expression of the human: colors, signs, gestures, and things could point to and admit the divine.

An important (and not widely known) principle of Aquinas serves as a guide to the realism of the sacraments. In the Eucharist Christ is present really: not physically but sacramentally.[95] Christ is present really, but reality has several modes (of which metaphor or pure symbol are not one). Jesus was really and bodily present on earth two millennia ago in a historical mode; the risen Jesus is present now in the Eucharist as sacrament. Historical and sacramental presences are both real. The sacramental presence, however, is real and substantial, but it is not physical. Although faith affirms that the substance of wine is changed into the substance of blood, obviously Jesus' blood is not present in the cup in its biological, physical characteristics. The employment of the Aristotelian dual framework for reality—substance and accident—helps theology explain how a sacramental reality can exist without being a physical reality, but like every philosophy applied to revelation it has limitations.

Aquinas always balanced theological ideas: for instance, he certainly supported the real presence of Christ in the Eucharist, but this presence is accessible to those with faith. The role of the priest consecrating bread and wine is necessary but he celebrates it within the people's liturgy, and as only a modest instrument of divine power. At the moment of communion grace comes through the sacramental blood and body of the risen Christ. David Power summarizes Aquinas' theology of Eucharist in this way:

> He puts his treatment of the Eucharist in context by opening it with a question that places it in the economy of grace and closing it with a question on the rite of celebration. Clearly the action of the Eucharist within the economy of redemption is his concern. At the

same time, his theology is centered around the presence of the living
Christ in the sacrament and looks to the gift that he makes of himself to the faithful in communion. In explaining all of this, within
the orbit of faith, Aquinas draws principally on the philosophy of
Aristotle, and thus on the categories of substance, matter and form,
and efficient causality.[96]

The spiritual and the material: Aquinas would not emphasize one at
the expense of the other. Consequently he has become known as a
source and proponent for a realism in the sacraments.

Finally, this central sacrament transcends time: it commemo-
rates the past, celebrates a historical man present now, and anticipates the future. Like the Eucharist which is the center and climax of
sacraments, every liturgy is oriented toward the future. Eucharistic
consecration and communion touch the three dimensions of time:
they recall in memory the passion, fill now the human spirit with
grace, and anticipate the future to come.[97]

We have seen that Aquinas so prized the activity of creatures that
even in the realm of grace he permitted men and women within life,
church, and liturgy to make grace present.[98] The sacraments are a difficult case of human and divine causality. The ministries of priests
and bishops, parents instructing their children, husbands and wives
living amid the joys and difficulties of married life, bearers of the
Eucharist to the sick and aged—ordinary people could be real causes
of grace. Strictly speaking, of course, only God could cause grace,
could effect the divine life shared with creatures. Moreover, a precise
and formal analysis concludes that strictly speaking there can be no
true created causes ("secondary causes") of grace. A creature (and certainly not a sinner) cannot cause out of its meager powers Trinitarian
life, that is, it could not be a cause of grace (I–II, 112, 1). Nevertheless,
in ways quite circumscribed, God did allow and encourage creatures
to act.

How then do people influence grace? Aquinas avoids three
extremes in sacramental theology: (1) making something or someone
into a enclosure or a controller of grace, (2) reducing the sacramental
to a symbolism of another world, and (3) channeling grace from the
Spirit to my soul apart from matter and sensation. In a sacrament
things represent the transcendent and bring to the senses not only
matter and words but the grace of Jesus Christ (III, 60, 3, 2). Bread,

water, wine do not have natural properties for making citizens of the reign of God, and so sacraments cause grace not as independent sources but as instrumental events or channels. In a creative application of a theology of instrumental cause to sacraments Aquinas avoided turning ritual things and actions into magic (a sacrament is not an independent, automatic source of grace). At the same time, he would have rejected banishing God to a remoteness away from human worship. The moments of liturgy are the historical actions of Christ present today in this world. "The sacraments of the church draw their particular power from the passion of Christ whose power is somehow conjoined to us through receiving them" (III, 62, 5). In the realm of divine presence the role of instrumental causality is real but minimal: its power and fluid form is incomplete and transitory (III, 62, 3). If this theology opposes creatures causing or manipulating the grace of God, it also opposes austere and empty Puritanism. As an instrument, a creature can publicly and visibly serve, point to, and realize the grace of God.

An instrumental cause is first of all an inanimate object, something used for a higher purpose, e.g., a hammer, a saw. The being of a tool contributes little to the principal cause. A pen wrote down in ink the words of Shakespeare, but formally this was a very minor contribution to the composition of *Hamlet* by a human being. Similarly, in the liturgy and ministry of grace the creature can direct, concretize, and symbolize grace but not originate, quantify or control grace. Aquinas intended two things: he wanted to further an incarnational theology by interactions of the human and the divine, and to safeguard the obvious, namely, that human beings do not bring into existence the divine. The instrumental causes of grace are of varying degrees. Instrumental causality has quite a different meaning when the instrument is a human being like a minister of the church. "An inanimate instrument, like a saw, is moved by the artisan through corporeal motion; an instrument animated by a rational soul is moved through its will, as a servant is moved to do something by the command of the master" (III, 18, 1, 2). Here instrumental causality is directed by individual life and free will. Speaking of the gifts of the Holy Spirit, Aquinas observed: "The human being is not that sort of instrument [an instrument which does not act but is only acted upon] but is moved by the Holy Spirit precisely in order to act in so far as it has free will." He explained the modest role, directive rather than causal, of the creature toward grace. "The interior influx of grace is from no one except Christ . . . but the influx into members of the church in terms of exterior direction can come from others. . . . A human being does not give grace interiorly by pouring it forth but externally by persuading for those things which are of grace. . . ." (III, 8, 6; I–II, 68, 3, 2). The concept of instrument undergoes a radical transformation with the introduction of freedom, knowing, and responsibility, but human beings do serve the reign of God.

The sacramental combines the created and the uncreated, the human and the revealed but without confusing either. Sacramentality does not include only the seven sacraments (they are, however, the subsections of the *ST*'s theology of sacrament). Contemporary theologies have developed how degrees of grace and creation can be extended in the model of circles of sacramentality radiating from the center which is Christ. Moreover, the activities of grace in men and women are broader than sacred symbols and words. God does not limit graced contact with the human personality to religious objects: "God has not bound his power to the sacraments so that he cannot confer the effects of the sacrament without the sacrament" (III, 64, 7).[99] As we approach the end of our tour of the *ST*, we see that in this theology of the High Middle Ages three realms—Trinity, people, and sacraments—stand out, while two issues which particularly interest modern people—sin and church—are in the background.

VIII. The End as Beginning

The *ST*'s pattern of exit and fulfillment does not imply a return in the sense of a going backwards. The line from source to telos passes through human history, and salvation-history is eschatological, that is, it is always moving ahead. Just as creation tends ever forward, so Trinitarian life, grace perceived by faith and active in love, is leading billions of men and women into the future. "The time of grace is like the dawn, like the morning in terms of the fullness of love in heaven."[100] The theology of the future is a theology of the present in the future. Aquinas did not attempt to describe a heaven and he takes pains to find the human and religious reality behind the symbols and fantasies of life beyond death. In brief, that absolute future in which God is directly present elevates and empowers the world of earth. Faith becomes vision, matter becomes transfigured, life is not replaced but resurrected, community triumphs over isolation and violence. The future of human history, however, is not an angelic future but a future of the universe and of earth, one which remains material and sacramental.

God is not the goal of the human being because divinity has dictated this as a pious imperative. Rather, the Trinity's missions in human salvation-history are themselves processes moving forward, forward to the fulfillment of their divine presence. The opening lines of the *ST* proclaimed its theme to be God as source and as goal: as *"principium"* and *"finis"* of a special human life. The wide range of the theology of Aquinas has led us to contemplate again and again how God is the source and destiny of the universe, of its being and of its participation in divine life in a future free of ignorance and violence. "God is the end of faith from the point of view that he is the unique good who by his eminence transcends the capacities of human beings. His generosity leads to a sharing of the goodness which is his own."[101] The universe evolves toward its goals and gives glory to God not through a fixed permanence but in movements and individuals, in these birds in this September or in that planet sparkling in the December sky, in that physician or monk, not yet born, whose life will inspire thousands.

Heaven cannot be a localized paradise nor an earthly anesthetic. Heaven is the fulfillment of the Spirit's life in men and women. Only Love and Wisdom intent on diffusing their gifts could have created our spirits so restless for happiness, so capable of living greater and greater interests and ecstasies. "The object of the will . . . is the Good without reserve, just as the object of the mind is the True without reserve. Clearly then, nothing can satisfy our will except that kind of good which is found not in anything created—every created good is a derivative good—but in God alone" (I–II, 2, 8). How often we think of God, Jesus, everything religious, as existing in a distant past, but in the *ST* grace is always teleological. In a way, each human being is already living in an inner time and in an inner place where origin and destiny meet; this is confirmed by the human imagination thinking of timeless times and longing for perfect states. These longings are the place to which the Trinity's missions come offering a different, eternal life.

The future will transform earth, and the resurrection of all will arrive in the train of the coming of Jesus Christ. For Aquinas, this future will not be bizarre nor a celestial amusement park of entertainment and pleasure. It will be the dramatic unfolding of each individual's graced life. Each personality has its own sanctity, and in the force-field of the future holiness and identity will only deepen. For the believer the sacrament of baptism has already been a resurrection into supernatural life. In a liturgical text he composed for the feast of *Corpus Christi,* Aquinas called grace "the seed of future glory." Dante's *Paradiso* vividly depicts grace as the light of heaven. In the ascending circles of paradise grace becomes the power to see more and more, and eventually to see God. The next life will not be an eternity of distractions but an unimaginable communion with Wisdom and Love, a life which never tires or bores. God not only gives happiness but is the reward: the Trinity is "the light of glory." No more challenging (or sublime) passage from Aquinas can be found than the one stating his conviction that "God's love for us is no greater in heaven than it is here and now."[102] Grace's destiny is always silently inviting and blessing human life.

In this theology of the future there is fulfillment but not replacement or rejection. One and the same supernatural power dwells in people on earth and flourishes in the billions in the eschaton. Sanctity is identity; beatitude will be fulfillment; the future is in the present. "The light of glory [in heaven] is the same as grace in its consummate stage; [it is] the same grace energizing us in the acts of our life."[103] We do not become someone utterly new, someone dramatically different from who we were in adult life on earth.

Life after death is the life not of a soul but of a human being, animal and spiritual. The future resurrection of a woman or a man is caused by and modeled after the rising of Jesus of Nazareth. The Risen Christ is the proximate, efficacious source of victory over death. "The resurrection of Christ is the exemplar of our resurrection . . . and the efficacy of the resurrection of Christ extends to the resurrection of both the good and the bad" (III, 56, 1, 3). Resurrection is the true beginning of life after death, for it restores and recreates in a new way what is a human being (people are not ethereal souls). "Resurrection cannot be the principle of nature although resurrection finds its goal in the life of nature" (*ST* III [Supplement], 75, 3). Passing beyond the mysterious wall of death, faith and hope become vision. Heaven's vision of God brings gifts which enable human beings to transcend the limitations of matter, and to fulfill on a higher plane individual personality. Love heightens as it expands toward vast communities of men and women. What was a sluggish and meager interest in God and religion on earth becomes a high level of wisdom. We see and learn endlessly, as the divine vision eternally inspires and amazes.

Whether one has elected heaven or hell, the eschaton is the flourishing of what has emerged, continued, and has been sustained in a person's life. The free and deliberate choice of self alone over all of the universe is a choice for what is not divine and not human. To be damned is for the will to be fixed in things, to be isolated with them alone. In this self-damnation the pains of hell are, above all, pains of loss. Fire is a symbol for absence, loneliness, and self-hatred. The absence of divine life brings the deepest pain, pain over all that has been relentlessly and freely destroyed. Memory is torture, for love and grace had been violently driven away in time.

At the end of time the same themes and chords sound as they did at the beginning of the *ST*: the divine activity overflowing with being and goodness and beauty, the divine image in men and women, activity and individuality, incarnational union. Free of competition and hostility, love introduces men and women to a vast realm where many kinds of beings live eternally. In a sermon for All Saints Thomas Aquinas depicted for his hearers how salvation fulfilled is social. The eschaton is a society reaching through many times and worlds. "One society of God and angels, a society in which all communicate in one destiny, namely beatitude . . . a society which belongs to God by essence and to angels and humans by participation. . . . Among all those who live in one society through one destiny there must be such a sharing of activity that those who have not yet reached the goal are helped toward it. . . . And so we celebrate the feasts of the saints who have reached beatitude so we might be helped by their prayer, encouraged by their example, and energized by their rewards."[104]

The missions of God's love continue, continue in the being of galaxies whose age is enormous and in grace offered to men and women entering adult life.

4. Traditions, Schools, and Students

— ✝ —

Time is, so to say, a discoverer and a kind of co-operator.
Commentary on the Ethics *of Aristotle*

History, far from banishing Thomas Aquinas to the reference rooms of libraries, presents him as one of the most important thinkers of faith and philosophy. His serene power has long influenced Western Christianity; it has reached modestly even to the Eastern churches and occasionally to Protestant Christianity. At first glance the theology of Aquinas appears simple, clear, dry. But time has disclosed its potential for stimulating further theologies and its capability of addressing issues which were never expected by its author. Individuals, universities, and religious orders have expanded his understanding of Christianity in a long history of interpretations. The history of Thomas Aquinas' theology in various metamorphoses is called "Thomism." This chapter sketches the interpretations of Aquinas in the centuries after his death.

Such a historical survey is not unlike seeing paintings of Thomas Aquinas executed in different cultural eras. In Francesco Traini's *Triumph of Saint Thomas*, painted in Pisa around 1350, we see a professor who has become a heavenly icon. A century later Fra Angelico in his frescoes for San Marco in Florence painted in the pure, intelligent expression of Thomas' face an approachable teacher whose inner light complements the book he holds, both being signs of holiness, energy, and wisdom. There are dramatic soaring representations from the Baroque era, while in the nineteenth century, corresponding to the flat style of that neo-Thomism, there is Ludwig Seitz' *Saint Thomas Offering His Writings to the Church* in the Vatican. On that canvas Thomas, in an allegorical setting surrounded by mother church, angels, and Aristotle, appears as a static figure whose facial expression is otherworldly. In each painting there is a man clothed in the white and black Dominican habit holding a book, but the artists have painted their own varied imaginations of that individual. Through different styles they have presented Aquinas as a symbol of different times.[1]

Like the paintings of him, the interpretations of his theology have an identity and a variety. In the history of Thomism people have selected this or that facet and drawn his theology into a framework which spoke to 1530 or to 1880. But none of those later ages is quite the same as the world of 1270. This does not mean the history of Thomism is a series of unrelated systems which are distortions. Rather, his theology retains its characteristics and its depth even as it encounters and responds to new questions and cultural paradigms. A history of Aquinas' philosophy and theology is a history of interpretation corresponding to epochs and cultures. Because it gives to many people in different time periods an important presentation of Christianity, it is part of Christian history, and it is also part of the intellectual history of humanity.

Interpretations can explain and enhance, or they can dilute and render distant. A copy of the *ST* may lie open, the paragraphs of an important article may be read, and yet the reader may lack access to the text's meaning. After all, these pages of theology were written down long ago, and since then there have been centuries of change. Then, too, research can bury genius, and sterile clichés might hide patterns and themes intended to assist in viewing the world and Christian revelation. Such a long history of influence, however, beginning centuries before Martin Luther or Thomas Jefferson, does argue that still today he has insights for life and faith.

I. A Perduring Influence

Thomas Aquinas has influenced an extraordinary number of men and women. Over seven centuries thousands of teachers and writers from Moravia to the Philippines, from Peru to Armenia have studied his writings. To think only of Dominicans, there was Diego de Deza who advised Christopher Columbus to explore what lay to the west of Portugal, or Anton de Montesinos and Bartolomé de Las Casas who early on defended the native Americans against the Spanish conquerors. His theology inspired women like Catherine of Siena who was a spiritual mentor for reform movements in the church. It inspired a painter like Fra Angelico, but it also suggested an executionary clarity to the Grand Inquisitor, Tomas de Torquemada. Bishops have condemned him and popes have praised him. Some readers of Aquinas like the Carmelites at Salamanca wrote multi-volume interpretations of his thought, and some like Ignatius Loyola developed a succinct, personal approach to imitating the life of Jesus. In this century he influenced men like M. J. Lagrange who furthered modern biblical studies by establishing a school in the land of the Bible, and Yves Congar who pioneered a Roman Catholic acceptance of ecumenism. Novelists as different as Sigrid Undset and Flannery O'Connor turned to the pages of Aquinas. Apparently, his thought is quite capable of surviving time and it can undergo metamorphoses as its deepest insights become new theologies.

Aquinas' progeny mediate him to us today. The different neo-Thomisms were not always exactly the same as Aquinas' own ideas written down in the thirteenth century. Many of his disciples transmitted his thought well, but in so doing they inevitably interpreted and expanded it. In the last analysis, to understand Aquinas with some maturity and accuracy, one should learn about Thomists and Thomisms past and present.

For over six hundred years this philosophy and theology brought forth schools of disciples in many countries. A "theological school" is a social grouping within a Christian church. These have developed a common theology or spirituality usually within universities, regions, or religious orders. They fashion particular ways of perceiving and applying their distinctive view of Christianity. When they live on, it is because they have fashioned a personalized theology capable of attracting people, a theology which escapes the debilitating touch of passing time, that touch which in its wake leaves most religious organizations moribund. There is, of course, no one or basic tradition in Christianity or in Western Catholicism: there are many traditions. Thomism or Scotism is not a text or an argument but an interpretation of faith, an interpretation verified and sustained against time by a group who have found this particular approach useful and illuminating. When a consistent approach to theology or spirituality moves from individuals to communities, a school emerges. The genius of a spiritual leader (Bernard of Clairvaux) or the needs of a ministry (Alphonsus Liguori) can summon from the gospel a new perspective. Mentioning Aristotelianism and Albertinism, Scotism and

Suarezianism, the Baroque École Francaise and the Tübingen school, Karl Rahner described theological schools as "structures which within the church and its creeds form a more or less deep and unified perspective on theology or spirituality. . . . The church has (one could say with some shock, in a generous and naive way) recognized, indulged, and protected the simultaneous existence (even in points where they were mutually contradictory) of diverse moral theologies."[2] These schools have their births and their demises. They may reach the point where they no longer understand their own origin or they may end in petty disputes; only a few last several centuries. The broader the original perspective the longer the school lasts. There are Thomistic schools of interpretation which are twice as old as the constitution of the United States.

There has never been one Thomism.[3] When someone speaks of "Thomism," those who know Aquinas (and who themselves belong to a particular school) become uneasy. Which school is meant— Carmelite, Dominican, Suarezian, Salamancan? Which Thomism— of Cardinal Cajetan or Bernard Lonergan? Gerald McCool writes: "Representatives of a philosophical or theological tradition differ from one another both in their interpretation of their founder's thought and in their systematic development of his heritage. Each of them, it is true, endeavors to 'recover' the 'perennially living essence' of their founder's thought. But to determine what precisely that 'living' essence might be is a task which calls for hermeneutic ability, historical knowledge, and sound speculative judgment."[4] The history of interpretations from the many Thomist schools ranges from careful late medieval commentators to recent innovators developing a dialogue between Aquinas and Kant. Through guides or through one's own personal research it is valuable to know the contours of the Thomist tradition of traditions.

Aquinas' theology is too rich in ideas, too rooted in cultures and sources to be abbreviated in a catechism or a handbook. His writings are not difficult to understand, and yet they have a depth which is more than the history of interpretations; they can still inspire new approaches. About Aquinas, Josef Pieper wrote once: "He undertook the enormous task of 'choosing everything'."[5] There is no one way to understand Aquinas: a number of readings are legitimate, for the emphasis of each—historical, transcendental, sacramental, metaphysical—is, while seeking to understand what Aquinas had in mind as he wrote down his ideas, only drawing out some facet of a theology which has a number of modalities mirroring or discovering some aspect of human life.

Aquinas' theology has been called "perennial." Such an exaggeration led a few to identify their Thomism with revelation, dogma, or with the teaching office of the church. This encomium, hastily imposed by anxious theologians and church authorities, presumed that time and culture had little impact on human consciousness, and implied that one philosophical theology could serve all people. By claiming too much it rendered Thomism bland or arrogant.

Aquinas' theology is only one Christian theology and Christianity flourished in many cultures before the thirteenth century. Thomism is itself diverse, and no one approach to his thought should claim a monopoly of understanding. Some approaches can be arid, or even hostile to his deepest sympathies. An isolated individual who claims innovation and dominance in his or her interpretation is, because of the absence of a complementary school or tradition, often idiosyncratic. Valuable interpretations build upon the past, but they are neither sensational nor the final stages of the founder's ideas. Thomas himself wrote of how all thinkers and students through time helped each other in the work of understanding, and of the benefits of each age collectively nourished by the discoveries of all who have gone before. The history we are sketching is a gallery of traditions inspired by a genial synthesis.

"Thomism" is a history of the influence of the religious worldview of a theologian unfolding in a family of traditions committed in different ways to the principles and insights of Thomas Aquinas' thought. The history of Thomism up to the present has had four periods: the age of defenses (the 1200s to 1400s); the age of commentaries (the mid-1400s to the early 1600s); the age of controversies, encyclopedias, and compendia (the mid-1500s to the early 1700s); the recent neo-Thomist revival (1840 to 1960).[6] Sometimes scholars speak of three Thomisms. The first, from the thirteenth to the fifteenth centuries, is a period of works defending Aquinas' ideas before other medieval philosophical and theological schools. The second, reaching from the sixteenth to the eighteenth centuries, is a time of commentaries and of encyclopedic compilations, and of expositions on controversial topics current at that time. A "third Thomism" is that revival begun in the 1840s and lasting to the 1960s (in the twentieth century the variety of interpreters and disciples of Aquinas has been remarkable). To observe this long and rich river of viewpoints is to perceive Aquinas' contribution and destiny.

II. First Medieval Attention

Dead at forty-nine or fifty in 1274, Aquinas left few mature, devoted disciples. Moreover, his thought immediately faced ecclesiastical censorship. As has been the case with other great theologians, Aquinas' ideas frightened authorities during and immediately after his lifetime. Albert the Great learned in 1276 that certain bishops were lumping together all who used Aristotle in theology and calling them "Averroists," implying by this that they were more Muslim than Christian.[7] Pope John XXI ordered Bishop Tempier of Paris to investigate the Aristotelianism of theologians, and on March 7, 1277 (curiously, the third anniversary of Aquinas' death) he proscribed over 200 propositions and excommunicated all who taught them. It was clear that some of the propositions were found in Aquinas' writings. Shortly after this ecclesiastical censure, across the channel in England the Archbishop of Canterbury, a Dominican, also condemned Aristotelian-Thomist ideas.[8]

Although the Dominican Order contained within itself a number of distinct directions in theology, philosophy, and spirituality, it increasingly defended and promulgated Aquinas from 1278 up through his canonization in 1323. The triumphal course of his thought began within the Order to which as a young man he had given his talents. Meetings of delegates from the Dominican Order's provinces ("general chapters") in Milan (1278), Saragossa (1309), and London (1314) made special recommendation of his teaching. By the 1280s there were disciples at Oxford and Paris who were not Dominicans, and Aquinas' thought had found followers among other religious orders like the Carmelites. In 1288 a Dominican wrote a summary of the Second Part, and by 1323 there was an abbreviated explanation of the entire *ST*.[9] From Paris in 1306 to London in 1314, the chapters of the Dominicans recommended and then imposed this teaching. The teacher, named "universal" in 1317 and "angelic" in 1450, was proclaimed by Pius V in 1567 "doctor" of the church, and in 1880 Leo XIII made him patron of all Catholic schools. Nevertheless, Aquinas' theology was not the only theology of the medieval schools. The Franciscan school flourished and Augustinianism continued within the theological pluralism of the Middle Ages.

Already before 1300, however, some university professors were skeptical of Aquinas' grand synthesis of creation and grace. They doubted that the being and activity of the universe mirrored slightly the divine being, and they had come to wonder if God was not so far above our powers of knowing as to be unattainable by reason or analogous logic. Some medieval theologians after Aquinas stressed God's will and omnipotence rather than his intellect and his incarnational project. In the fourteenth and fifteenth centuries, new directions in philosophy and theology made the choices of the divine will more important and decisive than God's intelligent plans grounding the rules and structures of being. The nature of the universe or of our happiness might be at odds with the transcendent divinity. These opposing philosophical theologies of the fourteenth century led to the late-medieval theologies of Scotism and Ockhamism. The age of synthesis visible in the cathedrals faded amid new intellectual currents among which Aquinas' Aristotelianism, a harmonious view of reality and grace, was but one.

III. Disciples of Aquinas in the Fourteenth and Fifteenth Centuries

In the fourteenth century manuscript copies of the *ST* multiplied, and there were translations into medieval German, Greek, and Armenian. Not only Dominicans wrote on Aquinas but so did other teachers and scholars like the diocesan priest and professor, Heinrich of Gorkum (c. 1386–1431) who composed Thomistic treatises on predestination and the just war and who wrote an introduction to the different sections of the great *summa* as well as a "compendium" drawing together key facets of the *ST.* Although the *Sentences* of Peter Lombard remained (along with the Bible) the normal text for the universities, the Dominican Order's leadership between 1286 and 1405 repeatedly insisted on Aquinas' writings as central texts for their schools. From Hungary with Peter Niger (†1451) to Spain with Diego de Deza (†1523), the advocate of Columbus, there were friars' expositions of Aquinas' thought. By the time of John Capreolus (†1444) a modest Dominican school was taking shape. Capreolus wrote the *"Princips Thomistarum,"* a long defense of Aquinas' theology, but that exposition was presented in a commentary on Lombard's *Sentences* using ideas from Aquinas' commentary on the same work and the *ST.* It set forth the differences between Aquinas and Scotus or Ockham, or their voluntarist disciples like Gregory of Rimini and Pierre d'Ailly.[10]

One creative figure of the early fifteenth century was Antoninus of Florence (†1459) whose *Summa theologiae moralis* treated new moral issues in an original format. Renaissance Florence at the time of the Medicis, where Antoninus was archbishop, brings to mind two other followers of Aquinas with different talents. There was Fra Angelico whose paintings depicted in vivid red and gold a harmony of grace and personality in the men and women enacting the stories of the Bible and church history. But there was also Jerome Savonarola. His apocalyptic and reformist preaching aimed at establishing under some form of religious leadership a republican government for the Florentines. Soon aristocracy, people, and papacy turned against him, and his calls for reform, sermons mixing politics and religion in dangerous prophecies presented in the language of cataclysm, ended in his being burned at the stake. His apologetic and theoretical works had found a resource in Aquinas' *Summa contra gentiles.*[11]

The history of the emergence of Thomism was not a mounting triumph of Thomas Aquinas. Religious orders and universities frequently turned to the new, and eventually the new was not Aquinas but criticism bordering on skepticism, diversity leading to fragmentation, words preferred to realities, and will over intellect. Many Thomists in Italy did not further the Renaissance, whose positive view of the human being's culture and intellect would have been congenial to Thomas. Increasingly Thomism fled the challenge of the new. North of the Alps, in the decades just before the Protestant Reformation, Thomism lacked vitality and originality. At the time of the Reformation, the Dominican school and Thomism in general were named by some the *via antiqua,* "the old way," over against the modern approach of the followers of William of Ockham whose theological and philosophical "modern way" questioned the harmony between faith and reason, and the links between the universe of being and Trinitarian grace. Rome neglected the legitimate concerns of Martin Luther in the second decade of the sixteenth century because it mistook them for annoying struggles between an Augustinian modern thinking and a Dominican retrospective Thomism, both

wrestling over Latin terms and Aristotelian definitions. In the sixteenth century, incapable of facing, much less of integrating the
epochal shifts of Renaissance humanism and Reformation upheaval,
it took up a defensive position.

Analyzing old and past issues, many followers of Aquinas in
the sixteenth century hid from the momentous changes latent in
Luther's word and Leonardo's paintings. Nevertheless, two Dominicans, Tomasso Campanella (1568–1639) and Giordano Bruno
(1548–1600), did create theories for a post-medieval world in politics
and cosmology. But their originality followed paths other than
Thomism, and hostility towards ideas not clearly Aristotelian led to
reactions against these innovators: imprisonment for Campanella
and execution for Bruno. Their destinies symbolize in a way the
choice made by Roman authorities, and by many philosophers and
theologians, not to pursue new intellectual directions in the sixteenth century but to restore the medieval and the scholastic: that is,
to bring forth a "neo-scholasticism."

In every vital period a school and a tradition must address new
ways of thinking; only thereby can it keep alive its traditions. The
thought of Thomas Aquinas is a concrete example of a theology
meeting the challenge to exist between ossification and dissolution.
In 1567 the Dominican reforming pope, Pius V, after proclaiming
Aquinas doctor of the church, further improved editions of his writings. But those papal gestures were intended to fix the conclusions of
texts rather than to open his principles up to new applications.

IV. The "Second Thomism" of the Counter-Reformation
and the Baroque

If the sixteenth century showed the limits of Thomist schools, it
also brought, particularly within Italy and Spain, a reawakened interest in Aquinas. Thomist theologians turned to new issues. The *ST*
was taught more and more in schools, and explanatory commentaries
on it (and on the *Summa contra gentiles*) were written. The tradition
of writing commentaries on the *ST* began with Johannes Tinctoris
around the middle of the fifteenth century in Cologne,[12] and in the
next hundred years large works on Thomism were composed in the
university centers of Europe. Eventually in Louvain a seven-year
course conducted by two professors was dedicated to the *ST* alone.

Some remarkable figures emerged from the Italian and Spanish Dominicans at this time (with the Americas discovered and the Reformation about to explode). An important theologian in Italy was Thomas de Vio who began his career by lecturing on Aquinas at Pavia at the end of the fifteenth century. He wrote between 1507 and 1520 what remains the outstanding commentary on the *ST.* As a young Dominican superior general de Vio delivered in 1512 a fiery address at the ecumenical council Lateran IV on the need for extensive church reform. Named cardinal in 1517, he was sent by Pope Leo X to a first meeting with Luther at Augsburg in the next year. Luther's ideas so impressed him that afterwards the Dominican set aside the writing of scholastic commentaries for smaller studies on the Bible and on understanding but refuting the views of the Protestant Reformers. At the same time Francisco de Sylvestris (†1528) assembled Aquinas' theology in a commentary arranged around the chapters of the *Summa contra gentiles.*

In Salamanca, Spain, a particularly prominent neo-Thomist tradition was developed after 1500 by professors who employed the new approach of lecturing directly on the *ST.* Francisco Vitoria (†1546), the founder of international law, was succeeded by Domingo de Soto (†1560), Domingo Bañez (†1604), theological adviser to Teresa of Avila, and Melchior Cano (†1604). Vitoria and his successors defended the indigenous Americans by calling on principles of Aquinas' theology: the goodness of creation, the human being created in God's image, the existence of implicit faith, a denial of categorical predestination to hell, the rejection of non-belief as a sin, the inseparability of human rights from human nature. They fought vigorously against the imperialism of state and commerce who excused their conquests with a theology holding that the Indians were non-human sinners and incapable of faith.[13] Cano served as the bridge between Thomism and Baroque-modern theological methods emphasizing sources. At this time, new issues were explored like the intricacy of certain moral issues, grace and free will, international law and natural rights, and the structure of the state.

In the sixteenth and seventeenth centuries, Italy, France, and Spain saw the emergence of countless movements in spirituality and ministry. Cloistered nuns and laymen, artists and bishops were drawn into the ideas and methods of Philip Neri, Ignatius Loyola, Teresa of Avila, or Pierre de Bérulle. Some of these mystics had been instructed in Thomism. For instance, Teresa of Avila, through her spiritual director Bañez, absorbed Thomist views on personality and grace. This vigorous "Second Thomism" emerged out of the scholasticisms developed in universities, but it also had ties to the schools and spiritualities of new and old religious orders.

Pausing for a moment, one can visualize this "second Thomism" by seeing how in Renaissance culture its spirit hovers around Raphael's paintings for papal offices done from 1508 to 1511. In a large room two wall frescos, the *School of Athens* and the *Disputa*, face each other. One shows Plato and Aristotle entering through classic and renaissance arches into an assembly where the great thinkers, artists, and scientists of Greece meet and converse. On the opposite wall, theological geniuses of history discuss the principle of incarnation, the dynamic meeting of God and man in Jesus Christ and then in the sacrament of his body and blood. In both frescos and in the ensemble of the two, the harmonizing synthesis of nature and grace, of Greek culture and Christian religion is unmistakable. The large frescos illustrate a milieu where some influence of Aquinas' wisdom of graced life continues, a theology heightened by the humanism of the late fifteenth century.

The church reacted to the Reformation by encouraging the scholastic propositions and definitions taught by the different religious orders. The Council of Trent (1545–1563) expressed its reforms through scholastic conclusions somewhat influenced by Aquinas. With Franciscans, Jesuits, Dominicans, and Carmelites in attendance, however, Trent's documents refrained from choosing one medieval scholasticism over the others. It did, however, insist on responding to the Protestants in a language their movements had already rejected, Latin scholasticism. In the period before and after Trent there were neo-scholastic schools apart from Thomism with their own interpretations of medieval masters like Bonaventure and Scotus, and the contributions of Franciscan and Augustinian medieval and late medieval schools should not be forgotten.

Differences among Thomistic schools became more marked with the emergence of the Society of Jesus in 1540. Ignatius Loyola intended Aquinas to play a central role in the education of his innovative order, and the early Jesuits were drawn into the circle of Thomist theology. John W. O'Malley narrates:

In time, nonetheless, the Jesuits definitively settled on Thomas Aquinas as their preferred author "for scholastic doctrine," a decision Ignatius enshrined in the *Constitutions*. . . . Several extrinsic factors had to incline them toward Aquinas. At the beginning of the sixteenth century, the Dominicans in Paris had displaced Thomas's early commentary on the Sentences of Peter Lombard with the *Summa theologiae,* the work of his maturity, as the subject of their lectures. . . . Its relative novelty probably attracted the attention of the companions during their stay in Paris and drew them to the lectures at the Dominican convent of Saint Jacques.[14]

Many of the leading Jesuits of the first generations of the Society like Francisco Toledo, Gregory of Valencia, and Francisco Suarez studied theology at Salamanca under Vitoria and Cano. More systematic and deductive than the philosophical theologies of the thirteenth century, scholasticism in the Jesuit tradition tended to be rather eclectic: it drew from Scotus and other medieval authorities as well as from Aquinas. Uninterested in efforts to repristinate the past, the Jesuits expected theology to address the issues of the times. In Spain where a Thomistic renaissance was accompanying the affluence of empire and a revival of asceticism and mysticism, the book of the Jesuit Luis de Molina, *Concordia liberi arbitrii cum gratiae donis,* appearing in 1588, sought to resolve the intricate problem of reconciling human free will with God's grace. It introduced creative theories emphasizing the role of freedom by affirming that God meets the future events of free men and women through "a middle knowledge" which does not determine what will happen. God surveys all possible events flowing from every choice which could be made by every individual. But God's graces are rendered efficacious partly by the consent of the human will. Suited to serve a spirituality for men and women working for God's realm, this theology fit the ministerial style and spirituality of the Jesuits. But Bañez at Salamanca found Molina's theory to be contrary to Aquinas. The controversy between the Jesuits and the Dominicans became international and heated. For almost twenty years prior to 1607 reports were sent to Roman commissions until Pope Paul V permitted each side to teach its theology. The Jesuit tradition reached a high point in Francisco Suarez (1548 to 1617) whose views on divine activity, metaphysics, and theology gave a certain emphasis to the self and to God in a stance more modern and less scholastic than that of the Dominicans. These two schools of theology within Roman Catholicism, Dominicans and Jesuits, disagreed with some acrimony from 1600 to Vatican II, and that history indicates the intra-Catholic pluralism of the theologies of religious orders and a difference of viewpoints over the authority and content of Aquinas.

Thus, in response to the Reformation, Catholicism expanding through the world underwent a period of renewal. If this vitalization was initiated by the Counter-Reformation, its deepest sources came from new movements and presentations of the spiritual life.

In the sixteenth and seventeenth centuries, however, Thomism played an increasingly small role in the emergence of the spiritualities of the new religious orders, in the establishment of schools and foreign missions or in the spread of Baroque art and architecture. Curiously, the decline in neo-scholasticism and consequently in neo-Thomism in the seventeenth and eighteenth centuries was furthered by the shift in theology from dogmatic themes to morality and spirituality. After 1600 Baroque Catholicism had its own perspective. There was an awareness of a vast world (Galileo and Newton but not Aristotle), and Christianity was centered anew on the humanity of Jesus Christ rather than on God's sovereign grace. Imagination and emotion, dedication and ministry—these dominated the seventeenth century, and the importance of speculative systems of theology faded.

Thomism was still sustained by the seminaries of some religious orders, and those orders brought it to the new universities they founded around the world from Lima to Manila. The forms of this neo-scholasticism mirrored the Baroque interest in detailed analyses of theological issues like degrees of freedom or faith. Baroque theological texts tended to be either all-encompassing compendia or minute analyses of ethical problems. A proliferation of topics and debates was arranged into textbooks and summaries, while the interest in *summa* and system faded. Those summaries and commentaries, however, often diluted the thought of Aquinas. The Thomistic schools, carried along by the currents of different countries, universities, or religious orders, increasingly disagreed over the issues which seemed of paramount importance to them. They developed different solutions to the relationship of actual grace to the life of virtue, and they opted for different methodologies in moral theology and different conclusions about how individual conscience discerns the morally good.

With an author of multi-volume systems like John of St. Thomas (Jean Poinset) (†1644), we have a prominent example of Baroque neo-Thomism. Educated at Louvain and professor in Alcala, he composed along with other works two multi-volume expositions in a style austere and clear: the *Cursus philosophicus Thomisticus* was printed over a dozen times after its publication in 1631, and the *Cursus theologicus* published from 1637 to 1643 was equally popular. That latter theology follows the order of the *ST* but does not treat every article as it pursues its goal of expounding, defending, and vindicating Aquinas.[15] The *Cursus* serves to order and incorporate large amounts of material from Aquinas' writings in dialogue with issues of the age raised, for instance, by Jansenism and new schools of the mystical life. Drawing on Cajetan and on the Salamancan school, the *Cursus theologicus* devotes particular space and energy to issues like divine and human liberty or the gifts of the Holy Spirit where John shows some originality. For some historians of Thomism, John of St. Thomas marks the climax of Baroque Thomism. Those several thousand pages of speculative Thomism lead on to the French writers of the great age of spirituality and ministry in the seventeenth century, and to a new genre of spiritual theology which will replace systematic Thomism for some time.[16] As a bridge from scholasticism to spirituality, one can single out, among the Dominicans, Vincent de Contenson (†1674). Standing apart from the many authors of handbooks of theological issues and Thomistic opinions, he strove still for a grand exposition, but for one which would integrate Aquinas' theology with the ideas of great spiritual writers before and during the seventeenth century.

Some Jesuits and Dominicans focused upon the order and logic of Thomism, while others employed it as an apologetics against Protestantism and Jansenism. John of St. Thomas with his systems of philosophy and philosophical theology, the Carmelites with their collections, the *Salmanticenses* and the *Complutenses*, Contenson with his volumes of parallel texts from scholastic theology adorned by Baroque spirituality, and Charles René Billuart's twenty-volume re-expression of Aquinas exemplify the forms of Thomism in the seventeenth and eighteenth centuries. "With these," Otto Pesch observes laconically, "the history of classical Thomism reaches its end."[17]

That particular historical period viewed Aquinas as one, albeit privileged, source, and, if it applied Thomism to new problems, nonetheless, it did not create an engaging systematic theological perspective for an increasingly secular world. Baroque Thomism lived from the energy and perspective of the seventeenth century, but, despite the tremendous accomplishment of the Baroque, we cannot overlook its shadow side. The church was often distracted from its real mission by internal disputes (the controversy *De Auxiliis,* Jansenism, Gallicanism, Probabilism, Chinese Rites). Theology became lost in erudition or emotion. New sciences were not really incorporated, while politically and socially the Baroque encouraged inequality and extravagance. The church failed to see, as the eighteenth century began, that a new rationalism and structuralism were replacing over-taxed emotionalism and individuality. The light of a Baroque heaven was replaced by the light of reason. Authors, lacking originality, severed texts from their context and arranged them around a particular theme: moral theology, the nature and work of a priest, or mystical theology.[18] Gerald Vann was right to evaluate Thomism from 1530 to 1730 with limited enthusiasm:

> In the main, however, the history of Thomism during these centuries is a history of failure; and a failure precisely to achieve the Dominican ideal in the way St. Thomas had so fully demonstrated and so clearly illustrated; a failure to meet the intellectual needs of the times. The vitality of the Spanish school did not spread; Thomists were preoccupied with their controversies with the nominalists; preoccupied also too exclusively with the working out of the purely theological implications of this or that particular doctrine, forgetting the main work of synthesis which is the stuff of Thomism.[19]

Nevertheless, Thomism had in quite different cultures been able to sustain not only tradition but creativity.

To choose the Dominican Order as an example of one Thomistic school, we have witnessed an intellectual tradition of length and diversity reaching from the Middle Ages to the Rococo: from Capreolus and Sylvester Ferrariensis to Vitoria and Melchior Cano, and on to John of St. Thomas. Around the world the basic principle of "grace leading human nature to its destiny" (*Gratia perficit naturam*) had sustained the meaning of the Incarnation and had been enhanced as basic to Catholic life. Nevertheless, systematic theology was largely replaced after 1640 by analyses of Christian ethics and spiritual life, and the style and content of Aquinas continued in fewer and fewer publications issuing from universities and religious orders.

V. The "Third Thomism" from 1860 to 1960

As the Enlightenment assumed a strong hold on European life, Roman Catholicism entered a period of weakness. For almost a century from 1740 to 1840 scholasticism, and with it Thomism, were little known outside of seminaries. The "Age of Light" was hostile toward a historical and supernatural revelation and toward what the second scholasticism had become by the early eighteenth century: exercises in the mechanics of human and divine contacts. The energy of Catholic theology had been drained off into conflicts between the religious orders over the nature of metaphysics, grace, and free will, and the casuistic solution of moral cases. Great theological topics like Trinity and Christ were little considered or were treated only in static views which had little religious appeal. And too, theology was dominated by apologetics: by volumes of arguments aimed at defeating the science, philosophy, democratic politics, and liberal Protestantism of the age of reason, books rarely read outside of clerical circles. This decline was furthered by the suppression in 1773 of the Society of Jesus with its many educational institutions and its scholastic tradition. Nevertheless, during the eighteenth century, in small numbers, Thomist schools survived among Dominicans and Carmelites in Spain, scholars in France and Belgium, and Benedictine centers in Austria and Baden. Their work often selected some neoscholastic texts to address specific issues, usually issues of the church and the spiritual life. They ignored the earthshaking changes of the age of Voltaire and Jefferson. The freedom, realism, and humanism of the Enlightenment might have found some positive philosophical relationship to the thought of Aquinas, but that period's hostility to faith and church made dialogue difficult.

Beginning in the 1790s, a new cultural epoch suddenly ushered in a renewal of Roman Catholicism. During the first half of the nineteenth century, as the Enlightenment yielded to romanticism, Catholic life was inspired by new directions in art and science. Even while conversing with modern philosophy, it underwent an expansion of church life. The new romantic style found in medicine, chemistry,

or literature as well as in philosophy emphasized religious intuition
and explored consciousness as the common history of God and
humanity. After 1810, Catholic intellectuals at the universities of
Tübingen and Munich like J. S. Drey and Johann Adam Möhler,
Joseph Görres and Franz von Baader developed theological systems
which drew on insights and approaches of philosophers after Kant,
particularly Schelling.[20] Theology and philosophy, freed from the
hegemony of a sterile rationalism, composed a new theology which
included mysticism, history, and art. That romantic idealism, organic
and aesthetic, revitalized Catholicism in the early nineteenth century through original theologies of church and tradition. Aquinas
and scholasticism, however, had little to do with that restoration.
Medieval theology was then little known: for Kant and Hegel the
scholastics were distant figures whose writings were not easily accessible and whose static, theocentric metaphysics were irrelevant.

    After 1850 it became clear that the optimistic expectations of the
previous decades of idealism—a universal science bringing the benefits of art, physics, and politics to all—had not been fulfilled. The
nineteenth century, and the Catholic Church with it, moved in mid-
century from a time of optimism and creativity to one of reaction and
positivism. The late idealist systems of Schopenhauer, Feuerbach,
and Engels convinced some church leaders that the result of modernity was inevitably pantheism, relativism, and subjectivism. Those
ideologies clearly undermined the gospel. Would they not be best
countered by a philosophy grounded in realism, revelation, and
church, and might this not be found in Aristotle and Aquinas? Thus
was born another revival of neo-scholastic philosophy and theology,
a "third Thomism."

    That neo-scholastic restoration began in the 1840s and lasted for
over a century up to the 1960s and Vatican II. More and more bishops and seminary professors were convinced of the value of a Thomist restoration, and in Mainz, Münster, Rome, and Louvain centers
were committed to uncovering and expounding Thomas Aquinas.
Somewhat self-taught scholars collected medieval texts, wrote
learned articles on Aristotelian and scholastic metaphysics, and composed neo-scholastic textbooks. Neo-scholasticism after 1880 dominated Catholic philosophy and theology. It was part of a larger neo-
Gothic revival whose branches could be found in architecture, the
restoration of medieval religious orders, and Gregorian chant. That

revival of a Greek and medieval neo-scholasticism provided the standard against which every Catholic intellectual movement from Vatican I through two world wars to Vatican II was to be measured.[21]

As often happens, a liberal epoch (1790 to 1840) had been followed by a conservative time when precision and certainty were sought. Science and socialism, Protestantism and idealist philosophy no longer appeared irenic after 1870 but increasingly hostile to Catholicism. That third neo-scholasticism assumed the unfortunate style of a reaction to all that was modern and contemporary. Catholic thinkers of romantic idealism were dismissed simply for having pursued the interplay between faith and modern philosophy. There were reasons for the return to medieval thought: for instance, to combat materialism and relativism, and to find a strong support for a metaphysical critique of modernity with its exaggerations and ideologies. And it should be remembered that the philosophies which neo-Thomism was to replace were rarely the great figures of German idealism but were minor Cartesians and ontologists, some of whose views had found their way into mediocre seminary textbooks.

The terms "neo-scholasticism" and "neo-Thomism" came into use in the late 1870s. The pioneering historian of medieval thought Martin Grabmann defined neo-scholasticism in this way: "That direction which has emerged since the mid-nineteenth century and is usually found in Catholic theology and philosophy; it takes up again the traditional links with [medieval and Baroque] ecclesiastical scholasticism which were broken by the Enlightenment; it searches to make fruitful for contemporary problems the thought-world of medieval scholasticism, particularly that of Thomas Aquinas."[22] The encyclical, *Aeterni Patris* (1879), singled out Aquinas as the outstanding teacher in the church and indicated his method as normative. His works were republished in several editions, particularly in a new critical edition begun by Leo XIII (the "Leonine edition"). Papal sponsorship increased in subsequent decades with the publication of *Doctoris Angelici* (1914) of Pius X, the controversial twenty-four theses from the Vatican in 1914, *Studiorum Ducem* (1923) of Pius XI, canon 1366 of the *Code of Canon Law* (1917/18), and *Humani Generis* (1950) of Pius XII. This restoration was of Aristotle as much as of Thomas Aquinas. The Greek philosopher's conceptual clarity was prized along with the Christian theologian's view of God.

Table 4.1 Representative Kinds of Neo-Thomism

Universities	Religious orders	Dialogue Partners	Styles
Louvain	Salamanca (OP)	History	Literal
Mainz	Le Saulchoir (Paris)	Politics	Historical
Piacenza	(OP)	Art	Philosophical
Munich	River Forest, Ill.	Modern Philo-	Theological
Toronto	(Chicago) (OP)	sophy	Transcendental
Montreal	Pullach (Munich) (SJ)		
Fordham	St. Louis (SJ)		
	Walberberg (OP)		
	Roman Schools:		
	Gregoriana		
	Angelicum		
	Lateran		

Of course, neo-Thomism was not identical with neo-scholasticism: restorations of the theology of Bonaventure and Scotus also occurred within the neo-scholastic movement. The Jesuits insisted that their own thinkers from Molina to Suarez were faithful to Aquinas. The Franciscans, however, were not forceful enough to establish their thinkers as the equals of Albert and Aquinas. This unfortunate situation kept official Catholic theology from noticing a medieval diversity, and from seeing similarities between the Augustinian-Franciscan tradition and idealist and existentialist philosophies.[23]

One can detect three stages in the course of that neo-scholasticism of the period from 1860 to 1914. The first years (1850 to 1875) saw the move from discovery to stability. Scholars educated in earlier German historical and idealist ways of thinking studied the medieval thinkers but did not fully replace modern thought with neo-scholasticism. At the same time, young enthusiasts assumed a rather ideological stance on behalf of Aristotelianism and insisted upon a proselytizing scholasticism as the dominant, indeed the sole philosophical stance for Catholics. Those first neo-Thomists did not always grasp the richness of Aquinas. Self-consciously non-scholastic thinkers like the Tübingen professors Johann Evangelist Kuhn or Paul Schanz understood the fabric of Aquinas' theology better than those who were culling passages for seminary textbooks. A second period from

1875 to 1890 presumed that Thomism and scholasticism were known in content (numerous books on Aquinas had appeared) and presented a theology destined by church authority to give the intellectual format of Catholicism. A third stage, beginning after 1890, held a variety of genres: (1) manuals and multi-volume textbooks; (2) works explaining the meaning of Aquinas, mainly on philosophical issues; (3) applications of Aquinas and Aristotle to social and ethical issues; (4) histories of medieval thought.

Neo-Thomism involved several shifts: the texts of Aquinas and Thomists rather than the "books" of creation and revelation were central; the teacher was a commentator on speculative texts rather than one who explained the Bible; the open spirit of research and dialogue became one of exposition of work already done; new questions and new sources (usually adversaries) were not integrated into the structures of Aquinas' thinking. In the years around 1900 Aquinas would be established as a judge ruling against what was new or different. Experience, change, development, pluralism were rejected by this specter. Consequently, many in European intellectual life linked the Catholic Church with the antiquarian and the imperious, stances supported by a Vatican politique which would last through the first half of the twentieth century. Because it insisted that scholasticism alone could do justice to the authentic Catholic doctrine on revelation and grace, this third neo-Thomism reinforced by papal documents did not just apply specific philosophical words to central Christian beliefs but to some extent altered theological content. Neo-scholasticism identified truth and life with immutability and rationality, it opposed being to history and ignored concreteness in human life and in the economy of salvation. Its Aristotelianism was too rigid and conceptual, and religious education at all levels consisted in little more than philosophical passages on God or virtue. In a child's catechism or a priest's manual Christian revelation appeared to be a sparse blueprint of laws and graced achievements. Scriptural themes, different periods in the history of doctrine, personal faith, and communal liturgy were neglected. Any other theology, not only modern but biblical, patristic or medieval, could be dangerous. If, viewed positively, scholastic thought warded off the absorption of Christian revelation by philosophy and by the liberal Protestant reduction of God's action in history, nevertheless, biblical faith was held in a castle guarded by metaphysics and canon law. The authority of the Catholic

Church replaced the intrinsic criteria of truth prized by Albert and Aquinas. Theology was to have the same narrow standards as dogma and to avoid growth, originality, and pluralism. All of this found its climax in the selection in 1914 by anonymous figures of twenty-four theses (all concerning philosophy) which would perfectly present the thought of Aquinas. While neo-Thomism aspired to become dominant in the classroom life of Catholicism from 1860 to 1960 through the authority of the Vatican, actually any superficial neo-scholasticism seemed to qualify. Some universities and religious orders with a long tradition of studying Aquinas were shocked at what claimed to be "scholastic" or "Thomist."

As the twentieth century progressed, narrow styles of neo-Thomist philosophy sought to be non-modern and timeless, and some identified their neo-Thomism with revelation or with the teaching office of the church. Written in a dead language, an artificial Latin imitating medieval or Baroque styles, it could protect but not vitalize Catholic life. Did its claim of timelessness come true in an unexpected way? The genres of system (*summae*) and open discussion (medieval disputation) were replaced by the seminary textbook and by the defense of artificial and irrelevant propositional theses. From 1878 to 1962 dogma, theology, philosophy, ecclesiology, liturgical rubrics, and canon law melded into a synthesis directed and furthered by the Roman schools and the Vatican. Many aspects of Catholic life were removed from their own age. Whether in Milan, Boston, or Nairobi—there was a kind of universal sociology of thinking and pedagogy of communication, one inspired and limited by a highly philosophical neo-scholasticism. This philosophy of Catholic Christianity, uncomplicated in its normal and normative seminary form, furthered a church which appeared isolated or asleep.

How did the introspective neo-Thomisms of the early twentieth century differ from Aquinas' writings? The former had: (1) a view of Aquinas primarily as a philosopher to the neglect of Christian revelation and theology; (2) an interest in syllogisms and proofs to the detriment of a dialectical and synthetic contemplation of theological ideas and sources; (3) an outdated physics and a shallow metaphysics which forced theology to be static, verbal, and timeless, and to be an exercise beginning with definitions and ending in conclusions; (4) a lack of knowledge of the historical context of Aquinas' career or of development in his writings; (5) a focus on the Aristotelianism in

Aquinas which overshadowed the Platonic influences at work. All this removed the study of Aquinas from preaching and education and located it in seminaries cut off from the life of society. Thus Thomas Aquinas, whom history records as a singular example of a creative synthesis of multiple sources and new philosophical currents, often became identified with a past ontology, a dead language, and a fear of one's own age.[24]

This third Thomism was to last until Vatican II. And yet, before and after World War I, science and culture were already stimulating some Catholics to reject the idea of a philosophy and theology which, angry at what was new, simply reproduced scholastic terms and syllogisms. In the 1890s, just when metaphysical rigidity was becoming sclerotic, new directions appeared, prototypes of what lay ahead. In quite different ways they expanded Thomism. One direction applied scholasticism to ethical and social issues; a second investigated the history of medieval thought. Joseph Mausbach at Münster and Viktor Cathrein applied Aquinas to issues of labor law and women's rights. In the broader and ultimately more influential area of history, the Jesuit Franz Ehrle focused on medieval Augustinianism, the Dominican Heinrich Denifle glimpsed in Meister Eckhart the diversity within the medieval period, and the younger Martin Grabmann explored the medieval universities and sciences. The reclaiming of the historical context of Aquinas took decades of work, but eventually understanding the variety in the Middle Ages illumined Aquinas' theological vision. Understanding the intellectual world and theological sources and goals of the theologian revealed his potential for later generations. Then, too, in the first years of this century, a third group emerged who argued that dialogue between modern philosophy and Aquinas would give perspectives seminal for Catholic thought and life.

These shifts within neo-Thomism in Europe involved a conviction that Aquinas was not the same as a philosophical neo-scholasticism. They forecast an expansion from an ontology of beings to a theology of human consciousness and history, and a move from logical tomes on theodicy to theological themes like grace and sacrament.[25]

VI. The Diversity of Thomisms in the Twentieth Century

Neo-Thomism in the twentieth century has its own history and diversity. During the time of the Third Thomism, which lasted up to the 1960s, a diverse group of people—logicians, theologians, political theoreticians, artists, and historians—produced books, periodicals, and approaches which employed the same philosophical and theological principles. Its variety is evident when we list figures like Reginald Garrigou-Lagrange, Étienne Gilson, and Karl Rahner, or schools like Salamanca, the Roman Angelicum, and Louvain. In the 1950s monopolistic rigidity and creative diversity struggled for coexistence, even for mastery. Some rejected a monopoly of one neoscholastic way of thinking and sought dialogue and creativity. Renewed Thomisms provided in the work of Edward Schillebeeckx or John Courtney Murray had an marked influence at Vatican II.

Gerald McCool sees in the twentieth century five distinct periods of neo-scholasticism.[26] (1) The period from the turn of the century to World War I was marked by expansion and consolidation; it flourished in universities and centers of religious orders like Louvain, Innsbruck, Valkenburg. Historical research was beginning, but the anti-modernist campaign attacked any opening of the intellectual life of the church. (2) The second period between the wars was a "flowering of the scholastic revival." Traditional Thomism was enriched by commentaries, the Middle Ages came alive through historical study, and transcendental Thomism emerged. There were some attempts to dialogue without arrogance with contemporary culture. (3) After World War II the Catholic Church became concerned with its pastoral life, and pursued not only practical areas like liturgy but non-scholastic theologies found in the Bible and the theologians of the first centuries. Increasingly neo-scholasticism was sometimes viewed as static and sterile, neither academically creative nor pastorally applicable, but church authorities were not favorable to any non-scholastic theology, although many Catholics learned only a neo-Thomism which was a succinct Aristotelian exposition of Christianity. (4) During the preparation and event of Vatican II theologians aided by Aquinas' theology developed the great conciliar themes. (5) While the ideology of Thomism faded quickly after the Council, after a respite of a few years, the study of Aquinas' theology in books, journals, and institutes, in Europe but also in North and South America, emerged in the late 1970s with renewed strength.

Before we look more closely at the currents which vivified and extended neo-Thomism in this century, we should note some of the benefits to Catholicism and to the Thomism coming from the restoration from 1860 to 1960. The understanding of Aquinas increased enormously.[27] Philosophy and speculative theology offered a real alternative to the modern ideologies which a priori excluded revelation. Catholicism presented a positive vision of the human person and human culture. The introduction of university students, laity, and even high school students to Thomism was a step beyond a merely catechetical religious education. A positive anthropology prepared for political activism, fostered new spiritualities, and prepared thousands to work for and to understand the renewal of the life of the church which would be formulated at Vatican II. Neo-Thomism itself had displayed a certain pluralism in the twentieth century. It had brought forth a rather meticulous and static Spanish school with figures like Norberto del Prado, Santiago Ramirez, and Juan Arintero. There were literal commentators like Reginald Garrigou-Lagrange or M. M. Labourdette, as well as creative, culturally open thinkers like A. D. Sertillanges, and Jacques Maritain. There were historians like Gilson and M.-D. Chenu. There were scholars like Carl Werner and Josef Pieper who drew Aquinas into modern German streams of thought.[28]

The following pages look briefly at a selection of important interpreters of Aquinas in the twentieth century. They transmitted his insights but they also rendered them attractive. There were three groups: the first brought together a variety of expositors of the ideas and texts of Aquinas, each with their own approach; the second group studied Aquinas in the context of the Middle Ages; the third established a conversation between Aquinas and modern philosophers. McCool, looking back at recent Thomist history, concludes:

> Contemporary Thomism would not have been possible without the intense historical research and the vigorous speculative confrontations which characterized the history of Thomism from the turn of the century until Vatican II. Furthermore, although Thomism has lost its dominant position, it has not lost its confidence in the rigor, speculative fruitfulness, and integrating power of Thomas's thought. Although it is much more sophisticated and sober in estimating the possibilities of a Scholastic synthesis, it is very conscious that Catholic theology would not have reached the present state of its development without the Scholastic Revival"[29]

A. A THOMIST SPECTRUM

Antonin Dalmais Sertillanges (1863–1948) had the greatest veneration for Aquinas' thought, but he developed his ideas in dialogue with
French cultural life around World War I. Expecting a harmony
between faith and reason and between human nature and grace,
Sertillanges rejected the ideology that modern philosophy, art, or politics are inevitably false, and he sought new applications of the orientations of Aquinas' thought to French philosophy and intellectual
life. He and others like Ambroise Gardeil (1859–1931), in the words
of McCool, faced "Immanence, voluntarism, relativation of the concept in favor of an immediate intuition of being, together with a
metaphysics of life and mobility rather than a stable metaphysics of
being. These seemed to be the challenges which the newer religious
thought in France, stimulated by Blondelianism and Bergsonianism
presented to Catholic theology."[30] Chenu saw Sertillanges and
Gardeil, "men who had received their Thomist formation in a spirit
of research and who knew instinctively that theology implies co-
essentially on-going research,"[31] as the sources of the dialogical and
historical Thomism which would flourish in Paris. The books of
these French Dominicans retain valuable insights as they sum up an
area of theology in a magisterial way or locate Aquinas in a social or
aesthetic context. The Dominicans were confident that their
Thomist view of the powers of the intellect and the intelligibility and
harmony of faith could respond to dialogue with modern views. The
writings and teaching of these men prepared for the work of the next
generation of French Thomist historians and philosophers, men as
different as Chenu and Reginald Garrigou-Lagrange.

Reginald Garrigou-Lagrange (1877–1964) took up anew the tradition of the Baroque Dominican school (Cajetan, Bañez, John of St.
Thomas), presuming that it was the best, indeed, the only interpretation of Aquinas' theology. He represents many conservative French
and Roman neo-Thomists of the first half of this century. A student
of philosophy at the Sorbonne, he heard Emil Durkheim and Henri
Bergson lecture and became friends with Jacques Maritain. Exposure
to secular and contemporary philosophy, however, made him suspi-
cious of the idea of a modern Catholic theology which would emphasize knowing over being and accept a too fluid development in
Christian dogma. After 1909 he was a professor at the Dominican

school in Rome, the Angelicum, and during his fifty years there he served frequently as an adviser to the Vatican's investigations of doctrinal aberrations. A historical interpretation of Aquinas drawn from the thirteenth century (Chenu) or a creative theology pondering cosmic evolution and social process in the twentieth century (Pierre Teilhard de Chardin) were directions he urged the Vatican to condemn. Garrigou's early works like *Common Sense, The Philosophy of Being and Dogmatic Formulae* (1909) and *God, His Existence and Nature* (1915) were philosophical in their subject matter, clear in their conception and style, but defensive toward all that was outside Thomism and Catholicism. His two-volume theological apologetics, *De Revelatione* (1918, 1932), stands out from the many mediocre works of neo-scholastic apologetics. If it mainly musters pages of dated arguments for the truths of Christianity and the Catholic Church, it does treat some speculative issues with originality. While moderately open to diversity within schools of spirituality and Thomism, he was incapable of appreciating any non-scholastic approach to Christianity. In the 1920s and 1930s Garrigou turned to the theology of the spiritual and mystical life extracted from Aquinas and from the Carmelite mystics like Teresa of Avila and John of the Cross (*Christian Perfection and Contemplation according to Thomas Aquinas and St. John of the Cross, The Three Ages of the Interior Life*). Those books (still of considerable value) present a Thomist spirituality which begins with the ordinariness of grace in human psychology and finds its fruition in the life of the gifts of the Spirit enabling mystical prayer. In the twenty years after 1936 he composed a commentary on the *ST* of which volumes on God, grace, the virtues, and Christ were completed. This commentary gives a close reading of the text illumined by an array of citations from other works; its principles of divine activity and grace as a new life exemplify its Dominican approach.

Louis Billot (1846–1931) entered the Jesuits at the end of his university studies. He was professor at the Gregorian University in Rome from 1885 to 1911. Active in the more mature stages of the Thomistic revival, he too wrote a series of lengthy commentaries on the *ST* as it treated central areas or "tracts" of the Christian faith like Christ or grace. In contrast to his Dominican contemporary, Garrigou-Lagrange, whose analysis served meticulously each phrase of Aquinas' text and who drew in patristic and scholastic texts, Billot expounded "theses" which were intended to focus on the important point of one or more articles in a question of the *ST*. His Latin exposition unfolded his own ideas with few references to other theologians or philosophers. Detached from the history of salvation in Christianity and biblical theologies, his personal stance was conceptual and juridical: while he retained the Jesuit orientation toward many issues in grace and spirituality, he sought the meaning of Aquinas' texts even when that meant accepting some approaches from the Dominican school (significantly this prominent Jesuit thinker had set aside Suarezianism). Speculatively gifted, he nonetheless displayed, in other writings more than in his commentary, the importance of "positive theology," that is, of the study of Scripture and patristic thinkers. He was able to offer a historical background for theological issues without giving support to modernist interpretations of dogmas empty of revelation. Pius X named him a cardinal, but because of his sympathy for the independent political movement, "*Action française,*" he had to resign that honor in 1927 and withdraw from the activities of curial cardinal and theologian.

Jacques Maritain (1882–1973) was raised in liberal Protestant circles, and the lectures of Henri Bergson led him during his university years at the turn of the century beyond the age's materialistic positivism into the realms of spirit and activity. Léon Bloy was active in his conversion to Catholicism in 1906. Maritain taught at Paris, Toronto, Chicago, and Princeton, serving from 1945 to 1948 as French Ambassador to the Vatican. This French philosopher advocated what he called "an open Thomism," a form of Thomism which in the period between the wars was viewed as liberal and eclectic (exemplified in works like *The Degrees of Knowledge, Science and Wisdom, Existence and the Existent*). Although negative in his evaluation of modern philosophy and Protestant thinkers,[32] he was no friend of a simplistic, clerical, neo-Gothic revivalism in the intellectual life. He wanted to address art, science, and society in the twentieth century, and he drew an international audience to his ideas on politics and aesthetics. He found in Aristotle and Aquinas a way of thinking which could be humanist and even existentialist. Appreciative of the contributions of science, he pursued, while many neo-scholasticisms were still advocating forms of monarchy, the themes of freedom and democracy. His aesthetics presented a scholastic theory of art even as it struggled to understand modern art.

He aspired to introduce a religious and synthetic direction over against the fragmentation of modernity and the theocentric legalism of some of Catholicism at the turn of the century. This "integral humanism" called attention to the value of the person and the claims of the common good.

And yet, while he addressed the wider world in some specific areas, ultimately there was only one healthy set of principles: Maritain's own neo-Thomism.[33] In metaphysics and speculative theology he could imagine little of value outside of neo-Thomism. Some Thomists found him too eclectic, too much held captive by recent scholastic interpretation rather than by the text of Aquinas; others judged him hostile to historical interpretations, while yet others criticized him for giving positive directions for the art and politics of the twentieth century. Nonetheless, from 1930 to 1960 he inspired many Catholics throughout the world to search for ways in which their church's life and thought could escape being hostile to European and American societies and to initiate a dialogue between Thomistic synthesis and contemporary culture. Although he was not a theologian, Maritain at the end of his life objected to the extra-European vitalization of the Roman Catholic Church at Vatican II.

Charles Journet (1891–1975) was a theologian of broad knowledge and considerable synthetic ability. Yves Congar described him as the most inventive theologian of ecclesiology in the first half of the twentieth century, and Journet influenced the writings and sermons of Paul VI. Journet was an independent thinker working outside any individual scholastic school (Jesuit, Dominican, Roman) but drawing from many of them. He complemented neo-scholastic logic and metaphysics with patristic, canonical, mystical, Baroque-scholastic, and papal texts. While he represented creative ecclesiology in the decades leading up to Vatican II, in retrospect one sees that a neo-Thomist framework often depicted a church which existed mainly in hierarchical functions or mystical states, a church whose ecclesiastical structures were too much a neo-Aristotelian delineation of a machinery of powers bestowed by the papacy.[34] Nevertheless, he brought a breadth of sources and a literary originality to areas of Christian revelation and church.

❖ ❖ ❖

Theology mediates between revelation and culture, and both of these poles have their histories. Eventually Catholic theology had to pass beyond a rejection of all that was not medieval, a rejection of history itself; furthermore, it needed to accept some of the aspects of modern philosophy and research. As we have mentioned, a deeper appreciation of Aquinas in the twentieth century came through two movements: (1) an understanding of the history of philosophy and theology in the Middle Ages; (2) a positive dialogue with modern philosophy. Those shifts occurred in the years around World War I. Political and economic changes led some philosophers and theologians to critique the enclosed ecclesiastical mentality sustained by the Vatican and to plan for some expansion in the life and thought of Catholicism. In history, the first generation of Denifle, Ehrle, and Grabmann was followed after 1930 by Gilson and Chenu. In philosophy, Jesuits like Pierre Rousselot, Joseph Maréchal, and Gaston Fessard were pioneers after 1900 in finding common ground between medieval and modern philosophies; they were followed by Erich Przywara, Emil Coreth, Lonergan, and Rahner. In these new directions neo-Thomism contained the forces of its own liberation and expansion. The rediscovery of Aquinas precisely as a theologian came from historians and from philosophers in touch with both the needs of Catholic life and the thinking of modernity.

B. HISTORICAL RESEARCH IN THE MIDDLE AGES

The historical context is the beginning of a competent understanding of any thinker. Thomas Aquinas was not an angelic mind operating above time, and the more we know of his sources and audiences the better we understand him. The following researchers uncovered the age of Aquinas, an enterprise freeing his theology for wider use. Paradoxically, the historical understanding of a theologian or a philosopher offers their potential to other times.

Étienne Gilson (1884–1978) taught in various universities until he was appointed professor of medieval philosophy at the Sorbonne and director of medieval philosophy at the Ecole Pratique des Hautes Etudes. A founder in 1929 of the Institute of Medieval Studies in Toronto, Canada, he was elected to the Academie Française in 1947. His critique of Cartesianism led him to the courses of Henri Bergson and from there to medieval philosophy and Thomism. His influence in medieval history was enormous, as he researched a variety of thinkers. Illustrating the relationship of mysticism to theology, Gilson wrote books on Augustine, Bonaventure, Dante, Bernard of Clairvaux, and Duns Scotus. In 1955 he delivered in Washington, D. C., the Mellon lectures on art (as Jacques Maritain had done earlier). He experienced Catholic intellectual life in the first decades of this century as a shallow philosophy which was often ignorant of Aquinas' writings, and as a metaphysics with few links to theology, medieval or otherwise.[35] Gilson was uninformed about and excessively critical of modern philosophy. He rejected too vigorously attempts by Catholic thinkers to discuss the role of human subjectivity, the central point of philosophy after Kant. While his emphasis upon the theological dimension of medieval thought (and of any true scholasticism) was valuable, he fashioned a theological context (one never accepted) for metaphysics which was eccentric; he thought that insights on being were derived from the revelation on Sinai of "I am who am" (Exodus 3:14). Other Thomists objected to his beginning philosophy with ontology rather than natural philosophy.[36] Nevertheless, after observing differences between Aquinas' texts and Cajetan's Thomism from the sixteenth century, he argued that one should not identify any neo-Thomism with its original source. His understanding of medieval and patristic thought and his transcendence of the logical textbooks of neo-Thomism made him an important influence.

M.-D. Chenu (1895–1990) wrote many important studies on theology in the twelfth and thirteenth centuries and founded the bibliographical survey *Bulletin Thomiste. Toward Understanding St. Thomas,* which remains decades later an orientation of high value, located masterfully the man and the *ST* in the world of the thirteenth century. Building upon the French Dominican tradition of a scholarly but open consideration of Aquinas (exemplified in Gardeil and Sertillanges), Chenu based his work upon a sense of the vitality and sublimity of revelation, the personal but supernatural quality of faith, and the social conditions of a period. The science and culture of an age offer the forms for expressing faith; science, architecture, politics, philosophy, and theology often have a certain cultural unity. Philosophy is the "history of the human spirit in search of first truths," and mature human reflection concerns itself not with logical games but with insight and understanding enhanced through his-

tory.[37] Truth is eternal, but its eternity is accessible to us through
temporality. Chenu directed his Dominican confreres at the school of
Le Saulchoir outside Paris where they established a new approach to
theology, a school devoted to historical context and to the contemporary life of the church. Theologians, not being archaeologists,
should study history not solely to isolate and compare past ideas (this
would imply that theology and Christianity were dead) but to discern
their meaning for the present. The historian said he wanted to do for
Aquinas' theology what M.-J. Lagrange had done for biblical studies
by establishing the Ecole Biblique in Jerusalem, that is, let history
bring vitality and contemporaneity.[38] To ignore history is to search
for one timeless philosophy and theology, to by-pass the reality of
revelation and to minimize both human nature and grace in history.
The incarnation of the Word in Jesus Christ takes place within creation, and the presence of Jesus' Spirit continues on in people: this
gives the pattern for the Gospel and the church to be at work in history and culture. This way of thinking led the historian of the Middle
Ages to be involved in the theological and pastoral renewal of France
after 1945. He had written as early as 1931:

> Those who enclose themselves in a scholastic Thomism hard-
> ened by generations of textbooks and manuals (and marginalized
> by the intrusion of a massive dose of Baroque scholasticism)
> oblige themselves thereby to summary condemnations of posi-
> tions of which they are largely ignorant. This would certainly not
> be the path for the disciples of Thomas Aquinas. And less help-
> ful is the way of those who, with a strange collusion of anti-
> modernism, hand over the great memory of the medieval Doctor
> to a positivist intellectualism and keep for themselves a Thomism
> which is only a paragon of their own pseudo-religious integrist
> position. But this exploitation of Thomism (which some naively
> view to be salutary) cannot hide the real intentions of others, pen-
> etrated with the spirit of Thomas and with the high demands of
> scientific or theological work. They meet honestly the problems
> legitimately posed by the philosophy of religion, biblical exegesis,
> and the history of dogma. Illumined by the experience of their
> teacher they know how to discern in new terrain the relation-
> ships of reason and faith. Precisely this is the intellectual regime
> of Catholicism.[39]

This critique would be accepted thirty years after it was written. The historian was convinced that the study of history showed the depth and applicability of the great thinker. To underscore this belief, he cited a phrase of Gilson: "It is impossible to conserve without creating."[40]

Yves Congar (1904–1995), a student and a co-worker of Chenu, exemplifies how the historical study of Aquinas can have the most practical effects. Congar's specialty was the history of the institutions and theologies of the church. He unfolded older and richer theologies of tradition and episcopacy, wrote the first theology of the laity, and introduced ecumenism to Roman Catholicism. His life's work was a major preparation for Vatican II. Congar emphasized the history of salvation and the pastoral and missionary dimensions of the word of God over against a Roman hierarchical neo-scholasticism. "What do I owe to St. Thomas, that I have gone back to him so often? First of all, a certain structure within the world of the human spirit. That's what makes him relevant even today. His ideas are well-ordered. There is too a sense of openness and even dialogue. Thomas, with his incredible dialectical power, spent all his life looking for new texts and having new translations made for himself."[41] Aided by his research into history and into the movements of his own age, Congar discovered a dynamic in Aquinas which reached out toward reality and empowered people. The historian of ecclesiology was critical of neo-Thomism as a monopoly, as an intellectual construct which mixed Aristotelian and neo-Platonic ontologies with a Baroque institutional politique, or as an ideology which brought homogeneity at almost any price. Beyond Aristotelian metaphysical logic, in the mid-twentieth century theologians had come to see an anthropocentricism, a history, and a Trinitarian salvation-history.

From his teacher Chenu, Congar learned to appreciate the role of history, a history which revealed that the church was both the same and different for various ages and cultures. Aquinas, Congar explained, understood the relationships between the secular and the spiritual as interplays of the human and the divine, and as the realm of the sacramental in the widest sense. The whole people of God (including the hierarchy) acts in faith and charity to serve the world. Congar's ecumenical work too was part of a larger vocation of the historical theologian. The separated churches, which had been born from particular theologies, might complement each other.[42] The division of theology into closed camps, neo-Thomism as a monopoly, the isolation of Rome from Eastern Orthodoxy, the rejection of new approaches for parishes, the narrow confines of a pyramidal ecclesiology—all of this was not the defense but the impoverishment of Catholicism. Congar's ideas, contemporary and yet rooted in the history of the church, introduced the new. But that advocacy of renewal in the 1950s brought censorship. Removed from teaching and publishing by Vatican officials under Pius XII, the French Dominican was rehabilitated by Pope John XXIII who personally insisted that he be asked to serve on a commission preparing for Vatican II. There his ideas in an extraordinary way found fulfillment.

The careers of Chenu and Congar show how the revitalization of Thomas Aquinas and other medieval theologians was part of a renewal of French Catholic life after World War II. When the French church accepted in 1945 the need for pastoral vitalization, one foreseen to be so extensive that France could truly be called a "missionary country," it set in motion wide-reaching tremors touching liturgy and modern church art, religious education, and the study of the Bible. Church renewal then meant dialogue with social classes, priests and nuns as factory workers, Mass in the vernacular. The French in the 1950s took Aquinas' thought out of libraries and put it into parishes, and factories; that employment exemplified the union of theory and practice as it had been affirmed by Aquinas at the opening of the *ST* (I, 1, 4).

C. DIALOGUE WITH MODERN PHILOSOPHERS

Running parallel to historical research was a conversation with modern philosophies. Was it possible that even Thomas Aquinas might offer insights for a theology of the person or for a morality of freedom?[43] The Roman neo-Thomist establishment often responded negatively during the years from 1910 to 1960 to any positive evaluation of the cultural theories and institutions of the modern age. Nevertheless, in the first years of the twentieth century there began a struggle of philosophers and theologians (responsible to church authorities as priests and members of religious orders) to ask whether the medieval Dominican's principles could be applied to contemporary philosophies and societies. Was Thomism merely an ancient metaphysics? Was it the only metaphysics? Of course, encyclicals of the popes had themselves already pursued the line of contemporary application in social questions. But a theology is only as vital as its thought-forms, and a living faith cannot avoid forever its own age.

Looking at the renewal of Thomism in the twentieth century, one can offer the generalization that the Dominicans pursued theologies in their historical context, while the Jesuits focused on modern philosophers. The Jesuits' writings were concerned with ways through which consciousness shapes reality, with the "Copernican revolution" of Kant, that is, the shift to the active forms of the personality. They thought that Thomism should halt its ignorant carping and escape its isolation from every modern theory. They also thought that modern philosophy could learn from Aristotle and Aquinas.

Philosophers and theologians in Europe explored active subjectivity in knowing and belief by describing Aquinas' psychology of an active light giving intellection, and of parallel lights of faith and mysticism. In France those efforts would influence the nature of faith, Christian existence, and spirituality. In Germany during the 1920s professors at universities and seminaries studied the relationship of Greek and medieval thinkers to the stages of modern philosophy. The phenomenologies of Edmund Husserl and Max Scheler found disciples among young Catholics and recent converts. Martin Heidegger composed his doctorate on Scotist medieval thought, while his colleague, Edith Stein, brought together phenomenology and Aquinas. Romano Guardini wrote on Bonaventure. That dialogue with modern culture, intent on transcending neo-Thomism, would, despite ecclesiastical censors, grow and establish partnerships with biblical and historical theologies. Thereby it prepared for Vatican II and for the Council's theologians.

Erich Przywara (1889–1972) was broadly educated and conversant with contemporary philosophies and theologies: he was an expositor and friend of Karl Barth and of Paul Tillich. The Jesuit heightened the essential message of Aquinas—divine grace was working in finite causalities—but he also showed in original ways how idealism and existentialism might converse with medieval theologians and Catholic mystics. "The method [of Catholic thought] cannot, precisely because it intends to remain authentically Catholic, consist in building as many walls as possible, strengthened by forbidding moats: rather, it should be a decisive and special way, able to seek out through obstruction and cacophony the illumination of the 'Logos' penetrating all."[44] Aquinas' teaching of the harmony of nature and grace, particularly as it overflows into the activities of human beings represents a kind of inner law of the Catholic mind. Consequently Aquinas should not be held captive in the confines of Suarezianism nor should Thomism flee hysterically before Hegel or Dilthey. Some similarities between medieval and modern issues, for instance, in the relationships of the knowing subject to freedom and the objective world were being recognized. The modern shifts from the cosmos to subjectivity and from ontology to the historicity of knowing were accepted; being and the human subject were not opposed to each other.

The sovereign dignity of human action is preserved and enhanced in Aquinas' theological axiom, "grace brings nature to completion." Przywara wrote:

> This basic proposition has a dual form, one concerning being and one consciousness: so it implies harmony both in the order of grace and of faith. While it is true that grace might seem to exist in order to serve the completion of nature, this is not true in terms of all of nature, of matter and atoms. Rather Aquinas wants to grasp the mystery of the world of grace somehow in the categories of being and nature . . . so questions are asked of the world of revelation as developed from philosophical categories.[45]

The goal is not to have either a rationalized faith or a nature adorned by something called grace. "Grace does not extinguish nature, faith does not extinguish reason, but each becomes a new vital form of nature or reason. The creature appears not as perfect nature in itself but as something which one can designate in an unusual expression as the existing being of grace."[46] Philosophy is itself an approximate theology, the ultimate form of the obediential potency leading towards the mystery of the supernatural.

Joseph Maréchal (1878–1944), a Belgian Jesuit, wrote eloquently on the natural drive of the intellect toward being and truth.[47] He argued that Aquinas too appreciated the activity of the personality, the intuition of the Infinite, and the judgment of what was concrete and experienced. Each being has its actualization, and every act has an innate drive to realize its identity and to seek a further good.

Maréchal devoted his efforts to restoring what he saw to be Aquinas' grounding of philosophy in the active teleology of the faculties. Aquinas' epistemology was not the same as Aristotle's: the former was open to the exploration of revelation and history. A Thomism which was not the static conceptuality of the Italian neo-Thomists might be both faithful to Aquinas and open to dialogue with approaches present in contemporary phenomenologies and neo-Kantians. "To have refused consistently to separate life and consciousness, activity and speculation, or, more generally, act and form (all unjustified separations)—this seems to me to be the main merit of Thomist epistemology and the secret of its lasting value."[48] Aquinas still had contributions to make.

Pierre Rousselot (1878–1915) received inspiration from Maréchal to pursue a vital and intellectualist understanding of Aquinas. This was possible, he began, only if one saw the sharp contrast between Aquinas and modern and medieval emphases upon the will. Sadly, voluntarist philosophies had crept even into neo-scholasticism. Rousselot was not so much concerned with the past, Kant and Hegel, as with the present in which Henri Bergson and Maurice Blondel, philosophers of life, were emphasizing experience and temporality. Could topics like analogy and God's being be examined through new approaches beyond those of an extrinsic physics and static ontology? His theology of faith offered an alternative to the unconvincing proofs or panoplies of cerebral apologetics which ended in fideism or in a confusion of knowing and believing. Faith, granted its unsupported darkness in this life and its bestowal by grace, was ultimately a knowing of the vision of God. The dynamic orientation toward eschatological fulfillment in the future had already begun on earth. A deeper reading of Aquinas showed how closely understanding and being, the dynamics of the mind and the goodness of being, were kept together; and how the finite personality was grounded in God. In Aquinas there is no conflict between thought and action. The intellect is not simply reason arranging sense-data but a knowing which grasps implicitly in every act the mystery of divine being. Rousselot's lectures on faith and love at the Institut Catholique in Paris after 1909 exercised a broad influence. His approach, by bringing faith and theology closer to human experience, would revivify Catholic intellectual life. But in 1915 the Jesuit was killed in World War I.[49]

These thinkers were not inserting dangerous modern ideas into an alien medieval thought but were observing that an active transcendental subjectivity and freedom had been present in some scholastics. Moreover, dialogue went both ways: if Catholic philosophy and theology could be stimulated by the direction of modernity, haughty ideologies always in danger of being swept away by subjectivism and relativism could learn from Aquinas. Because they appreciated the transcendental (Kant's term for the analysis of active human subjectivity), the philosophers of the conversation between idealism and Thomism whether in Paris, Innsbruck, or Munich, became known as "transcendental Thomists." McCool sums up: "Together Rousselot and Maréchal took Thomism a long way from the Scholasticism of their nineteenth-century confreres. Both were resolute Thomists in their metaphysics of man and being, but the Suarezian tradition represented by Liberatore and Kleutgen no longer had any part in their philosophy and theology. . . . Both of them felt that, properly understood and consistently employed, Kant's transcendental method could vindicate a Thomistic metaphysics of man and being."[50] It is important to see that they did not all mix or compromise Aquinas with Kant but explored a Thomism which had a transcendental direction actually rooted in Aquinas. An even more creative generation—one which included Max Müller, Gustav Siewerth, Emil Coreth, J. B. Lotz, Bernhard Welte, and Rahner—followed Rousselot and Maréchal.

Bernard Lonergan (1904–1984) was a Canadian Jesuit who taught most of his life in Rome. He pondered with a courageous originality the relationship of modern philosophy to Aquinas. His early works on grace and word in the Dominican theologian exemplified a more sophisticated approach to historical interpretation than what was found in the neo-scholastic textbooks of the time. Lonergan realized that beyond the reconstruction of a past theology there was the need to understand the dynamics of experience, understanding, judging, imagination, and decision which were at work in any theology. The important book *Insight* looked at the different ways in which people, who are inevitably yearning to know, understand: it studied the methods of human culture, the illumination and limitation of each knower and each object known, and then the paths in which human beings enter into the realm of religion. Subsequent writings elaborated a transcendental approach which was neither Cartesian nor

Kantian but, nonetheless, modern, one which emphasized the active affirmation of judgments about things rather than a mental photograph. They offered an alternative method for Catholic theology, one which sought to keep a balance between the drive toward specialization and a deeper theological program. Lonergan, however, left to others the application of his important ideas to specific areas of revelation and theology.[51]

Karl Rahner (1904–1984) emerged as the most important Catholic theologian after Vatican II (Yves Congar was the most important one prior to the Council). Rahner's Jesuit education made him knowledgeable in the thought of Aquinas (his doctoral dissertation in philosophy *Spirit in the World* related a few articles in the *ST* to issues in modern philosophy). His studies with Maréchal and Heidegger exposed him to the latest directions within modern philosophy in this century. Of the attitude of young Germans in the 1930s he wrote: "We read the works of Thomas: we allowed him to alert us to certain problems, but ultimately we approached him with our own questions and problems. And so we didn't really practice a Thomistic scholasticism but tried to maintain toward him a stance comparable to that toward Augustine, Origen, and other great thinkers. . . . And I think that a similar relation to Thomas would be advisable also for the present generation of theologians."[52] Scholasticism ("school-theology") meant to Rahner three things: (1) the theology taught in seminary classrooms from 1880 to 1960; (2) forms of neo-scholasticism in the nineteenth and twentieth centuries; (3) the theology found in seminary textbooks after 1850. This boring, abstract, and static theology addressed no vital theoretical or pastoral issues. Rahner rejected the idea that there was only one way of looking at reality, a neo-scholastic way, or that the thought of Aquinas meant a war with the motifs of modernity. He wrote of new directions:

> In the middle of the present century a profound change took place in Catholic theology. Neo-scholasticism had been dominant until that time; its mentality had an effect on the methods in the historical branches of theology as well as on exegesis and the writing of church history. It was essentially an ecclesiastical science which preferred to use Latin; by and large it had its established, clearly defined canon of topics and problems promulgated throughout the world.

Neo-scholasticism resolutely worked within the framework of these topics but rarely considered that its methodology was questionable. . . . One tried to live as far as possible in an ecclesial autarchy.[53]

New theologies should replace the neo-scholasticism dominant between 1850 and 1950. "The new theology must not view neo-scholasticism as the defeated predecessor which it can simply leave behind. This past history is likewise a reality whose values are to be acquired anew. . . . On the other hand, despite spasmodic efforts, there can be no return to neo-scholasticism."[54] Rahner, however, went ahead; he did not just repeat Aquinas but employed some central theses of Aquinas' theology to express Christianity in modern thought-forms and to address contemporary problems of society and church.

Rahner was first and foremost a theologian, a theologian of originality and expertise. He was also a gifted philosopher, a keen observer of the history of doctrine, and a masterful presenter of Christianity in terms of contemporary issues. A first book *Hearers of the Word* pondered the conditions in the individual—analogous discourse, personal contact, freedom, historicity, and openness to religion—which would both condition and enable a revelation from God. Catholicism can develop a theology in dialogue with modernity, and modern theology need not always be fashioned in a liberal Protestant mode where the forms absorb revelation's message.

> We must say that the epoch-making situation of today demands a framework and method which are transcendental and anthropological. Plato, Aristotle and Thomas will remain sources of our learning. But that does not change the fact (even if this fact has only been recognized by thinkers in the Catholic Church for about forty years) that philosophy and theology today cannot remain back before the transcendental-anthropological turn of modern philosophy. . . . An inner ambiguity marks not just modern philosophy but human life (and so, philosophy) at all times. But this should not keep us from seeing how Christianity will relate to this historical epoch of modernity which is itself a moment in Christian philosophy and theology.[55]

By 1964 the Jesuit was lecturing on and composing something new and exceptional for Catholic theology in this century: a modern systematic theology, modern in the sense of proceeding from a subject analyzed transcendentally, existentially, and historically. While the subject does not fashion revelation, he or she is the place where revelation speaks. The human person with a culture, language, and temporality is the grammar, as Rahner put it, for the word of God. What we call revelation and grace are a special presence, silent and unexpressed but real, of the divine Triune God in its "self-communication" to men and women. Rahner's analysis of the individual man or woman is located in the midst of grace, grace as the divine life, as a personal subject who loves each individual in their temporality. The Trinity freely chooses to offer a deeper and future life, and for this goal enters history, in God's incarnation in Jesus' Kingdom and Spirit. Revelation discloses, faith ponders, grace shares, and liturgy realizes God's life, radical mystery in history. Reflecting Heidegger, Rahner understood how time brought to every form and idea a cultural context and how history enabled sacraments and theologies to emerge into the light of human encounter. Grace is the theme of Rahner's theological system just as grace was an underlying theme of Aquinas' *ST*. Rahner's divine self-communication is not unrelated to Aquinas' Trinitarian missions, while the concrete, intimate offer of grace to all in the depths of their conscious life (the "supernatural existential") is a variation on the *ST*'s supernatural order selected by God. A transcendental approach to grace vivifying sacraments resembles Aquinas' view of the new law of Christ as the Spirit of Jesus, as well as his theology of faith as a grasp of divine First Truth. In short, the idealist distinction of transcendental and categorical was central in Rahner's theology, whether it was treating the essential message of Jesus' reign of God among religious customs or the historical chain of liturgical and ecclesiastical forms.

Edward Schillebeeckx (1914–) is a Belgian Dominican and long-time professor at Nijmegen in the Netherlands. In his years of philosophy in the Dominican *studium* he had as one of his teachers, Dominic de Petter. That Flemish philosopher had been working on a synthesis between Thomism and the phenomenology of Husserl, an enterprise which showed how theology could incorporate an anthropological dimension as well as taking into account the development of doctrine. At Le Saulchoir, Schillebeeckx "met the greats. . . . Under the guidance of Chenu I read St. Thomas from a historical perspective and not just literally, but in the context of the philosophy of the time.

I learned to tackle a problem from a historical perspective."[56] In the milieu of Parisian Thomisms, he could attend the lectures of Gilson and write a doctorate under Chenu. Schillebeeckx found in Aquinas intuition as well as logic; a dynamic understanding of personality led to a comprehension of symbols as active; realism and the individual did not remain with the subject but moved into history. In 1957 he wrote an essay about aspects of the theology of the medieval Dominican which still has a particular relevance for today: for instance, the various meanings of authority and the role of past sources in reflection on revelation, faith as act as well as content, the affective side of theology. "It is always instructive to find out how great theologians went to work in their own time, not in order to imitate them, but so that we may also do independently in our own time what they did in theirs."[57] An important book from the period just before Vatican II described the sacraments as encounters with Jesus Christ, with the living God present in matter. Aquinas' theology of sacrament implies that the first, primal sacrament is Jesus Christ. His incarnation continues the depth-sacramentality of the church and flows into specific sacraments and rites. Those ideas would appear in the conciliar documents. Phenomenology helped Schillebeeckx' explain the humanity of Jesus as the presence of the Word of God. What the ancient metaphysics of "person" guarded for the Word did not deny what modern philosophies and psychologies would have described as the personality of Jesus of Nazareth.[58] Serving the bishops at Vatican II as a theological adviser, Schillebeeckx spoke there on the relationship of theology to the Bible, on Aquinas as an important but not unique voice from tradition, on salvation-history, and on the nature of church authority. In recent years he has turned to an examination of topics in the theology of ministry today, and, in a multi-volume study of Jesus Christ and salvation, to a more direct confrontation between the New Testament and social issues. In this later theology, by his own admission one which leaves behind earlier Thomistic and phenomenological foundations, Schillebeeckx now incorporates insights from contemporary discussions on hermeneutics and critical theory.

VII. Neo-Thomism in the United States

What was the history of Thomism in North America from 1880 to 1960? It certainly had a dominant, almost monopolistic presence in the Catholic Church in the United States, while Canada was open to European, particularly French, developments. By 1930 Gilson had arrived in North America and institutes of medieval studies were underway in Toronto, Quebec, and Montreal. If it lacked any significant creative development, nevertheless, as McCool points out, in the years before 1960 neo-scholastic thought made a contribution to American Catholic education.[59] Seminary professors were educated in Rome or at the Catholic University of America, and journals focusing on scholasticism were begun. Then, after World War II, as Catholic colleges and universities expanded, neo-Thomism's positive, clear, and realistic world-view had an impact at schools like Fordham University, St. Louis University, the University of Notre Dame, Catholic University, and De Paul University in Chicago. A few professors were aware of the diversity of neo-Thomisms, and they welcomed the thought of a Gilson or a Maritain and had some knowledge of transcendental currents in Europe. Most schools, however, were obedient to the Vatican politique of not straying from the all too clearly marked borders of a general neo-scholastic philosophy. Seminaries (a great deal of philosophy and theology existed in seminaries), of course, had as their purpose not to be centers of intellectual life but to provide more and more priests for an expanding number of parishes. To be a priest in America was to minister to the sacramental and moral life of people and not to ponder American democracy or the culture of modernity. Seminaries and houses of studies of religious congregations cultivated a mechanical Aristotelianism isolated not only from the imagined threat of pantheism but from American social life. One can find a record of American neo-Thomism by looking at the contents of neo-scholastic journals of that time. They rarely touch on theology but reconsider aspects of Thomist and Aristotelian ethics or metaphysics. Thomist philosophy (but not theology) was seen by some as offering an integrating force for Catholic culture. Certainly its realism, dynamism, and positive view of humanity, as well as the inclusion of God offered a different perspective from those of the philosophy departments of secular universities. But the success of this cultural view, whose potential was great, could for several reasons only be quite limited. Its tone was apologetic and even arrogant; it seemed to be based on Vatican authority or on an antiquated logic and not on intellectual insight. Content with neo-scholastic problems, it rarely expressed philosophy's relationship to Christianity or Catholicism in America.

Neo-Thomism by and large stayed a philosophical enterprise. Occasionally scholars employed Aquinas in some field beyond the issues of natures and causes, for instance, in social ethics, but the lack of education and the obedient stance of the American immigrant church prior to the late 1950s discouraged intellectual initiative. The Dominicans in a Chicago suburb established a center for the study of Aquinas and modern science, while the Jesuits in St. Louis pursued Aquinas and epistemology. Neither succeeded in contacting many in the worlds of education or science. Neo-scholasticism, however, did bring some benefits to this multi-national church whose interests were life rather than ontology. McCool notes: "Catholic philosophy, associated with the scholastic tradition of Thomas, gave Catholic schools a realistic epistemology and a metaphysics of man and being which fostered the integration of knowledge which Catholic education often proposed as the aim justifying its institutional existence."[60] But this must be qualified by recognizing how few Catholic schools presented neo-Thomism rather than some neo-scholastic variation and how few found a pedagogy for this philosophy which was at all interesting.

In the 1950s American Catholicism, moving beyond its immigrant condition, developed a modest, alternative Catholic intellectual life. Magazines such as *Commonweal* and *Jubilee* gave some information on European thinkers like Romano Guardini and Jean Daniélou or on monastic liturgy and modern church art. Figures like John La Farge, Dorothy Day, Sister Madeleva, or Thomas Merton did not express themselves on American social issues in scholastic abstractions. Their success in reaching a broad audience flowed from their development of theologies in other keys. The few educated and culturally open directions in American Catholicism were evidently seeking ways around the neo-scholastic monopoly. The eve of Vatican II, then, found the American church conducting an industry of collegiate and clerical neo-scholasticisms which made no claim to influence parish or society, but also containing a small group of men and women with intimations of other approaches to Christianity.

Around the world, neo-Thomism was a spectrum of schools and opinions, drawn from different countries and cities, religious orders and universities. From Maynooth to Nairobi, it had made Aquinas' thought known. The third neo-Thomism had lasted about a century, from 1860 to 1960. It attained its widest international audience just as the Council began. At that time Aquinas' thought existed in five modes: (1) largely philosophical and isolationist neo-Thomisms; (2) historical research on Aquinas; (3) tentative applications of Thomism to ethical and political issues; (4) dialogues between Aquinas and post-Kantian philosophers; (5) reconsiderations of supernatural grace present in human history. This spectrum of offerings ranged from Chenu's conviction that the historical context of Aquinas would reveal his genius to Garrigou-Lagrange's lack of interest in a historical context, from a neo-Thomist manual's description of "idealism" as the denial of extra-subjective objects in knowledge[61] to Rousselot's (and Heidegger's) knowledgeable dialogue with Kant. McCool writes: "Neo-Thomism was not imposed on the church by the sheer exercise of power; it managed to win a good measure of legitimacy on its own merits. Nevertheless, like every intellectual movement, Neo-Thomism had a limited life span. Neo-Thomism was accused of blindness to the claims of history; and once the problems posed to the church by history became all-important, Neo-Thomism had to yield its place to the newer theologies which claimed that they could handle them."[62] Nevertheless, although little known in the English-speaking Catholic churches throughout the world, the European renewal, the extensive body of articles and books by historians like Grabmann and Chenu or by theologians like Congar or Rahner, was developing further implications of Aquinas. Thus the twentieth century produced a renewal of Thomism—one of unusual depth and breadth—but it was not the triumph of apologetics and ontology that many had expected. The Council would create an atmosphere in which theological education would rapidly extend to young and old, clergy, religious, and laity. Thereby it would expand the role of Aquinas through the pluralism of theologies active at Vatican II.

VIII. Aquinas, Theology, and Vatican II

Since Vatican II a number of German theologians have observed that passing beyond neo-scholasticism and going back to biblical and patristic sources and forward to theologies of history and personality was the most important challenge to the Catholic Church in the twentieth century. Karl Rahner expressed the shift in this way: "The new theology [of Vatican II] is conversant with modern philosophy since Descartes and Kant. It sees modern philosophies not simply as the enemy to be opposed, as they were for traditional neo-scholasticism, but rather—without compromising its own individuality or shunning critical dialogue with these philosophies— purely and simply as the index of that milieu in which a Christian must live and critically discern how to be a Christian. More than in the past the new theology is consciously affected by the concrete questions of the present-day individual . . ."[63] For the neo-Thomists Aquinas had answered every question so rapidly that little by little there was no longer any need for inquiry. But for the historical and transcendental Thomists, Aquinas' thought was challenged to disclose its depths, the depths of a theology which had lived through seven centuries and which might still respond to the problems and life-forms of the twentieth century. In the 1960s a new ecumenical direction stepped forth: studies appeared on Aquinas and Protestant figures, comparisons with Martin Luther, John Calvin, Paul Tillich, and Karl Barth showing similarities and differences. This ecumenical research dispelled many prejudices about a theologian often viewed as Pelagian or rationalist.[64] But as the writings of Otto Pesch showed so well, the thought-form of Aquinas was quite different from that of Luther. An emphasis upon grace as a new life, the divine principle as intellect, a sacramental and dynamic approach to theology and religion, creation and predestination and incarnation as the overflow of goodness, the positive view of humanity even fallen, the knowability and goodness of creation, the absence of fideism and voluntarism, the distinction between divine presence in creation and in the supernatural order retained the distinctive Catholic incarnationalism. As thinkers from Erich Przywara to Karl Barth have observed, the original and permanent ecumenical issue is the relationship of divine grace to human nature.[65]

Perhaps the very spirit of Aquinas was urging his followers to break out of their prison of dry interpretations and was prompting the historical and transcendental Thomists to go forward. Certainly the medieval Dominican's own vision of divine wisdom, of analogous realms of universe and grace resembled that of the theologians who fashioned the documents of Vatican II which permitted the Catholic Church to live in its own age and on a scale which was international.

A human cultural movement is reaching its high point even as, unperceived, the cultural forces of its decline are already at work. The largest Gothic cathedrals were completed as their medieval era had passed its cultural climax. Similarly, the opening of Pope John XXIII's ecumenical council in 1962 occurred within a church which on the surface was united through a monoform international network of canon law, neo-scholasticism, and papal centralism. But that was also a church in which dozens of creative minds were working to interpret the gospel anew. In 1946 Jean Daniélou surveyed the state of theology, and he concluded that the neo-scholastic monopoly gave "the impression of absence and unreality."[66] It avoided the challenge to treat God as God and did not speak to the modern person living in a world of science, nor did it describe meaningfully Christian life within the struggles of human existence and a free society. From this and from many other calls for biblical and pastoral theologies in the French church at this time a "new theology" was born. Theology rediscovered the Christian world-views of the early Eastern and Western churches, pursued biblical studies, accepted ecumenism, developed the schools of spirituality past and present, and conversed without hostility with modern and contemporary philosophies. Was Latin neo-Thomism to be the sole means of expression for a universal church in council in 1962? Otto Pesch speaks of neo-Thomism holding "Thomas Aquinas under house arrest" prior to 1962 and of the period around the Council as a reversal "from Thomism to Thomas."[67] Imbibing the spirit of Aquinas' theology of grace in human spirit, the Council looked positively on the aspirations of the world, on the religions of humanity, and on the quests of all people of good will. The church again conversed with its religious past and its human future.

Did Aquinas contribute to the deliberations of the Council? A comparison between Vatican II and the two previous councils, Trent and Vatican I, is illuminating. As we saw, remaining above the quarrels of theological schools, Trent borrowed fundamental ideas from the medieval schoolmen. Vatican I drew only on a general scholastic language to express its ideas on faith, revelation, and human reason. Vatican II, however, broke with both these approaches; it expressed its theology and pastoral renewal in biblical and modern theological terms. The Council of the 1960s showed the same attitude of selective employment toward Aquinas that it adopted vis-à-vis other theologies within that living tradition which is the church. By incorporating biblical, patristic, and liturgical sources, the Council professed a faith in the Spirit at work in each age. To renew the local church, however, the Council needed new plans, new languages, and new ideas. This obviously meant much more than neo-scholasticism. Nevertheless, in the conciliar years it was obvious that Aquinas had inspired the great theologians like Henri de Lubac, Chenu, Congar, John Courtney Murray, Rahner, and others.

The Brazilian theologian Jose Pinto de Oliveira holds that Vatican II gave Aquinas' theology the opportunity to return to its basic principles and to reestablish a theological breadth. A positive view of humanity and an optimism toward God assisted the Council to lead the church into the world around it. "To connect Aquinas' doctrine with all of tradition as a rallying point and not as a rupture, and to extol his method and his spirit as an incitement to research and to dialogue in the church within different forms of culture—this is essentially the practice and orientation of the Council."[68] The mission of the Spirit, the law of the Gospel, liberty at the heart of faith, the anticipation in justice of eschatology, the intuitive side of grace, Christ as the head of the human race—these were aspects of Aquinas' theology which neo-Thomism had not much employed. They became productive, however, in that springtime which the Council initiated in the church and the world. In short, the role of the Spirit in the life of the church and in the history of peoples gave the principles of the *ST* a new vigor and put them to work. *Gratia perficit naturam*—Vatican II re-emphasized a grace active in society where humanity, church, and liturgy were sacramental under the aegis of the Incarnate Word.[69]

IX. Beyond Vatican II

The effect of the Second Vatican Council upon Thomism, however, seemed to be a disaster. The world-wide neo-scholastic monopoly collapsed after 1965. Aquinas' influence was reduced, as contemporary or biblical theologies replaced neo-scholasticism. The theocentric order of his thought as well as the Aristotelian conceptuality pushed his writings into the background of a Catholic life intent upon experimentation and inculturation.

In 1974 Pope Paul VI, on the occasion of the seventh centenary of Aquinas' death issued a commemorative letter. The pope spotlighted the realism and objectivity of his thought, a thought which both respects and reaches towards the mystery of God, a theology which

stands between the false options of naturalism and fideism, which is
"opposed to every exaggerated supernaturalism."[70] Aquinas was not
an ideologue, the pope continued, and his theology was born out
of the "conditions of his culture" and followed a "dialectical"
method.[71] He appreciated the distinctions between free speculative
theology and the dogmas of the church. A suspicion of other theological traditions or of modernity is not the main reason for interest
in Aquinas. The emphasis upon activity, freedom, and subjectivity
furthers a mature understanding of God and of the human person.
That anniversary year of 1974, coming less than ten years after the
Council, displayed an interest in Aquinas which was beginning to
reassert itself as evidenced in the number of congresses and multi-
volume commemorative collections which appeared then.[72] Centers
of Thomism nourished by his theology more than by his
Aristotelianism with their publications continued. If there was an
understandable reaction, after a time of reservation interest in
Aquinas has again been growing. One of the paradoxes of the post-
conciliar period is that, despite the rapid decline which Vatican II
brought to neo-scholasticism, from the 1970s on abundant new
resources and studies have appeared. Recently a bibliography of
works on Aquinas issued during only the last two decades has been
published: it lists 3500 entries.[73] These range from the many volumes
of essays drawn from international congresses to the IBM *Index
Thomisticus.* The last decades of the twentieth century have been
marked by major studies by Ghislain Lafont, Albert Patfoort, Otto
Pesch, and Jean-Pierre Torrell. Their works are a crown and a conclusion to the vast research into Aquinas' thought in the twentieth
century.

❖ ❖ ❖

Aquinas reaches us through centuries and civilizations, and
through people and schools who understood and developed his ideas.
To look back on the history of this theology is to be struck by its
longevity and fecundity. Is this history of interpretations Thomism's
great accomplishment?

When one ponders this history threading its way through many
cultures, it is clear that, first, there was no single Thomism, no one
interpretation, but many. Second, this theology was not timeless but

culturally fashioned: it flourished in Salamanca in the sixteenth century and in Paris in the twentieth century as it faced new questions and found new ways of expressing a medieval synthesis. Third, one cannot be a disciple of Aquinas and think that some major cultural periods are intrinsically or mainly evil, or hold that one culture or age has monopolized intellect and grace.

Genius and idea express themselves in history, and historians are still sketching the history of Thomism with its responses to issues as diverse as the morality of war or the rise of labor unions. If one does not know something of this history, the student mistakes a particular interpretation for the source itself. For us in the West, scholars in medieval studies still help us understand the richness of the past, while we await new reconsiderations of Aquinas coming from Africa and Asia. Because Aquinas' thinking was a tireless dialogue with the largest number of resources, he would be awed and stimulated by today's possibilities for preaching, holiness, insight, and ministry in a world growing closer and a church growing larger.

5. Thomas Aquinas Today

————— ✛ —————

> The human being is a kind of boundary line of spiritual and corporeal creatures, existing in a horizon of eternity and time.
>
> *Summa contra gentiles*

The words of Thomas Aquinas filling the pages of his writings are much more than linguistic signs of abstract ideas lodged in an effortless logic. They intend to express and touch divine and human realities, and they hold an impetus to speak to people. The history of their influence just outlined displays their power to influence science and art, church and society.

I. Theology and Culture

Culture enables genius to shine forth, but culture often receives new life from creative spirits. Gifted painters or philosophers, far from escaping the intersection of their world and age, find that they live and work out of the worlds around them. A genius transcends time not by avoiding its forms and limits but by letting insight in materials and models create a world. Culture gave birth to Aquinas' theology, and culture for over seven hundred years has called forth different applications of his ideas. Early in this century the German medievalist Martin Grabmann reflected the opinion of many in noting, "Thomas is without doubt a particularly great researcher of culture, even in many areas excelling what Dante achieved." Aquinas gives to individual information coming from the classical and patristic life of culture a structure which organizes the data; second, both individual and society appear in this system within an affirmation of individuality in the totality of creation.[1] Aquinas did not compose a modern theory of cultural history. Nevertheless, because he was in contact with the movements of a great age, his ideas can be drawn out

201

as facets of a theology of culture. His basic perspectives are cultural principles: the goodness of creation, the generosity of the Creator in the power of creation, the independence of the orders of being and grace, the capability of word or symbol to disclose what is good or holy. As the beings of the cosmos are the messengers of their Creator, the forms of culture can become the sacraments of grace.

By the presence of Aquinas in culture we mean much more than his image in a painting or his books bound in leather. His theology has served as a religious horizon for politicians and novelists. Scholars tell us that they can see his influence in government constitutions, papal writings, or mystical narratives. For countless others, his way of thinking about the seen and the unseen reaches them directly through his writings or indirectly through their influence on Western Christianity and on the Catholic Church. Catechisms, sermons, textbooks, and the documents of bishops and popes have contained general directions derived from one Thomism or another. In the history of Catholicism the cultural streams of the Middle Ages and the Counter-Reformation as well as those of the Baroque and of the nineteenth and twentieth centuries have been channels of Aquinas' theology and influence. Aquinas' use of Aristotelian psychology in the thirteenth century helped find a place for theology in the new universities, while his approach to the interplay of grace and nature has in recent decades entered into the theologies and programs of Vatican II. If Dante made some of the Dominican's ideas serve as images for a panoramic journey in poetry, seven centuries later contemporary Thomists have seen how this theology leads to a positive evaluation of human religions. One reason for Aquinas' wide presence is that his theological interpretation of Christianity is profoundly incarnational, and Christianity is a faith centered in incarnation. This chapter treats theology within cultural realms like psychology, politics, art, spirituality, church, and the world religions. These topics permit us to look again, from different perspectives, at great themes in Aquinas' theology.

In the Spanish Chapel at the Dominican priory of Santa Maria Novella in Florence there is a large painting from the fourteenth century which shows Aquinas holding his *Summa theologiae*. He is seated amid women and men like the Muses or Euclid, representing the humanities and sciences. The painting presents through the figures, including Thomas, a synthetic wisdom looking at all of creation, a love of beauty, and a human cultural community. Albert the Great noted how arts could lead to truth: "Whatever other holy comparisons might be drawn in, for instance, out of forms and pictures, they exist not as deceptions but as introductions into truth . . . and they use all kinds of images to depict God."[2] Aquinas' theology does not demand a choice between God and creation nor does it mistrust the self or presume that every story has a tragic ending. His ideas and conclusions, far from being an academic game of theories, reach into the new even as they nourish the past's respect for being and beauty. As an artist makes preliminary drawings on the pages of a sketchbook for a later painting, the following pages would trace a few facets of contemporary life which Aquinas' principles might address and inspire.

A. PSYCHOLOGY

The *Summa contra gentiles* observes that the human being lives on the boundary between spirit and cosmos, eternity and time.[3] Aquinas' theology is very much a psychology: the incarnation, sacraments, morality, and grace emerge within an anthropology and a psychology. For the thirteenth century the latest analysis of personality was the psychology of Aristotle. Because creation mirrors the intelligence and goodness of God's being, the human race despite its bloody history is at every moment full of potentialities for invention, creativity, and holiness. Thomas Merton wrote:

> The theology of St. Thomas is a theology of intellectual reconciliation, which, instead of maintaining itself in existence by the insistence on those opposites which create problems, justifies itself by uniting opposites and looking beyond the stereotyped solution of problems. This archetypal reconciliation was present in his own vocation which, as he lived it, told him daily that the confrontation of apparently irreconcilable opposites presented no problem at all. One could love and serve God in the city, teaching Christian clerks from the book of a pagan philosopher.[4]

People are wonderfully gifted: they can reach the cosmos by mathematical equations or turn blue and gold stones into mosaics. The free, active, knowing person is the image of God.

While Aquinas intended his theology to be centered dynamically on God, there is an anthropocentric dimension to it. The First Part of the *ST* concludes with the arrival of the human person. The remaining two Parts are centered on the dialogue of the human personality with created grace, and the metaphysical conversation of Jesus of Nazareth with uncreated grace. The supernatural order itself exists to serve the human race so that humanity in several ways might glorify God. This positive view of the human personality explains why, as long as psychotherapies do not become irreligious ideologies (as once with Freud), psychologies are congenial to the Catholic mind. Catholicism in the latter decades of the twentieth century admitted various psychologies into moral theology, spirituality, education for ministry, and pastoral theology. Moreover, healthy psychologies are the stimuli and the inner framework of spiritualities. For instance, the theories of Jung have been applied to Carmelite spirituality, itself born of experience, Scripture, and Thomism. There is nothing to fear from knowing yourself. The knowing and loving person is a special creation into whom the Spirit of grace enters. The voice of the honest self is a voice of human nature about freedom and love, and it can bring messages from the one God. In the *ST* Aquinas explored the healthy personality at length.

A bright emphasis upon human potential did not deny widespread, debilitating influences from original sin. But the metaphor for the fallen human condition chosen by Aquinas was not slavery or death but illness. Whatever its source or name, that personal debilitation has its own psychological dimensions. The sinful condition which weakens the human race is manifest in a lack of harmonious interaction between emotions, judgment, and will power. A homiletics of hated humans judged by a wrathful God or the ugliness and pride of every enterprise is the opposite of Aquinas' theology, as is a religion of failure, willfulness, and meanness. The human personality, even if it is prompt to sin, begins and remains the recipient of the offer of grace. Sin as a personal action flows from complex degrees of freedom and culpability. Strictly speaking, Aquinas observed, only that seriously violent and disordered action born of calculating freedom deserves the name of sin. Personal sin is the rejection of human as well as graced life, and that occurs in a psychological world.

Original sin and personal sins are not the only legacy of the fallen human condition at work within people: emotional illnesses too can pose an obstacle to grace. Those distortions of nature, freely chosen and habitually assumed over time become the tyrants of the personality, blocking grace just as they block human life. Neurosis can to a lesser or greater degree impede the exercise of virtuous choice. God's grace moves in secret and mysterious ways, but compulsions and self-centeredness, anxiety and depression will hamper it. Pathology diminishes freedom and reduces sinful culpability. Indeed, the addictive or self-absorbed personalities prevalent today are present in Aquinas' analysis of men and women held by the tenacious negative habits he called vices. When he pursued in detail the psychology of disordered human enterprises, he described their various forms not first as passing actions but as the malformations of the personality. They were engendered by repeated bad acts and became the source of sin. By contrast, a positive and energetic psychology describes a self capable of responding to hope, love, and grace (or however one names the presence of God). By nature and grace the image of God can dissipate debilitating, enclosed religion and counters authoritarianism and elitism with their accompanying cults of failure and fear. Grace as a new life principle, Aquinas concluded, enables the actions of a citizen of the reign of God to be spontaneous and enjoyable (I–II, 110, 2).

For Aquinas, each individual personality is a direct creation of God, a loved existence, and each one awaits a further presence of grace. Evidently God is not first of all condemnatory or hostile. An Aristotelian psychology plays a positive role here. Each personality is endowed with the proper actions of their own life, and, as grace is a life-principle, the individual's Christian life must ultimately be just that—a life. Grace reaches an individual through her personality, and her sanctity will reveal itself out of her own psychological terrain. Responsibility and commitment come first from within the person and not just from religious imperatives which are no more than obedience to an authority, to a text, or to a vision. Merton's moving prose unfolds in metaphors a Thomist theology of grace and personality.

> The seeds that are planted in my liberty at every moment, by God's will, are the seeds of my own identity, my own reality, my own happiness, my own sanctity. For me to be a saint means to be myself. Therefore the problem of sanctity and salvation is in fact the problem of finding out who I am and of discovering my true self. . . . The secret of my identity is hidden in the love and mercy

of God. Therefore there is only one problem on which all my existence, my peace and my happiness depend: to discover myself in
discovering God. . . . But although this looks simple, it is in reality
immensely difficult. In fact if I am left to myself it will be utterly
impossible. For although I can know something of God's existence
and nature by my own reason, there is no human and rational way
in which I can arrive at that contact, that possession of Him which
will be the discovery of Who He really is and of Who I am in Him.[5]

The God who creates me and who offers redeeming grace are one, and
my personality has its own geography of vocation and identity. Thus
Merton can offer the unusual idea that my identity, reality, happiness,
and sanctity are familiarly related, all being offspring of nature and
grace.

Religious enthusiasm is not the same as the quest for freedom or
the life-long dialogue with divine grace. The presence of Word and
Spirit are antidotes to the idolatry of things and to the elitism of con-
trolling God, characteristics of every fundamentalism. This psychology of grace is, as we stressed earlier, the opposite of every religiosity
born of compulsion and anxiety, and of every ideology offering legalism and oppression.

B. ART

Aquinas drew upon the world of the arts in several ways. First, he
offered a brief theory of the beautiful and the practical arts. He also
used analogies drawn from artists and arts for theology: for instance,
God as artist, sacraments as signs, the illuminating power of light.
Finally there was a poetic side to his theological mind; he enjoyed the
varieties of discourse and elaborated the role of metaphor and allegory. Moreover, the friar composed poems for the liturgy.

His thought brought together ideas about art current in the 1200s.
The neo-Platonic tradition represented by the writings of Pseudo-
Dionysius affirmed a unity between the good and the beautiful: God
is the sublime consonance and luminosity behind being and truth.
Aquinas agreed that the beauty of creatures flows from the causal
action of God and bears a faint likeness to the beauty of God.[6] But
Aristotle's writings, too, offered a theory for understanding the char-
acteristics of a work of art: form, clarity, brilliance, and the striking

impact of a painted statue or of a play's ending. A third theoretician of aesthetics, Augustine, spoke of the suitability and proportion of parts in what was beautiful. Aquinas drew these three approaches together when he explained that a work of art—this might be a song or a mosaic but it might also be a well-made chair or cup—is a reality communicating to our senses and mind the ensemble of striking forms and characteristics. "Things are beautiful which when seen give pleasure" (I, 5, 4, 1).

Beauty is both objective and subjective: it is found in forms encountering human seeing, knowing, and hearing. Art is an illumination of senses and mind. What distinguishes artistic works is their sensual attraction. The work of art brings pleasure for the senses, meaning for the intellect, and emotion for the feelings. The colors, sounds, and words of the arts are so formed as to draw us intuitively to a depth of meaning within symbolic forms; they disclose the invisible in the visible. While it can shock with jagged incoherence or bizarre perversion, something formally ugly cannot be human art in its form or in its effects. Human creativity has great potential and countless options, but the art which links nature, intellect, and passion will not mock reality or dismiss the human. Although Aquinas had emphasized in the worlds of nature, existence, and grace the mirrored beauty of God, in a specific work of art he emphasized the beauty of this particular object. Art is paradoxical: on the one hand we get a glimpse of some reality as its stands momentarily apart from the flux of time, and, on the other hand, we have an intimation of some future fullness. What is fragmentary and passing points to more as it endures and shines. And ultimately there is "the beauty of truth."[7]

An artist is someone with talent and skill who can make things. The separation between the fine arts and other arts was not prominent in the Middle Ages, and Aquinas had in mind the saddle-maker as well as the sculptor. Art is the inspired application of correct knowledge within the realm of objects (I–II, 57, 3). In previous chapters we saw how Aquinas mentioned the Creator as an artist in the medieval sense of the term. God's art active in creation's array of beings proceeds not from a capricious will but from plan and order: "God produces his effects according to his wisdom."[8] Like the director of the entire fabric of a cathedral, the divine source is an architectonic artist. Beauty is particularly referred to the Word of the Triune God who as the image of the Father has a divine luminosity and a striking glory (I, 39, 8). Through creation God is seen to be beautiful, and the Trinity in its inner shared community of life is radiant. Both beauties are ours to share. Art leads to light: Aquinas, thinker of light, was a theologian for whom God has diffused light in various modes. The reality and the metaphor of light recur often in his writings. Light, suitability, and brilliance explained an aesthetics of stone or symbol. Like the light playing over the Italian hill country or the light streaming in through the windows of French churches, God as sub-sistent Being is the source of countless modalities and entities which are lights existing out of a darkness of non-being. Parallel to the sun giving light and illumining things, God bestows grace and revelation, participations in further divine light. Grace is a light which vitalizes the personality and illumines consciousness with faith, with richer understanding, and with discerning prudence.

An incarnational theology inevitably has an aesthetic distinction. Incarnation brings the Word of God who is wisdom and beauty into the matter of a human life. Christ is the icon of God even as he is the head of the human race moving through history. In religious symbols, sacraments and rites, color and movement make the divine present. Art, Aquinas wrote, had been introduced into the church at an early date for three reasons: to teach the basic truths of faith; to present through pictorial forms the incarnation of the Word in Jesus and the lives of the saints as examples for us; and finally to stimulate devotion, for seeing is more powerful than hearing.[9]

Imagining God as an artist throws some light on the knotty, un-solvable problem of the relationship of Creator to creation. Christian and Greek thinkers have stressed the distance, the disparity in being or goodness between the Infinite and the finite. And yet an analogical bridge of concepts drawn from infinitely faint but real facets reaches from the beings of the universe to the divine act which began those primal elements of hydrogen and oxygen. Is the Creator modified by creation? We might ask, Does the artist find joy, fulfillment in the production of the play? Certainly. But the colors of the painting or the acts of the play do not in a significant way surprise or extend the artist. She has already conceived out of many options every detail. So it is with God. Creation and history do glorify God but human achievements, lives and cultures, events born of good or divinely per-mitted evil, do not surprise the Godhead.

A work of art is produced by intelligence, planning, and instinct.

A poem is fired by the desire to share experience, and a sonata bears the stamp of the composer: both are the gifts of the depths of talent. Paying attention to the subjective side of a work of art, Aquinas located art in the personality where talent, emotion, and intuition meet. Art is not a completely rational affair but flows from the intuitive side of a personality. Like the athlete or the loving parent or the saint,[10] the artist not only thinks and sees but feels and touches and suffers. Aquinas noted how mind, will, and emotions together "mutually contain one another" (I, 16, 4, 1), and how through interaction they experience and create. Artistic knowing is knowing—but it is a knowing of intuition and insight. Insight contacts directly what is loved; intuition engenders a supra-rational, perceptive oneness with what is known. "Loving draws us out to things more than knowing does" (I–II, 22, 2). Intuition is fired by emotion and love, and this kind of knowledge comes through feelings. Aquinas explained insight and artistic understanding through the ecstasy of sympathy and empathy. Through likeness a union emerged, a "connaturality." Love and enjoyment make similar the knower and the known or the lover and the loved (II–II, 32, 3). The artist is one with the object of art. By loving the beautiful in objects, he has a feeling for how to work and how to make, and so the maker lives out of sympathy with the artistic endeavor.

Abilities—mathematical or artistic or athletic—flow from heredity and cultivation. In art Aquinas kept distinct the realms of life and grace. Artistic talents emerge from their proper psychological realm and are not bestowed by grace or removed by sin. The contours of a personality with its talents and limitations come from nature, from genes and education. While a moral life will enhance the conditions of any human endeavor, and while the Christian faith will open windows to a real interplay between grace and sin, still grace and moral behavior do not produce great talent. Prayer will not transform an average musician into a second Beethoven, nor will reading the Bible change a poor painter into a Monet. Personality and the presence of divine grace influence each individual, but natural gifts have their own independence and power. Since sin and vice cripple the personality, they may also impede creativity, but, as the history of the arts shows, promiscuity and meanness do not terminate talent.

In a very modest way Aquinas was an artist. The *ST* embracing countless ideas and quotations has not only order but symmetry. He paid attention to etymologies, to literary genres, and even to the symbolism of numbers.[11] There are aphoristic insights like the view that "faith moves toward the highest truth while hope is drawn to the most majestic power," or that creatures have been given "the gift of being a cause."[12] His theological themes or the forms linking sections are in their way beautiful. But order and attractiveness do not mean that his theology is an aesthetic theology. It is far too much an exposition of realities to be such. The theologian became the poet as he composed the texts for the liturgy of the monastic office and the public Eucharist for the feast of Corpus Christi. For that he had to write antiphons and arrange selected readings. He wrote a number of hymns whose images and Latin rhymes have through the centuries inspired many: *"Tantum ergo sacramentum, veneremur cernui"* ("Bowing low, we venerate so great a sacrament"). Andreas Speer thinks that Aquinas' subjective, experiential appreciation of art did not emerge from aesthetic theories but from the liturgy. The liturgy mediates and brings to life in symbol and action the architecture of the cathedrals and abbeys. Aquinas' poems, metaphors, and hymns have stirred the spirits of men and women crowded into those mystical spaces decorated by works of art.[13]

We can see facets of Aquinas' theology of human activity amid grace and sin in the poems of John of the Cross or Gerard Manley Hopkins. Or under masks of sin and irony in the novels of Graham Greene and Flannery O'Connor. We can hear a certain happy striving for the disclosure of the holy in composers like Francis Poulenc and Olivier Messiaen. In the arts, human actions receive or flee grace, and the forces of evil, though powerful, are never predestined or fixed. Neither the divine nor the human is incoherent or sensational. Inevitably an ordinariness in life and grace provides the framework for art as it does for theology.

The goal of the artist's talent is to provide insight into the world of nature and of human culture. Ultimately art is a creation not a destruction, and the aesthetic experience is a discovery, an acceptance of a revelation. The intuitive energy of the human personality is also important for Aquinas' theology of prayer, contemplation, and mysticism. The genial and emotional sharing-in-being, the connaturality which characterized the creative artist is related to the mystics, for the contemplative's prayer is intuitive, a knowing empowered by love (III, 7, 2, 2; 45, 4).

C. SPIRITUALITY

A spirituality is a theological psychology. A person selects and arranges certain teachings from within the Christian faith. Men and women fashion a view of self, world, and church, in short, a theology of Jesus Christ which appeals to them. In mystics and prophetic social activists, in popularly revered saints and in founders of religious orders, we meet striking individuals who have fashioned their personal theology, that is, a spirituality. The word "spirituality," meaning a personalized and applied faith, is rather recent. Aquinas did not use the term in the modern sense; he employed it for the spiritual side of our life, faculties higher than carnal desire; only a few times did he mean the Spirit's life in us, the life of grace.[14] History and psyche create a spirituality: a theology realized in prayer, a personal arrangement of gospel truths and powers, a pattern of belief stimulated by one's own times. In different countries and times there appear individuals whose personal interpretation of the gospel appeals to others; its receptivity in other men and women reflects similar experiences with the gospel. A spirituality, whether Cistercian or Carmelite, can attract followers into a religious order, into the monastery or school of the founder. Patterns of prayer or ministry—one thinks of the followers of Charles de Foucauld or Dorothy Day—can also draw Christians to serve society. A psychologically oriented age, whether in the Baroque or in the contemporary period, is particularly interested in spiritualities: in finding in them ways of praying and in their techniques of meditation.

A spirituality influences and survives only when it attracts followers, kindred spirits in several cultures over centuries. Christianity is so rich that it can be active in many spiritualities: in varied journeys and world-views born of different times. Spiritualities exemplify, as do politics and art, theology become concrete. Aquinas' teaching, with the assistance of the large family of Dominican men and women, spread far. It touched the Rhenish Dominican mystics like Johannes Tauler and inspired a popular preacher like Johannes Nider. In the fourteenth century Catherine of Siena and John Dominici took theological principles and personal experience and put them into movements of reform. In Spain during the sixteenth century innovative founders of religious communities like the Jesuits of Ignatius Loyola or the Carmelites of Teresa of Avila and John of the Cross drew from Aquinas. In the birth of spiritual schools in France in the seventeenth century, Pierre de Bérulle was the spiritual director for men and women founding schools of prayer and religious congregations, and he too read Aquinas. In the pastoral renewal of the French church in the 1950s leading to Vatican II or in the writings of Edith Stein or Gerald Vann one can see the spiritual theology of Aquinas.

A great theology is simultaneously theoretical and practical; it is a way of seeing Christianity and it is a way of living. Healthy theology overflows into spirituality, and vice versa. In Friar Thomas of Aquino we find a professor who is holy, a theologian who is a saint. The principles of Aquinas' spirituality are the same as those of his theology: presence of the Trinity, human life, a universe of actions, revelation and grace realized in individual faith and love. We saw how, as Thomas became an adult, his life pursued a rather courageous and independent quest for God and theology, and for people and ministry and teaching. In Ulrich Horst's words, "Thomas Aquinas in all the important stages of his scholarly career treated questions which resulted from his thinking about the ideal of evangelical poverty and of discipleship to Jesus and the Apostles."[15] His mature works examine the following of Christ in light of the Gospels and the traditions of great theologians. They balance poverty with effective ministry, and external religious practice with an honest and modest inner orientation of the individual spirit to God.[16] His prayer and theology sought God through knowledge and faith as these flowed through emotions and love. His writings were the gift and the documentation of his spiritual life; teaching and writing were not only ministry but worship. Aquinas wrote almost nothing about retreats, techniques of meditation, or kinds of mystical visions. In the Middle Ages Christian spirituality did not separate theology from considerations of Christ, morality, or the liturgy. Christian reflection and life was a totality, and the narratives of Scripture or the theological interpretations of a sacrament fed the spiritual life.

Through the centuries the Dominican school of commentators on Aquinas has tried to retain his view that theology is spirituality, and that spirituality is more than ascetic practices or guides for stages of meditation. Aquinas treated daily life and the life of prayer within considerations of God, Jesus Christ, grace, and human life. Because his perspective affirms the goodness of creation and the incarnation of grace, his theology has empowered political theologies and mystical spiritualities suitable for different types of men and women. Chenu writes: "In an abusive way both the Reformation and the Renaissance, and also the origins of modernity have, in our view, torn asunder the central issue—humanity and the grace of God—from its varied realization in different spiritualities. Thomas Aquinas is the spiritual master of a conception of grace and of nature, and their conjuncture is sharply illumined out of its original juxtaposition but also the conception of each holds its own particular truth."[17]

Some prominent directions of spirituality are opposed to a Thomist theology of the spiritual life. They insist on a fissure between the secular and the sacred, on a depiction of mysticism as extraordinary, or they reduce Christian life to an obedience to the will of God or to the will of church leaders. Others offer a theater of religion resulting from God's whimsy or wrath, a severe and self-induced asceticism, or a reduction of the gospel to the cross. In Aquinas' theology of the human person as the image of God and the disciple of the law of love, holiness flows from a psychological maturity which draws on God's wisdom. Whatever forms of self-deprivation might be pursued they are always subservient to life. Before God as Wisdom and Love there is little room for blind obedience, pious but unrealistic intentions, or for seeking after suffering as an end in itself. Fleeing, then, any hint that the Christian life is cramped, masochistic, or unrealistic, this theology does not support religious groups calling for the sacrifice of reason, talent, or individuality to authorities. It does not encourage a fearful passivity before a capricious will of God. Suffering is an evil: the climax of Jesus' life is not the cross but his teaching and resurrection. A healthy human response to grace should not control or escape individuality through pious ideas or ecclesiastical machinery. Thomist spirituality is positive and dynamic; it is psychologically realistic; it enhances the individual. The experiences of a life (not ones sentimentally sketched in legends about some distant saint) will fashion the images and attractions of the divine.

A number of scholars have listed what they believe are basic lines in Thomas Aquinas' spirituality. Early in this century Martin Grabmann arranged it around the motifs of wisdom, charity, and peace, and then joined those three to the incarnation of Jesus Christ. Recently, Walter Principe has selected the themes of the value of each person as the image of God and the interior new law of the Spirit with its gifts. Principe also emphasizes the wholeness of the human being who is not a loosely joined duality of body and soul. The Christian life is not concerned solely with souls, now or in heaven, but with human beings whose sexuality, appetites, and emotions are facets of the personality touched by grace. God's will does not bypass my life but includes not only my intellect and faith but my emotions, my totality body and soul. All contribute to making ethical decisions and to living a spiritual life. If each personality is in its own way unique and if grace inspires human nature, God leads through, not apart from, my personality. "God in eternity is actively present here and now to help me find the divine will. It is here and now that I am to try to judge what is the best, the most just and loving thing to do."[18] As faith is deeper than propositions, so grace is more than religious observances. Principe concludes with a meditation on how Jesus Christ, as human being and savior, is present to all of human history. "We should seek to reflect on and discover the active presence and influence, usually hidden, of Jesus Christ, the Risen Lord, in all of Christian life and in all of human history. For Christ is Lord of the whole of human history and of our cosmos and its development. He intervenes not to destroy the good developments of the created order but rather to further its advancement until his final coming when his rule will be visible and will be explicitly recognized by all."[19]

Jean-Pierre Torrell traces a trajectory of Aquinas' spirituality from the Trinity to the human being living in the world. This spirituality is "a presentation of the totality of the realities of the gospel in a dynamic balance."[20] He finds its sources in the Bible (particularly in Paul, and in the gospels according to John and Matthew), in the liturgy, and in Augustine and Greek theologians. Thomistic spirituality, always possessed of a certain balanced objectivity, begins with active and free men and women, and with a profoundly influential grace. Its spiritual realism comes from the human spirit living in the world and in a body, and from the objectivity of creation and of divine grace. Creation is good and society calls for renewal; asceticism and detachment do not exist for themselves but for the engaged life of grace. Several themes from the theology of the *Gospel according to John* like worship in spirit and in truth and the life of the children of God are influential. This can also be called an ecclesial spirituality because it emphasizes people as social creatures and because it describes a new social status flowing from the leader of grace, the risen Christ. "If Christ's bodily weaknesses hide his divinity, still they reveal his humanity, and it is this humanity which is the way for us to arrive at divinity, as *Romans* says, 'We have access to God through Jesus Christ' [5:1f.]" (III, 14, 1, 4).

A person makes their theology concrete in his or her own life. Thomas' biographer noted that he was not only modest about his accomplishments but inevitably "gentle and courteous."[21] At home in the Dominican priory's library or arguing in a public disputation in Paris, Aquinas never lost the contemplative's affability or love of inquiry. His theology leads away from a religion of fear, neurosis, and ritual legalism. Like his own life, contemplation was a journey, and research a quest for truth. The ideas found in new books were uncovered in a search motivated by a hope for human virtue and by a love of the self-revealing God.

The spiritual life is vivified by prayer. Aquinas wrote on prayer and composed his own prayers. Prayer is an "ascent of the mind toward God" (II–II, 83, 13, 2) and not a list of events which we insist should happen in the future; prayer is a turning of one's attention to the God of grace, in suffering or in joy. Prayer is liturgical and personal, ecclesial and social. We pray for other people, they pray for us, and the communion of saints in heaven and on earth is united by prayer. Simon Tugwell writes: "The great achievement of Thomas in his treatise on prayer was to explain theologically both how prayer, in its traditional sense of petition, makes sense and how it is an authentic religious activity. He thereby shores up prayer, precisely in the sense in which all Christians are commanded to practice it. But at the same time he shows how unnecessary are a lot of the practical difficulties that people have claimed to find in prayer."[22] God is not an incomplete, suffering deity like Wotan, nor a watcher of human events like Jupiter. Compassionate and loving but transcendent in an infinity of joyous modes of being, God knows and wills all out of plans born of love. But, in our prayers are we true agents? How, Aquinas inquired, do we bring together the One who knows and influences the future and the one who prays for it? "In presenting the value of prayer we must neither impose a necessity upon human affairs subject to divine providence nor describe the divine disposition as mutable" (II–II, 83, 2). A difficult task. Aquinas suggested that

> divine providence does not merely arrange what effects are to occur; it also arranges the causes of those effects and the pattern by which

they occur. Among the many causes influencing human life, the actions of humans are causes of some events. So it is right for human beings to do certain things, not because through their actions they will change the divine disposition but because through their actions they will fulfill certain effects according to the plan of God. We do not pray in order to change God's plan but in order to obtain by our prayers those things which God planned to bring about by means of prayers. (II–II, 83, 2)

Living apart from time, God sees all things in the present. "In time, one thing is the indivisible, namely the instant, and something quite different is what has duration, namely time itself. But in eternity the now is indivisible and always perduring" (I, 42, 2, 4). This particular prayer and this life, within a delicate interplay of human freedom and divine influence, are real agents of what God plans and foresees, and what despite rebellious sin, he accomplishes.

Still, if prayer is not easy access to miracles, then why pray? The first answer we have already seen: God's knowing love includes our prayers within the divine plan. Aquinas wanted to explain how prayer in its traditional sense of petition—but petition to an all-powerful God—makes sense. His solution to this difficult problem involves our activity in our temporality.[23] Tugwell notes how, on the one hand, prayer is an exercise of our causality within the wider, guided realms of divine causality, and how, even as God respects our freedom, "asking God for something is intrinsically an act of worship . . . it is a sacrifice of our own planning minds to God."[24] We are invited to act through prayer, but within our communion with his Spirit, God remains God. A second reason for prayer is that it lifts up and empowers the person. Much of what is called "miraculous" or "extraordinary" in the imprecision of ordinary talk comes from the complex interplay of brain and spirit, personality and grace. Just as a mental attitude can further a physical illness, the power and hope of prayer can further human endeavors, whether those be the difficult exam or the dangerous operation. This view of prayer is clearly far removed from manipulating God or displaying self.

Prayer is making our life present to God, and it is unavoidable and human that prayers of petition emerge from the moments of our lives. We pray for what we and others need. The spiritual life begins with prayers petitioning God. Aquinas judged the *Lord's Prayer* to be "the most perfect of all prayers, giving form to all our inner aspirations" (II–II, 83, 9). Otto Pesch summarizes Aquinas' theology of prayer in this way: (1) human longing is the basic drive behind our prayer; (2) prayer is an interpretation of hope; (3) the "Our Father" gives form to prayer and hope; (4) in prayer one learns to trust God; (5) prayer is the human virtue for the path of life; (6) prayer gives a form to life.[25] Prayer is where personality and spirituality meet.

As it matures, prayer leads through meditation to contemplation. Contemplation, the pinnacle of human knowing and loving, is an intuitive, loving gaze on something. Contemplation meant for Aquinas not only the mysticism of a Carthusian nun but any quiet study of deep issues. Study, reading and prayer, the pondering of revelation and faith are contemplation.[26] The contemplative ponders out of calm and leisure the beautiful and the true. In contemplative prayer faith becomes an emotion-born insight into life within the Kingdom of God. Contemplation is a communion with God's love active in me, an intuition in faith empowered by love.[27] Mysticism for Aquinas— and for those schools of spirituality which follow him—does not involve extraordinary cures and visions but a prayer which is more and more simple, more and more intuitive. Mystical contemplation leaves images behind and rests darkly in the divine presence as God becomes both the subject and the object of praying. Prayer is not theology. Praying does not ordinarily give certain, explicit solutions to personal or social problems, and certainly it is not the preparation for a miracle. Prayer and solitude can be sweet, liturgy can move us to tears, because we are emotional creatures, and emotions and insight are accompanied by pleasure.[28] Ultimately prayer is an expression of the life of grace, while the ground of prayer is the personal, loving ground of all, God. Finally, contemplation leads to truth but also to ministry. On earth the divine love which fuels a contemplative love also leads us to go out of ourselves into the world. Since prayer is love, it suggests service.

As one would expect, those effects of grace in contemplation and mysticism are ordinary. Mystical experiences are not visions but the intensification and simplification of prayerful contact with grace. They are available to all who persevere in prayer. Thomists like John of St. Thomas in the seventeenth century or Reginald Garrigou-Lagrange in the twentieth held that mystical experiences born by grace and unfolded by the Spirit are very much gifts to Christian existence.

The substratum of mystical experiences, moreover, do not cease to involve the psychological activities of the human personality.[29] Of course, there can be intense human experiences which can be designated natural mystical experiences, but in the realm of faith and charity Aquinas separated the extraordinary from the ordinary. Whatever might be truly miraculous comes from transient charisms (II–II, 17), while contemplative union comes from the gifts of the Spirit within the life-principle of grace active during the journey of our life. While one can distinguish artistic and natural mystical experiences from the deeper prayer of the Spirit in us, these psychological spheres are not opposed and they do influence each other. In the last analysis spirituality is my life within grace, my journey to the eschatological goal offered to me by God. My identity cannot come from outside myself; it cannot come from a religious or civil authority, nor from a slavish imitation of Elizabeth Seton or George Washington. Even when a personality silently opens to God in faith, the self retains its identity, its images, its own contours. An accurate awareness of myself will create a receptive silence for God's word within me and will keep me from the extremes Aquinas' psychology of graced virtue set aside: a consuming acquisition of possessions, an exhausting sensuality, a neurotic religion of self-exaltation and the control of God.

Art and spirituality are similar. Both are intuitive and powerful; both give access to the transcendent. We have been looking at the worlds of the individual's personality and spirituality, but now let us turn to human community: to society and to religion.

D. POLITICS

Over the past hundred years the principles of Thomas Aquinas have influenced political theory and social movements. They have entered into the structures of religious orders and political parties. The universality of shared social life and the dignity of human beings appear in the writings of thinkers like Jacques Maritain and John Courtney Murray, in the theoretician of social development Louis Joseph Lebret, in the deliberations of bishops' conferences and in the authors of papal documents reaching from Leo XIII to John Paul II. Latin American theologians of liberation and contemporary North American moral theologians recognize a debt to Aquinas. This is somewhat surprising. The society Aquinas knew was largely feudal in its political order and sacral in its neo-Platonic hierarchies. The thirteenth century, however, did have its social innovations: it was a time of new social groupings and new styles of organizations. That age witnessed the rise of corporations like the universities, of less formal structures in business and trade, and of original Christian communities like the friars. Aquinas lived at a time when attention to Roman law increased, replacing local customs and awkward regional legal systems, and when the exposition and application of church law expanded.[30]

In Aquinas' view, a society is a gathering of human beings, a gathering which has its own life and goals from which no member is excluded. Forms of government exist for one purpose: to help human beings attain their destiny.[31] The common good and not just freedom of choice are standards for civic life. Human destiny, moreover, is both natural and supernatural. Consequently, governments should further the association of human beings for sustenance, procreation, and defense, but they should also support the life of the spirit in the sciences and the arts, and in faith and worship. The state is greater than individuals and communities within it, but its greatness is ministerial, serving freedom, life, cooperation, and virtue. As with the universe the good of the totality of creatures comes from a certain interplay and that common good enhances the individuals (I, 103, 2).

The Dominican theologian explored the forms of social life not mainly from the point of view of passages found in the Bible but from principles flowing from reason and experience, and from texts of theoreticians of law and political process.[32] The Hebrew Bible offers some anecdotal insights about politics but no programs. The evangelical law of the Spirit brought people further support for natural law and justice but the New Testament does not outline a form of government. Thomas drew no line from the Bible to any kind of imperium, kingly or papal; the realm of politics belongs to human social reason.[33] Nevertheless, without collapsing nature and grace, God can be at work not just in the church's books and rites but in human moral life and in the just institutions of humanity. The role of the Spirit is to help all in the society pursue virtue and to perceive where justice and injustice are to be found (I–II, 108, 1, 2).[34] Humanity and the world are good despite the nefarious woundings furthered by the human condition, while grace holds out at every moment the potentiality for healing and enlightenment. Chenu observed: "When

I learned theology, I was taught that the human being was only passing briefly on earth and that the world was a provisional reality condemned to be destroyed when one passed on to another world. . . . But
I, disciple of Thomas, reacted against this and was persuaded that the
reign of God is already in the world. . . . 'Development' names the progressive influence of humans on things but today we meet the word,
'liberation,' which has a political expression. . . . There is always for
the Christian the dialectic between creation and incarnation."[35] The
affirmation of creation as the milieu of grace encourages research and
creativity even as it defends the poor, the worker, the fetus, the psy-
chotic invalid.[36]

Aquinas' contribution to political theory flows from the great
themes of the Second Part of the *ST*; there the activities of the human
image of God assist political reason through supernatural prudence.
Society is like a collective human personality. Aquinas' theology furthers a politics of optimism and of effort, one defending a pluralism of
groups working for the common good. As Torrell observes, "The
development of a theology with a perspective toward the future city
of God confers upon this diverse activity a special quality, the imitation of the divine generosity."[37] Political life and human laws should
mirror personhood and creation; there too grace can heal the effects of
sin (selfishness, violence, intolerance) and can invite all to work for
community and justice. On the other hand, Aquinas' graced anthropology precludes sectarianism. Christianity is not mainly a lonely
prophetic voice in an evil world, nor a small church with radical ideas
about society. Politics is not a dirty business nor is it a metaphysical
arrangement of laws by which large populations become instantly and
totally virtuous. The religious contribution to politics begins with the
observation of how well God has ordered the universe where creative
power is joined to the independence and interplay of creatures and
moves out to biblical standards of justice and love. As he drew guide-
lines for the virtuous life of the individual from both nature and revelation, Aquinas presumed the stability of institutions bestowed by
human nature. He did not think that political rights and dominion
were bestowed on people by religion, that is, by faith, baptism, or
church membership. They came with human nature. The church
cannot remove or replace the rights of parents or social leaders.
Natural societies and rulers do not derive their being from baptism or
faith but from the natural union of men and women to live well. If

Aquinas spoke a few times of kings being subject to priests, his principles interpret that axiom as theological in a general sense. In the political world, revelation and grace should ground a higher realm of the virtuous life but they do not control the social dimension of the human spirit. Secular rulers have their proper autonomy. Pesch notes: "Thomas . . . cannot imagine a state without the foundation of faith, and still it is significant how in the midst of the Christian society of the European Middle Ages a genuine Christian impulse brings the basic distinction between faith and politics, law and morality."[38]

More than one political form has contributed to human society. In the abstract the best form of government is the one in which all participate in the selection of those who rule (I–II, 105, 1). The rule of a group or of a large number has precedent, but in Aquinas' orderly mind the rule of one, when the ruler is enlightened and virtuous, was preferable to that of a group. That perspective was supported by his experience of cities and provinces ruled by groups being torn by a series of dissensions. "It is clear that unity is more effectively brought about by that which is one in itself than by many" (I–II, 105, 1). If the definition of good politics is the practical direction of the society toward a good life, then tyranny begins when the ruler seeks only the benefit of his person, a solitary authority zealous for a solitary purpose. What does the citizen do when the ruler becomes unjust? This can reach an intolerable point. Then society has a right to demand an end to what is essentially and resolutely destructive of the common good, for in the last analysis the intention of rulers and lawgivers is primarily the common good, secondarily an order of justice and of virtue which permits the existence and attainment of the common good (I–II, 100, 8).

Justice is the means through which society pursues its goals. Justice means not the maintenance of any civil order but the relationships among people which give each his or her due (III, 61, 4 & 5). Among the different kinds of justice, general justice serves the common good of the whole community, particular justice safeguards the rights of an individual or an association, and legal justice is the expression (but not the full realization) of rights in laws. The purpose of law is to serve the order of the community, to promote virtue and peace (I–II, 95, 1). Law is made "by the whole community or by the one representing it" (I–II, 90, 3). Good human laws are facets of that "law" which is divine wisdom.[39] Civic laws are not absolute and unchangeable, nor are they always moral and virtuous. Bad laws are not truly laws for they subvert order and goodness. In a rather radical view the medieval Dominican held that an unjust law, a law which does violence to creation and oppresses people, should not be obeyed (I–II, 95, 2). Human reflection on the given nature of humanity is a kind of law of creation, but this natural law is not an easily deduced set of exceptionless rules. History and culture have drawn out of the human race's reflections different levels of moral maturity. The law of nature has different degrees of knowability, certitude, and universality. One recognizes differences in the human reception of morality, as history has witnessed even degrees of faith, revelation, and grace. Natures, laws, principles, societies—these exist in a teleological theology for a goal. For Aquinas their goal is the enhancement of the human family and the service of the graced person, ministries which tend toward the eschatological fulfillment of people and communities in spheres of life beyond death. In this theology of harmony, laws are not usually opposed to the gospel. In conclusion, it is important to note that neither the reality of communities and societies nor forms of government are given by special divine revelations but come from human nature with its cultural diversity and political potential. Creator of beings and natures, God is the *gubernator mundi*, "the director of the universe," but not the royal designator of earthly kings. In the last analysis, a theology of creation and of the grace-empowered individual is the source of a Christian view of society.

Aquinas' social thought refuses individualism or legalism by spotlighting the reality and priority of communal justice. Since the gifts and demands of society have a foundation in human nature and creation (I, 96, 4), civil laws or ecclesiastical censures will not by-pass human beings to create an unrealistic utopia. It is important for the individual to search for justice outside of law books and mental theories and to find it in life itself. Statesmanship involves more than the application of laws. Politics is an art more than a science, "a kind of art for giving order and institutions to human life" (I–II, 104, 4). Political direction is the employment of principles for the good of a group, and so its exercise flows from the practical intellect, from prudence searching out concrete policies which further human community. While the goal of society is the good and virtuous life, sometimes this can be accomplished only step-by-step. A community's leader is not obliged to eradicate every immorality at once nor to impose by law every virtuous aspect of human life (I–II, 96, 2 & 3; II–II, 10, 11). People cannot be forced to be virtuous citizens or saints. Thomas Gilby concluded: "St. Thomas was the first Western writer to bring out the difference of politics from the other sciences and to distinguish the operation of civil law from moral law."[40]

Aquinas was a social realist. He did not think human beings were angels. He recognized the influence of psychological, social, religious, and educational factors upon people. He had no illusions about the difficulties of political life: neither monarchy nor republican assemblies guaranteed responsible government. Laws could be evaluated and changed; tolerated wars had to meet certain conditions; regicide and revolution were permissible as last resorts undertaken against widespread evil. The condition of the city and state in which one lived affected human life. In short, the theologian spotlighted a justice within society which would look not just at private or legal issues but at the health or the disharmony of the state as a whole.

Aquinas stands opposed to any nihilism or anarchy which despairs of human beings achieving anything. He would oppose the abuse of creation since he prized the divine gift of the order of creation so highly, and he condemned the inhuman, shallow materialism of sensuality and avarice. Countering positivism with realism, he would disagree with the modern claim of state or corporation to absolute freedom, or with the legitimization of morality solely by civil law. The dialogue of human psychology and divine grace (and communities and societies are collective personalities with their own natures and forms) challenges, on the one hand, secularism's denial of grace and of a graced future, and, on the other hand, fanatical piety's rejection of the human family or of the rights of others.[41]

For over a hundred years popes have drawn on Aquinas' principles to treat social issues ranging from labor unions to genetics: it is no coincidence that Leo XIII initiated both a Thomistic renewal (*Aeterni Patris*, 1879) and the modern line of important social encyclicals (*Rerum Novarum*, 1891).[42] In terms of social issues, both the early *Rerum Novarum* and the later *Centessimus Annus* celebrating the centennial of that first social encyclical built upon Aquinas' approach from the intrinsic value of creation and of the human being. Private property is natural and beneficial; justice, however, also needs to be enhanced by charity. Degrees of individual and social justice, a critique of capitalism (ownership and wealth are not absolutes but are subject to the interests of society as a whole) along with a defense of individual rights, an advocacy of the common good and a respect for private property are developed as principles for limiting materialist greed and for employing resources for the poor. Private property is natural and beneficial but justice also needs to be enhanced by charity. Paul VI in his encyclical on Aquinas mentioned how his thought supports the legitimate structures and claims of political society. Religion should not impede or deny the natural order in the name of a fideism; Thomism rejects a political system whose ground is some forceful but blind act of personal faith which is in fact a theological ideology.[43]

The bishops at Vatican II wrote that the expectation of the eschaton, of a future "new earth," ought not to weaken but should stimulate global concern for life on the planet we inhabit. "For here grows the body of a new human family, a body which even now is able to give some kind of foreshadowing of the new age."[44] Neither the gospel nor Thomism is a guidebook for passivity, or for an apolitical attendance on an angelic heaven yet to come. Aquinas would applaud the church's social stances since Vatican II: "The Council brings to mankind light kindled from the gospel, and puts at its disposal those saving resources which the church itself, under the guidance of the Holy Spirit, receives from its founder. For the human person deserves to be preserved; human society deserves to be renewed."[45] Since the ecumenical council of the 1960s Catholic leadership has set aside seeing the development of the world as evil, and the church has left the sacristy to address and enter public life. The incarnational nature of the theology of the *ST* expects humanitarian forms and social reforms.

E. THE CHRISTIAN COMMUNITY

As we saw in chapter three, Thomas Aquinas did not include in the *ST* a section of questions on the theology of the church. In the thirteenth century canon law was attracting a growing body of interpreters and applications. Canonists appeared to some to be the dutiful bureaucrats of a system of clerical offices who would give the church indiscriminate political power and turn the body of Christ into a machinery of rules, but Aquinas refused that direction. In his theology the church is first the body of Christ and a people vivified by the Spirit. Chenu wrote:

It is significant that this theology [of the church] is not formed into a separate treatise . . . but develops totally—both as institution and sacrament—within a theology of Christ and the incarnation. The church is the very body of Christ animated by the Spirit; its organic realities come from its apostolic foundation under the guidance of the pope. The church is at the same time both a body (a corporation in the sociological sense of the word) and a mystery of Christ living on mystically and sacramentally.[46]

Aquinas mentioned canonical questions in his systems of theology, but his ecclesiology is biblical and theological. The following pages present some ecclesial insights from Aquinas which support the renewal of church and ministry, topics which have been widely discussed in this century and will continue to be important. Aquinas spoke of Jesus, the Incarnate Word, the leader of the new humanity, as full of graces, graces of charisms and ministries and offices. John Mahoney writes:

For Aquinas the Church is essentially "the Church of the Holy Spirit," and this underlies his teaching that those in authority in the Church be sensitive to the purpose of their decisions and decrees as providing a timely, and when necessary temporary, expression of the grace of the Spirit in the community of the faithful. And not only should all in the Church be open to the possibility of the unexpected from the Spirit, and to the Spirit's response through his Church to the needs of men in every generation. They should also respect the Christian dignity of all the faithful and realise that the New Law of the spirit is not . . . a burden . . . but a clearly visible expression of the love and freedom which the Spirit imparts.[47]

As we have just seen, communities large and small are not necessary evils but correspond to and fulfill the convivial nature of humanity. The family, the clan, the city, the parish or the religious order, the state, and the church express the social nature of men and women who enjoy creating social bonds. Just as the forms of life for men and women lead to societies, the forms of grace too should reveal a community. Yet, the church is not a regional kingdom, a rigid hierarchy serving its directorate, a sacral fortress, nor a merely human organization. "In the body of the church the peace among diverse members is sustained by the power of the Holy Spirit who vivifies the body of the church. . . . Someone moves away from the unity of the Spirit by seeking to transform the church's good into their own. Just as in the terrestrial state peace is removed by the fact that individual citizens seek their own benefit" (II–II, 183, 2, 3). The church is society in the supernatural order. The called gathering (*ecclesia*) is the community where grace lives explicitly and visibly. If the church is a visible society with institutions, offices, and laws, these forms serve the reign of God on earth and help human beings in this life which is the state of pilgrimage and embattlement. In the next life, while the Body of Christ unfolds in a greater power of its animating Spirit, the church's degrees of authority and active roles will not survive. A different community, living already in the eschaton, draws the pilgrim church on earth forward (III, 61, 4, 1; 63, 5, 3). Now, however, the terrestrial church mixes the good and the bad. It struggles to be the Spirit's new creation, but its members can pursue misdirected goals and prefer selfish power to holy service. The church is not on the same level as God or Christ but remains a place, a means, a voice of God in Christ. So the *ST* does not contain a full ecclesiology.

Aquinas used various metaphors and theological terms, some biblical and some political, to describe the church. He compared states and groups in secular society with "that people which is called a church,"[48] a people coming from all nations and from all levels of society. A note of universality implies an openness to all, while an active diversity suggests different roles within the church. "The aggregation of believers, which is both the church and the house of God, is drawn from diverse kinds of men and women, for instance, from Jews and Greeks, from slaves and free."[49] This congregation also is universal in time, enduring from Abel to the end of the world.[50] It includes all men and women potentially: all those who will respond to grace and to the revelation of God, and those who, remaining in degrees of potentiality to Christ, will choose evil (III, 8, 4, 1). If "congregation" brings the notions of breadth and universality, the phrase "body of Christ" implies activity and diversity. Drawn from the Pauline letters, the metaphor "body" expresses the variety of activities in the members of the church (III, 8, 1; 48 2, 1). The actions and ministries of all these people further the institutional and social organism of the church.

If the church is not simply a religious version of a state or a collectivity of states (Aquinas' employment of "*Christianitas*" is rare[51]), it is also not a natural society with a veneer of theism, nor an active evangelizing cell. Thomas had no interest in a solely interior Christianity, a spiritual church without forms, or a small gathering of the elect from which institutional problems are absent. He is human enough to appreciate the difficulties of living in any institution; he had plenty of experience in Dominican province, Parisian university, and papal court of how frequently ignorance and passion disrupt communities and how challenging are new structures.

His ecclesiology is clearly a sacramental one, continuing the work of Jesus the Christ. Living from the missions of the Trinity, the church continues the saving work on earth of Jesus Christ, source of grace and head of graced humanity, while the Spirit, the divine life-principle, brings ways for the church to serve the reign of God. The church is evidently a context or a ground for the seven sacraments, but Aquinas did not develop an explicit theology of the church as sacrament: he left other theologians to depict the Body of Jesus at the center of circles of the forms of grace in cultures, an approach developed in the twentieth century.

Liturgy is a primary activity of the Christian community. Sacraments bring spiritual life to the members, and in this theology realism and adaptability in ritual and ministry are important. Although grace in sacramental signs and personal ministry were centered in the thirteenth century in the Eucharist, that communal and sacramental theological ground permits those living centuries later to imagine various unions of grace and service in ministry. Liturgy is the source and expression of ministry, and both liturgy and ministry exist for people. Aquinas evaluated liturgy's signs and the activities of monastery or parish not by asceticism or power but by how well they brought people together with God. On the one hand, visible and effective sacraments serve the unseen, while, on the other hand, externals serve inner worship, that dialogue of Spirit and personality.

Preaching, the community hearing the gospel proclaimed, is a central ministry. The primacy Aquinas gave to the senses—particularly to seeing which encouraged incarnation and sacramentality—did not reduce the high regard in which he held preaching. The friars labored to reestablish content and vigor in sermons. For Aquinas, preaching and teaching went together, and both were inconceivable without study and reflection. There is no preaching without theology, since preaching is the communication of the gospel through a vital interpretation. The preached word leads to the Word incarnate in Jesus Christ. Yet, the visibility which the sacraments brought to the community is placed higher than words proposing realities in an audible, linguistic form.[52] Words are transitory and less tangible than material symbols.

One basic reason for the sacrament of orders was to depute some to give the community information about faith. Preachers were to explain the gospel, and not to offer just a few phrases from catechisms, creeds, or dogmas. He concluded that everyone preaching should know enough Scripture and theology to deal with the issues brought up in daily life, while bishops and theologians ought to be able to present more difficult issues and resolve problems (Supplement, 36, 2, 1).

Church and society by the thirteenth century had partly replaced the biblical term *diakonia* ("ministry") with Roman legal terms like *officium, status,* and *ordo;* the variety of the church's ministries had been quite reduced. For instance, the diaconate had for some centuries existed only in its liturgical form, and the forms of service attached to that liturgical presence in the early church were entrusted to religious orders and lay confraternities: clergy or laity acted without a commissioning in what were in fact diaconal roles. Ministry in a public way existed only in the priesthood—the bishop was for Aquinas by and large a higher form of priest. Aquinas ended his theology of the Christian life in the Second Part of the *ST* by treating charisms, the active and contemplative lives, a few church offices, and general states of life.

Despite the monoformity of offices in the thirteenth and subsequent centuries, Aquinas' theology can today be employed to support some newness and diversity in the church's structures. After all, it had once served the expansion of ministry. What was ecclesially new in the thirteenth century was not the restoration of the ministries of the first century of the Christian era or the granting of public roles beyond monastic ones to women (there were attempts in the decades before Francis and Dominic, all suppressed, to give women evangelizing ministries of preaching) but forms of a poor, apostolic life. The controversy over whether new orders like Franciscans and Dominicans (regional gatherings of mobile brothers imitating the life of

Christ and his preaching) had the right to restore evangelical forms and to fashion new approaches to holiness and preaching was a controversy over the possibility of new forms of ministry in the church. What diversity there was in ministry appeared in religious orders or in local lay brotherhoods.

To Aquinas the Pauline theology of the Body of Christ suggests a diversity of activities and gifts: "Each human being has a body and a soul and through them diverse members. So it is with the Catholic church: one body and yet different members; the soul which vivifies this body is the Holy Spirit."[53] Significantly, in his analogy with the body, the church is almost always compared to a physiological organism owning an inner life with diverse functions, and not to a sociological city or state.[54] Some arrangements of the structures of the church come not from revelation but from church law. Some are of divine tradition, but not a few change with the times (I–II, 97, 1); the latter are matters not of dogma but of polity, policy, and church law (II–II, 184).

Aquinas did not divinize every ecclesiastical office as he treated the important offices under the sacrament of orders (II–II, 184). He situated church offices in a dialectic of form and tradition. Each office, like every being, was teleological. If all ministries point to the Eucharist, it is equally true that every office has as its telos the making of grace accessible and stands at the service of the divine.[55] A charism, an office, a ministry, an ordination—these had their purposes, goals to be achieved for the church. Offices are not solely positions of ecclesiastical governance or honors but continue the work of Jesus and his Spirit. Some ensemble of different ministries has always existed, and Aquinas gave three reasons for a diversity of roles in the church (II–II, 183, 2). First, in nature, the universe, and in political groups we see how diversity assists order; similarly grace centered in Christ seeks a diversity in the members of the body of Christ. Second, the church needs to have a variety of services to help people. Third, the church displays a beauty through this diversity. Church offices, ecclesiastical teachings, church laws are not the products of definitions but are actions with forms structured by human beings. In the age of the apostles the basic ministries were present, but their names and descriptions were not the same then as those appearing in later ecclesial organization.[56] Although his pastoral theology of bishop, priest, and deacon was considerably limited by the ecclesiastical practice of his time, Aquinas' theological principles do not exclude a diversity of orders. Still, how to account for the one sacrament of orders having different forms and ordinations, e.g., bishop, sub-deacon, acolyte? He explained orders as a unity within diversity. The various church orders composed a "potestative whole" (Supplement, 37, 1, 2). The one sacrament of orders is a vital totality, an organism from whose life various powers could emerge. This theory leaves open the issue of whether in theory and practice ministries beyond those of leadership might be different in kind and number from age to age, culture to culture.

The bishop's office, not so clearly an order distinct from the priesthood but definitely an important office,[57] is to instruct and govern the church. Explaining and interpreting the gospel, he teaches and preaches at a high level, and his teaching office cannot be delegated to others (II–II, 185, 3; III, 67, 2, 1; I, 43, 7, 6). Preaching and teaching find a climax in the ministry of the bishop: the placing of the book of the Gospels on the bishop's head at his ordination is a symbol of his knowledgeable and inspired communication of the Christian faith. The bishop illumines the people in his local church. Aquinas, however, contrasted those who might define the truths of Christianity in rare papal and conciliar texts with the bishops who interpret in an ordinary, pastoral way the sacred teaching of the gospel in terms of pressing issues. Bishops as teachers in the church have the "pastoral teaching office" (*magisterium*), but theologians also have a teaching office. It is not one of pastoral care and of the preaching of revealed doctrines but a teaching role given by the academic professorship. Nonetheless, the *cathedra magistralis* is also destined for the explanation of revelation. Both have their roles. In the area of important church teaching, the bishops present the basics of Christian faith. Nevertheless, this does not replace theological interpretations needed for new times or new problems. Research and teaching, creative theology and the solution of issues are done by theologians. "Some [theological] disputation belongs to the university and has as its goal not to remove errors but to instruct people and to lead them toward an understanding of the truth. It is right for this to use investigative reasons to reach the heart of the truth . . . and not to determine questions by authority alone."[58]

Aquinas lived in a Europe which was enjoying a new universality. The particularity of individual churches, the differences of regions and rites were not what the cultural moment held up as significant.

Dioceses were administrative segments of the one church. Religious orders were universal and supra-national; they were not subject to local bishops but to each order's central administration in Rome and to the papacy. The office of bishop belongs to the local church, but bishops' leadership of their churches was sometimes compromised by being temporal rulers or delegates of Rome. Nevertheless, the goal of the office remains the good of the community and its service. "A prelate exists for the good of the church, and not vice-versa."[59] While Aquinas saw bishops receiving areas of their jurisdiction from the bishop of Rome, he did not think that the sacramental power and the central ministerial identity of the bishop are derived from the papacy.[60] In the church as in the world of nature a universal politique joining a multitude of regional groups is necessary. Yves Congar noted that the new contexts of friar and theology would lead to an emphasis on the universal church over a previous monastic and national regionalization.[61] The bishop of Rome has a central, hence important, role. That bishop directs the universal church: his administration and jurisdiction, saving the rights of local churches, can extend to each church.

Despite the role of the papacy in the creation and sustenance of the friars, Aquinas' theology did not overly magnify the See of Peter. As the questions on faith unfold (II–II, 1), the *ST* discusses how the express statement of Christian faith takes place publicly. The verbal elements, the "articles" of faith are gathered together to be more easily preached, and this collection is called a *symbolum* or "creed." When in time errors arise, there needs to be a new "edition" of the creed. Since the pope is the only permanent entity which has the care of the entire church, it belongs to him to call an ecumenical council or "to determine those things which are of faith" (II–II, 1, 10). "Just as a later council has the power both of interpreting the creed formulated by an earlier one and of adding certain things, so also the Roman Pontiff can do this by his authority."[62] The context of the *ST* suggests that the papal determination (a technical term meaning to give a high level of ecclesial formulation and advocacy), while of a special, that is, universal nature, is not solitary or charismatically isolated. Determination involves some approval and reception within the church and its councils (II–II, 1, 10, 3). Expressing the most central teachings of the faith has been entrusted to the papacy, but not without some involvement of the church. "The universal church cannot err" (II–II, 1, 9). Apart from a very few articles the papacy is not treated formally in the *ST*, and later questions, precise and difficult, about this ministry are left unmentioned.[63] The bishop of Rome has impressive powers, but the term "infallible" is not used of him. In the precise meaning of the word for Aquinas only God could be *infallibilis:* revelation and the church's teaching about revelation can have a participatory lack of error.[64] Aquinas saw degrees and levels of authorities, sources, and media of revelation. He had a sophisticated approach to the interpretation of sacred teaching by witnesses living and dead. The source of any charism or role in teaching was the Holy Spirit and its goal was to serve one faith among the faithful (II–II 1, 1 & 10).

We should recall that the broad strokes of Thomist thought over time introduced and penetrated something of the church's self-interpretation. In ecclesiology nature and grace remain distinct and independent but harmoniously interactive. Divine charism and apostolic office build upon natural gifts for ministry. Aquinas would not have understood a church without a basic unity in faith and doctrinal expression, for a society requires unanimity in spirit and in form, internally and externally. Grace brings not only activity and theological creativity, the servants of faith and church, but some consensus about belief and a moral life. In short, the unity of the church is not one solely of rubrics or administration but begins with a unity in understanding faith's truth. This becomes active in love and is realized symbolically in sacrament. Mahoney sums up the role of authority for Aquinas. "The exercise of authority in the church is obviously to be a ministry of the Spirit, sensitive to his guidance in order to provide the family of God with suitable means of expressing and professing, according to circumstance of time and place, the love of God which has been poured out in their hearts."[65]

Of course, Aquinas' view of the church could not escape some Platonic or feudal elements. A pyramid of hierarchy had long before replaced the primal concentric circles of ministries. With the angels as analogue and with a neo-Platonic theology of light as inspiration, the pattern of hierarchy (which is not the only model suitable to Christian authority) was for Aquinas prominent both theologically and ecclesially. Hierarchy was a ladder of descending illuminations. There was, too, the unfortunate principle that a higher office and order contains the lower.[66] If so, what could the lower contribute to higher ranks? Little or nothing. Finally, in this ecclesiology diversity in offices, orders, and jurisdiction was, except for abbesses, clerical and male. Nonetheless, the motifs of Spirit and individuality were never fully captured by feudal clericalism. Movements, religious orders, mystics, and charismatics were visible representatives of freedom and diversity in the Spirit. Aquinas applies Jesus' preaching of servanthood to church offices. Church ministry as a reward for ambition or as a control of society would be unacceptable to Aquinas: the goal, the insignia, the style of all members remained love. Grace lives deeper than Platonic forms and will not be held captive by one set of social structures. "Adults in the faith adhere to God alone. . . if they adhere to their prelates it is only because those prelates adhere to Christ" (II–II, 43, 5). Aquinas' psychological theology of the Second Part would encourage the ministerial and charismatic contribution of all the baptized. It argues that in terms of nature and grace, people should be selected for church ministries because of their qualifications, and these qualifications are evident in their lives and activities. Authority should not be didactic but concerned with the individuality of Christians and of their churches, for the function of the church is to serve the Christian life (I–II, 106, 1, 1). Endowed with virtues and gifts, men and women are baptized to extend the work of the Trinity. One of the effects of the sacraments of baptism and confirmation is to depute, through a theology of a bestowed spiritual form (a "character"), a man or a woman to Christian worship. Those sacraments qualify the person to enter fully and maturely into the liturgy of the church: they bestow a certain participation in the priestly office of Jesus Christ, the redeemer of the world. Ordination to special ministries in the church, e.g., deacon or priest, builds on this initial baptismal priesthood. Here we might recall that the application in recent years of what baptism, ministry, and liturgy were in the New Testament churches to the contemporary church has been furthered by the pioneering ecclesiology of Yves Congar, Edward Schillebeeckx, J.-M. Tillard, and others who have used Thomist principles to deepen and expand the forms of church life.

Women active in the church—what did Aquinas think? His theology could hardly have transcended the long tradition before him or the medieval social forms in which he lived. But why are women not ordained? No argument from a papal document or New Testament passage was offered.[67] The fact that the church has not ordained women does not come merely from canon law but from some more serious factor (Supplement, 39, 1). On the topics of women preaching or being ordained to lead the local church, he also did not argue from biblical examples or from maleness in Jesus and his disciples. We do not have his mature thinking on that point for he dies before treating the sacrament of orders in the *ST.* In the young Dominican's treatise on orders, part of a commentary on Lombard's *Sentences* which is reproduced in editions of the *ST,* the reason given for excluding women from priesthood and episcopacy is that state of subjection drawn from the Jewish Scriptures (an idea prominent in the creation of women in the First Part): a passage from Genesis argued that after the fall women are subject to men (I, 92, 1, 2). A personal (or religious) subjection given by the Fall brings apparently a social diminishment.

But Aquinas also gives an argument from medieval sociology. Mention is made of a lack of "a grade of eminence" necessary for the symbolic aspect of leadership in the ordained (Supplement, 39, 1).[68] Significantly Aquinas replied to questions about women as priests and preachers in terms of the sociological symbolism of the woman. Ordained public ministry was withheld from women because of their image in public life. They lacked de facto authority and direction in society and this was reinforced by theology. This has to do with masculine and feminine roles in society, with their general social impact on people. On the other hand, Aquinas cited Paul in Colossians to support without discussion women baptizing and being sponsors at confirmation as "ministers of Christ" (III, 67, 4) and of course charisms from grace, the milieu and gift of the supernatural order, like prophecy or mystical experience are no less accessible to women than to men. Individual women could have high qualities of human spirit and special ecclesial charisms (and also limited leadership in monasteries) but not the universal church's offices with their extensive civil accoutrements in the Middle Ages. What could this idea that women do not have the signification of being a public figure mean? The medieval theologian might have meant that an abbess or a duchess did not appear to her (medieval) society as a public leader. When the question of women preaching arose, he argued that women can preach privately and to small groups. "Privately" suggests a woman teaching and preaching to a few within a community (II–II, 177, 2). Again the only reason briefly stated against public preaching is the subjection of Genesis 3:16.[69] So we have a theology on this topic which is sparse in claims on Christian revelation and explicitly located in a social context.

When we say we believe in the church, Thomas Aquinas wrote, this means we believe in the Holy Spirit animating the church (II–II, 1, 9, 5). As grace comes through sacraments, the illumination and animation to speak and act on behalf of Christ comes through the Spirit. In terms of an institutional model Aquinas retained something of the forms of pyramid and hierarchy with clerical offices culminating in the pope. That ecclesiology, however, was inserted in the larger missions of Word and Spirit among a people.

F. THE WORLD'S RELIGIONS

What is the role of Christ and his kingdom in a lengthy history of religions? This is a most important topic for today and for the future. Not so much books and theories but contact with peoples on earth with their array of religions demands that Christians ponder the centrality of Christ. Vatican II encouraged a positive appreciation of the degrees of grace and of revelatory rays touching billions. But did Thomas Aquinas, centuries before, discern salvation for those living outside of faith in Christ?[70]

Aquinas could hardly have known how culturally diverse was the human race or how lengthy its history. At first his experience of human religion outside of Christian faith and baptism was limited to the Jewish communities in the medieval cities and to ancient texts about Greek and Roman religion. Of course his theology was done in dialogue with important (but past) Greek, Jewish, and Muslim minds. In his room or in a nearby library were the works of the great philosophers and theologians from other religious traditions, and he saw no reason why they could not help him find truth. All truths came from God who is Truth. Scholars, however, no longer think that the *summa* disputing with the great gentiles was written as a handbook for missionaries, and while a few points of the Koran are touched on there is no systematic consideration of the book. R. A. Gauthier concludes: "In the last analysis most of the non-believers whose errors St. Thomas wants to refute are pagans . . . but of missions to pagans of his own time there is no mention. . . . Thomas never speaks in the *Summa contra gentiles* of the pagans of his time. The pagans he is refuting are always the pagans of antiquity."[71]

Aquinas may have slowly become aware that the Christianity of Europe included only a part of the human race and that the world was much larger. We know that the thirteenth century witnessed new contacts with cultures and religions outside of Christendom. Francis of Assisi established irenic missions in Egypt after 1217. Both the Franciscans and the Dominicans had traveled far into Asia. Frederick II had drawn to his court and university at Palermo a spectrum of scholars. In the years around 1240 two of Thomas' brothers fought with the Emperor's army, and some think that in this force Europeans saw for the first time a number of North and Sub-Saharan Africans.[72]

For Aquinas this topic of wider grace does not concern the Jews. They stand in the line of God's covenant of the supernatural order and are in an always distinguished way the source of the Christ and his gospel. "The passion of Christ had the effect of salvation among the Jews, and then through the preaching of Jews the effect of the passion of Christ passed on to the peoples" (III, 47, 4). The Jews had—and still retain—covenantal beliefs and sacramental rites (I–II, 101, 4; 102, 5; 111, 62, 6), some of which anticipated prior to Pentecost the Messiah. Some of the theologically educated, the *majores*, had an intimation of Trinity and Incarnation (II–II, 2, 7). Aquinas interpreted the Jewish rituals as valuable, even in his own time to Christian as well as to Jew; they were sacraments (II–II, 10, 11; I–II, 101, 4). Aquinas felt the civil authority should take a dim view of non-Christian rituals which insulted or mocked that faith, but those are special, if unfortunate, cases. There are no circumstances which would permit the forced baptism of Jewish adults or children, because of their sovereignty as human beings (III, 68, 10).[73] Aquinas showed particular interest in the writings of Jewish scholars, accepting them as privileged guides. As he looked at the plan of salvation history, he concluded: "The conversion of the nations belongs solely to the mercy of God, but the salvation of the Jews belongs to his justice" (I, 21, 4, 2).[74] He saw Judaism beyond making explicit the natural law (II–II, 174, 6) as the object of God's gracious and unmerited love bringing it "a special kind of sanctification" (I–II, 98, 4). The interiority of the Spirit's gospel law of grace is also found in the prophets (I–II, 104). As one would expect, the reality of this chosen people always has an eschatological dynamic as it anticipates and brings the Messiah.

The issue of salvation for those who had not heard of the gospel did not attract much explicit treatment from the medieval Dominican:

no question in the *ST* considers this topic formally. For theologians in the century before him the traditional academic case exemplifying this problem described a minor, rather bizarre, hypothetical incident: how would grace reach an orphan raised by animals and thus unavoidably ignorant of the gospel? Later in his life Aquinas stopped mentioning that case and began to speak in general terms of people apart from baptism or faith. Perhaps through the reports of his Dominican brothers who had been in the lands of the Mongols he had become aware of large groups of peoples to the South and East. He did not compare or evaluate the rituals of other religions. Rather, his theology of the extent of grace was developed from the areas of grace, faith, and baptism but not from the issues of God's being or through comparisons of doctrines from different religions. Themes like the deepest orientation of the individual, life in touch with personal salvation, responsibility before the natural moral law join with faith, baptism, and Christ to treat this issue. Is there access to grace for those who, without any culpability, have not encountered personally the means selected by Scripture and tradition as ordinary: being a Jew, faith in Jesus, Christian baptism, and church-membership?

Aquinas opened his questions on faith by describing faith not as a willed acceptance of divine curiosities but as a kind of knowledge of the realm of grace. Faith, "a power of understanding intensified by divine grace" (I, 12, 3; II–II, 4, 1), brings knowledge. Faith is important not because of a divine command or a gnostic initiation, but because knowing directs people in their activities, and we de facto live in a world and telos of grace. Does one need some faith, he asked, and does one need faith in the Incarnation and in the Trinity? Christ definitely belongs to the object of faith, but he has been the object of faith at different historical stages in different cognitive modes. "Consequently the mystery of Christ's Incarnation was to be believed in all ages and by all peoples in some fashion—but in diverse ways according to the differences of times and peoples" (II–II, 2, 7). What of those living after Christ who have neither heard of him nor received a special revelation? Aquinas replied by introducing the distinction between implicit and explicit faith. "Those, however, who were saved and to whom revelation was not given were not saved without faith in a mediator. Because even if they did not have an explicit faith, still they had an implicit faith in divine providence, believing God to be the liberator of people according to ways which pleased him, and according to which he would have revealed the divine self to some knowing the truth" (II–II, 2, 7, 3). Similarly, the article on faith in the Trinity pursues not a mathematical secret for Christians but a revelation connected to the Incarnation. "In every age and for all human beings it has been necessary to believe these two truths in *Hebrews* about God (that he is, and that he rewards; 11:6), but still that is not all there is [to believe] for every age and every person" (II–II, 2, 8, 1). The lack of Christian faith is not a sin.

Not every non-Christian religious ritual is evil. The dialectic of ground and realization is true also of religion. The expressions of religion, its propositions and rites, have a secondary role; their divine ground and goal come first. "To worship God belongs to a moral precept, but the determination of this precept . . . belongs to rules about ceremonies" (I–II, 99, 3, 3). Religion with its doctrines and rituals serve (or distort) something higher and deeper: the "new law" which is the presence of the Holy Spirit. "The New Law's foundation consists in that grace which is given to believers interiorly. . . . Secondarily it consists in certain facts, moral teaching and sacraments" (I–II, 107, 1, 3). Is baptism absolutely necessary for grace to reach a woman or a man? Aquinas distinguished between baptism as a suitable visible sign of faith and baptism as a cause of salvation. "The sacrament of baptism can be absent from someone in two ways. One way, in *re* and in *voto*, happens in those who neither are baptized nor wish to be, and here there is a kind of contempt of the sacrament by those who have free will. . . . In another way, the sacrament of baptism can be absent in *re* but not in *voto*. Someone desires to be baptized but for some reason death intervenes. This person can attain salvation without actual baptism because of the desire of baptism" (III, 68, 2). Later theologies expanded this *votum*, which here seems to imply a desire for the sacrament, to mean a general desire to follow God's plan. Baptism sacramentalizes the reality of grace (whatever it might be called) which a person accepts. "Someone can attain the effect of baptism through the power of the Holy Spirit without baptism of water or blood: for someone's heart can be moved by the Holy Spirit to believe, to love God and to have sorrow for sins" (III, 66, 11).

Because grace is ultimately a presence of the Trinity there cannot be intrinsically different kinds of grace, e.g., a general grace apart from Christ, for people in other religions, nor can there be a world apart from sin and grace (III, 62, 6, 3). Related to this intention of attaining what baptism liturgically symbolizes is Aquinas' theology of how each individual comes to an adult awareness of serious moral decisions. Maturity brings the choice of a fundamental orientation of life. That decision will involve a movement of the will, and in that movement there is an acceptance or a rejection, implicit or explicit, of the grace of God (I, 89, 6). This is a pattern for all adults. All human beings receive grace, but in the interplay of grace and freedom not all receive grace with the same intensity, and some do freely will to abandon grace (I, 23, 5; 23, 3, 2). The medieval Dominican spoke of degrees of the presence of the New Law of the Spirit just as he spoke of degrees of implicit and explicit faith. Grace which is the life of the Holy Spirit has an unchanging divine source, and yet "the state of the New Law is subject to change with regard to various places, times and persons" (I–II, 106, 4).

Aquinas had a modest theology of history, of history influencing the modes of God's grace present on earth. Jesus is the head of humanity, the first citizen of the reign of God. But is he the head of men and women who do not know him? Different groups of people have varied contacts in history with the event of Christ. One redeemer is sent to effect the "salvation of the entire human race" (III, 8, 3, 1), but several passages indicate that grace comes to individuals in their own particular moral and religious situations. "In all places the new law is proposed, but, however, not in all times, although in every time there were people who belonged to the New Law" (I–II, 106, 1, 3).[75] Apparently people outside of baptism and belief in Christ are not cut off from grace. While Christ is the center of the history of religion, God is not so stingy with grace that the billions who have never known Christ are, without any fault of theirs, destined to be without grace forever. Grace is not withheld from large groups for temporal or geographical deficiencies.

The few passages on how original sin in individuals is strong and how it can lead to vice are nowhere expanded into global damnation. Except for an oblique reference to turning from grace through sins (in contrast to an inculpable lack of explicit faith [II–II, 10, 1]), the dynamic of Aquinas' theology is positive: God's loving predestination to grace for intelligent creatures, a presumption that beings reach their goals, the offer of grace at key moments of moral choice. The devastating contagion of primal sin comes to each individual by birth, but grace, whether before or after Calvary, comes by a personal encounter with God (III, 8, 1). Within human freedom the Trinitarian life-principle can be rejected by sin (II–II, 10, 1) or contempt (III, 68, 2) but not by conditions of birth or by an inculpable ignorance of religious truths.

Aquinas' general theological motifs are at work in this topic of the breadth of grace. For instance, God does not create creatures and then leave them crippled, randomly excluded from their activities and goals. Neither God nor the theologian should ask more from a nature —including a graced nature—than it can give. An absent revelation does not bring damnation nor does creation bring for many men and women exclusion from the new creation.

> It is not suitable that God would provide more for creatures being led to a natural good by divine love than for those creatures to whom that love offers a supernatural good. For natural creatures God provides generously . . . forms and powers which are principle of acts so that they are inclined to activity through their own beings. . . . Even more for those moved to reach an eternal supernatural good he infuses certain forms or qualities of the supernatural order according to which easily and enthusiastically they are moved by God to attain that good which is eternal. (I–II, 110, 2)

The exclusion of blocks of loving creatures from God's love apart from their activity does not fit with Aquinas' theology of Creator or Redeemer. God would aim in the world of grace, as in the world of beings, at maximum life.

Although the legal and administrative side of Roman Catholicism has at times through the centuries appeared condescending and exclusivistic toward others, Aquinas' theology of implicit faith and degrees of contact by grace, a grace which in history becomes "more abundant" (I–II, 108, 2, 1), has furthered theological and ecclesial views that the intimate presence of God on earth is not tied to baptism, belief, or belonging to a church. While faith in the gospel and membership in the church are the central ways of God's grace working in history, grace does exist outside Christianity. Christ died for all men and women: not just for a small, select group predestined by an unpredictable and unpleasant deity millions of years ago. Jesus Christ is the unique, intense center and cause of grace, but his work visibly celebrated by Christmas, Good Friday, and Easter invisibly contacts all men and women in their lives.[76] Nevertheless, there is a lack of explicit treatment here, and Aquinas' ideas lack completeness and resolution. Max Seckler thinks that the scholastics first confused and then never fully untangled two issues—individuals hidden from society and peoples never evangelized—and that the lines of his theology were left unresolved: "Thomas Aquinas offers to our topic no clear answer. Opposite a series of optimistic statements stands the silence of his later writings on decisive points. . . . One might think that Thomas did not write down all his thoughts, or that he did not see the problem of salvation of non-Christians in its true sharpness."[77]

After Thomas Aquinas, ahead in the future, was the discovery of not just clusters of peoples and religions living outside of Christendom but of entire continents not yet touched by evangelization. Within fifteen years after Spain's first contacts with the Americas, Dominicans like Francisco Vitoria and Bartolomé de Las Casas, themselves caught up in a neo-Thomist revival—were drawing upon texts in the *ST* to defend the natural rights of the indigenous. Aquinas viewed human and political rights as coming from nature and not from religion; this was employed through the sixteenth century to challenge the Spanish conquests advanced with the excuse that peoples had not accepted baptism and so had no legitimate life now or in the hereafter. They rejected the idea that lack of faith damns and that all rites of other religions are evil; they argued that grace can exist outside of baptism. Three centuries later, a second neo-Thomism rooted in a theology of personality and grace addressed the issues of the extent of grace in lengthy discussions over the degree of implicit faith necessary and over the sources of Hindu or Muslim mysticism. After 1950, gifted students of Aquinas as diverse as Jacques Maritain and Karl Rahner considered the topic anew. Aquinas' principles have continued on in the documents of Vatican II considering other religions and in the growing dialogue with the varied religions of humanity, a conversation which begins by affirming God's grace within them.[78]

II. "Grace Drawing Creation Forward"

With this vast but indistinct issue of the history and extent of God's presence, we have reached the edge of the mystery of God which, as Aquinas saw it, lay beyond "a kind of deep, dark mist."[79] His theology has pointed toward what future theologies will explore, namely, how Christ is the historical cause, teacher, and icon of the one supernatural order on earth.

Grace draws forward human striving to all that is good.

While Aquinas wants his disciples to distinguish between the realm of creation and that of grace and between the abilities of the personality and the gifts of the Spirit, we should not conclude that there is in the entire universe only two presences of God, both of which we can thoroughly describe. Nor that what little we know of the divine Trinity exhausts the Godhead. The theology we have been studying in this book did not intend to exhaust the divine presence but to give some view of its reality within the parameters of terrestrial life. The dialectic of affirmation and negation in every article of the *ST* gives general orientations and suggests that grace and reality are rich realms of God. Life and revelation on earth while communicating something real in God are infinitely particular. There are, one would suppose, many kinds and degrees of divine presence in the universes of matter and spirit. As artists have often said, it is precisely limits and focus which enable greatness and genius. Aquinas' thought is always inviting us to enter further into Creation and the Kingdom of God, and then, guided by the insights and narratives of the gospel, to accept the maturity and responsibility of passing beyond definition and analysis to discernment and communion.

With allusions to Trinitarian presence on earth and in the universe we have reached the limits of a theology of culture. The arts and sciences of individuals and peoples can never be the enemy of grace; they are the places, the spirits, the grammars, and the laboratories for the higher order Jesus called the reign of God. "Now God bestows grace upon people in the manner appropriate to them" (III, 61, 1, 2). Aquinas' general principles have guided us in the right direction, offering perspectives which have stimulated people over the centuries, and from whose breadth further ages can summon forth new insights. Nevertheless, in each of the above areas we seem to be novice believers and thinkers standing before complex worlds.

The last two chapters of this book have suggested a paradox. It was not flight and hostility which best served Aquinas' theology but self-confident encounters with different intellectual landscapes. Thomism became sterile when it isolated itself from all that was different or new. In this century it has had unusual influence, from liturgy to politics, when it conversed openly with great thinkers, past and present. Aquinas is the theologian of the more: the more present now in grace, the more at the edge of human powers. Words are limited—they do not express all that lies within the leaf or the poem. In a woman, a man, a cloud of gas and stars, a forest, a song there is always more, not in the ahistorical and cerebral style of replacement or destruction but in the sense of revelation and disclosure. "A word which comes to expression in us . . . does not take possession of all that is in that from which it arose, for the intellect expresses in the word conceived only some facet of what it holds in habitual awareness. Similarly, in reflection upon a conclusion, the entire force of a principle is never expressed."[80] A great theology both sums up and points ahead. Thinking of Thomas Aquinas while musing on truth in history, Chenu wrote that sometimes we are privileged to witness a powerful thinking, one so immersed in time that precisely in that act it touches eternity.[81]

Conclusion

——— ✦ ———

*The present time of grace is like a dawn, like a morning, when it
is compared to the fullness of love which lies ahead in heaven.*
                                        Commentary on the Sentences,
                                              Prologue to Book Four

Time, whether of a life or of an age, passes quickly. It is the thirteenth
century and a boy in his late teens, resolute about the directions his
life will take, is traveling from Naples to Paris with the innovative
friars preachers. A decade or so later a young university professor, tall,
strongly built, with thinning blond hair, is already a phenomenon as
a teacher. Later a man in his forties preoccupied with a number of
projects is dining with Louis IX at the end of a week of public disputations during which he was rudely interrupted by those hostile to
Aristotle; later that night he steals a few minutes to write on paper of
poor quality ideas which will survive centuries.

Thomas Aquinas' theology of Christian revelation has been the
subject of these chapters, pages which have offered little more than
an orientation. Aquinas' thought has lived on beyond the destruction
of feudalism and of monarchy, surviving reformers who burnt his
works and ecclesiastics who idolized them. In George Eliot's *Middle-
march* enlightened English visitors to Rome in the nineteenth century dismissed him as austere and obsolete, but a century later interest in him supports a dozen institutes devoted to his thought, and the
resources of IBM are harnessed to produce a computerized index list-
ing every word in all his writings.

Thomas is the outstanding theologian of the Middle Ages. Why?
In his thought medieval thinking brings together in harmony culture
and revelation. Some think that Aquinas transcends the style and
limitation of the Middle Ages—otherwise, how to explain his continuing influence? If in Aquinas the worlds of antiquity, of Augustine
and Aristotle, find a new vitalization, perhaps even the modern world

244

is slightly anticipated by this theology where the individual human person with freedom and various activities emerges to be touched by facets of Trinitarian life. History shows that Aquinas' theology has flourished when it courageously and creatively entered into dialogue with a different age having its own viewpoints.

This theology is free, inviting, life-affirming, serene. Some, like G. K. Chesterton, have noticed a generous optimism pervading Aquinas' thought, an optimism born of knowing who God is, and who we are and will be. In Aquinas' world of beings-in-act both creation and grace are bestowed by God so creatures can act and interact. Chenu writes of his own work: "The law of my theology as a good disciple of St. Thomas sought for terrestrial realities under the grace of God and under the preaching of the gospel to maintain an autonomy of action, method, and impact. You know that in the great controversies over theology in the thirteenth century Thomas was the only one to defend this position attacked by a certain Augustinianism which wanted grace to control the phenomena of nature. Thomas himself, maintained that the more grace is grace, the more nature is nature; the more faith is faith, the more reason is reason."[1] Catholic Christianity is served not by a theology of propositions and methods but by a theory of divine power enabling free persons. As in any great thinker or artist, certain basic themes recur, and anyone who has read Aquinas over some years finds a tonality in his lines and ideas, a tonality as distinctive as that running through the music of Vivaldi or Rachmaninoff. Thomas Aquinas' theology leads:

> —to the autonomy of creation; to the variety of creatures with their activities, and to the order and beauty of nature;
>
> —to the capacities, independence, and responsibility of the human person;
>
> —to the depth of God disclosed in creation and revealed by Jesus;
>
> —to the ecstasy of life and action, and to their goal of happiness;
>
> —to a human race called to share in the Wisdom and Love of the Trinity and endowed through Christ with a new life principle.

These characteristics—Godhead, Trinity, grace, human knowing and desire, incarnation, and sacrament—have retained seven centuries later the bright realism of a mountain range lit up by the dawn and awaiting exploration.

✣ ✣ ✣

After observing over several decades a number of Thomisms, I would conclude that the work of the scholars and theologians of this century have left behind various opportunities to understand the theology of Aquinas. The historical research of this century and the changes brought by the Council did not affect Aquinas as much as neo-Thomism, and the theological principles of renewal have often been extensions of his theology. No longer ignored by secular society as someone darkly "medieval" or superstitiously "Catholic," he has been given back his own history and theological depth. If Chenu, Congar, Rahner, Schillebeeckx, and others had to escape from the neo-scholastic monopoly, their theologies of personality and sacrament never lost sight of the genius and spirit of the medieval Dominican theologian. Jose Pinto de Oliveira and Otto Pesch are not alone in thinking that Vatican II had set Aquinas' theology free for new accomplishments.

Aquinas' theology is not the same as the revelation of God in Jesus Christ; not the same as every other Christian theology, nor is it the best or only way of thinking about God and Christ. Neo-Thomism is not Western Christianity nor was it ever Roman Catholicism. The limits of a theology should never be forgotten, for exaggeration is the parent of neglect. If culture gives birth to science and philosophy, then Aquinas' thought enthusiastically drawn from Aristotelianism and Platonism can never escape its medieval thought-forms. We are living in the late modern era, while Aquinas lived in the High Middle Ages; Aquinas and his commentators reflected European Christianity, but today Christianity is called to incarnation and inculturation in a much wider world. His thinking is largely theocentric, and from the eighteenth century on, human subjectivity, freedom, and science are the points of departure for human reflection and exploration. Catholicism should not rehabilitate an abstract, logical, and theocentric theology (which Aquinas never was), nor continue its past struggle against all the modes of living and thinking which have emerged over the past two centuries.[2] To parade the Aquinas of neo-Aristotelian metaphysics is a form of historicism, a fundamentalism of the past removing him from contemporary life. Pesch observes:

> The contemporary value of Aquinas can only be indicated by recognizing a basic distance of him from us. Thomas did not begin with our issues, nor did he take up our theological questions. Admittedly it is important to value the suggestions he gives and to see our connection with the problems he faces. Thomas is certainly an outstanding example of how basic problems of Christian theology, i.e., basic questions of faith and existence, perdure through changing forms of expression. Recognizing their lasting importance, however, and seeing the historical continuity with Thomas doesn't happen without work or without living and thinking in another period. The reward is clear: the experience of an important and graced period in history out of which we come and in which we still live to some extent. This mentality brings also an effective protection against instant, fashionable applications of Aquinas which think that his thought can be presented without its historical roots; and against the opposite presumption that real Christianity only began with our modern age.[3]

Pondering what might be Aquinas' influence today begins with understanding the medieval world as the context for the theology's insights and conclusions as well as a recognition of the distinction between medieval theology and the Greek conceptuality and Latin language expressing its ideas. It is not a question of resuscitating a medieval system, or of extracting definitions or syllogisms but of encouraging today's teacher, preacher, and intellectual to meet the insights and thought-forms of Aquinas. Then one can ask how the truths of Christianity and of human religious life might be illumined by his thought.

❖ ❖ ❖

There is a new interest in Aquinas today as theology and medieval research attract interest.[4] Pesch thinks that "in recent decades a remarkable change has taken place. In German, French, Anglophone, and of course in Italian and Spanish circles highly qualified works on Thomas have sprung up like mushrooms."[5] Congresses, periodicals, and institutes discuss his thought. But can a medieval theology assist faith, church, society? The following are a few suggestions.

(1) All of medieval life was deeply influenced by church and theology. Art and architecture, liturgy, monastic or feudal structures, any concrete form of religion are not intelligible without knowing something of their theological background. Acquaintance with the organizing perspectives of an Aquinas or a Bonaventure illumines medieval life in its sweep and details. Theology often explains art, daily life, and politics. So art history should offer more than the identification of a particular saint standing forth in a window or in a sculptured facade.

(2) If accurate knowledge of medieval theology is indispensable for understanding the subsequent Renaissance and the Reformation, even more, many forms of the Catholic Church from the Council of Trent to Vatican II were rooted in different interpretations of scholasticism, often of Thomism. For instance, some positions in the controversies over freedom and grace, which dominated theology during the four centuries after 1600 are variations on scholastic theologians. There is much to be done in setting out the history of the various Thomisms. Some knowledge of Baroque or nineteenth-century scholastic theologies in moral theology or sacramental theology is indispensable for understanding the life of the church which today is leaving the Baroque.

(3) Aquinas' theology, so long neglected for its philosophical frame, still offers aspects awaiting exploration. The patterns and forms of the *ST* are not well known or fully uncovered. They have much to disclose and can assist new applications of his principles (they will be different in Chicago, Lisbon, or Lagos).

(4) Modern philosophy begins with the free subject in process and history. Catholic theology can be done out of the thought-forms of modernity but not out of the ideology of modernity. Modern theology need not always be fashioned in a liberal Protestant form where humanity is tragic and divinity incomplete, and where finite ideas and forms inevitably distort historical revelation. Catholic theology can engage the three characteristics of subjectivity, freedom, and history without losing its commitment to a real, supernatural revelation. The modern distinction between objects and the horizons of knowing and loving is unavoidable in fashioning a theology which explains grace in millions of diverse lives even as it reflects Jesus'

Kingdom of God. Only a theology which takes seriously degrees of process, historicity, and individuality can respond to the pastoral issues of today as the church exists within global unity and cultural diversity, within world religions and free individuality, but also amid sin and suffering.

There appear to be some modern dynamics at work in Aquinas' theology. In a theology seeking to be free of prejudices and of merely edifying arguments, God does not enter to substitute for creation or to frighten creatures; faith and the supernatural have their place but they do not overwhelm sciences and sources as they are received through the free human appropriation of a person. All three parts of the *ST* are about active persons, divine or human. The First Part ends with the human being existing out of matter and spirit, existence and grace. This individual's freedom and various mental activities are highlighted, for they are where revelation and grace enter. The *ST's* general approach to personality and Spirit, even to the history of religion, is developmental. The structures of nature and the presence of the Spirit of Jesus have degrees of engagement with men and women in history. There is an exposition of the transcendental (or divine) depth in multitudes of truth and goodness as well as an affirmation that their varied realizations are good although limited. The modern search for the underlying realm or ground of a realm in the world is not unlike Aquinas' theories of implicit faith seeking First Truth, or from the description of the New Law first of all as the grace of the Spirit.

The value of Aquinas' theology lies very much in its expansive vision of divine and human life. If Catholic theology has taken a few steps into a post-modern era, this move is neither a return to scholasticism nor an enthusiastic embrace of the sterile directions of modernity. A self without God, texts without reference, ethics without responsibility, consciousness without community and sacrament, methods without realities, mechanisms apart from telos—this modernity is coming to an end. Late modern or postmodern moods imply some liberation from the confines of cultural formalisms born of abstraction and mathematics; they seek a union of theory and life, respect past cultures and present diversity, and recognize the end of the monopoly of words. There is a new conviction that the power of Christianity cannot be expressed solely in modern terms, i.e., in self-absorbed and non-supernatural systems which after one hundred and fifty years show themselves incapable of explaining faith and religion to people. Aquinas' thought is different from modern theology not because, as some neo-scholastics held, he rejected all subjectivity, freedom, and history, but because he affirmed reality, human and divine. Aquinas' system is essentially dialogical and expansive; he is not a Protestant fundamentalist, not a clerical restorationist, and not a late modern nihilist.

(5) A few pages comparing Aquinas and Latin American liberation theology have appeared, but the stimulus of that medieval theology for the churches and peoples in continents outside of Europe awaits new correlations.[6] What would he contribute to societies living apart from the ways of thinking drawn from Greece and Rome, thought-forms so dominant in Europe but absent from many areas of the globe? For them what is person and nature? Activity and sign? Can one remain with Aristotelian virtues or Alexandrine hypostases in societies living amid networks of life-forces pictured in non-Hellenic ways? The world is not composed of Aristotelian cultures, and so the role of Aquinas, for instance in Africa, awaits an African Thomism. Francois de Mediros observes basic differences in thought-form between the African mind and Aquinas: the influence of symbol and name in the realm of act and being; a proper African "logic" and "metaphysics"; the African religious milieu which is neither solely that of Christian revelation nor of ancient European paganisms. As points of contact with Aquinas, he selects an emphasis upon life, degrees of being and life, and the active life of the human being; the motif of harmony; and an ethics of happiness and respon-sible action.[7] Vatican II brought the world church, and theology has brought contacts with cultures new and old. Some Thomist insights lead outward into a pluralism of theologies among a broad human religious history.

With Aquinas and his theology, however, there is always a "scandal." A scandal of goodness, a scandal of reality, a scandal of limits. This independent thinker who drew on all the resources of a great epoch to re-think Christianity was confident of the creature's potential and of God's love. Moreover, Aquinas believed that education should not be divorced from the moral life, and that study should lead to prayer, life to art and liturgy, and realism in theology to praxis. That explains why Aquinas' theology always has some potential for liberating and refreshing Christianity.

❖ ❖ ❖

Aquinas' theology is an opening, a path, a synthesis, and a center. If today there are opportunities, there are also obstacles to understanding Aquinas' theology. First, due to the ending of neo-scholastic seminary and college education there is a considerable ignorance of the style and language of scholasticism and consequently of the principles and thought-forms of any theology related to them. Second, there is a tendency in medieval studies in North America to focus upon any area except religion, church, and theology. Third, unfortunately a slight recurrence of the fixation on Aquinas' logic and metaphysics is implying again that ontology was his life's work and authoritarian rigidity his style. By enshrining a poorly understood segment of the recent past, it closes itself off from the world-wide Catholic Church as it exists since Vatican II.[8] The future of Thomist theology lies elsewhere: within the future of the Incarnation whose servant and sacrament this theology is.

Who will see that Aquinas' theology is more widely appreciated, more deeply understood, more honestly applied to our times? It will be people who are well-educated in both content and context, in both philosophy and history. To work with Aquinas demands an entry into two worlds: access to his own, knowing as well as possible the cultural and historical conditions of the production of his writings, and an awareness of this age. The study of Aquinas in his historical context prepares for understanding his theology, while the history of the Thomist schools shows the value and limits of applications.

An internship lies ahead for the student of Thomas Aquinas. It takes time to understand the thought-forms and the organization of that great thinker, and the volumes of his writings offer no end of analyses and arrangements. It is important to understand not merely a few pages of one book but the general forms of that thought which is Aristotelian, Platonic, and Augustinian. In the twentieth century scholars have composed a context for Aquinas' thought. They emphasize: (a) attention to the historical context of the twelfth and thirteenth centuries; (b) awareness of underlying theological motifs; (c) discernment of shifts in his thinking and his sources; (d) knowledge of the various families of interpretations, the many Thomisms.

Aquinas' thinking offers insights and principles but it does not give final systems or universal conclusions. His theology of the virtues is not the totality of moral theology; his elaboration of the hypostasis of Christ is not a contemporary Christology; his theology of the priest-hood makes only a small contribution to the theology of a parish or dio-cese today. The future of his thought lies with us.

❖ ❖ ❖

Sometimes one can find a spirit or a memory in a place. One can imagine a person in a landscape. The atmosphere of a hillside or a street seems for a moment or two to transcend time and to intimate a presence from the past: an important person, or a past event. Places like art are companions to thought and prayer.

One senses a medieval *genius loci* in the Sainte-Chapelle in Paris. Its vertical lines of stone frame the stained-glass windows. The colors give access through art to the flesh and blood of the biblical stories and to the history of the church. The church is a marriage of architecture and theology accomplished by master-builders, design-ers, engineers, and workers seven centuries ago. Sculpture, ceramics, friezes, windows, paintings present a detailed, harmonious but sumptuous decoration. An enormous stone and glass jewel box, it was built to display Christ's crown of thorns and was completed after perhaps less than five years of labor. Nearby during the years of con-struction Thomas was studying the architectonics of pseudo-Dionysius and Aristotle. The solemn consecration of the Sainte-Chapelle took place on April 26, 1248. A few months after that ceremony in the summer of 1248, he left with Albert for Cologne. His career shares in the affluence of an age which could so quickly build this royal chapel, and his pages of synthesis flow from the same cultural spirit as does the chapel's art.

In the countryside of Lazio south of Rome, the tan stones of the abbey of Fossanova still glimmer today in the sun against the green background of fields and woods. Now staffed by Franciscans rather than by the Cistercians who cared for Aquinas' last days, its spacious church and cloister seem little changed from the thirteenth century. In a building used for storage and farm equipment worn stone stairs lead upward to the room where Aquinas died. There a simple terra-cotta plaque mentions that passing. The cool room seems still caught in the dismay and reverence of death, while outside fertile valleys lead to the hills where members of his family once lived.

And finally, a place can recall the past even as it continues that distant moment in the present. Today, as a century and a millennium end, to walk across the stone bridge from the Isle de Paris, where Notre Dame and the Sainte-Chappelle soar into a spring or autumn evening, is to enter the "Left Bank." In that quarter, at the time of Aquinas' professorship, the students drawn from the countries of Europe spoke with each other and their teachers through the common language of a direct, simple Latin. Today on the students' side of the Seine is the church of Saint Julien le Pauvre where Aquinas preached. Outside the church are narrow, short, crowded streets lined with bookstores and eating places. There we sense how Thomas Aquinas' journey has continued over the years. His message of the value of the intellectual life, his optimism about discovery, his quest for transcendence and for the presence of the divine in men and women is never alien to any honest science or human art. His thought spoke to Meister Eckhart and to Etienne Gilson in the different centuries when they were students here. It has survived the politics of Richelieu and has heard the music coming from an organ played by Cesar Franck; it has not disappeared with the innovations of Debussy and Picasso or with those of James Joyce or Olivier Messiaen. Today the windows of the book stores present a biography of Hemingway or a study of Simone de Beauvoir. But they also hold new books about Thomas Aquinas and new editions of his works. Centuries of literature on his thought fill bibliographies, and yet how little we know about the force of his genius or the fabric of his theology.

❖ ❖ ❖

The momentous journeys in Thomas Aquinas' life—to the university world of the thirteenth century, to the Dominicans and to Aristotle, to Paris and Rome, back to Paris and then to Naples, to the controversies of university or papal court—perhaps influenced his giving theology the form of a journey. In the procession of all things from the Godhead each existent is moving forward. In the plan of the *ST* the spiral of emergence and journey from the generous Godhead accompanies all things forward. The human journey, "a road to happiness" (II–II, 1, 7), finds a first climax in the creature of spirit and matter, personality and grace, who is ourselves. It finds its center in

Jesus Christ who "displays for us the journey of truth in himself" (III, Prologue).

Thomism itself has been a religious thought on a journey through seven centuries. How that journey will continue, not in a medieval school or a Baroque monastery but in the twenty-first century, remains to be seen.

A true journey is one always moving further into reality, and for Thomas Aquinas reality could be expressed as being or as light. "The actualization of a reality is, in a way, its light."[9] When he was at the height of his powers Aquinas wrote a hymn for the liturgy of the feast of Corpus Christi, and one poetic line from it sums up his personality and his theology, "*Vetustatem novitas, umbrae fugat veritas, noctem lux eliminat.*" The Latin poem is speaking of the sacramental newness of the revelation of the Word in Jesus. "The old yields to something new, the truth puts shadows to flight, eliminating night is light."[10]

NOTES

✛

Introduction

1. That pioneer of the history of medieval thought Étienne Gilson wrote a book on Aquinas' system, *Le Thomisme*, which was given, however, the English title of *The Philosophy of St. Thomas Aquinas* (St. Louis, 1924).

2. See the bibliography of this book. Apart from major works, English secondary literature is cited in notes.

3. The work did not develop the content or forms of Aquinas' theology.

4. References to the *Summa theologiae* will be in the text according to part, question, article and objection; references to other works by Aquinas will be in footnotes. Translations from the Latin works of Aquinas are by the author.

5. Cited in Peter Hebblethwaite, *The Runaway Church* (London, 1975), p. 102.

6. Y. Congar, "Introduction (1983)," in *Thomas d'Aquin: Sa vision de théologie et de l'église* (London, 1983), p. ii.

7. *De Unitate intellectus contra Averroistas*, 5 *Opuscula philosophica* (Turin, 1954), p. 90.

8. Otto Pesch sketches four stages on the journey toward "the real Thomas Aquinas." The first stage discovers that his philosophy is quite different from a logic or an ethics done for its own sake; it differs too from any neo-Thomism which juxtaposes Aristotelianism with some Christian dogmas. The second stage is a decisive turn to Aquinas as theologian. The third stage is the discovery of history: the historical context of Aquinas' own age, the history of Thomism, and the forms of history and process in his own theology reaching from the Trinity creating to the grace of Jesus Christ amid the human race. The fourth stage is to view Thomas in dialogue: for instance, with other Eastern and Western churches, with contemporary philosophy and science, with the world religions. See Otto Pesch, *Thomas von Aquin. Grenze und Grösse einer mittelalterlichen Theologie. Eine Einführung* (Mainz, 1988), p. 36.

1. The Life and Career of Thomas Aquinas

1. Recent biographical sources are Jean-Pierre Torrell, *Initiation à saint Thomas d'Aquin. Sa personne et son oeuvre* (Paris, 1993) and J. A. Weisheipl, *Friar Thomas d'Aquino* (New York, 1974). There is a summary article by Torrell, "Thomas d'Aquin," *Dictionnaire de spiritualité* 15 (Paris, 1991), 718f., and one by Weisheipl, "Thomas Aquinas, St." *New Catholic Ency-*

clopedia 14 (New York, 1967), 102f. See also Simon Tugwell, "Thomas Aquinas. Introduction," in *Albert and Thomas. Selected Writings* (New York, 1988), p. 201f.; Walter Principe, "Aquinas, St. Thomas," in *The HarperCollins Encyclopedia of Catholicism*, ed. R. McBrien (San Francisco, 1995), pp. 83–89.

2. M.–D. Chenu, *Toward Understanding St. Thomas* (Chicago, 1964), p. 131f.

3. Angelus Walz, *Saint Thomas Aquinas* (Westminster, 1951), p. 15.

4. Weisheipl, *Friar Thomas d'Aquino*, p. 18.

5. On Peter of Ireland, see Torrell, *Initiation à saint Thomas d'Aquin*, p. 10; Weisheipl, *Friar Thomas d'Aquino*, p. 15f.; M. B. Crowe, "Peter of Ireland: Aquinas' Teacher for the Artes Liberales," *Arts libéraux et Philosophie au Moyen Age* (Montreal, 1969), p. 617f.

6. On the predecessors to Dominic and Francis in the century before them, see Herbert Grundmann, *Religious Movements in the Middle Ages* (Berlin, 1935; Notre Dame, Ind., 1994); Otto Pesch argues that scholasticism too is developed in the framework of these evangelical movements ("Paul as Professor of Theology. The Image of the Apostle in St. Thomas' Theology," *The Thomist* 38 [1974]: 587).

7. See Leonard Boyle, "The Dominican Order and Theological Study," *Providence* 2 (1964): 241f.

8. Pierre Mandonnet, *Saint Dominique. L'idee, l'homme et l'oeuvre 2* (Paris, 1938), p. 83; see J. B. Freed, *The Friars and German Society in the Thirteenth Century* (Cambridge, 1977). With papal approval in 1217 the Dominican brothers were preachers not only in activity but in commission and ministry; see Alain Boureau, "Au coeur du Moyen Age: Les dominicains et la maitrise narrative," *L'Evenement sans fin. Récit et christianism au Moyen Age* (Paris, 1993), p. 55f.

9. M.–D. Chenu, *St Thomas d'Aquin et la Théologie* (Paris, 1959), p. 11.

10. Torrell, *Initiation à saint Thomas d'Aquin*, p. 22.

11. Tugwell, "Thomas Aquinas," p. 206.

12. If there was an incident of seducing Thomas with a prostitute (and scholars disagree over its historicity), this seems to have been an escapade of the brothers at Montesangiovanni occuring before Thomas met his mother at Roccasecca; see Weisheipl, *Friar Thomas d'Aquino*, p. 31.

13. See Torrell, *Initiation à saint Thomas d'Aquin*, pp. 16f., 403f.

14. Texts from the acts of provincial and general councils around 1275 cited in M. H. Vicaire, "L'homme que fut S. Thomas," in *L'Anthropologie de Saint Thomas* (Fribourg, 1974), p. 29.

15. Chenu, *St Thomas d'Aquin*, p. 11.

16. Quoted in Joan Evans, *Life in Medieval France* (New York, 1969), p. 14f.

17. Otto von Simson, "Die Kunst des hohen Mittelalters. 'Lichtvolle Geistigkeit'," in *Das Mittelalter II. Das Hohe Mittelalter, Propyläen Kunstgeschichte* 6 (Berlin, 1972), p. 11; see *The Year 1200* (New York, 1970), 2 vols.

18. See J. Le Goff, *Intellectuals in the Middle Ages* (Cambridge, 1993), p. 65f.

19. Ibid., p. 81.

20. Chenu, *Toward Understanding St. Thomas*, p. 20.

21. The words of the professors who requested upon his death the body of Aquinas; see Chenu, *Toward Understanding St. Thomas*, p. 23.

22. Chenu, *St Thomas d'Aquin*, p. 27.

23. Tugwell, "Thomas Aquinas" p. 207.

24. See J. A. Weisheipl, *Thomas d'Aquino and Albert His Teacher* (Toronto, 1980).

25. R. Imbach, Prologe, p. xliii in *Prologe zu den Aristoteles-kommentaren*, ed. F. Cheneval and R. Imbach (Frankfurt, 1993). Tugwell also thinks that Aquinas heard Albert lecture on Aristotle's psychology and on the theology of Pseudo-Denis ("Thomas Aquinas,"p. 208). "The solution [to various opinions] seems to be that the time of study in Paris was a time of mixed formation. When Thomas' superiors, aware of his intellectual gifts, permitted him to begin his theology even while receiving his formation in philosophy. . . . Nothing hinders us from thinking that at Saint-Jacques he followed at the same time certain courses in theology with Albert for whom he re-copied the *De caelesti hierarchica*" (Torrell, *Initiation à saint Thomas d'Aquin*, p. 35f.).

26. See particularly Loris Sturlese, "Der philosophische und naturwisen-schaftliche Rationalismus Alberts des Grossen,"in *Die deutsche Philosophie im Mittelalter* (Munich, 1993), p. 324f.

27. Albert the Great, *Physica* 1, tr. 1, c. 1.

28. Chenu, *St Thomas d'Aquin*, p. 31

29. Weisheipl, *Friar Thomas d'Aquino*, p. 41f.

30. Alain de Libera, *Introduction à la mystique Rhénane. D'Albert le Grand à Maître Eckhart* (Paris, 1984), p. 36f.

31. Cited in E. Schillebeeckx, "Thomas Aquinas: Servant of the Word,"in *The Schillebeeckx Reader*, ed. R. Schreiter (New York, 1984), p. 291. Albert complained that anti-Aristotelian Dominicans were "blaspheming about what they did not understand . . . namely the use of this philosophy" (cited in Y. Congar, "In Dulcedine societatis quaerere veritatem. Notes sur le travail en équipe chez s. Albert et chez les Precheurs au XIIIe siècle," in *Albertus Magnus Doctor Universalis, 1280/1980*, ed. G. Meyer [Mainz, 1980], p. 56).

32. Weisheipl, *Thomas d'Aquino and Albert his teacher*, p. 13. R.-A. Gauthier finds in Aquinas' commentary on the *Ethics* 350 passages where the influence of Albert is evident. Still, by the time of the composition of this commentary and the composition of the *ST* Thomas saw some deficiences in his teacher's work (cited in Torrell, *Initiation à saint Thomas d'Aquin*, p. 38f.).

33. Tugwell, "Thomas Aquinas," p. 212f.

34. Tugwell, "Thomas Aquinas," p. 213.

35. Weisheipl, *Friar Thomas d'Aquino*, p. 85.

36. *Contra pestiferam doctrinam retrahentium homines a religionis ingressu* 15, *Opuscula theologica* 2 (Turin, 1952), p. 185.

37. See Torrell, *Initiation à saint Thomas d'Aquin*, p. 54f.

38. *Principium Fratris Thomae de Commendatione et Partitione Sacrae Scripturae, Opuscula theologica* 1 (Turin, 1954), p. 435.

39. *Breve Principium Fratris Thomae de Commendatione Sacrae Scripturae, Opuscula theologica* 1 (Turin, 1954), p. 441f.

40. Peter Calo, *Fontes vitae S. Thomas Aquinatis auctore Petro Calo*, ed. D. Prummer (Toulouse, 1912), p. 30.

41. Weisheipl, "Thomas Aquinas, St.," 105.

42. For an overview on Aquinas and platonism, see C. D'Ancona Costa, "Historiographie du platonisme médiéval. Le cas de saint Thomas," in *Saint Thomas au XXe siècle*, ed. S-T. Bonino (Paris, 1994), p. 198f.

43. William of Tocco, *The Life of St. Thomas Aquinas*, cited in Torrell, *Initiation à saint Thomas d'Aquin*, p. 61.

44. R. W. Southern, *Medieval Humanism* (New York, 1970), p. 48.

45. Chenu, *Toward Understanding St. Thomas*, p. 36f.

46. Chenu counted two thousand quotations from Aristotle in the earlier commentary on Peter Lombard and one thousand from Augustine (Torrell, "Thomas d'Aquin," 725). It is not certain that Aquinas gave a title to his greatest work, but the oldest title is *Summa theologiae*; see A. Walz, "De genuino titulo *Summa theologiae*," *Angelicum* 18 (1941): 142f.

47. "Thomas von Aquin," *Herrlichkeit* 3:1, Part 1 (Einsiedeln, 1965), p. 356.

48. Tugwell, "Thomas Aquinas" p. 221.

49. See R. A. Gauthier, *Saint Thomas d'Aquin. Somme contre les gentils* (Paris, 1993). On the medieval *summa*, see Chenu, *Toward Understanding St. Thomas*, p. 298f.

50. See Torrell, *Initiation à saint Thomas d'Aquin*, p. 154f. "The non-believers whose errors St. Thomas wants to refute are largely pagans . . . but of missions to pagans of his own time there is no mention" (R.-A. Gauthier, *Saint Thomas d'Aquin*, p. 112.) On the similarities between this earlier *summa* and the *ST*, see Torrell, *Initiation à saint Thomas d'Aquin*, p. 170.

51. Chenu, *Toward Understanding St. Thomas*, p. 258.

52. Leonard Boyle describes this conventual education of the young friars in "Notes on the Education of the *Fratres communes* in the Dominican Order in the Thirteenth Century," in *Xenia medii aevi historiam illustrantia oblata Th. Kappeli, O.P.* (Rome, 1978), p. 249f.

53. See Torrell, *Initiation à saint Thomas d'Aquin*, p. 250f.; L.-J. Bataillon, "Saint Thomas et les Pères: de la Catena à la *Tertia Pars*," in *Ordo sapientiae et amoris*, ed. C. J. Pinto de Oliveira (Paris, 1993), p. 15f.; W. Principe, "Thomas Aquinas' Principles for the Interpretation of Patristic Texts," *Studies in Medieval Culture* 8–9 (Kalamazoo, 1976), p. 111f.; C. Pera, *Le Fonti del pensiero di S. Tommaso d'Aquino nella Somma teologica* (Turin, 1979); G. G. Geenen, "The Council of Chalcedon in the Theology of St. Thomas," in *From an Abundant Spring* (New York, 1952), p. 123f. and

"St. Thomas et les Pères," *Dictionnaire de théologie catholique* 15: 1 (Paris, 1946), 743f.; see Weisheipl, *Friar Thomas d'Aquino*, p. 168; Leo J. Elders, "Santo Tomas de Aquino y los Padres de la Iglesia," *Doctor Communis* 48 (1995): 55f.

54. Weisheipl, *Friar Thomas d'Aquino*, p. 171; O. Pesch and A. Peters, *Einführung in die Lehre von Gnade und Rechtfertigung* (Darmstadt, 1981), p. 66f.; H. Bouillard, *Conversion et grâce chez s. Thomas d'Aquin* (Paris, 1944), p. 64f.

55. Weisheipl, *Friar Thomas d'Aquino*, p. 244f.

56. Ibid., p. 121. Aquinas' commentary shows that by the time of the lectures on Matthew he had found a copy of Chrysostom.

57. See Torrell, *Initiation à saint Thomas d'Aquin*, p. 254f.

58. "The commentary on the *De anima* had been finished, and would be published in Italy in the autumn of 1268; so there is nothing which contradicts the view that Thomas could have left around this time (probably in September). . . . One can add that the invasion of Rome by Conradin in July, 1268 (Santa Sabina itself was pillaged) furnished a further reason for this early departure. For Gauthier there is no doubt that Thomas left Rome at that time and traveled by boat from Civitavecchia to Aigues-Mortes, and then up the Rhone by boat. . . . This would have brought Thomas as quickly as possible and by the most rapid means to Paris, arriving a little after the fourteenth of September, the beginning of the school year" (Torrell, *Initiation à saint Thomas d'Aquin*, p. 264f.).

59. Cited in Weisheipl, *Friar Thomas d'Aquino*, p. 288.

60. Martin D'Arcy, *Thomas Aquinas* (Westminster, 1944), p. 12.

61. Chenu, *St Thomas d'Aquin*, p. 110.

62. Weisheipl, *Friar Thomas d'Aquino*, p. 272f.

63. Torrell, *Initiation à saint Thomas d'Aquin*, pp. 347, 349.

64. Weisheipl, *Friar Thomas d'Aquino*, p. 281.

65. Chenu, *Toward Understanding St. Thomas*, p. 214. Rudi Imbach writes: "Thomas Aquinas is a theologian: whoever does not understand or interpret him as a theologian misunderstands him completely; in research on Aquinas since E. Gilson and M.-D. Chenu this thesis has been represented and practiced with the greatest force" (*Prologue*, pp. ix, lviii). Gauthier concludes: "Thomas never was and never wished to be anything but a theologian. If, at the time he was presenting moral theology in the Second Part of the *ST*, he was commenting on the Nichomachaean ethics, that was solely because he saw in the moral philosophy of Aristotle the rational instrument by which he could give an account of what faith teaches about the purpose of human life. Thomas then never wrote a moral philosophy, nor an interpretation of Aristotle, solely for Aristotle but used the moral philosophy of Aristotle in a theology animated by a spirit alien to Aristotle" (*Aristote. L'Ethique à Nicomaque* [Louvain, 1970], p. 275); see "Le Métier de sage," *Saint Thomas d'Aquin. Somme contre les gentils* , p. 143f. "One important factor in this theology was the conviction he shared with Albert that philosophy has to be taken seriously. The faith is not served by invoking dogmatic considerations

to impose solutions to philosophical problems, nor is sound theology fostered by disowning philosophical conclusions that are genuinely cogent. . . . Thomas was sometimes seen as conceding too much ground to the philosophers, but what was at stake in Thomas' position was the very possibility of a coherent Christian understanding: if Christianity is true, then it must make sense and it must make sense in terms which are related to the ordinary, untheological ways in which human beings try to make sense of things" (Tugwell, "Thomas Aquinas," p. 227).

66. W. Principe, "Aquinas, St. Thomas," *The HarperCollins Encyclopedia of Catholicism*, p. 84.

67. L. Hödl, "Philosophische Ethik und Moral-Theologie," in *Thomas von Aquin*, ed. A. Zimmermann (Berlin, 1987), p. 34.

68. See A. Dondaine, *Les secrétaires de S. Thomas* (Rome, 1956); on the role of memory in Aquinas' writings, see M. J. Carruthers, *The Book of Memory. A Study of Memory in Medieval Culture* (Cambridge, 1990), pp. 5, 152f., 172f.

69. See J. A. Weisheipl, "An Introduction to the Commentary on the Gospel of Saint John,"in *St. Thomas Aquinas, Commentary on the Gospel of St. John* 1 (Albany, 1980), p. 3f.; M.-D. Philippe, "Préface," in *Thomas d'Aquin, Commentaire sur l'Evangile de saint Jean* (Versailles-Buxy, 1981–1987), 3 vols.

70. See Torrell, *Initiation à saint Thomas d'Aquin*, pp. 351, 355.

71. Ibid., 362.

72. Weisheipl, *Friar Thomas d'Aquino*, p. 319, with a quotation from the process of canonization.

73. Bartholomew of Capua cited in Weisheipl, *Friar Thomas d'Aquino*, p. 320.

74. William of Tocco cited in Weisheipl, *Friar Thomas d'Aquino*, p. 321.

75. Weisheipl, *Friar Thomas d'Aquino*, p. 321f.; Torrell, *Initiation à saint Thomas d'Aquin*, p. 422f.

76. Rejecting the view that Albert went to Paris to defend Aquinas against the proposed episcopal condemnation is Weisheipl, *Thomas d'Aquino and Albert*, p. 19f.

77. M.-D. Chenu, *Une école de théologie: Le Saulchoir*, ed. G. Alberigo (Paris, 1985), p. 173.

78. Chenu, *St Thomas d'Aquin*, p. 113.

79. Chenu, "*Veritas liberabit vos*," (1936), *Sources* 16 (1990): 100f.

80. Ch.-D. Boulogne, *S. Thomas d'Aquin* (Paris, 1968), p. 91f. Torrell observes some trips involving boats would reduce this time. (Torrell, *Initiation à saint Thomas d'Aquin*, pp. 410, 264).

81. Vicaire, "L'homme," p. 7f.

82. Torrell, *Initiation à saint Thomas d'Aquin*, p. 138f. Torrell writes of Aquinas engaged by many controversies during his second professorship in Paris: "We should underscore that in these controversies Thomas appeared as he had in his earlier years in Paris. He is like a fighter who fights when he has to and who is ready to respond to any challenge. He is loyal and rigorous

but also impatient when arguing with his opponents who do not understand the weight of an argument, indignant when faced with their kind of radical questioning which weakened faith, and even ironic when he asks, in paraphrasing Job, if they are the only intelligent beings in whom wisdom had appeared" (*Initiation à saint Thomas d'Aquin*, p. 284f.).

83. "S. Thomas écrivain," *Super Boetium De Trinitate . . . De Hebdomadibus, Opera Omnia* 50 [Leonine ed.] (Rome, 1992), p. 209; see also G. Moretti, "St. Thomas Aquinas," in *The Saints through Their Handwriting* (London, 1964), p. 248f.

84. *Questiones . . . Duodecim Quodlibetales*, 2, 4 and 5 in *Opera Omnia* 3, pp. 447f., 464f.

85. *In Aristotelis Libros de Caelo et Mundo*, 1, 22 Turin, 1952), p. 109.

86. *In XII Libros Metaphysicorum Aristotelis Expositio*, 12, 9 (Turin, 1950), p. 599.

87. A. G. Sertillanges *St. Thomas Aquinas and His Work* (London, 1932), p. 51.

88. Torrell, "La pratique pastorale d'un théologie du XIIIe siècle. Thomas d'Aquin predicateur," *Revue Thomiste* 82 (1982): 223f.; see L-J. Bataillon, "Approaches to the Study of Medieval Sermons," *Leeds Studies in English* 9 (1980): 19f.

89. Unedited Sermon, "Osanno fillo David," cited in Torrell, "La pratique," p. 227.

90. Vicaire, "L'homme," p. 28f.

2. Patterns in the *Summa theologiae*

1. "The guiding intuition which directs the plan of the *Summa theologiae* wants to lead us to place human reason at the very heart of religious reality" (A.-I. Mennessier, *Saint Thomas d'Aquin, L'Homme chrétien* [Paris, 1965], 25).

2. M.-D. Chenu, *Toward Understanding St. Thomas* (Chicago, 1964), p. 46; see B. Coffey, "The Notion of Order according to St. Thomas Aquinas," *The Modern Schoolman* 27 (1949): 1f. The opening of the *SCG* (1,1) holds a counterpoint of three themes: the wise person discerning and ordering; the artist directing through art good beings to their goals; order and goodness in the universe as resulting from truth, from divine Truth.

3. *SCG* 1, 1.

4. Martin Grabmann, *Introduction to the Theological Summa of St. Thomas* (St. Louis, 1930), p. 7.

5. Martin Grabmann, *Die Kulturphilosophie des hl. Thomas von Aquin* (Augsburg, 1925), p. 23.

6. Around 1260, at S. Jacques in Paris, another Dominican, Jerome of Moravia, was teaching music, and writing a "*summula*" on the musical theory of his time. He noted that new texts were needed because the multiplicity of forms was engendering confusion and boredom among students; see

A. Gastoue, "Un Dominican professeur de musique au XIIIe siècle. Fr. Jérome de Moravie et son oeuvre," *Archivum Fratrum Praedicatorum* 2 (1932): 232.

7. Otto von Simson, "Die Kunst des Hohen Mittelalters. 'Lichtvolle Geistigkeit'," *Das Mittelalter II. Das Hohe Mittelalter, Propyläen Kunstgeschichte* 6 (Berlin, 1972), p. 11.

8. Arnold Hauser, *The Social History of Art* (New York, 1958), vol. 2, pp. 10f.

9. Chenu, *Toward Understanding St. Thomas*, p. 67. Jacques Maritain observed: ". . . In Gothic architecture's times, and especially after St. Francis of Assisi—mystery discloses its more human depths. This is the age of Duccio, Giotto, Angelico . . . Art is still dominated by sacred inspiration, and Christ is still at the center. But this time it is Christ in his humanity, in his torment and redeeming passion . . . and all the saints with their individual features and adventures, and mankind with all the characters who play their part in human life, and all nature reconciled with man in the grace of the Gospel. The human soul gleams everywhere through the barred windows of the objective world, the human self is more and more present on the stage" (*Creative Intuition in Art and Poetry* [New York, 1953], p. 22).

10. See G. A. Zinn, Jr., "Suger, Theology, and the Pseudo-Dionysian Tradition," in *Abbot Suger and Saint-Denis: A Symposium* (New York, 1986), p. 33f.

11. Suger, *De Rebus administratione sua gestis* in *Abbot Suger on the Abbey Church of St.-Denis*, ed. E. Panofsky (Princeton, 1946), pp. 63, 65.

12. M.-D. Chenu, Preface to H. Petitot, *Life and Spirit of Thomas Aquinas* (Chicago, 1966), p. 6.

13. Otto von Simson, "The Gothic Cathedral. Design and Meaning," in *Change in Medieval Society*, ed. S. Thrupp (New York, 1964), p. 169. Von Simson stressed the "functionalism" of this art; the teleology of Aquinas is a kind of functionalism.

14. E. Panofsky, *Gothic Architecture and Scholasticism* (New York, 1957), p. 29 "Is Panofsky's problematic about a possible connection between gothic architecture and scholasticism illegitimate? Not at all, for certainly a century like the unusual thirteenth raises the issue of the inner dependence and mutual relationships of so many cultural streams and innovations" (A. Speer, "Thomas von Aquin und die Kunst," *Archiv für Kulturgeschichte* 72 [1990]: 343.) "Manifestation" is a significant word in Aquinas. Light manifests itself and other things; creation and grace manifest the Trinity, Jesus makes the Logos manifest. Words are manifested in emotions, and each existent manifests the Creator and the act of creation. See *"manifestatio,"* *Index Thomisticus* 13 (Stuttgart, 1974), p. 421f.

15. J. Le Goff cited in von Simson, "Die Kunst des hohen Mittelalters. 'Lichtvolle Geistigkeit'," p. 11.

16. Chenu, *Toward Understanding St. Thomas*, p. 298. R. A. Gauthier observes that a *summa* is a manual which should be both a summary and a complete overview (*Saint Thomas d'Aquin. Somme contre les Gentils* [Paris, 1993], p. 146).

17. Chenu, *Toward Understanding St. Thomas*, p. 299.

18. Richard Heinzmann, "Die Theologie auf dem Weg zur Wissenschaft," *Münchener Theologische Zeitschrift* 25 (1974): 6; see *De Veritate*, 8, 10. See N. Senger, "Der Begriff '*architector*' bei Thomas von Aquin," in *Mittelalterliches Kunsterleben nach Quellen des 11. bis 13. Jahrhunderts*, ed. A. Speer (Stuttgart, 1993), p. 208f.

19. See Panofsky, *Gothic Architecture* and Christopher Wilson, *The Gothic Cathedral* (New York, 1990), 141. A. D. Sertillanges found an aesthetic side of order: "There is a real musical symmetry about the *Summa*, not because of some artifice in the distribution of its materials, but in its very structure: it has emerged like a Gothic cathedral; a lyric of pure thought" (*St. Thomas Aquinas and His Work* [London, 1932], p. 113). "In St. Thomas, doctrine has become harmonious after the manner of a symphony. It vibrates freely in all its parts and undulates from end to end, without any of those intermissions which falsify the key and break the harmony, without unresolved discords or any but expressive silences, by which I mean mysteries. Mysteries are not empty voids. They are more full of meaning than anything else, and it is their depth that makes them unfathomable. . . . Their purpose in a synthesis is to give unity and strength, and indeed, beauty to the whole" (ibid.).

20. Leonard Boyle, *The Setting of the "Summa theologiae" of Thomas Aquinas* (Toronto, 1982), pp. 17f.; see L. Boyle, "Notes on the Education of the *Fratres Communes* in the Dominican Order in the Thirteenth Century," in *Xenia Medii Aevi Historiam Illustrantia*, ed. R. Creytens and P. Künzle (Rome, 1978), p. 249f.

21. Boyle, *The Setting*, 11.

22. Ibid., 16.

23. Ibid. Boyle notes that the Second Part of the *ST* with its theology of the Christian life, theoretical and practical, was widely circulated on its own apart from the two parts which framed it. It might have been that his confreres and colleagues did not fully appreciate Aquinas' broader accomplishment within the *ST* (ibid., 23).

24. This book gives only a general orientation to texts and translation of Aquinas' writings; J. A. Weisheipl, *Friar Thomas d'Aquino* (New York, 1974) and J.-P. Torrell, *Initiation à saint Thomas d'Aquin. Sa personne et son oeuvre* (Paris, 1993) study the genesis of each work .

25. Boyle, *The Setting*, p. 14.

26. A. Patfoort, *Saint Thomas d'Aquin. Les clefs d'une théologie* (Paris, 1983), p. 12.

27. Ibid., 64.

28. On Aquinas' diverse sources, see Ceslao Pera, *Le Fonti del pensiero di S. Tommaso d'Aquino nella Somma teologica* (Turin, 1979).

29. Chenu, *Toward Understanding St. Thomas*, p. 301. To look at the charts by J. J. Berthier or G. Q. Friel (see Bibliography) is to see static divisions and clusters divorced from their Aristotelian and Thomist vitality.

30. Aquinas' theology contained no small amount of Platonism coming not only from newly accessible neo-Platonic writings but from Greek theologies

and from Augustine; cf. R. J. Henle, *Saint Thomas and Platonism* (The Hague, 1956), and the writings of L. Hödl. A pattern of emergence and return had been a popular one from Christian theologians like Origen to German idealists like Schelling.

31. *In 1 Sent.*, d. 14, q. 2, a. 2.

32. *In Librum beati Dionysii de Divinis Nominibus expositio*, bk 4, lect. 11 (Turin, 1950), p. 148; *In 3 Sent.* d. 2, q. 1., a. 1.

33. *Compendium theologiae*, #201.

34. *De Perfectione Vitae Spiritualis, Opuscula theologica* 2 (Turin, 1954), p. 116.

35. See O. Pesch, "Um den Plan der Summa Theologiae des hl. Thomas von Aquin," in *Thomas von Aquin* ed. K. Bernath (Darmstadt, 1978) 1, p. 128f.; A. Patfoort, "L'unité de Ia Pars et le mouvement interne de la Somme théologique de s. Thomas d'Aquin," *Revue des sciences philosophiques et théologiques* 47 (1963): 514f.

36. Y. Congar, "Tradition et sacra doctrina chez Saint Thomas d'Aquin," in *Thomas d'Aquin: Sa vision de théologie et de l'église* (London, 1964) 2, p. 164.

37. M. Seckler, *Das Heil in der Geschichte* (Munich, 1964), p. 35.; see Otto Pesch, *Thomas von Aquin. Grenze und Grösse einer mitelalterlichen Theologie: Eine Einführung* (Mainz, 1988), p. 390f.

38. Congar, "Traditio et sacra doctrina," p. 162.

39. G. Lafont, *Structures et méthode dans la Somme théologique de Saint Thomas d'Aquin* (Paris, 1961), p. 435.

40. "The prologue to the first part of the Second Part in the *ST*—a passage which begins the entire Second Part—recalls intentionally the anthropology of the First Part (q. 93), the human being made in the image of God" (Y. Congar, "Le sens de 'l'économie' salutaire de S. Thomas d'Aquin [*Somme theologique*]," in *Glaube und Geschichte* 2, ed. E. Iserloh [Baden-Baden, 1957], p. 105).

41. Chenu, *Toward Understanding St. Thomas*, p. 86.

42. Grabmann, *Introduction to the Summa*, p. 139.

43. *De Potentia* (Turin, 1949), 4, 1, p. 104.

44. *Miscellanea* 1, 75 cited in Chenu, *Toward Understanding St. Thomas*, p. 259.

45. *The Sermon-Conferences of St. Thomas Aquinas on the Apostles' Creed*, ed. N. Ayo (Notre Dame, Ind.,1988), 4, p. 51.

46. *Principium Fratris Thomae de Commendatione et Partitione Sacrae Scripturae*, p. 439.

47. Ibid., 443.

48. On Aquinas and Scripture, see Torrell, *Initiation à saint Thomas d'Aquin*, p. 49f.

49. "Prologus," *Super Epistolas S. Pauli lectura* (Turin, 1953), 1, p. 3; *Super Epistolam ad Romanos lectura* (Turin, 1953) p. 116f. "Roughly speaking, the *Summa* contains three sections wherein there is a direct elaboration of Holy Scripture: of *Genesis*, in the treatise on creation (*Ia Pars*, qq. 65–74),

of the books on the Law . . . (*I–IIa*, qq. 98–105), and finally of the gospels in the treatise on the life of Christ (*IIIa Pars*, qq. 27–59)" (Chenu, *Toward Understanding St. Thomas*, p. 259).

50. Pesch, *Thomas von Aquin*, p. 88.

51. Aquinas at the beginning of a commentary might generally expound its structure in terms of the four Aristotelian causes, but Henri de Lubac also points to his use of an ancient theological triad of shadow, image, and true reality ("Le 'Nouveauté' de Saint Thomas," *Exégèse médiévale* II [Paris, 1964], p. 286f.).

52. See B. Smalley, *The Study of the Bible in the Middle Ages* (Oxford, 1983). "Just as Aristotelianism refused to dissect soul from body, so it refused a dichotomy between the spirit and the letter. The spiritual sense was not to be studied separately from the literal as if it were superimposed, but through and in the literal" (R. Brown, *The "Sensus Plenior" of Sacred Scripture* [Baltimore, 1955], p. 61); see P. Benoit, *Inspiration in the Bible* (New York, 1965).

53. *Super Evangelium S. Matthaei Lectura* [3: 1] (Turin, 1951), ch. 3, lect. 1, p. 171.

54. *Super Epistolam Primam ad Corinthios Lectura* [5: 1] (Turin, 1953), ch. 15, lect. 1, p. 405.

55. M. A. Reyero, *Thomas von Aquin als Exeget* (Einsiedeln, 1971), p. 247f.

56. "Preface," *In Psalmos, Opera Omnia 6*, p. 48.

57. *Super Evangelium S. Johannis Lectura* [21: 6], c. 21, lect. 6 (Turin, 1952), p. 488.

58. Pesch, *Thomas von Aquin*, p. 345.

59. See W. G. M. B. Valkenberg, *Did Not Our Heart Burn! Place and Function of Holy Scripture in the Theology of Aquinas* (Utrecht, 1990). Ceslaus Spicq's opinion was that in textual criticism and its theory Aquinas was inferior to some of his contemporaries, and that his subjections of the biblical text to countless, logical divisions can appear excessive ("Thomas d'Aquin," *Dictionnaire de théologie catholique* [Paris, 1946], 15:1, 708).

60. "By the very fact of being a cause, a being has a certain likeness to God" (*SCG* 3, 75).

61. *De Spiritualibus Creaturis* 1, q. 10, ad 16 in *Quaestiones Disputatae* 2 (Turin, 1911), p. l, 411.

62. *SCG* 3, 70. "If . . . [God] communicates to others his likeness in terms of being it would follow that he would give a likeness in terms of action, so that created things would have their proper actions" (*SCG* 3, 69).

63. Thomas Aquinas, a sermon for the Second Sunday of Advent, cited in Chenu, *St Thomas d'Aquin*, p. 74.

64. Sertillanges, *Saint Thomas Aquinas and His Work*, p. 37.

65. Cf. Y. Congar, "Le moment 'économique' et le moment 'ontologique' dans la sacra doctrina," in *Mélanges offerts à M. D. Chenu* (Paris, 1967), p. 135f. U. Horst, "Über die Frage einer heilsökonomischen Theologie bei Thomas von Aquin," in *Thomas von Aquin*, ed. K. Bernath, 1, p. 373f. "Thomas sees the *ordo salutis* in a radical way as salvation-history: salvation

is realized in an event, and too, every event between heaven and earth is either salvation-history or its opposite" (M. Seckler, *Das Heil in der Geschichte* [Munich, 1964], p. 121).

66. Chenu, *Toward Understanding St. Thomas*, p. 309.

67. Ibid., 319.

68. Lafont, *Structures et méthode*, p. 483.

69. Patfoort, *Saint Thomas d'Aquin*, p. 87.

70. E. Schillebeekx, "Salut, Redemption et Émancipation," *Problemi di Teologia, Tommaso d'Aquino nel suo settimo centenario* 4 (Naples, 1974), p. 276.

71. O. Pesch and A. Peters, *Einführung in die Lehre von Gnade und Rechtfertigung* (Darmstadt, 1981), p. 79.

72. For the axiom, "to the one doing what is within his powers God gives grace," compare the interpretation in the *Commentary on the Sentences* (II Sent. 5, 2, 2; 28, 1, 4) with that of the *ST* (I–II, 109, 6) which teaches that any act leading to or deepening grace is itself possible only under the influence of grace.

73. Lafont, *Structures et méthode*, p. 469.

74. A. D. Sertillanges, *Saint Thomas d'Aquin* (Paris, 1925) 2, p. 327.

75. Chenu, *Toward Understanding St. Thomas*, p. 167f.

3. A Theological World

1. "Tradition et 'Sacra Doctrina' chez Saint Thomas d'Aquin," in *Eglise et tradition*, ed. H. Fries (Le Puy, 1963), p. 168; see G. van Ackeren, *Sacra doctrina. The Subject of the First Question of the Summa Theologica of St. Thomas Aquinas* (Rome, 1952) with its introduction by Congar; T. C. O'Brien, "'Sacred Doctrine' Revisited: The Context of Medieval Education," *The Thomist* 41 (1977): 475f.

2. *Quaestiones . . . Duodecim Quodlibetales*, 4, q. 3, *Opera Omnia* (Rome, 1992), 3, p. 461.

3. A. D. Sertillanges, *St. Thomas Aquinas and His Work* (London, 1933), p. 38.

4. *In 1 Sent.*, d. 8, q. 1, a. 1, ad 4.

5. *In 1 Sent.*, d. 22, q. 1, a. 3.

6. *Expositio super Librum De Causis*, 6, *Opera Omnia* 4, p. 580.

7. *In 1 Sent.*, d. 27, q. 2, a. 4.

8. *In 1 Sent.*, d. 36, q. 2, a. 1.

9. See John F. Wippel, *Thomas Aquinas on the Divine Ideas* (Toronto, 1993); especially, pp. 37f. and 46f.

10. J.-P. Torrell, "Thomas d'Aquin," in *Dictionnaire de Spiritualité* 15 (Paris, 1990), 763f.

11. *SCG* 2, 2; see 2, 21. Although Aquinas lived long before the thinkers of evolution like Schelling, Darwin, and Teilhard de Chardin, there is a faint line of process or development in his theology. God can create and influence directly, or he can act through creatures; this latter approach through secondary causes points to divine power in an intense format (I, 92, 4, 3).

12. A. D. Sertillanges, *Foundations of Thomistic Philosophy* (St. Louis, 1931), p. 102.

13. *De Potentia*, q. 3, a. 10, ad 2.

14. S. Tugwell, *Albert and Thomas: Selected Writings* (New York, 1988), p. 213. Thomas Merton writes: "A tree gives glory to God first of all by being a tree. For in being what God means it to be, it is imitating an idea which is in God and which is not distinct from the essence of God, and therefore a tree imitates God by being a tree. The forms and individual characters of living and growing things and of inanimate things and of animals and flowers and all nature, constitute their holiness in the sight of God" (*Seeds of Contemplation* [New York, 1949], p. 24f.).

15. *In Librum B. Dionysii de Divinis Nominibus*, 4, 5 (Turin, 1950), p. 115; see J. Kovach, "Divine Art in Saint Thomas Aquinas," in *Arts libéraux et philosophie au moyen âge* (Montreal, 1969), p. 663f. "The analogous names of God refer to a—granted, much higher—kind of metaphor. From his theoretical basis Thomas could have evaluated the images of the Bible in a less positive way than he did, and he could have worried about the 'poetic gifts' of God which in his personal word, the Scripture, reveal themselves with so much 'imagination.' But Thomas did not pursue that course. Despite a quite agnostic element in his teaching on analogous discourse about God (something usually overlooked by scholars), he accented the relatively meager moment of 'similarity' in analogy. He was following convictions expressed in the *Summa contra gentiles* where he said the greatest pleasure comes from the most modest knowledge of the highest things. God is then not a 'poet'; but he certainly is an 'artist'—in the way that the Middle Ages understood art" (Otto Pesch, *Thomas von Aquin. Grenze und Grösse einer mittelalterlichen Theologie: Eine Einführung* [Mainz, 1988], p. 346).

16. *SCG* 3, 97.

17. Sermon # 6, *Opera Omnia* 6, p. 583.

18. *Super Evangelium Ioannis Lectura* (1:4) (Turin, 1952) ch. 1, lect. 3, p. 20. These extensions of love are a kind of mercy (I, 21, 3).

19. *SCG* 3, 97

20. Contemporary phrases are too succinct and open to misunderstanding when they say that everything in the *ST* is treated "under the referential modality of God." The opening of the *ST* presumes that readers understand "reference" in the multiple and active senses of God as efficient, formal, and final cause. Moreover "God" should be understood primarily as the source of the supernatural order, the reign of God

21. Sertillanges, *Saint Thomas Aquinas and His Work*, p. 97. On the image of God, see D. Juvenal Merriell, *To the Image of the Trinity. A Study in the Development of Aquinas' Teaching* (Toronto, 1990).

22. No true God, no source of all of being realized in billions of galaxies, is so tied to one planet as to be involved in a process of becoming God solely through the meager history of earth. Certainly, in the parables of Jesus' teaching we do not meet any of these incomplete or suffering gods. Aquinas' views on the characteristics of God are enhancements, openings to transcendence,

not limitations. But they do protect theology from falling into terrestrial anthropomorphisms, even very modern and pessimistic ones.

23. M.-D. Chenu, *St Thomas d'Aquin* (Paris, 1959), p. 116.

24. Ibid., 122.

25. *SCG* 2, 81.

26. *In De Anima* 2, 1 (Turin, 1936), p. 89.

27. See N. Luytens, "L'homme dans la conception de saint Thomas," in *L'Anthropologie de Saint Thomas* (Fribourg, 1974), p. 48f.; Jean Drapeau, "Selon saint Thomas d'Aquin, l'homme est-il maître de la nature?" *Écologie et environnement* 5 (1986): 135f.

28. Thomas is a theologian, not a biologist or a physician. In his time Aristotelian views had an extraordinary weight. Today, it is less than two centuries since empirical science definitively showed the Aristotelian view of conception to be false.

29. Women are easily enticed into adultery (I–II, 105, 4, ad 9); curiously the biblical text from Job is in fact referring not to an adulteress but to an adulterer (I–II, 105, 4, ad 5).

30. Pesch, *Thomas von Aquin*, p. 217. Aquinas' theology of God is eminently one of an active, infinite spirit and of three persons whose biblical names are partly metaphorical and always analogous (that is, partly equivocal). A patriarchal God is not the divine being of this theology. When we recall the various polemics against the Middle Ages because scholastics were too independent of the Bible, it is ironic to realize that it was the Bible which presented Aquinas with the primal motif from Genesis of subjection, and with that of I Corinthians on women keeping silence. On some negative effects of Thomist views in subsequent centuries, see Pesch, *Thomas von Aquin*, p. 225f.

31. See Kari E. Børresen, *Subordination and Equivalence. The Nature and Role of Woman in Augustine and Thomas Aquinas* (Washington, 1981); C. Kiesling, "Aquinas on Persons' Representation in Sacraments," in *Women Priests* (New York, 1977), p. 253f.

32. Pesch, *Thomas von Aquin*, p. 386f. "The prologue for the I–II of the *Summa theologiae*, which opens the entire second part, intentionally recalls the anthropology of the first part, the human being made in the image of God" (Y. Congar, "Le sens de l'économie salutaire de S. Thomas d'Aquin (*Somme théologique*)," in *Glaube und Geschichte* 2, ed. E. Iserloh (Baden-Baden, 1957), p. 105f.

33. J. Tonneau, *Morale et théologie* (Paris, 1952) 3, p. 13f.

34. C-J. Pinto de Oliveira, "Ordo rationis, ordo amoris. La notion d'ordre au centre de l'univers éthique de S. Thomas," in *Ordo Sapientiae et Amoris* (Fribourg, 1993), p. 285f. See T. O'Meara, "Grace as a Theological Structure in the *Summa theologiae* of Thomas Aquinas," *Recherches de Théologie ancienne et médiévale* 55 (1988): 130f.

35. *De Veritate*, 27, 1; I–II, 110, 1–4.

36. *In XII Libros Metaphysicorum* (Turin, 1950), bk 5, lect. 5, p. 224.

37. *SCG* 4, 22.

38. "Grace is that creative presence of the eternal love of God in the midst of the human personality, a personality which is thereby drawn out of the limitations of nature and brought to a shared life with God" (O. Pesch, *Einführung in die Lehre von Gnade und Rechtfertigung* [Darmstadt, 1981], p. 89).

39. O. Pesch, "Die bleibende Bedeutung der thomanischen Tugendlehre," *Freiburger Zeitschrift für Philosophie und Theologie* 21 (1974): 378f.

40. See O. Lottin, *Le Droit naturel chez Saint Thomas et ses prédécesseurs* (Bruges, 1931).

41. Chenu, *St Thomas d'Aquin*, p. 115.

42. R. Garrigou-Lagrange, *The Three Ages of the Interior Life* (St. Louis, 1947) 1, p. 78.

43. *Super Evangelium Sancti Matthaei Lectura* (4: 19) (Turin, 1951) ch. 4, lect. 2, p. 58.

44. *SCG* 3, 69.

45. A. M. Carré, *Les Maîtres que Dieu m'a donnés* (Paris, 1982), p. 72.

46. Aquinas asked if the infusion of grace into the human personality ("justification") is a miracle. He answered that, although "the good of grace in one is greater than the natural good of the entire universe," it is not a miracle in the ordinary understanding because it is unperceived (I–II, 113, 9, 2).

47. "[Aquinas avoided] two opposite errors: naturalism where God is removed from the world and particularly from human culture, and supernaturalism or fideism where in doctrinal and spiritual matters . . . the legitimate postulates of reason and progress of the natural order are denigrated by the force of some authority" (Paul VI, *Lumen ecclesiae* #8).

48. J.-H. Nicolas comments: "Redoubtable difficulties begin when one confronts the sovereign divine will with its own production of the created universe. . . . Thomas inflexibly maintains all the proper dimensions of the two terms encountering each other: he maintains without making any concessions the absolute sovereignty of the divine will, and the reality of the causality of the created will, particularly human freedom and the responsibility resulting from it. The reconciliation [of the two], while maintaining the conditions of an unyielding rigor, is difficult" (*Somme théologique* 1 [Paris, 1984], p. 299f.).

49. *SCG* 3, 71. "For there would be no evil, if the order of good were removed, whose privation evil is. And this order would not exist, if God did not exist" (*SCG* 3, 71).

50. Chenu, *St Thomas d'Aquin*, p. 126.

51. For Ludwig Hödl, Aquinas' thought through in a new way the theology of grace precisely by pondering the relationship of virtue to grace. He speaks of the "*lumen gratiae*," a new illumination of the existence of the person, a light which relates both to the light of intellect and to the light of glory. Grace achieves a centrality when the treatise on law was extracted from the section on creation and located as leading to the new law which is grace. The ethic of virtue retains its natural foundation gained in creation but receives a depth in grace and is a transformation of an ethic of law. "The

moral theology of Thomas is formally and essentially theology, for God is the source and the goal of the moral activity. The employment of philosophical concepts and statements does not alter the basic theological intention of Thomas; in the *Summa theologiae* we find no trace or element of a philosophical ethic which does not find in a theological syntheisis a theological character" (L. Hödl, "Philosophische Ethik und Moral-Theologie," in *Thomas von Aquin*, ed. A. Zimmermann (Berlin, 1987), p. 30.

52. *De Veritate* 27, 2.

53. Chenu, *St Thomas d'Aquin*, p. 67

54. *Super Evangelium Sancti Matthaei Lectura* [5:2] (Turin, 1951), ch. 5. lect. 1, p. 65.

55. *In Decem Libros Ethicorum . . . Expositio*, bk. 8, l. 5 (Turin, 1949), p. 425. Mary Ann Fatula has arranged a study of Aquinas' spirituality around the motif of friendship: *Thomas Aquinas. Preacher and Friend* (Collegeville, 1993); see also Fergus Kerr, "Charity as Friendship," in *Language, Meaning and God* , ed. B. Davies (London, 1987), p. 21f.

56. *De Veritate* 17, 2.

57. G. Lafont, *Structures et méthode dans la Somme théologique de Saint Thomas d'Aquin* (Paris, 1961), p. 216.

58. *The Sermon-Conferences of St. Thomas Aquinas on the Apostles' Creed*, ed. N. Ayo (Notre Dame, Ind., 1988), p. 43.

59. Illness and death kept Aquinas from completing the Third Part, and the eschatology presented in the text of the *ST* is excerpted from the early commentary on Peter Lombard's *Sentences*.

60. Jesus as way, truth, and life is developed in Aquinas' commentary on the Gospel according to John.

61. M.–D. Chenu, *Toward Understanding St. Thomas* (Chicago, 1964), p. 270f. Chenu adds: "If this embarrasses you, then you will find Aquinas embarrassing" (p. 9). Aquinas' ordering of his *summa* explains why in the Catholic mind Jesus is not the sole actor in salvation: Trinity and Holy Spirit, saints and sacraments are also active. This primacy of grace with a christological center in various degrees before, during, and after Jesus Christ is frequently found in contemporary Catholic theology after Vatican II: e.g., E. Schillebeeckx, P. Teilhard de Chardin, K. Rahner.

62. Chenu, *Toward Understanding St. Thomas*, p. 315. "The incarnation is for Thomas Aquinas both the extreme point of the mystery of God, since it is an expansion reaching the creature from the mystery of the Trinity, and the extreme point of the mystery of the human person, for it is the attainment of the absolute summit in the order of creation, as human nature transcends itself by this union and in this union with a divine person" (M. J. Nicolas, "Introduction," *Thomas d'Aquin. Somme théologique* 1, p. 51).

63. Lafont, *Structures et méthode*, p. 262f.

64. "Thomist Christology is introduced in the *ST* as expressing two principles of the theology of Pseudo-Denis . . . the process moving outward and returning . . . and the principle that goodness diffuses itself" (T. A.

Audet, "Approches historiques de la *Summa theologiae*," in *Études d'histoire littéraire et doctrinale* [Paris, 1962], p. 24).

65. *Super Epistolam ad Ephesios Lectura* [3: 18] (Turin, 1953), ch. 3., lect. 5, p. 45.

66. *SCG* 4, 27.

67. Aquinas was "the first scholastic of the 13th century to quote the texts of Chalcedon and other early councils" (J. A. Weisheipl, *Friar Thomas d'Aquino* [New York, 1974], p. 164f.).

68. The incarnate Word is not simply in or with human nature but brings the personality (in the Greek sense), the hypostasis of a concrete individual existing in human nature, a *homo*. There is, however, no insistence that the human nature assumed by the Word in that individual had as its unavoidable goal, rather than one conditioned by symbolic and social reasons, the maleness of Jesus, that he was a *vir* (III, 17, 1). Aquinas' discussions of masculine and neuter often have to do with Latin grammatical forms. Aquinas rejected the idea that only generative forces (in his view they would be in name or reality linked to maleness) should be involved in the incarnation (so Joseph would be involved and not Mary) because the incarnation has for its terms the "nature of the species," and for its work "the redemption of both sexes." "And nevertheless it must be simply concluded that it [the Word] was able to assume the feminine sex according to its absolute power, although it would not have been so suitable" (*In III Sent.*, d. 12, q. 2, a. 2, quest. 2).

69. "Through the individual events of the human life of Jesus the continuing meaning and effect of the incarnation of God precisely in these events express the human life of Christ, but they also address the lives of Christians. . . . Because Christ is the human son of God, Thomas' theology of incarnation rejects a mythologizing interpretation in which the events of Jesus' life are not really historical mysteries and not really a theology for us. [His theology rejects] the view that the events of the life of that one man would not really be the event of the Son of God and so not the places where salvation occurs, and that these mysteries would not be indications of the lasting meaning of salvation of the Incarnation of God [for us]" (Gerd Lohaus, *Die Geheimnisse des Lebens Jesu in der Summa theologiae des heiligen Thomas von Aquin* [Freiburg, 1985], p. 256); see R. Schenk, "*Omnis Christi Actio Nostra est Instructio*. The Deeds and Sayings of Jesus as Revelation in the View of Thomas Aquinas," in *La doctrine de la révélation divine de saint Thomas d'Aquin*, ed. L. Elders (Vatican City, 1990), p. 105f.

70. Pesch, *Thomas von Aquin*, p. 178.

71. *Super Epistolam ad Ephesios Lectura* [2: 18] (Turin, 1953), ch. 2. lect. 5, p. 31; on instrument in patristic Christology and Aquinas, see W. Metzger, *Der Organongedanke in der Christologie der griechischen Kirchenväter* (Munsterschwarzach, 1968), p. xxf., essays by H. Bouësse in *Revue Thomiste*, and T. Tschipke, *Die Menschheit Christi als Heilsorgan der Gottheit* (Freiburg, 1940).

72. *Super Evangelium S. Johannis Lectura* [8:1] (Turin, 1952), ch. 8, lect. 1, p. 223.

73. *Super Epistolam ad Hebraeos Lectura* [10: 1] (Turin, 1953), ch. 10, lect. 1, p. 441.

74. *De Veritate*, 29, 7.

75. Chenu, *St Thomas d'Aquin*, p. 130. Commenting on the main portal of Notre Dame in Paris, Alain Erlande-Brandenburg observes: "The annunciation of the end of the world and of the return of Christ is no longer conceived as an apocalyptic vision. Here the more humane depiction from the *Gospel according to Matthew* is basic. . . . Christ appears in the tympanum as redeemer, showing his wounds and surrounded by angels with the instruments of his Passion. The Virgin and John are prominent as intercessors for humanity . . . and angels watch this dramatic event" (*Notre Dame in Paris, Geschichte, Architektur, Skulptur* [Freiburg, 1992], p. 108).

76. M. Grabmann, *Die Lehre des heiligen Thomas von Aquin von der Kirche als Gotteswerk* (Regensburg, 1903), p. 89f.; Yves Congar, *Esquisses du mystère de l'église* (Paris, 1953), p. 88; Y. Congar, "'Ecclesia' et 'Populus (Fidelis)' dans l'écclésiologie de S. Thomas," in *St. Thomas Aquinas, 1274–1974: Commemorative Studies* (Toronto, 1974) 1, p. 159f.

77. Yves Congar, *L'Église de saint Augustin à l'époque moderne* (Paris, 1970), p. 234.

78. Yves Congar, "The Idea of the Church in Thomas Aquinas," in *The Mystery of the Church* (London, 1960), pp. 103, 106. "It is significant that this theology (of the church) is not formed into a separate treatise . . . but develops totally—both as institution and sacrament—within a theology of Christ and the incarnation. The church is the very body of Christ animated by the Spirit whose organic realities come from its apostolic foundation under the guidance of the pope. The church is at the same time a body (a corporation in the sociological sense of the word) and a mystery of Christ living on mystically and sacramentally" (Chenu, *St Thomas d'Aquin*, p. 98). See also A. Dulles, "The Church according to Thomas Aquinas," in *A Church to Believe In* (New York, 1982), p. 149f.

79. See G. Sabra, *Thomas Aquinas' Vision of the Church* (Mainz, 1987), chapter two.

80. Recent experts find in Aquinas an emphasis upon sacrament and an experience of liturgy; and perhaps also some acquaintance with Jewish liturgy; see A. Schencker, "Die Rolle der Religion bei Maimonides und Thomas von Aqûin," in *Ordo sapientiae et amoris* (Fribourg, 1993), p. 193.

81. *In 4 Sent.*, d. 15, q. 3, a. 1, ad 1.

82. *Super Evangelium secundum Johannem Lectura* [13:35] (Turin, 1952), ch. 13, lect. 6, p. 345.

83. *The Sermon-Conferences of St. Thomas Aquinas on the Apostles' Creed*, p. 125.

84. Congar, *L'Église de saint Augustin à l'époque moderne*, p. 234.

85. See David E. Luscombe, "Thomas Aquinas and Conceptions of Hierarchy," in *Thomas von Aquin: Werk und Wirkung im Lichte neuerer Forschungen*, ed. A. Zimmermann (Berlin, 1988), p. 261f.

86. Congar, "The Idea of the Church," p. 103.

87. *The Sermon-Conferences of St. Thomas Aquinas on the Apostles' Creed*, p. 129.

88. *In 4 Sent.*, d. 4, q. 3, a. 1.

89. John Mahoney, " 'The Church of the Holy Spirit' in Aquinas," in *Seeking the Spirit* (London, 1981), p. 101f.

90. See chapter five for further reflections on church and ministry.

91. D. Bourke, "Introduction," to *St. Thomas Aquinas, Summa theologiae*, vol. 56, *The Sacraments* (New York, 1978), p. xx.

92. "The divine office was the daily occupation of Thomas and there are coincidences between his theology and the celebration of the liturgical year. . . . He has furthered his vocation of theologian through a lived experience of the liturgy, and one finds an echo of this in his preaching" (J.-P. Torrell, "Thomas d'Aquin," *Dictionnaire de Spiritualité* 15, 772).

93. The exemplary manuscript of Humbert of Romans of 1254 still exists at the Dominican headquarters, Santa Sabina in Rome; on the Dominican rite, see W. R. Bonniwell, *A History of the Dominican Liturgy* (New York, 1944).

94. L. Walsh, "The Divine and the Human in St. Thomas' Theology of the Sacraments," in *Ordo Sapientiae et Amoris* (Fribourg, 1993), p. 345. Some sacraments, particularly baptism bring a mark, a "little sign of divine predestination" (III, 63, 1, 1) which has been traditionally called a character; this, however, is not at all a static badge but a further potentiality which as a participation in the priesthood of Christ enables people to act within and on behalf of the church (63, 3 & 6).

95. *In 4 Sent.* d. 10, q. 1, a 1.

96. David Power, "Thomas Aquinas on the Eucharist: Focal Point of Medieval Thought," in *The Eucharistic Mystery. Revitalizing the Tradition* (New York, 1992), p. 236; Niels Krogh Rasmussen, *Saint Thomas et les rites de la messe*, doctoral dissertation, Le Saulchoir, 1965.

97. "*O Sacrum Convivium in quo Christus sumitur: recolitur memoria passionis eius, mens impletur gratia, et futurae gloriae nobis pignus datur*" (Aquinas' antiphon for the "*Magnificat*" at Second Vespers of the Feast of Corpus Christi).

98. "Christ, the spiritual physician," works in two ways: one way interiorly through himself as he prepares the human will so that it might will good and hate evil; in another way he works through ministers externally offering sacraments and in this way he works to bring to fullness that which is begun externally" (III, 68, 4, 2).

99. "By the excellence of the power of Christ he can certainly confer the effect of the sacraments without the external sacrament" (III, 64, 3; 66, 12). We should note that in early works an evangelist comes to the isolated person not to baptize but first to teach. Interestingly, an *infidelis* can administer a sacrament. "Although one might believe that from what is externally done no interior effect follows, still that one is not ignorant of what the Catholic church intends and through the external actions offers the sacrament. And so infidelity is not an obstacle if what the church intends is

intended, even though [the infidel] might consider it to be nothing" (III, 64, 9, 1).

100. "Prologus," *In 4 Sent.*

101. *In 3 Sent.* d. 23, a. 2, ad 1.

102. *Quaestiones Quodlibetales* 5, q. 3, a. 6, ad 2.

103. *In 3 Sent.* d. 13, q. 1, a. 1, ad 5.

104. The sermon *Beati qui habitant"* in T. Kaeppeli, "Una raccolta di prediche attribuite a S. Tommaso d'Aquino," *Archivum Fratrum Praedicatorum* 13 (1943): 88f.

4. Traditions, Schools, and Students

1. For a view of Thomas Aquinas in the history of art, see G. M. Lechner, "Iconographia Thomasiana. Thomas von Aquin und seine Darstellungen in der bildenden Kunst," in *Thomas von Aquino. Interpretation und Rezeption,* ed. W. P. Eckert (Mainz, 1974), p. 933f.; M. Grabmann, *The Interior Life of St. Thomas Aquinas* (Milwaukee, 1951), pp. 1f., 19f., 58f.; Maria Chiara Celletti, "Tommaso d'Aquino," *Biblioteca Sanctorum* 12 (Rome, 1969), p. 544f.

2. Karl Rahner, "Schulen, theologische Schulen," *Lexikon für Theologie und Kirche* 9, 509f.; see A. Landgraf, *Einführung in die Geschichte der theologischen Literatur der Frühscholastik unter dem Geschichtspunkte der Schulenbildung* (Regensburg, 1948).

3. Anyone who studied in Catholic schools before Vatican II recognizes the following portrait of a seminary professor in southern France who had "the intimate conviction that he incarnated perfectly Thomism, that his work is the ideal toward which our Thomistic school has been leading, a Thomism most apt to heal the many evils of our time. . . . It is not necessary for him to read opinions to reject them and everything is equally certain. . . . This intellectual absolutism is accompanied with the most stupifying lack; its ignorance of scientific things surpasses all imagination" (from a letter of July 8, 1926 to the provincial of the Toulouse province of Dominicans about a professor at the studium at Saint-Maximim, cited in H. Donneaud, "Une vie au service de la théologie," *Revue Thomiste* 92 [1992]: 19).

4. Gerald McCool, "Neo-Thomism and the Tradition of St. Thomas," *Thought* 62 (1987): 132. See the bibliography of this book for studies on the history of neo-Thomism.

5. J. Pieper, *Guide to Thomas Aquinas* (New York, 1962), p. 21.

6. J. A. Weisheipl, "Thomism," *New Catholic Encyclopedia* 14 (New York, 1967), 126f.; O. Pesch, "Thomismus," *Lexikon für Theologie und Kirche* 10 (Freiburg, 1965), 157; see L. Kennedy, *A Catalogue of Thomists, 1270–1900* (Houston, 1987). Francis A. Cunningham, *Essence and Existence in Thomism* (Lanham, 1988) is a particular exercise in the history of Thomism as it traces one particular metaphysical theme; similarly, in theology there is L. B. Cunningham, *The Indwelling of the Trinity. A Historico-Doctrinal Study of the Theology of St. Thomas Aquinas* (Dubuque, 1955).

7. On the first years after Aquinas' death see Simon Tugwell, *Albert and Thomas. Selected Writings* (New York, 1988), p. 236f.

8. For a summary of these controversies and the first espousal by the Dominican Order of Aquinas' thought, see Tugwell, *Albert and Thomas*, p. 236f., and J.-P. Torrell, *Initiation à saint Thomas d'Aquin. Sa Personne et son oeuvre* (Paris, 1993), p. 436f.

9. See Martin Grabmann, "History of the Theological *Summa*. Its Commentators," *Introduction to the Theological Summa of St. Thomas* (St. Louis, 1930), p. 43f.

10. Indices and tables for the *ST* and then for the entire corpus as well as compendia appeared in the century or so after 1350; a Greek translation of the *ST* appeared in the fourteenth century.

11. See William Hood, *Fra Angelico at San Marco* (New York, 1993), and D. Weinstein, *Savonarola* (Princeton, 1970).

12. Pesch, "Thomismus," p. 159.

13. See the writings listed in T. O'Meara, "The Dominican School of Salamanca and the Spanish Conquest of America: Some Bibliographical Notes," *The Thomist* 56 (1992): 555f.

14. See John W. O'Malley, *The First Jesuits* (Cambridge, 1993), p. 247f.; Avery Dulles, "Jesuits and Theology: Yesterday and Today," *Theological Studies* 52 (1991): 527.

15. On the role of Aquinas at this time of Baroque neo-Thomism, see John of St. Thomas, *De Approbatione et auctoritate doctrinae angelicae divi Thomae*, one of three introductory treatises with which the author begins his theological system, *Cursus Theologicus* 1 (Paris, 1931), pp. 221–301.

16. R. Garrigou-Lagrange, "Thomisme," *Dictionnaire de théologie catholique* 15:1 (Paris, 1946), 829f.

17. Pesch, "Thomismus," p. 160.

18. Grabmann, *Introduction to the Theological Summa*, p. 164f.

19. G. Vann, *Saint Thomas Aquinas* (New York, 1940), p. 70f.

20. See T. O'Meara, *Romantic Idealism and Roman Catholicism. Schelling and the Theologians* (Notre Dame, Ind., 1982).

21. See G. McCool, *Nineteenth Century Scholasticism: The Search for a Unitary Method* (New York, 1989); T. O'Meara, *Church and Culture* (Notre Dame, Ind., 1991).

22. M. Grabmann, "Neuscholastik," *Lexikon für Theologie und Kirche* 7 (lst ed.) (Freiburg, 1935), p. 522.

23. On Leo XIII and the restoration of Thomism, see G. McCool, "The Nineteenth Century Heritage" in *From Unity to Pluralism. The Internal Evolution of Thomism* (New York, 1989), p. 5f.

24. Rigid and philosophical neo-Thomists did not in fact cultivate a mature knowledge of Aquinas' writings. Before 1960, outside of northern Europe, in some schools and faculties claiming to be most devoted to neo-Thomism, one could often not find good editions of Aquinas or important secondary literature. What posed as devotion to Aquinas was occasionally indolence, an easy presumption that everyone could be instantly an authority

in this game of concepts and terms. Catholic intellectual life from 1860 to 1960 shows that a simplistic restoration of medieval logic or neo-scholastic ethics falsifies Aquinas' contribution and skews his influence, making him into the plaything of neo-Gothic fundamentalists and ensuring eventual neglect. In 1946 Gerald Vann mentioned that those who found themselves attracted by the breadth and depth of Aquinas' wisdom were repelled by a rationalism fashioned by recent Thomists (*St. Thomas Aquinas* [New York, 1947], p. 164f.).

25. Otto Pesch, *Thomas von Aquin. Grenze und Grösse einer mittelalterlichen Theologie: Eine Einführung* (Mainz, 1988), p. 34f.

26. G. McCool, "Twentieth-Century Scholasticism," in *Celebrating the Medieval Heritage: A Colloquy on the Thought of Aquinas and Bonaventure. The Journal of Religion (Supplement)* 58 (1978): S198f.; "Neo-Thomism and the Tradition of St. Thomas," *Thought* 62 (1987): 131f.; for a study of the basic types of neo-Thomism in the twentieth century, see Helen James John, *The Thomist Spectrum* (New York, 1966), and Gerald McCool, *The Neo-Thomists* (Milwaukee, 1994).

27. "Up to 1924 one can count no less than 218 commentaries on the first part of the *Summa theologiae* and 90 on the whole *Summa*" (Hans Kung, *Great Christian Thinkers* [New York, 1994], p. 114; see also Pesch, "Thomismus," p. 159).

28. For the views, positive and negative, on the restoration of Aquinas by Werner and other early writers in Germany and Austria, see T. O'Meara, "Thomas Aquinas and German Intellectuals," *Gregorianum* 68 (1987): 719f.

29. McCool, "Twentieth-Century Scholasticism," p. S221.

30. G. McCool, "Blondel, Bergson, and the French Dominicans," in *The Neo-Thomists* (Milwaukee, 1994), p. 43f.; for Gardeil, *Introduction to the Philosophy of St. Thomas* (St. Louis, 1956); R. G. Perez Robles, *The Experimental Cognition of the Indwelling Trinity in the Just Soul: The Thought of Fr. Ambroise Gardeil*, doctoral dissertation at the Angelicum in Rome, 1987; for Sertillanges, see *Foundations of Thomistic Philosophy* (1931), *Philosophie Morale de Saint Thomas d'Aquin* (1946), *Saint Thomas Aquinas and His Work* (1933).

31. *Jacques Duquesne interroge le Père Chenu* (Paris, 1975), p. 44.

32. For examples see Maritain, *Bergsonian Philosophy and Thomism, Three Reformers*, and *The Dream of Descartes*; see G. McCool, "Maritain: A Neo-Thomist Classic," *Journal of Religion* 58 (1978): 380f.

33. "If I am anti-modern, it is certainly not out of personal inclination, but because the spirit of all modern things that have proceeded from the anti-Christian revolution compels me to be so" (*Antimoderne*, quoted in "Preface," *The Angelic Doctor* [New York, 1931], pp. xi–xii).

34. On Journet, see J.-P. Torrell, "Paul VI et le Cardinal Journet. Aux sources d'une ecclésiologie," *Nova et Vetera* 61 (1986: 161f). Having written widely on dogmatic theology and spirituality, in the 1940s the Swiss priest began a four-part ecclesiological system: the framework for treating the church would be the four causes of Aristotle. The first volume treats the efficient

cause, the apostolic hierarchy; the second volume considers the intrinsic formal cause (the "soul" of the church), grounded in charity and active in sacraments, and presents the intrinsic final cause of the church, the sanctity of its members; the third volume treats the formal reality of the church in action, within salvation-history, reaching from creation through the church to the eschaton. One volume appeared in English; the others are in French: *The Church of the Word Incarnate*, I. *The Apostolic Hierarchy* (New York: Sheed and Ward, 1954); see T. O'Meara, "The Teaching Office of Bishops in the Ecclesiology of Charles Journet," *The Jurist* 49 (1989): 23f.

35. His autobiography describes the emergence of a mature and accurate knowledge of Aquinas the theologian amid the secular intellectual life of France after 1900: *The Philosopher and Theology* (New York, 1962); see John M. Quinn, *The Thomism of Étienne Gilson. A Critical Study* (Villanova, 1971); S.-T. Bonino "Historiographie de l'école thomiste. Le cas Gilson," in *Saint Thomas au XXe siècle* (Paris, 1994), p. 299f. Norman F. Cantor, "The Christian Philosopher," in *Inventing the Middle Ages. The Lives, Works, and Ideas of the Great Medievalists of the Twentieth Century* (New York, 1991), p. 326f. In 1962 Étienne Gilson wrote at the beginning of *The Philosopher and Theology* that as a philosopher he has no past and as a Christian he lives in an inner solitude.

36. For a critique of Gilson by the Dominican school, see T. C. O'Brien, "Reflecting on the Question of God's Existence in Contemporary Metaphysics," *The Thomist* 23 (1961): 1f., 211f., 362f.; other Dominicans critical of Gilson were W. A. Wallace, Louis-Marie Régis, and Lawrence Dewan. From the perspective of the freedom of philosophy, James Collins warned: "The work of philosophizing is never totally governed by the laws discovered by the historian of philosophy" ("Toward a Philosophically Ordered Thomism," *New Scholasticism* 32 [1958], 315f.). The contributions of those sympathetic to Gilson, like Anton Pegis, Armand Maurer Joseph Owens, Eric Mascall, and J. Henle, were valuable. The name of the Anglican Mascall reminds us that there were a few Thomists who were not Catholics, for instance, the important Mortimer Adler.

37. *Une école de théologie: Le Saulchoir* (Paris, 1985), p. 162. Rome came to view the Saulchoir Dominicans as dangerous precisely because of their historical studies. Did not understanding Aquinas in his age and culture imply that he was not uniquely perennial? Chenu's book of 1937 describing the importance of understanding the historical context of medieval thought at Le Saulchoir was put on the *Index* of prohibited books in 1942.

38. *Jacques Duquesne interroge le Père Chenu*, p. 49.

39. M.-D. Chenu, "Le Sens et les leçons d'une crise religieuse," *La Vie intellectuelle* 13 (1931): 380. In 1954 he was removed from teaching for fashioning a theology for the priest-workers; see F. Leprieur, *Quand Rome condamne* (Paris, 1989); T. O'Meara, "Raid on the Dominicans. The Repression of 1954," *America* 170 (1994): 8f.

40. Cited in Chenu, "La Liberté de la théologie," in *Le Père Chenu. La Liberté dans la foi* (Paris, 1969), p. 45.

41. *Fifty Years of Catholic Theology. Conversations with Yves Congar* (Philadelphia, 1988), p. 70.

42. See J. P. Jossua, *Yves Congar* (Dubuque, 1968); Richard McBrien, "Church and Ministry: The Achievement of Yves Congar," *Theological Digest* 32:3 (1985): 203f.

43. In 1945 the Dominican moral theologian M. Labourdette wrote to his provincial: "In terms of the future of the Dominican students, it is foolish and dangerous to make what should be a positive formation into one of barriers and controls. . . . Can we continue to let the students leave [their theological education] without having seriously spoken of communism, socialism? Then we would be like the first sons of Dominic who would never have known anything about Albigensianism and or who would never have studied the heresies of Nestorius and Eutyches. We teach our students to refute Baius and Jansens; but we never speak of Marx and Lenin" (from a letter from Marie-Michel Labourdette cited in H. Donneaud, "Une vie au service de la théologie," 30).

44. E. Przywara, "Zwei Gräber: Paul Natorp-Clemens Baeumker," *Stimmen der Zeit* 108 (1925): 317; see Przywara, *Polarity* (London, 1953); J. Zeitz, *Spirituality and Analogia Entis according to Erich Przywara* (Washington, 1987); T. F. O'Meara, "Paul Tillich in Catholic Thought: The Past and the Future," in *Paul Tillich: A New Catholic Assessment* (Collegeville, 1994), p. 9f.

45. E. Przywara, "Der Grundsatz 'Gratia non destruit sed supponit et perficit naturam'. Eine ideengeschichtliche Interpretation," *Scholastik* 2 (1942): 180.

46. Ibid., 183.

47. Otto Muck, *The Transcendental Method* (New York, 1968); on Rousselot, Maréchal, Gilson, and Maritain, see McCool, *From Unity to Pluralism*, and *The Neo-Thomists*.

48. Joseph Maréchal, *Le point de départ de la metaphysique (V). Le Thomisme devant la Philosophie Critique* (Paris, 1926), p. 461.

49. See McCool's chapters on Rousselot in *From Unity to Pluralism*, p. 39f.

50. McCool, *From Unity to Pluralism*, p. 110. Cornelius Fabro pursues a Thomism, largely philosophical, away from a scholasticism of essences but within neo-Platonic themes like participation; see *God in Exile* (Westminster, 1968); *Tomismo e Pensiero moderno* (Rome, 1969).

51. See Frederick Crowe, *The Lonergan Enterprise* (Cambridge, 1980); D. Tracy, *Achievement of Bernard Lonergan* (New York, 1970).

52. Karl Rahner, "The Importance of Thomas Aquinas," in *Faith in a Wintry Season* (New York, 1989), p. 45; Rahner has in his sermons and meditative reflections some beautiful and illuminating passages on Aquinas; see "Thomas Aquinas: Monk, Theologian and Mystic," and "Thomas Aquinas, Patron of Theology" in Karl Rahner, *The Great Church Year* (New York, 1993), p. 309f.

53. Karl Rahner, "The Present Situation of Catholic Theology," in *Theological Investigations* 21 (New York, 1988): 71.

54. Ibid., 73; on Aquinas and Rahner, see G. McCool, "Karl Rahner and the Christian Philosophy of Saint Thomas Aquinas," in *Theology and*

Discovery. Essays in Honor of Karl Rahner (Milwaukee, 1980), p. 63f.; Thomas Sheehan, *Karl Rahner: The Philosophical Foundations* (Athens, 1987).

55. Karl Rahner, "Theology and Anthropology," *Theological Investigations* 9 (1968): 28.

56. Edward Schillebeeckx, *I Am a Happy Theologian* (New York, 1994), p. 8.

57. Edward Schillebeeckx, "Scholasticism and Theology," in *Revelation and Theology* (New York, 1967), p. 258.

58. Edward Schillebeeckx, *Christ the Sacrament of the Encounter with God* (New York, 1963). "If theology drew from new viewpoints, for instance, from a philosophical anthropology which favored a non-dualist conception of the human being, it could better explain that this had already been the case in the past with some of the basic intuitions of Thomist Christology and with Aquinas' appreciation of the human being of Christ. It would understand better the import of the position of Aquinas which refuses to depersonalize the humanity of Christ" (G. Vergauwen, "Edward Schillebeeckx— Lecteur de saint Thomas," in *Ordo Sapientiae et Amoris*, ed. C. J. Pinto de Oliveira (Fribourg, 1993), p. 669; see J. Bowden, *E. Schillebeeckx, In Search of the Kingdom of God* (New York, 1983).

59. See G. McCool, "The Tradition of Saint Thomas in North America: at 50 Years," *The Modern Schoolman* 65 (1988): 185f. Charles Hart sketched the history and role of neo-scholastic philosophy in the United States in the first third of the twentieth century in "Neo-scholastic Philosophy in American Catholic Culture," in G. Vann, *Saint Thomas Aquinas* (New York, 1947), pp. ix–xxv.

60. McCool, "Neo-Thomism and the Tradition of St. Thomas," *Thought* 62 (1987): 134.

61. J. Gredt, *Elementa Philosophiae Aristotelico-Thomisticae* 2 (Freiburg, 1953), p. 71.

62. McCool, "Neo-Thomism and the Tradition," p. 136.

63. Rahner, "The Present Situation of Catholic Theology," p. 72.

64. See S. Pfürtner, *Luther and Aquinas on Salvation* (New York, 1965); H. Kung, *Justification: The Doctrine of Karl Barth and Catholic Reflection* (Philadelphia, 1964); O. Pesch, *The God Question in Thomas Aquinas and Martin Luther* (Philadelphia, 1972).

65. See O. Pesch, "Existential and Sapiential Theology—the Theological Confrontation between Luther and Thomas Aquinas," in *Catholic Scholars Dialogue with Luther* (Chicago, 1969), p. 61f.

66. Daniélou, "Les orientations présentes de la pensée religieuse," *Etudes* 79 (1946): 5.

67. Pesch, *Thomas von Aquin*, pp. 27, 32. As the post-conciliar eclipse of Aquinas began, Thomas Merton wrote: "The current popular reaction against St. Thomas is not due to anything in Thomas himself. . . . No one who takes the trouble to read St. Thomas and understand him will be surprised to find that the values people now seek elsewhere have been present

in him and can always be made accessible without too much difficulty. There is first of all that 'turning to the world'—that awareness of the modern world, the world of poor people, of cities. . . . The spirit and perspectives of St. Thomas are 'modern' in the soundest sense of the world. . . . The whole difficulty of St. Thomas today arises, not from Aquinas himself, but (as has been said so often) from Thomists. Where Thomas was open to the world, they have closed him in upon himself in a little triumphalistic universe of airtight correctness. They have unconsciously sealed off his thought in such a way that in order to embrace Thomism one has to renounce everything else. . . . Now the windows are open in the *Summa* too, and there is a little peace and fresh air!"(*Conjectures of a Guilty Bystander* [New York, 1966], p. 186).

68. C. J. Pinto de Oliveira, "Thomas d'Aquin, Vatican II, et la théologie contemporaine," in *Ethique chrétienne et dignité de l'homme* (Fribourg, 1992), p. 111f. Avery Dulles lists twenty-four ways in which documents of Vatican II draw on the theology of Aquinas; "The Church according to Thomas Aquinas," in *A Church to Believe In* (New York, 1982), p. 165f.

69. In the recognition of the mystery of the Trinity's presence in people on earth and of the non-objectified offer of grace in individual lives there is a shift from neo-Thomist mechanisms of actual graces to a perspective more in harmony with Aquinas. There are the shifts (a) from actual grace to uncreated grace (the divine being); (b) from actual grace and virtues which are not intrinsically supernatural to an emphasis upon one supernatural grace subtly and diversely present in the personality; (c) from grace conceived as efficient causality to grace as formal causality.

70. *Lumen ecclesiae* (Naples, 1975), #9.

71. *Lumen ecclesiae*, # 19, 25. Addresses by Pope Paul VI in 1964 and 1965 had anticipated the letter which stated that fidelity to St. Thomas far from resulting in a system unproductively turned in on itself can inspire principles, methods, and spirit for new tasks and issues of today (*Lumen ecclesiae*, #25f.). The Code of Canon Law of 1989 speaks of Catholic theological institutes studying the mysteries of salvation as presented by Scripture and tradition "with St. Thomas as a special teacher." (Can. 252). An address of Pope John Paul II stresses faith as light and the moral life as a path of God ("Aquinas: Defender of Human Dignity," *The Pope Speaks* 36 [1991], 78f.).

72. For instance, W. P. Eckert, *Thomas von Aquino. Interpretation und Reception* (Mainz, 1974), 980 pages; *Tommaso d'Aquino* (Naples, 1975), 9 vols.; four the *The Thomist* for 1974; *St. Thomas Aquinas, 1274–1974, Commemorative Studies* (Toronto, 1974), 2 vols. For further Thomistic congresses see the fifty volumes of *Studi Tomistici* (Rome, 1974–).

73. Richard Ingardia, *Thomas Aquinas. International Bibliography, 1977–1990* (Bowling Green, 1993).

5. Thomas Aquinas Today

1. Fritz Kern cited in Martin Grabmann, *Die Kulturphilosophie des hl. Thomas von Aquin* (Augsburg, 1925), p. 15f.; on Dante's admiration for Aquinas joined to a quite limited theological discipleship, see Kenelm Foster, "St. Thomas and Dante," *The Two Dantes and Other Studies* (London, 1977), p. 56f. For a survey of Aquinas portrayed in painting and poetry, see works cited in chapter four, note 1. An insightful essay on Aquinas and art is Thomas Gilby, *Poetic Experience: An Introduction to Thomist Aesthetics* (New York, 1934); see also writings in this area by Etienne Gilson, Jacques Maritain, and Umberto Eco. To begin an exposition of the dialectic of nature and grace in society and politics, John Paul II cites Aquinas: "*Genus humanum arte et ratione vivit* ('Humanity lives by creativity and intellect'). These words go beyond the contemporary meaning of Western culture, whether it is Mediterranean or Atlantic. They have a meaning that applies to humanity as a whole, where the different traditions that constitute its spiritual heritage and the different periods of its culture meet.... Culture is a specific way of human 'existing' and 'being' " (Pope John Paul II, "Man's Entire Humanity Is Expressed in Culture," in *The Church and Culture since Vatican II. The Experience of North and Latin America*, ed. J. Gremillion [Notre Dame, Ind., 1985], p. 189).

2. Albert the Great, *Super Dionysii Mysticam Theologiam et Epistolas, Epistola 9* (Cologne, 1978), p. 533.

3. *SCG* 2, 81

4. Thomas Merton, *Conjectures of a Guilty Bystander* (New York, 1966), p. 187.

5. Thomas Merton, *Seeds of Contemplation* (New York, 1949), p. 25f.

6. "All things are said to be caused by divine beauty because they have the real aspect of harmony which is a facet of beauty" (Thomas Aquinas, *In Librum De Divinis Nominibus Expositio*, c. 4, lect. 6 [Turin, 1950], p. 119).

7. *In Psalmos* 44, 2, *Opera Omnia* (Rome, 1992), 6, p. 115.

8. *SCG* 2, 24.

9. *In 3 Sent.*, d. 9, q. 1, a. 2, ad 3.

10. The saint is a personality responding to the instinctual gifts of the Spirit (I–II, 68); family relations are founded on a "conjunction of natural origin" (II–II, 26, 8); a game is like contemplation for it brings pleasure in its activity (*In I Sent.* d. 2, q. 1, a. 5; see II–II, 168, 4).

11. On the symbolism of numbers, see J. Tonneau, "Appendice I," *La Loi Nouvelle (Somme théologique)* (Paris, 1981), p. 98f.

12. *De Spe*, q. 4, a. 4, ad 14, *Opera Omnia*, 3, p. 433.

13. Andreas Speer, "Thomas von Aquin und die Kunst," *Archiv für Kulturgeschichte* 72 (1990): 343f. Like some of his contemporaries, often religious authorities, Thomas criticized polyphony, the introduction into church of singing in "a theatrical manner" (II–II, 91, 2, 3 & 4). Elsewhere he wrote that for what is lacking in singing the psalms of the divine office, in comparison to the beautiful rites of angelic praise, there might be compensation in

the work of writing about the excellence of angels (*De Substantiis Separatis seu de Angelorum Natura*, "Proemium, *Opuscula philosophica* [Turin, 1954], p. 21). See C. Pera, "Le Testimonianze della liturgia cattolica," *Le Fonti del pensiero di S. Tommaso d'Aquino nella Somma teologica* (Turin, 1979), p. 62f. In the opening question of his Christology when he asked why the Word became a human being he mentioned the human fall and redemption from sin, and added that "the blessing of the Easter candle ("the *Exultet*")" mentions the "happy fault," the fall of Adam and Eve, which earned such a Redeemer (III, 1, 3).

14. J.-P. Torrell, " 'Spiritualitas' chez S. Thomas d'Aquin," *Revue des sciences philosophiques et théologiques* 73 (1989): 575f. Spiritual is often applied to the act of intellection; less frequent are references like "the spiritual incorporation into Christ" (referring to the Eucharist) (*In 4 Sent.*, d. 9, q. 1, a. 1).

15. Ulrich Horst, *Evangelische Armut und Kirche* (Berlin, 1992), p. 29.

16. Ibid., 224.

17. M.–D. Chenu, *St Thomas d'Aquin et la théologie* (Paris, 1955), p. 113. L. Hödl observes: "You will find the spirituality of Thomas Aquinas in the 'Second Part' of the *Summa theologiae*: it is a complicated, applied theology of grace" ("*Lumen Gratiae*,"in *Mysterium der Gnade* [Regensburg, 1975], p. 239). For overviews of Aquinas' spirituality in the modern sense, see Matin Grabmann, *The Interior Life of St. Thomas Aquinas* (Milwaukee, 1951); *Dominican Spirituality*, ed. A Townsend (Milwaukee, 1934); W. Principe, *Thomas Aquinas' Spirituality* (Toronto, 1984); "Affectivity and the Heart in the Theological Spirituality of Thomas Aquinas," *Spiritualities of the Heart* (New York, 1990); S. Tugwell, *Albert and Thomas. Selected Writings* (New York, 1988); J.-P. Torrell, "Thomas d'Aquin," *Dictionnaire de Spiritualité* 15 (1990), 718f.; Mary Ann Fatula, "*Contemplata Aliis Tradere:* Spirituality and Thomas Aquinas, The Preacher," *Spirituality Today* 43 (1991): 19f.; B. M. Ashley, *Thomas Aquinas. The Gifts of the Spirit: Selected Writings* (Hyde Park, 1995).

18. W. Principe, "Aquinas' Spirituality for Christ's Faithful Living in the World," *Spirituality Today* 44 (1992): 118f. To these he adds an ecological perspective. "Thomas is no monist; he exults in the diversity of creatures (as well as of individuals) since more glory is given to God by this diversity. . . . Preserving each individual species is for Thomas a service of God's glory" (122).

19. Ibid., 129f.

20. Torrell, "Thomas d'Aquin," p. 772; Torrell sees five stages in Aquinas' view of the spiritual journey (ibid., 763f.).

21. Bartholomew of Capua quoted in J. A. Weisheipl, *Friar Thomas d'Aquino* (New York, 1974), p. 255.

22. Tugwell, *Albert and Thomas*, p. 278

23. For an exposition of Aquinas' position among medieval theologies of prayer, see Tugwell, *Albert and Thomas*, p. 275f.

24. Ibid., 276.

25. L. Maidl and O. Pesch, *Thomas von Aquin. Gestalt, Begegnung, Gebet* (Freiburg, 1994), p. 30f.

26. "The different sciences in different ways correspond to three modes of contemplation . . . moral science, natural science and metaphysics. But the Gospel of John contains as a present totality what sciences consider in a fragmentary way" ("Prologue," *Super Evangelium S. Ioannis Lectura* [Turin, 1952], p. 2f.).

27. Grabmann wrote: "Speculative theology, which has found in the *Summa theologiae* of Thomas Aquinas its highest completion, mediates a deeper knowledge of the mysteries of Christianity, and gives to Christian thinking great and fruitful ideas. . . . In the history of theology we see again and again the inner and interior connection between the metaphysics of being, speculative dogmatics, and mysticism" (*Die Idee des Lebens in der Theologie des hl. Thomas von Aquin* [Paderborn, 1922], p. 4).

28. *In Psalmos* 30, 16. 9, *Opera Omnia* 6, p. 90.

29. One finds in various writings of Reginald Garrigou-Lagrange a thorough presentation of Aquinas' spirituality as a journey through the Christian life. A psychology of activity in stages of maturity is the framework for that theology of spirituality and prayer; see *The Three Ages of the Interior Life* (St. Louis, 1947), 2 vols. Karl Rahner wrote: "In every human being . . . there is something like an anonymous, unthematic, perhaps repressed, basic experience of being oriented to God, which is constitutive of man in his concrete make-up (of nature and grace), which can be repressed but not destroyed, which is 'mystical' or (if you prefer a more cautious terminology) has its climax in what the older teachers called infused contemplation" ("Teresa of Avila," in *Opportunities for the Faith* [New York, 1970], p. 125).

30. The two great summas contain 193 references to Gratian's compendium of canon law and ninety-one to collections on Roman law; see Thomas Gilby, *The Political Thought of Thomas Aquinas* (Chicago, 1958), p. 161; J. M. Aubert, *Le Droit romain dans l'oeuvre de saint Thomas* (Paris, 1955). Gilby discussed at some length Aquinas' thought (and that of the Dominicans in general) as independent and practical; as reflecting the urban, entreprenurial middle class (pp. 213, 312f.).

31. The following is drawn from *De Regimine Principum*, cc. 1–5; see Louis Lachance, *L'Humanisme politique de Saint Thomas d'Aquin. Individu et État* (Montreal, 1965).

32. Where Aristotle employs "political" Aquinas prefers "social." See E. Scully, "The Place of the State in Society according to Thomas Aquinas," *The Thomist* 45 (1981): 407f.

33. Otto H. Pesch, "Theologie und Politik," in *Summa theologica, Die deutsche Thomas-Ausgabe* 13 (Heidelberg, 1977), p. 739f.

34. Commenting on Aristotle, Aquinas observed that a love which existed outside of the social order would belong either to a monster or an angel; see *Jacques Duquesne interroge le Père Chenu* (Paris, 1975), p. 110.

35. Ibid., 74.

36. See Clodovis Boff, "Saint Thomas Aquinas and the Theology of Liberation," *Dominican Ashram* 5 (1986): 128f.

37. Torrell, "Thomas d'Aquin," 768.

38. Pesch, "Theologie und Politik," p. 741.

39. J. Collins, "God's Eternal Law," *The Thomist* 23 (1960): 497f.

40. Gilby, *The Political Thought*, p. 315.

41. Torrell, "Thomas d'Aquin," 768f.

42. Recent documents of Catholic social teaching from the magisterium are collected in David O'Brien and Thomas Shannon, *Catholic Social Thought. The Documentary Heritage* (Maryknoll, 1992); the index shows the influence of Aquinas.

43. *Lumen Ecclesiae* (Naples, 1975), #8; see Pius XI, *Studiorum Ducem* (an encyclical on Aquinas from 1923), *AAS* 15 (1923): 309f.; Y. Calvez and J. Perrin, *The Church and Social Justice: The Social Teaching of the Popes from Leo XIII to Pius XII (1878–958)* (Chicago, 1961); M. Schuck, *That They Be One: The Social Teaching of the Papal Encyclicals 1740–1989* (Washington, 1991). For a collection of texts and excerpts from writings drawing on Aquinas, see Paul E. Sigmund, *St. Thomas Aquinas on Politics and Ethics* (New York, 1988); on major themes and papal uses of them see Robert Barry, "Aquinas' Social Thought and Catholic Social Teachings: An Historical Perspective," *Providence* 1 (1992): 131f.; J. Hennesey, "Leo XIII's Thomistic Revival: A Political and Philosophical Event," *Journal of Religion* (Supplement) 58 (1978): 185f.; the essays in Oliver F. Williams and John W. Houck, *Catholic Social Thought and the New World Order. Building on One Hundred Years* (Notre Dame, Ind., 1993).

44. Vatican II, *The Church in the Modern World*, #39.

45. Ibid., # 3.

46. Chenu, *St Thomas d'Aquin*, p. 98; see "The Idea of the Church in Thomas Aquinas," in *The Mystery of the Church* (London, 1960); A. Dulles, "The Church according to Thomas Aquinas," in *A Church to Believe In* (New York, 1982), p. 149f.; G. Sabra, *Thomas Aquinas' Vision of the Church* (Mainz, 1987); T. O'Meara, *Theology of Ministry* (New York, 1983), p. 110f.

47. John Mahoney, "The Church of the Holy Spirit in Aquinas," in *Seeking the Spirit* (London, 1981), p. 115.

48. *In 4 Sent.*, d. 20, q. 1, a. 4. There are also passages where the social and ministerial structure of the church does resemble that of feudal society, where the bishop is a prince and other ministers derive their powers from him (*In 4 Sent.*, d. 7, q. 2, a. 1).

49. *Super Epistolam ad Hebraeos* (3:1) (Turin, 1953), ch. 3, lect. 1, p. 373.

50. See Congar, "Ecclesia ab Abel," in *Abhandlungen über Theologie und Kirche* (Festschrift Karl Adam), ed. M. Reding (Dusseldorf, 1952), p. 79f.

51. See *Index Thomisticus, Concordantia Prima* 4 (Stuttgart, 1974), p. 74.

52. See various places in the commentary on Romans as listed in G. Sabra, *Thomas Aquinas' Vision of the Church*, p. 144f.

53. *The Sermon-Conferences of St. Thomas Aquinas on the Apostles' Creed*, ed. N. Ayo (Notre Dame, Ind., 1988), p. 125.

54. Sabra, *Aquinas' Vision of the Church*, p. 66.

55. *In 4 Sent.*, d. 24, q. 2, a. 1, ad 3.

56. "Since in one city there are not many bishops, this expression in the plural must include the presbyters. . . . In the beginning, although the orders were distinct, still the names of the orders were not" (*Super Epistolam ad Philippenses* [1:1] [Turin, 1953], ch. 1, lect 1, p. 91). "In the early church, because of the small number of faithful, all lower ministries were confided to deacons. . . . All those powers were contained in the single diaconal power. But with time, divine service was expanded and that which the church possessed in one order it has distributed in many" (*In 4 Sent.*, d. 24, q. 2, a. 1, ad 2., *Opera Omnia* 1, p. 574). Still, Aquinas spoke of the beginnings of the church and its completion but also of its progress which is the subject of the apostles' letters in the New Testament (*Principium Fratris Thomae de Commendatione Sacrae Scripturae, Opuscula theologica* 1 [Turin, 1954], p. 439).

57. *SCG* 4, 76.

58. *Quaestiones . . . Duodecim Quodlibetales* 4, 18 (Turin, 1942), p. 317; see A. Dulles, "The Teaching Role of the Magisterium and of Theologians," *Proceedings of the Catholic Theological Society of America* 24 (1969): 239f.

59. *Super Epistolam ad Colossenses* (4:1) (Turin, 1953), ch. 4, lect. 1, p. 161.

60. Y. Congar, *L'Église de saint Augustin a l'epoque moderne* (Paris, 1970), p. 237.

61. Y. Congar, "Saint Thomas et les archidiacres," *Revue Thomiste* 57 (1957): 670.

62. *De Potentia*, 10, 4, ad 13. The creeds articulate what the Bible holds and the church believes (II–II, 1, 6, 1; II–II, 1, 9; II–II, 110, 3, 1).

63. On Aquinas and papal roles see Sabra, *Aquinas' Vision of the Church*, p. 137f.

64. Ulrich Horst, "Kirche und Papst nach Thomas von Aquin," *Catholica* 31 (1977): 152.

65. John Mahoney, "The Church of the Holy Spirit in Aquinas" in *Seeking the Spirit*, p. 99.

66. *In 4 Sent.*, d. 24, q. 2. a. 1, ad 1, *Opera Omnia*, 1, p. 574.

67. We do not have this question treated in the *ST*, because that work was left incomplete before it treated of the sacrament of orders. The "Supplement" gives the teaching of his commentary on the *Sentences*. Hilary Martin notes that the pages of the commentary on *First Corinthians* treating this topic is not the text of Aquinas but the report of a student ("The Injustice of Not Ordaining Women: A Problem for Medieval Theologians," *Theological Studies* 48 [1987]: 303f.). Dennis Michael Ferrara argues convincingly that the phrase concerning the priest acting "in the person of Christ" meant for Aquinas the recitation of Jesus' consecratory words at the last supper and not that the priest as a male is a symbol of the incarnate Word ("Representation or Self-Effacement: The Axiom *In Persona Christi* in St. Thomas and the Magisterium," *Theological Studies* 55 [1994]: 195f.); see

K. E. Borresen, *Subordination and Equivalence: The Nature and Role of Woman in Augustine and Thomas Aquinas* (Washington, 1981); C. Kiesling, "Aquinas on Persons' Representation in Sacraments," in *Women Priests. A Catholic Commentary on the Vatican Declaration,* ed. L. and A. Swidler (New York, 1977), p. 253f.

68. This passage has been taken from the early *In 4 Sent.,* d. 25, q. 2, a. 1. It can be left to sociologists of the Middle Ages to research the meaning of this subjection and eminence in that society. He would not have accepted that the Word of God became incarnate in a "male" rather than in a human being, for the Word assumed human nature in an individual human being (III, 4, 3).

69. To this he added two arguments: one about women inciting to sensuality, and one about women being not well educated (II–II, 177, 2). On the other hand, asking whether women can be the sponsors at confirmation for men, Aquinas responded abruptly: "*Colossians* says that 'in Christ Jesus there is neither male nor female,' and therefore it makes no different whether a man or a woman is a sponsor in confirmation" (III, 72, 10, 3).

70. Vatican II, *Declaration on the Relationship of the Church to Non-Christian Religions,* #1.

71. R.-A. Gauthier, *Saint Thomas d'Aquin. Somme contre les Gentils* (Paris, 1993), p. 112; see J.-P. Torrell, *Initiation à saint Thomas d'Aquin. Sa personne et son oeuvre* (Paris, 1993), p. 153f.; see a different view in A. Patfoort, *Saint Thomas d'Aquin. Les clefs d'une théologie* (Paris, 1983), p. 127f.

72. Otto Pesch, *Thomas von Aquin. Grenze und Grösse einer mittelalterlichen Theologie: Eine Einführung* (Mainz, 1988), p. 56.

73. For literature on the Dominican opposition to any forced baptism of Jews, see U. Horst and B. Faes de Mottoni, "Die Zwangstaufe jüdischer Kinder im Urteil scholastischer Theologen," *Munchener Theologische Zeitschrift* 40 (1989): 173f.; see, too, Pesch, *Thomas von Aquin,* pp. 64, 313; D. Berg, *Servitus Judaeorum* (Berlin, 1988); W. Eckert, "Thomas von Aquino und seine Stellung zu den Juden und zum Judentum," *Freiburger Rundschau* 20 (1968): 30f.; A. M. Hoffmann, "Die Gnade der Gerechten des Alten Bundes nach Thomas von Aquin," *Divus Thomas* 17 (1939): 30f.; Marcel Dubois, "Thomas Aquinas on the Place of the Jews in the Divine Plan," *Immanuel* 24/25 (1990): 241f.

74. *In 4 Sent.,* d. 46, q. 2, a. 26. Aquinas' letters on Jews in the Duchy of Brabant-Flanders is a letter of a few pages indicating little interest in the topic and offering nothing original. Torrell concludes: "On the Jews, he is content to reproduce the common teaching of his time on the state of servitude which is theirs; he underlines that they should be treated moderately, and if they are punished for disobeying laws on usury so should those who are not Jews. In fact, the interest of these few pages resides less in the treatment of Jews than in the general foundation of the legitimacy of taxes imposed by the prince and the demands of the public good" (Torrell, *Initiation à saint Thomas d'Aquin,* p. 321f.). A negative view of Jewish ceremonies is given in

terms of Christians, mainly in the past, who insist upon observing those rituals (I–II, 103, 4).

75. "Through Christ and then through the Apostles it [faith in the Trinity] was made manifest to the whole world" (II–II, 2, 8, 2). But medieval theologians had questions. Had the Gospel actually been proclaimed to all peoples? When did the hearing of the Gospel become normally or universally linked with the reception of grace, and did it arrive automatically at Pentecost, or end with the death of John the Evangelist? Aquinas changed his viewpoint as he grew older and became more reluctant to say that the Gospel had reached all nations. The commentary on the *Sentences* affirmed three ages in the human race's faith in the redeemer but then concluded that after Christ the mystery of redemption was visibly fulfilled corporeally, was universally "preached," and all are expected to believe explicitly: "And if anyone does not have an instructor God would reveal to that one so that the fault would be removed" (*In 3 Sent.*, d. 25, q. 2, a. 2, ad 2). Later, commenting on Matthew and Romans Aquinas was reluctant to assert that some nations had not at all been contacted by preaching (the view of Augustine); he held Chrysostom to be saying that, if some preaching had reached all nations, nonetheless, the church was not established everywhere. Curiously here Aquinas did not clearly leave the issue of world-wide evangelization in the fourth century and address the new issues of his own time. "But the explanation by Chrysostom is in better agreement with the present meaning of the Apostle than that of Augustine. For the mere fact that they were going to hear sometime in the future would be no basis for depriving unbelievers of an excuse. And yet one does not maintain because of this that news of the apostles' preaching reached every individual, even though it did reach all nations" (*Super Evangelium S. Matthaei Lectura* [24:14] [Turin, 1951], ch. 24, lect. 8, p. 299; *Super Epistolam ad Romanos lecturas* [10:18], ch. 10, lect. 3, p. 158). Sabra (*Aquinas' Vision of the Church*, p. 163f.), W. Schacten (*Ordo Salutis* [Munster, 1980]), and others think that the rise of Joachimitism (the end would come since the Gospel had been universally preached) made Aquinas cautious. This unresolved ambiguity entered the *ST*: "The preaching of the Gospel can be understood in two ways: in one way with regards to the divulgation of the idea of Christ, and in this way the Gospel was preached in the entire world even in the times of the Apostles. . . . In another way the preaching of the Gospel in the entire world can be understood in terms of its full effect, so that in each people the church has been founded . . . and in this sense the Gospel has not been preached in the entire world" (I–II, 106, 4, 4). See J. Theisen, *The Ultimate Church and the Promise of Salvation* (Collegeville, 1976), p. 1f.; Y. Congar, "No Salvation outside the Church?" in *Wide World My Parish* (Baltimore, 1961), p. 93f. For a survey of various Thomisms on this topic, see F. Sullivan, *Salvation Outside the Church? Tracing the History of the Catholic Response* (New York, 1992); Sabra, *Thomas Aquinas' Vision of the Church*. A bibliographical summary of Thomist theology concerning the Indies can be found in T. O'Meara, "The Dominican School of Salamanca and the Spanish Conquest of America,"

The Thomist 56 (1992): 555f., and "The School of Thomism at Salamanca and the Presence of Grace in the Americas," *Angelicum* 71 (1994): 321f.

76. If Aquinas was aware of his Dominican brothers' trips to the court of the Mongols or of their publication of studies on the Koran, why does he not have a formal treatment of faith and grace outside of European Christendom? Is it because Europe contacted Islam through bloody wars or learned of the Mongols through their frightening invasions? Is it because Aquinas, despite his positive anthropology of grace in theory, saw too much of the violence of life among Christians to make salvation impersonal or automatic? Caperan concluded in the 1930s: "Thomas Aquinas consistently taught that the non-believers themselves in whatever milieu the chance of birth has placed them have the means to be saved. . . . Without denying any essential element of Augustinian teaching, he takes us far from St. Augustine in whose perspective the darkness of ignorance covering the nations seems to resist any penetration of a ray of divine grace" (*Le Problème du salut des infidèles* [Toulouse, 1934] 1, p. 199).

77. M. Seckler, "Das Heil der Nichtevangelisierten in thomistischer Sicht," *Theologische Quartalschrift* 140 (1960): 45, 39; for new ways of dialogue between Indian thought and Aquinas see F. X. Clooney, *Theology after Vedanta: An Experiment in Comparative Theology* (Albany, 1993).

78. The following words of the Salamancans bring to mind Karl Rahner. "One might respond that it is sufficient that they be Christians in reality, for they have implicit faith—of course this would not suffice for them to be called Christians" (Domingo Bañez, *Commentaria in 2am 2ae . . .* [Venice, 1586], p. 419). "Although nothing is expressed in the gospel concerning baptism of desire, it is manifest that where the reality itself is not possible . . . the intention [for it] has an effect with respect to justifying grace" (Domingo de Soto, *De Natura et Gratia* [Paris, 1549], 1, 12, p. 130).

79. *In 1 Sent.*, d. 8, q. 1, a. 1, ad 4.

80. *De Veritate*, q. 4, a. 4.

81. Chenu, "L'étude historique de Saint Thomas," *Revue philosophique de Louvain* 49 (1951): 737f.

Conclusion

1. *Jacques Duquesne interroge le Père Chenu* (Paris, 1975), p. 100.

2. There are also curiosities such as articles on paradise as a place or on the legitimacy of military religious orders.

3. Otto Pesch, *Thomas von Aquin. Grenze und Grösse einer mittelalterlichen Theologie: Eine Einführung* (Mainz, 1088), p. 27.

4. In the 1980s the semioticist and novelist Umberto Eco observed: "We are witnessing . . . a period of renewed interest in the Middle Ages, with a curious oscillation between fantastic neo-medievalism and responsible philological examination" (*Travels in Hyper-Reality* [San Diego, 1986], p. 63).

5. L. Maidl and O. Pesch, *Thomas von Aquin. Gestalt, Begegnung, Gebet* (Freiburg, 1994), p. 13f.

6. See Hors Rzepkowski, *Thomas von Aquin und Japan. Versuch einer Begegnung* (Steyl, 1967) as well as the writings of Chlodovis and Leonardo Boff and other liberation theologians.

7. François de Mediros, "Les Cultures africaines face à la pensée de S. Thomas," in *1274—Année Charnière—Mutations et Continuités* (Paris, 1977), p. 769f.

8. Christian Duquoc notes that Aquinas' thought can be criticized not only as being too Aristotelian but as belonging totally to an "onto-theology" which not only linguistic studies has found outdated but which Heidegger in his existential ontology considered an obstacle to reaching "the godly God." But Duquoc responds: Aquinas' theology, when understood anew, safeguards the otherness of God and points to its transcendent mystery even as it affirms the finite openness and search of men and women ("De L'Actualité de S. Thomas," *Interpréter* [Paris, 1992]: 13f.).

9. *In De Causis*, Prop. 6, *Opera Omnia* (Rome, 1992), 4, p. 511.

10. Sequence for the Feast of Corpus Christi.

BIBLIOGRAPHY

——— ✝ ———

I. The Writings of Thomas Aquinas

The complete writings of Aquinas (including some texts incorrectly attributed to him) can be found in a Piana edition (1570), a Parma edition (1852–1873) (reprinted in New York in 1948), and a Paris edition (1871–1880). In this century many works, in theology and philosophy, have been published by Marietti in Turin. The books by J. A. Weisheipl and J.-P. Torrell (listed below) give a detailed study of the conditions of authorship of each work as well as editions and translations.

The Leonine Commission of the Vatican and the Dominican Order are working slowly and painstakingly to produce a critical text of all the writings. This version establishes through families of manuscripts a text close to Aquinas' original. The *Summa contra gentiles* and the *ST* were published in the last decade of the nineteenth century (with the commentaries of Silvester Ferrariensis and Thomas de Vio, Cardinal Cajetan, respectively). In the 1960s the work of the Commission was taken up again, and further texts of Aquinas have been published.

Early in the twentieth century the English Dominicans produced a translation of the *ST* (New York, 1912–1925), and some decades later this translation was reprinted by English and American Dominicans who added explanatory essays (St. Louis, 1948, 3 vols.; reprinted in 1981 by Christian Classics in five volumes). In the 1960s the English-speaking Dominicans presented a new translation of the *ST* in sixty volumes; the English translation faces the Latin text, and the volumes contain valuable notes and appendices (New York: McGraw-Hill, 1964). Doubleday Image Books began to publish this translation in paperback but ceased after a very few volumes. *Summa theologiae. A Concise Translation* is an abbreviated presentation in English of the entire *ST* as assembled by T. McDermott (Westminster, 1989). There is also a collection of philosophical passages from the *ST*: P. J. Kreeft, *A Summa of the Summa. The Essential Philosophical Passages of St. Thomas Aquinas' Summa Theologica* (San Francisco, 1990). Walter Farrell engagingly summarized and explained the entire *ST* in his *A Companion to the Summa* (New York, 1945), 4 vols; and a summary is found in W. Farrell and Martin J. Healy, *My Way of Life. Pocket Edition of St. Thomas. The Summa Simplified for Everyone* (Brooklyn, 1952). Paul J. Glenn's *A Tour of the Summa* (St. Louis, 1978) is a sparse summary of the work's main points. A number of other writings by Aquinas have been translated into English: the commentaries on Aristotle's *On Interpretation, Posterior Analytics, On the Soul, Metaphysics, Physics, Nichomachaean Ethics;* the *Compendium of Theology (The Light of Faith* [1993]) and the *Summa contra gentiles;* the disputations *On Truth* and *On Power; On Spiritual Creatures, On Charity;* the biblical commentaries on Job, John, Philippians, Ephesians, Galatians, and 1 Thessalonians, and the *Catena Aurea.*

There are also collections of texts from Aquinas: J. Dawson, ed., *Aquinas: Selected Political Writings* (Oxford, 1948); T. Gilby, ed., *Philosophical Texts* (London, 1951; Durham, 1982), and *Theological Texts* (London, 1955; Durham, 1982); Mary Clark, *An Aquinas Reader* (New York, 1972); Vernon J. Bourke, *The Pocket Aquinas* (New York, 1973). In Italian there is a recent dictionary of Thomist terms: B. Mondin, *Dizionario Enciclopedico del Pensiero di San Tommaso d' Aquino* (Bologne, 1991).

Valuable sources for studying Aquinas are the editions and notes of the *ST* in other languages; these editions resemble the McGraw-Hill edition in English: *Die deutsche Thomas-Ausgabe* (Salzburg, 1933; Cologne, 1955–); *Somme théologique* [Edition des jeunes] (Paris, 1925–1947) and more recently, *Somme théologique* (Paris, 1984–); *Summa theologiae* (Madrid, 1961–1965).

There are two booklets which depict the *ST* in static charts: J. J. Berthier, *Tabulae synopticae totius Summae theologicae S. Thomae Aquinatis* (Freiburg, 1893; Washington, 1946) and G. Q. Friel, *St. Thomas Aquinas: An Outline of the Summa theologicae* (Providence, 1950). There are also synopses in a few lines of every article from every question in the entire work: P. Alagona, *Theologicae Summae Compendium* (Turin, 1900), and G. M. Paris, *Synopsis totius Summae theologicae S. Thomae* (Naples, 1950).

II. Indices of Thomas Aquinas' Writings

Besides M. Stockhammer, *Thomas Aquinas Dictionary* (New York, 1965), there is an index to the *ST* by Roy Defarrari, *A Complete Index of the Summa theologica of St. Thomas Aquinas* (Baltimore, 1956; Boston, 1986). There is the valuable index produced by IBM: *Index Thomisticus*, ed. R. Busa (Stuttgart, 1974); these many volumes developed by computer technology offer from all of Aquinas' works an index of every word; the pages give the Latin word in each of its locations with its context of six or seven words. This index is also available on CD-ROM as *Thomae Aquinatis Opera Omnia cum hypertextibus in CD-ROM*, ed. R. Busa (Milan: Editoria Ellettronica Editel, 1992). Another computerized index of Aquinas is available from *Past Masters* (Clayton, Ga.: InteLex Corporation, 1993). There are indices of articles on Aquinas covering secondary literature over some decades at the Pontifical University of St. Thomas Aquinas (Angelicum) in Rome and at the Pontifical Institute of Medieval Studies (Toronto).

Thomistic studies are fortunate in having not only recent, computerized indices but a long-term and thorough bibliographical survey. For much of this century the *Bulletin Thomiste* (1924–1965)—which in 1965 became *Rassegna della letteratura tomistica* (Rome)—has attempted to list and review the large literature of books and articles on Thomas Aquinas in languages ranging from Portugese to Polish. Vernon Bourke compiled a *Thomist Bibliography, 1920–1940* (St. Louis, 1945), and a *Thomistic Bibliography, 1940–1978* (Westport, 1980). There is also a *Bibliographie thomiste* (Paris, 1960) begun by P. Mandonnet and expanded by M. D. Chenu. A recent bibliography is Richard Ingardia, *Thomas Aquinas. International Bibliography, 1977–1990* (Bowling Green, 1993). There are also bibliographies on special areas such as A. Pedrini, *Bibliografia Tomistica sulla Pneumatologia* (Vatican City, 1994).

III. Studies on Thomas Aquinas

Two internationally recognized studies on Aquinas' life and career and the historical context and genre of his writings are J. A. Weisheipl, *Friar Thomas d'Aquino: His Life, Thought and Work* (New York, 1974), of which there is a summary: "Thomas Aquinas"

New Catholic Encyclopedia, 14, p. 102f., and recently, J.-P. Torrell, *Initiation à saint Thomas d'Aquin. Sa personne et son oeuvre*, 2 vols. (Paris, 1993, 1996) (for a summary see Torrell, "Thomas d'Aquin," in *Dictionnaire de Spiritualité* 15 [Paris, 1990], 718–773).

M. D. Chenu's *Towards Understanding St. Thomas* (Chicago, 1964) remains a particularly helpful presentation of the context of his activity as a theologian. Treating Aquinas' sources is C. Pera, *Le Fonti del pensiero di S. Tommaso d' Aquino nella Somma teologica* (Turin, 1979). The writings of Chenu, Congar, and other French scholars remain valuable as is E. Gilson's *The Christian Philosophy of St. Thomas Aquinas* (New York, 1956). A penetrating study of the *ST* is G. Lafont, *Structures et méthode dans la somme théologique de S. Thomas d'Aquin* (Paris, 1961, 1995) to which can be added the literature cited in T. F. O' Meara, "Grace as a Theological Structure in the *Summa theologiae* of Thomas Aquinas," *Recherches de théologie ancienne et médiévale* 55 (1988): 130f. Looking at Aquinas' life and theology from the point of view of the spiritual life is S. Tugwell, *Albert and Thomas. Selected Writings* (New York, 1988), and a fine summary is W. Principe, "Aquinas, St. Thomas," in *The HarperCollins Encyclopedia of Catholicism*, ed. Richard McBrien (San Francisco, 1995), 83–89. There is a collection of passages from Aquinas juxtaposed with observations on American spirituality in M. Fox, *Sheer Joy. Conversations with Thomas Aquinas on Creation Spirituality* (San Francisco, 1992), and a collection of texts on the spiritual life, B. M. Ashley, *Thomas Aquinas. The Gifts of the Spirit. Selected Writings* (Hyde Park, 1995). See also the writings listed in chapter five on Aquinas' theology as a spirituality. Among European scholars Otto Pesch must be noted: building upon his lengthy study on Aquinas and Luther are *The God Question in Thomas Aquinas and Martin Luther* (Philadelphia, 1972), *Thomas von Aquin. Grenze und Grösse mittelatlerlicher Theologie* (Mainz, 1989), and "Thomas von Aquin," *Lexikon für Theologie und Kirche*, 10, 119f., 157f. Other recent studies are A. Patfoort, *Saint Thomas d'Aquin. Les clefs d' une théologie* (Paris, 1983) and Brian Davies, *The Thought of Thomas Aquinas* (Oxford, 1992). Articles on Aquinas, Thomism, and major Thomists can be found in encyclopedias like *The New Catholic Encyclopedia, Lexikon für Theologie und Kirche*, and *The HarperCollins Encyclopedia of Catholicism*.

In this century a number of biographies and studies appeared, each with its own perspective and limits: J. Maritain, *Angelic Doctor. Life and Thought of St. Thomas Aquinas* (New York, 1931); A. D.

Sertillanges, *St. Thomas Aquinas and His Work* (London, 1932); G. K. Chesterton, *St. Thomas Aquinas* (New York, 1935); Gerald Vann, *St. Thomas Aquinas* (New York, 1947); Martin D' Arcy, *Thomas Aquinas* (Westminster, 1954); and F. C. Coppleston, *Aquinas* (Baltimore, 1955). Joseph Pieper offered *The Silence of St. Thomas* (New York, 1957) and *Guide to Thomas Aquinas* (New York, 1962). The distinguished German medievalist from the beginning of the century, Martin Grabmann, wrote *The Interior Life of St. Thomas Aquinas* (Milwaukee, 1951), *Thomas Aquinas. His Personality and Thought* [1928] (New York, 1963), *Introduction to the Theological Summa of St. Thomas* (St. Louis, 1930), and *Die Kulturphilosophie des hl. Thomas von Aquin* (Augsburg, 1925).

During the neo-scholastic revival a number of periodicals began in European countries, some of which are still active: *Divus Thomas* (Piacenza) (1880–); *Revue Thomiste* (1893–) edited by the French Dominicans; *Ciencia Tomista* edited by the Spanish Dominicans (1910–); *Scholastik* (1926–1965) (Freiburg im Breisgau); *Revue néoscholastique de philosophie* (1894–) from Louvain; *Rivista Italiana di filosofia neoscolastica* (1909–) (Milan). To these could be added: *Angelicum* (Rome), *The Thomist* (Washington), *The Modern Schoolman* (St. Louis), *New Scholasticism* (begun in 1927, it becomes in 1989 *American Catholic Philosophical Quarterly*), *Recherches de théologie ancienne et médiévale* (Mont César), *Revue des sciences philosophiques et théologiques* (Paris) as well as general journals like *Medieval Studies* (Toronto).

IV. Surveys of the History of Thomism

For nineteenth-century surveys of the history of Thomism there are M. Schneid, "Die neuere thomistische Literatur," *Literarischer Handweiser* 20 (1881) in five parts and G. Feldnor, "Die Neu-Thomisten," *Jahrbuch für Philosophie und spekulative Theologie* 8, 9, (1894, 1895), five parts. In this century, see G. La Piana, "Recent Tendencies in Roman Catholic Theology," *Harvard Theological Review* 15 (1922): 122f.; M. Grabmann, *Die Geschichte der katholischen Theologie seit dem Ausgang der Väterzeit* (Freiburg, 1933), 218f. and "History of the Theological *Summa*. Its Commentators," in *Introduction to the Theological Summa of St. Thomas* (St. Louis, 1930), 43f.; P. Dezza, *I neotomisti italiani del secolo XIX* (Milan,

1942/44), 2 vols.; J. L. Perrier, *The Revival of Scholastic Philosophy* (New York, 1948); G. F. Rossi, *Le origini del neotomismo* (Piacenza, 1957); J. P. Golinas, *La restauration du Thomisme sous Léon XIII et la philosophie nouvelle* (Washington, 1959); E. Hocedez, *Histoire de la théologie au XIXe siècle* (Bruxelles, 1947–1952), 3 vols.; R. Aubert, "Aspects divers du néo-thomisme sous le pontificat de Léon XIII," in *Aspetti della cultura cattolica nell' eta die Leone XIII* (Rome, 1961), pp. 133–227; A. Walz, "Sguardo sul movimento tomista nel secolo XIX final all'enciclica Aet. Patris," *Aquinas* 8 (1965): 315f.

More recent are F. J. Roesch, *Early Thomistic School* (Dubuque, 1964); Helen James John, *The Thomist Spectrum* (New York, 1966); Thomas J. A. Hartley, *Thomistic Revival and the Modernist Era* (Toronto, 1971); L. A. Kennedy, *A Catalogue of Thomists, 1270–1900* (Houston, 1987). General overviews are provided by F. van Steenberghen, "Die neu-scholastische Philosophie," in *Bilanz der Theologie*, ed. H. Vorgrimler (Freiburg, 1969) 1, p. 352f.; J. Weisheipl, "Thomism," *New Catholic Encyclopedia* 14 (New York, 1967), 126–135 and "Scholasticism," *New Catholic Encyclopedia* 12 (New York, 1967), 1167f.; O. Pesch, "Thomismus," *Lexikon für Theologie und Kirche* 10 (Freiburg, 1965), 160; G. Sohngen, "Neuscholastik," *Lexikon für Theologie und Kirche* 7 (Freiburg, 1962), 923; O. Kohler, "Neo-Thomism, Scholasticism, and Modern Philosophies," in *Handbook of Church History*, ed. H. Jedin, 6:2 (New York, 1974), p. 316f.; Paulus Engelhardt, "Thomism," *Sacramentum Mundi* 6 (New York, 1970), 249; Marcel Regnier, "Le Thomisme depuis 1870," *Histoire de la Philosophie* 3, *Encyclopédie de la pléiade* (Gallimard, 1974), 483f; Norman F. Cantor, "After the Fall," in *Inventing the Middle Ages. The Lives, Works, and Ideas of the Great Medievalists of the Twentieth Century* (New York, 1991), p. 287f.; Wayne Hankey, "Making Theology Practical: Thomas Aquinas and the Nineteenth Century Religious Revival," *Dionysius* 9 (1985): 85f.; G. McCool, *Nineteenth Century Scholasticism* (revision of *Catholic Theology in the Nineteenth Century*) (New York, 1989), "Neo-Thomism and the Tradition of St. Thomas," *Thought* 62 (1987): 131f., "The Tradition of Saint Thomas in North America: at 50 Years," *The Modern Schoolman* 65 (1988): 185f., *From Unity to Pluralism. The Internal Evolution of Thomism* (New York, 1989), and *The Neo-Thomists* (Milwaukee, 1994); T. O' Meara, "The Two Directions of German Catholic Theology (1864–1914)," in *Church and Culture. German*

Catholic Theology, 1860–1914 (Notre Dame, 1991), p. 25f., and "Thomas Aquinas and German Intellectuals," *Gregorianum* 68 (1987): 719f.; *The Future of Thomism* , ed. D. Hudson and D. Moran (Notre Dame, 1992); and individual essays in *Christliche Philosophie im katholischen Denken des 19. und 20. Jahrhunderts*, ed. E. Coreth (Graz, 1988–1990), 3 vols. A volume of the ninth International Thomistic Congress treats this area: *Studi Tomistici 6, Storia del Tomismo (fonti e riflessi)* (Vatican City, 1994). The histories of the Dominican Order by W. Hinnebusch and B. M. Ashley discuss Thomism in various periods.

INDEX

✛